479

THE

HERO

TRAN

Ray B. Browne
&
Marshall W. Fishwick

IN

SITION

Bowling Green University Popular Press
Bowling Green, Ohio 43403

Contents

The Hero Box—called "The Historoscope" by 19th century toy makers—produced a chromo lithograph panorama when the knobs were turned. A century later, it looks surprisingly like the television box on which today's heroes make their brief, flickering appearances.

Toys, like heroes, are always in transition. But George Washington remains—first in everything.

The Hero in Transition

Marshall W. Fishwick

"Truth is one, the sages speak of it by many names."
The Vedas

"The heroes whom we see everyday through the TV screen may be the gods of our age."
Hidetoshi Kato

"Does not the pebble, entering the water, begin fresh journeys?"
Kung Fu Mediations

Introduction

*H*eroes light up the heaven; and like the moon, they wax and wane. When my study of *American Heroes: Myth and Reality* appeared (1954), they were waxing. We believed in Mom, Marilyn Monroe, and apple pie...to say nothing of Honest Abe, George Washington, and Thomas Jefferson. They were safe on our Olympus; their myth had become reality. Right?

> George Washington and Thomas Jefferson owned hundreds of slaves. Every president since Lincoln connived politically and cynically with the issues affecting the human rights of most people.[1]

We entered the time of the Great Against—not only against the Establishment, the Man, poverty, parents, but also against God (rumored to be dead), virginity and apple pie. (I still have period buttons which read: "Stamp Out Virginity" and "Apple Pie Makes You Sterile.") The hero waned.

So did the "Consensus School" of history, which held that most of our past conflicts were hyperbolic ritual warfare associated with politics.[2] They pictured the heroes I had studied (Jefferson, Lincoln, Roosevelt) as pragmatists, seeking sensible moderate solutions.

5

Nonsense, the "New Left" school insisted; tension, not consensus, explained our history and our heroes. We must fight the "systematic moronization" of the American past, insisted Herbert Marcuse. Living in what Michael Harrington called *The Accidental Century*, we must move quickly *Toward a Democratic Left.* And what of those of us who hesitated to capitulate and move? *Burn, Baby, Burn.*[3] Ugly became beautiful, odd got even. Heroic was out; anti-heroic was in.

Changes in America during those years have been so profound, so rapid, that no one can fully evaluate them. "What has happened," a Japanese observer notes, "is that substantial and structural problems have so shaken American society and politics that institutions have lost their ability to restore themselves." Heroes lost their ability to inspire, generals to lead. Arthur Schlesinger, Jr., wrote a much-quoted 1962 essay on "The Decline of Greatness." "Ours is an age without heroes . . . . We have no giants who play roles which one can imagine no one else playing in their stead."

Certainly there are few heroes modeled on those serenely confident generals, elegant 18th century squires, bold 19th century industrial tycoons. The presidency itself suffered a sea-change under Kennedy: first president born in the 20th century, first from the political vortex of megalopolis, first Roman Catholic. The term "popular" took on a new meaning with Kennedy. So did "politics." Out went purple prose and pious platitudes. His press conferences were masterpieces of relaxed, popular exposition. The young aristocrat was at home with new media, ideas and lifestyles.

The Communication Revolution was pumping into the human psyche an unending stream of images, information and value judgments. The outcome of the hard-fought Nixon-Kennedy presidential race of 1960 was, by common consent, determined by a series of television debates. Did man control the media, or did the media control man?

Kennedy's assassination, in 1963, was the crucial event in the heroic history of our generation. Because of the times and technology, Kennedy had a global popularity unlike that of any other president, or of any man then alive. That he should be killed senselessly by an ex-Marine, who was in turn killed on television before millions, formed an unbelievable historic episode—a happening.

Just how much the American mood changed in those fateful years is reflected in comic book characters. Consider Superman.

One morning we found him standing on top of a skyscraper, looking at ant-like humans below, musing: "For the first time in many years I feel that I'm alone ...."

For women and men, the heroic proposition is linked in to the new politics of visibility. We are dominated by images rather than words. Instant information cries out for instant solutions. Yet it does not follow that the heroic process is deteriorating, or the instinct for admiration and acclaim slipping. It may be that a generation which is better educated, more sophisticated, more travelled and media-exposed than any in history will demand and expect more than heroes. Because no highly publicized figure can any longer hide his contradictions, shortcomings, and recorded blunders, the old one-dimensional hero or paragon is finished. We have to accept the new crop warts and all, or not at all. Might this propagate the anti-hero?

Repetition and revolution go hand in hand. Ours was not the first age in which heroes were cut short and hair was worn long. Parents of the 1960s, bemoaning uncouth youth and the new barbarism, merely echoed Thomas Hall's advice in the 1660s:

> Go, Gallants, to the Barbers go
> Bid them your hairy bushes mow.
> God in a Bush did once appear
> But there is nothing of Him here.

If hair had not changed much in three centuries, the media had. First print, then radio and wireless, then television, then satellites wrought incredible changes. Myths which had served Western man well languished and died. When an old mythology disintegrates, a new one originates—along with new heroes. Instead of *discovering* a new mythos, we find ourselves *participating* in it. Was that not what our artists and heroes were doing; what our children were seeking with their new music, morals, hairstyles?

A whole series of studies reflected the down-grading of heroes. One of them, Harold Lubin's *Heroes and Anti-Heroes*, raised "serious questions about our contemporary culture heroes." Their styles are their fortunes, he complained, and their styles pass like any other fad of the moment—mini skirt, long hair, mod boots:

> Today's heroes rise with a dazzling brilliancy, but they are extinguished with all the finality of a shooting star.[4]

Roger R. Rollin published another *Hero/Anti-Hero* (1973) and made essentially the same points. The "hero" in Society A becomes the "villain" in Society B; you can't tell one from the other without a program. The title of Alice Childress' 1977 book put the idea in groovy slang: *Hero Ain't Nothing but a Sandwich.*

What had happened to charisma—that endowment of an individual with supernatural power what had been, for centuries, at the very heart of heroics? Why had our very political survival been reduced to a mixture of image projection, cynical self-seeking and ruthless ambition? Bryan Wilson summarized the answer given by many American intellectuals in the 70s:

> We have not produced an alternative language of persuasion with which to manipulate the electronic masses .... The basis of confidence that comprises the charismatic relationship is no longer there—and it appears unlikely to be recovered.[5]

This volume is an attempt to evaluate the heroic climate in the 80s; to see what a new generation of Americans is thinking and writing on this subject; and to trace the hero in transition.

For this much we *do* know: the hero, like Proteus of old, takes on all manner of shapes and guises. Today he hangs out in the video-game arcade, disguised as Pac Man, Black Knight, Tron or Jungle King. The Electronic Revolution has created new environments of invisible power—new patterns, new space, new style. The basis of that style is electronic popular culture.

So great is the change, so unprecedented the transition, that we have no place or discipline from which to view it all. Perhaps the best place would be in a skylab or satellite, looking down on our whirling green ball; but we must be content with this earth-bound book, to which various scholars have brought their thoughts and perspectives. Through various angles or vision and disciplines, they ask how fares today's hero? Is the era of the Anti-Hero ending? Where will the transition take us?

*   *   *

But first, a brief overview of the heroic environment over the centuries, and the field in which we shall be working. *Heros* (from the Greek) means superior man, directly related to the social and religious structure of his society. A gift of heaven, the *Heros* is a force sent by destiny.

Civilizations which flourished long before the Greeks knew this.

"The entire Sumerian civilization," writes Hidetoshi Kato, "can be seen as one great pantheon." Live heroes became deified in death; for the people of the Shang dynasty of China (1400 B.C.) the worship of heaven was synonymous with ancestor worship. In Japan, too, man's worship was tied to service to gods. Kunioi Ynagita notes that (the verb "massuru" (to worship) is akin to the verb "matsurau" (to be at the service of ...)[6] When Tokyo emerged as the Japanese capital in the mid-19th century, it was necessary to establish not only new sacred place but also new gods: the emperor himself had to be invented instantaneously.

The search and need for heroes is inherent in human history. Pre-literate societies allow men, heroes and gods to stand on a footing of tolerable equality. "Throughout the inhabited world, in all times and under every circumstance, the myths of man have flourished," writes Joseph Campbell. "It is necessary for men to understand, and be able to see, that through various symbols the same redemption is revealed."[7] The hero's story is a monomyth— and it has endless variations.

When one takes seriously the task of a *comparative* study of heroes, and to see if (as Joseph Campbell implies) one monomythic hero has a thousand faces, he quickly realizes the magnitude of his task. How can a Westerner come to understand the "Middle" or "Far" East? The terms themselves are significant—Occidental inventions implying distance from the West. That distance, Kenneth Scott Latourette points out, is not only geographical but cultural:

> Until the latter part of the 19th century, fewer contacts and less interchange existed between Western European and Far Eastern people than between the Occident and any other of the civilized folk of Asia.[8]

Latourette goes on to point out that the term Far East had its counterpart in the Far East itself: Nippon, in its more familar form Japan, means the land where the sun rises.

If history has forced most Westerners to deal with the great and expansive cultures of Japan, China and India in the twentieth century, it has still kept the historic and heroic patterns of many other Oriental cultures removed from wide understanding: Tibet, Sinkiang, Mongolia, Korea, Thailand, Burma, Laos, Cambodia,

Ceylon, the Malay Peninsula, the East Indies and the Philippines, for example. How many Westerners can name "the four Buddhist lands of the White Elephant and the Sacred Sword—"⁹ let alone name the nations' heroes? Or tell us why there are memorial parks to M. Ohmura and T. Saigo in Japan?

Yet a surprising number of young Westerners know the name of India's Ravi Shankar who became a superstar in the global culture of the 1960s. He and other Eastern musicians brought about what is called the "sitar explosion." By 1968 Shankar could write: "I find myself adored like a movie star or singer. I love young people very much, and since they know I love them, they listen to me and are very receptive."¹⁰ This appeal, Israel's Yehudi Menuhin comments, "is a tribute both to his great art and to the intuitive wisdom of the searching young."

This intuitive wisdom, and this search, takes on the guise not only of the culture but the epoch. In what Westerners call classic times, their heroes were god-men; in the Middle Ages, God's men; in the Renaissance, universal men; in the eighteenth century, gentlemen; in the nineteenth century, self-made men. Our century has seen the common man and the outsider become heroic. In keeping with the times they have reacted to our social and scientific revolutions. Some of them now go where once only gods could dwell—in outer space. Heroes must act their ages. History is not meaningful without people, and people are ineffective without leaders. The search for paragons is inherent in human nature. In remote areas of the world men are still deified in their own lifetimes. The idea of aloofness in superhuman power comes late in history.

Just as there are many roles, so are there many meanings. Historians see heroes as shaping the flow of events, philosophers as altering thought patterns, social scientists as evoking attitudes of behavior, folklorists as evoking legends and ballads, politicians as winning elections. Messiah, emancipator, founding father, preserver, creative genius are related terms for one whose influence or personality captivates the people. Emerging at a moment when men's emotions are deeply stirred, the hero appeals to both imagination and reason. No one knows just when and why he comes. The gift of heaven, he is a force and a rallying point.

Like a stream, history moves in one direction for a time, then veers off into another. Gaining momentum it washes away old banks and gouges out new channels. Those who perceive and justify this, altering with the flow of events, are heroes.

Some men flash into prominence—one-issue politicians,

matinee idols, sports champions—only to disappear like a flash flood. During their golden moments, however, the maxim is "Winner take all." We quote and misquote them with equal ease. At this juncture no one knows if they are true culture heroes or faddish meteors. (Marshall McLuhan, oracle of yesterday's media revolution, is a contemporary example.) Every age has thousands of aspiring heroes. Some carry through to the second generation, which feels the hero's power in stories told by their fathers. By the third generation his exploits take on a certain remoteness. Always susceptible to legend, a hero becomes superhistorical in myth.

This magic of leadership the Greeks called charisma. They imagined that the peaks of Mount Olympus were reserved for the men-gods who showed charismatic leadership. Such a figure was Heracles, called Hercules by the Romans. Beginning as a petty ruler subject to the order of a more powerful king at Argos, Heracles benefited from known exploits plus mythical stories attributed to him. Finally, he emerged as the Greek Happy Warrior, meeting (as Socrates points out in the *Gorgias*) deep psychological needs of his people. The Athenians, craving a hero of their own, elevated the soldier-seducer Theseus, strong in battle "for rich-haired Helen's sake." Ionian in spirit, he was fond of dancing and music, though city fathers toned down his amorous stories. They deleted Hesiod's references to Theseus' passion for Aegle. Bolstered by his role in plays by Aeschylus, Sophocles and Euripides, Theseus becomes more deliberate, lofty and Olympian over the centuries. Cimon brought Theseus' bones to Athens from Scyros, buried them in the heart of the city, and established his cult.[11] History has blotted out this particular shrine; but one can visit Francis' bones in Assisi, Lenin's in Moscow, or Kennedy's in Washington and see the same phenomenon at work.

In contemplating Theseus (or Francis or Lenin or Kennedy), his admirer found courage and faith. On Hadrian's Arch was inscribed "Athens, formerly the City of Theseus." Athenians did not respect him because he was Theseus; he was Theseus because they respected him.

Still a third Greek hero was chosen by Homer to tower over his great epic poem—Odysseus. His ten-year wandering after the Trojan War not only provided the material for one of the world's greatest stories; it also gave us the notion of odyssey—the long wandering marked by many changes of fortune. Adventurer-warriors all—but how different are Heracles, with his prowess and brute strength; Theseus, with his balanced personality; and

Odysseus, with his craftiness and political sagacity. In neither Greek nor American culture is the heroic style monolithic. Perhaps, as Emerson suggests, the one characteristic of a genuine heroism is its persistency.[12]

That persistency does not center on reputation or interpretation—the durability of heroes exists deep in our subconscious, emotions and not reason dominates. This is that magic place where dreams are stored and primordial ideas nurtured. "We share our heroes' thirst for glory," C.A. Burland writes, "wish we were as brave as they, and appreciate those who set the course."[13]

But who is setting the course—and what indeed *is* our course? We are involved in conflicts in which victory is nearly impossible to define, let alone achieve. In our "Never Go Out Alone" and "Exact Change After Dark" society, it is not rapture but rape which best describes urban living. How can anyone control nuclear arms, restore the economy, clean up the environment, restore America's competitive position? Where will our hero emerge, and just what will he do?

The heroic scene is changing too rapidly and we are too close to it to give final answers to long-range questions. We can say that changes in media, lifestyle, priorities, ideologies are reflected in our heroes. Motion pictures and television confer celebrity, for example—not just on people, but on acts, objects, places, ways of life. Everything is visible with the Big Eye.

To recognize the absence of myth is the first step toward resurrecting it. Today, that recognition is widespread in the Western world. When heroic style is refashioned, remythology thrives. By 1982, neo-conservativism controls key political positions throughout the world; nostalgia is a universal movement; the Hippies and Crazies of the 60s are finding Jesus and selling encyclopedias.

The media are changing not only our views of the hero, but of "the great globe itself." Travel, research, translations, documentaries and satellites are eliminating old barriers and frontiers. Only a few men have been on the moon—tens of millions have watched them once they got there. C.P. Snow's "two cultures" dilemma is outmoded. The sharp line between the arts and sciences is disappearing. Think of words that apply equally well to both: far out, experimental, interface, turned on, dynamic, nebular, freefall, random, fused, amorphous. Traditional disciplines have come tumbling down.

Cultural relocations and heroic transformations always go

hand in hand. Freed by technology, fed by media, image-makers are engaged in a worldwide scavenger hunt involving Mali masks, Zen fables, raga music, the camp style of Victoria, and the click-clack of computers. By telescoping time, tradition and geography the first universal heroic tradition may emerge. So we must ask such questions as:

1. How has the media affected heroic style around the world?
2. Has the line between elite, national, regional and popular heroes diminished or even disappeared?
3. How does the celebrity or entertainer become a hero?
4. Can and will the media create a new pantheon of heroes?

These and many other intriquing questions are raised in the essays which follow. The framework is set by Roger Rollin, who distinguishes between celebrity and hero. Then he adopts Northrup Frye's typology, (super hero, supreme leader, leader hero, Everyman hero, subordinate hero), relates mythos to logos, and examines our "crisis in heroism." Other essayists show us heroes that are accidental, unlikely, befuddled, rhetorical. Still others depict heroes and heroines in comic books, in orbit, on the tennis court. Some are retired (like Walter Cronkite), some dead (like Elvis Presley), others dead but resurrected (like Marilyn Monroe). From many quarters, and in many areas, the hero and heroine are waxing. That is a fact. But we must not get bogged down with mere facts. Emerson explained why, in a line that still rings true:

"Who cares what the fact was, when we have made a constellation of it to hand in heaven an immortal sign?"

Notes

[1] Eldridge Cleaver, *Souls on Ice* (New York: McGraw-Hill, 1968). Cleaver himself has gone through startling transitions since then. In 1982 he was peddling the Bible and the American flag for the Moonies, a fundamental religious sect.

[2] See John A. Garraty, "A Then for Now," New York *Times* (May 12, 1967), Section 7, p. 1.

[3] My summary of the period appears as chapter XIV ("Counter Culture" in *Common Culture and the Great Tradition* (Westport: Greenwood Press, 1982). See also William L. O'Neill's *Coming Apart: An Informal History of America in the 1960s* (New York: Random House, 1972).

[4] Harold Lubin, *Heroes and Anti-Heroes* (San Francisco: Chandler, 1969), p. 309.

[5] Bryan R. Wilson, *The Noble Savages: The Primitive Origins of Charisma and its Contemporary Survival* (Berkeley: Univ. of California Press, 1975).

[6] Hidestoshi Kato, "From Pantheon to Presley: Changes in Urban Symbolism," in *Communication and the City: The Changing Environment*, (Paper 7 of the East-West Communication Institute, Honolulu, Nov. 1973).

[7] Joseph Campbell, *The Hero With A Thousand Faces* (New York: Pantheon, 1949).

The Lone Ranger and
Lenny Skutnik:
The Hero as Popular Culture

Roger R. Rollin

...mankind's common instinct for reality...has always held the world
to be a *theatre* for heroism.

—William James[1]

On God and Godlike men we build our trust.

—Tennyson[2]

*T*he *sine qua non* of heroism is publicity. Without publicity an
act of heroism is like the sound made by the tree that falls in
the empty forest. A hypothetical case in point: the farm
woman who risks her life to save her two-year-old from a rampaging
bull and mentions the incident to no one. Even she may not think of
herself as a hero, only as a negligent mother or as someone who just
did what had to be done. But most of us would impute high values to
her act—courage, selflessness, and so on—or, more precisely, to her.
Values, however, can *only* be imputed: they *inhere* in nothing and
no one, for they are created by human consciousness. Such a woman
might impute value to her act and to herself. But if no one becomes
aware of what she did other than her two-year-old, who might not
understand the event and would at any rate soon forget it—if she
were never, in other words, to receive publicity for it—she would only
be a hero to the gods. And the gods have long been silent, even about
heroes.

Publicizing the heroic act and celebrating its performer,
therefore, are crucial, whether the individual in question is a tribal
or national figure acclaimed by a Homer or a Herodotus, or a citizen
who receives sixty seconds of attention on a local television
newscast. All heroes then are celebrities; no hero is not a celebrity.
As James Monaco has remarked, "The record—history—exists only

in the media, and the people who make the media, make history."[3]
This is so whether the medium is speech (a witness's account of that
day's extraordinary exploit by a tribal hunter), the legend of a great
warrior passed down by oral transmission (Homer's Hector), a feat
immortalized in a written text (Herodotus recapitulating the Battle
of Marathon), or a deed preserved on videotape (the firefighter's
rescue of an elderly citizen). Perception and identification of the
heroic by the non-heroic are fundamental. "Heroism is in the eye of
the beholder," says Edward Hoagland,[4] or (it might be added) in the
hearing, but always in the beholder's conscious mind.

A more traditional view is represented by Daniel Boorstin. It is
easy enough to agree with him when he argues that "all heroes are
self-made" in the sense that they are doers of "great deeds."[5]
However, it does not follow that "we can make a celebrity, but we
can never make a hero" (p. 48), that "celebrities are made by the
people" whereas the hero fulfills outside standards" (p. 74). For who
is to apply those standards and thus "make" heroes? Not the heroes
themselves, surely, for then their status would merely be self-
proclaimed. All that is left is "the people," the non-heroes who
witness and communicate the heroism and those who accept and
validate that communication.

i. The Hero as Celebrity: The Celebrity as Hero

Although all heroes are celebrities, not all celebrities of course
are heroes. It is to Boorstin that we are indebted for his definition of
the celebrity as "a person who is known for his well-knownness."[6]
They are, literally, creatures of media, created things, "human
pseudo-events,"[7] the heirs of "Buffalo Bill." As Monaco explains,
"Celebrities ... needn't have done—needn't do—anything special.
Their function isn't to act—just to be."[8] It could be argued that
William F. Cody, successful hunter, army scout, the slayer of Yellow
Hand, had indeed done something special and thus was no mere
celebrity. On the other hand, he did not achieve either celebrity-
status or real hero-status until he became the favorite subject of the
inventor of the dime novel, "Ned Buntline" (himself the celebrated
creation of E.Z.C. Hudson).

Before the advent of the mass media, only those born to great
place, royalty and nobility, could be classified as celebrities in
Boorstin's sense of the term. Boorstin himself argues that monarchs
were *not* mere celebrities, being persons of "illustrious lineage" and
possessing "impressive actual and symbolic powers."[9] But neither
lineage nor power together or separately is sufficient for

transcending celebrity-status. Kings and queens, dukes and duchesses, the blue-blooded lot, simply *were*—they did not need to *do* anything to become well known, and more often than not, did not. The sobriquet "celebrity" is only titular, and prior to the communications revolution, most of them were the titled.

Contemporary celebrities may simply be "beautiful people" or those who are married to (or living with or who are merely seen with) the powerful or the successful. Whatever the reason, they become the foci of the mass media and thus the cynosures of the mass audience. At least a significant part of the mass audience. For celebrity-status is fundamentally a quantitative matter, like the rest of popular culture. (Perhaps the most functional, if necessarily hedged, definition of the slippery term "popularity" is "that which gains the attention and involvement of as much or more of its 'target audience' than its competition for that audience"). Celebrities then, rather like Willy Loman's ideal man, are not just known: they are well-known.

Only half facetiously, Monaco offers two criteria for celebrity classification: "The first test of celebrityhood is passed when there is a significant number of people who know your name and face even though you don't know theirs." However, real celebrityhood, he continues, "doesn't come until you realize that there are images of yourself being propagated that don't quite jibe with what you know about yourself."[10]

Neither of Monaco's criteria holds up very well. Teachers, for example, are known by more students than they themselves know, and doubtless there are few teachers who find that the images of themselves fashioned by their students square well with their self-images. Another of Monaco's points, about celebrityhood, however, is well taken: "It's not what they are or what they do, but what we think they are that fascinates us." As students are interested in teachers, sometimes even fascinated by them, so too must some significant portion of the mass audience be at least interested, at most fascinated, by a given individual for him or her to be accounted a true celebrity.

The particular nature of such interest is unimportant. A given celebrity may be liked or disliked; what is important is his or her recognition-level. *Knowing* the name and/or face and/or personality enough to like or to dislike the celebrity is what counts. Non-recognition or, to a lesser extent, indifference, on the part of sufficient members of the mass audience in effect denies celebrity-status to a given individual. Celebrities then are doubly dependent, being not only the creatures of the mass media but the creatures of the mass audience as well. Bianca Jagger's life as a celebrity is in my hands and yours. If enough of us would not cross the street to see Bianca Jagger, she becomes that which celebrities seem to dread more than being a non-person—a non-celebrity.

"We control them," as Monaco points out, but there is a sense, he adds, in which they also control us.[12] Such control is exercised in part by the very proliferation of celebrities and their ubiquity. Whether or not one agrees with him that "Increasingly, our lives are acted out in a social sea of celebrityhood," as a result of which "we seem to be suffering more and more from an overload of this sort of collective celebration,"[13] the phenomenon of the celebrity is one element which distinguises twentieth-century popular culture from its earlier manifestations. Transitory though their condition may be, their tribe flourishes. For technology has done for the beautiful people and their ilk what mere word-of-mouth and the hand-operated printing press could not do for medieval and Renaissance princes and their entourages.

Yet the very existence of royalty and aristocracy, whether of birth or of the media, implies that celebrities fulfill human needs: since they did not exist, we had to create them. One such need, clearly, is economic: celebrities are good business. Some newspapers (e.g., *The National Inquirer*), some magazines (e.g., *People*), some television programs (and all talk shows) are glitter palaces built upon the shifting sands of celebrityhood. It is also possible to discern political and social needs. In spite of the often ephemeral nature of celebrityhood, for at least a millenium governments have found celebrities to be useful agents for symbolizing national attitudes and beliefs, for focusing national feelings, and for diverting national attention away from unpleasant national realities—witness the present British monarchy. By so functioning celebrities become a useful means of social control—celebrities as the opiate of the people.

None of these needs or uses, however, exists primarily in the collective consciousness (of unconsciousness) of the community, but only in those individual subjectivities which together make up the community. Whatever needs celebrities fulfill they fulfill them first in my head or yours. Morris Dickstein has claimed that "The cult of celebrity is the substitution of vicarious individuality for the real thing,"[14] but much of our experience (and almost all of our cultural experience) is vicarious, regardless of how individualistic we may be. The fact remains that the establishment of a cult of a given celebrity is entirely dependent upon the development of a consensus among a significant number of discrete individuals who make up the collective whole. Unless the celebrity figures somehow in the psychical lives of sufficient numbers of the "little people" they themselves become little people.

For the celebrity-conscious then celebrities fill some kind of psychological vacuum—what kind of vacuum can differ radically from one person to another. For some, utterly loathing Pat Nixon, for example, may be a sublimation of aggression or guilt. The hostility the loather feels towards Mrs. Nixon, in spite of the fact that she has *done* nothing but simply *is*, functions as a socially inconsequential displacement of unconscious aggression towards others (or even towards the self). On the other hand, a positive interest in, say, a Jacqueline Kennedy, is more likely to involve wish-fulfillment. The celebrant imagines her to be an improvement upon what he or she is as a person. This may only consist of being well-known, or of being one of the beautiful people. But where is the American of such Puritan rectitude who has not fantasized about such possibilities? For others such values as exceptional beauty, charm or sophistication may be imputed to the celebrity. Since many of these are qualities often associated with heroes, some celebrity-struck individuals, themselves unstudious of definitions, may perceive their idols as heroes even though these luminaries have *done* nothing except exhibit luminosity. Boorstin inveighs against such transformations:

> The hero was distinguished by his achievement; the celebrity by his image or trademark. The hero created himself; the celebrity is created by the media. The hero is a big man; the celebrity is a big name.[15]

What is implied here, of course, is modern decadence, the moral bankruptcy of deriving inspiration and role models from these "human pseudo-events." For Boorstin the celebrity, unlike the true hero, is "morally neutral,"[16] and thus to participate in his or her cult is to celebrate the superficial, to ritualize emptiness. But, it might be added, such celebrations are in the main socially harmless and on an individual level possibly helpful, therapeutic, a form of needed ego-reinforcement. Such is not always the case with the celebration of heroes, as Robert Burton pointed out more than three centuries ago; in his polemic on the madness of warfare he scathingly exposes the dark side of hero-worship:

> ...every nation hath their Hectors, Scipios, Caesars, and Alexanders. Our Edward the Fourth was in 26 battles afoot; and

as they do all, he glories in it, 'tis related to his honour. . . . *They commonly call the . . . strongest thieves, the most desperate villains, treacherous rogues, inhuman monsters . . . courageous and generous spirits, heroical and worthy Captains, brave men* at arms, valiant and renowned soldiers . . . *they put a note of divinity upon the most cruel, & pernicious plague of human kind,* adore such men with grand titles, degrees, statues, images, honour, applaud, highly reward them for their good service. . . .[17]

Since our heroes are often killers, it becomes more of a question than Boorstin acknowledges as to whether a wish-fulfillment fantasy concerning an Audie Murphy is more socially and psychologically adaptive than a fantasy about a Merv Griffin.

One fact about fantasy is that facts are unimportant. Whatever gratifies is what counts, and when it comes to gratification, "factoids" (Norman Mailer's term for fictive facts)[18] can be as viable, often more viable, than mere facts. What is important to the celebrity-struck is that they be able, consciously or unconsciously, to "project" qualities which they believe themselves to possess upon the celebrity-figure and/or to "introject" qualities they associate with the celebrity into their own psychical personalities. It is by such mental processes that identification with the celebrity takes place.

As a psychological phenomenon identification reinforces the ego, the mind's mediatorial and management subsystem. Due to the constant demands placed upon the ego by external reality, by the mind's emotive and intuitive subsystem (the id), and by the subsystem concerned with beliefs and values (the superego), the ego requires regular shoring up. Identification with a positive object like a hero or even a celebrity can provide such necessary psychical support. Because narcissism is necessary, celebrities are functional. We have invented them because we need them or, at the very least, we accept such inventions because we have found that we can use them. They fill the gaps left by the absence of heroes or serve as substitutes for heroes who evoke anxiety or guilty. It can be argued that the mass media impose celebrities upon us, but the mass media can impose nothing: the mass audience can, and frequently does, ignore or reject proposed celebrities for reasons that are seldom conscious and are ultimately personal.

The mass media then cannot make a celebrity a hero. That power is reserved for the individual member of the mass audience who, in violation of all definitions of terms, consensus and even common sense, do so for reasons of their own. The late Duke of

Windsor, the former Edward VIII, may have been a neglible human being, but he was undoubtedly a celebrity and certainly to some a hero. Beside a Mark Anthony, who also gave "all for love" (or so Shakespeare and Dryden would have us believe), Windsor lolling on the beaches of St. Tropez, looks vaguely ridiculous. Not a few British subjects still regard him as something of a bounder if not a villain. Yet if those who write the biographies and the histories, who script the movies and the television specials, should over time side with those who perceive the abdicator as a hero, a hero in history he could become.

ii. The Hero as Media Creation and Media Victim

James Monaco is bearish on heroes. "Before we had celebrities," he says, seconding Boorstin, "we had heroes." In his view celebrities are driving heroes out of the market: there are fewer heroes around because "other types of celebrities are so powerful that they outshine figures who might, in other times, have been heroes."[19] But to imply that celebrities are a quite recent phenomenon is not, as has been suggested above, historically accurate. If, in primitive societies, heroes were usually leaders and vice-versa, down through recorded history relatively few members of royalty and the nobility were either true leaders or true heroes; for every Henry V there were scores of regal and titled celebrities. Further, Monaco's opinion that in contemporary society true heroes are being outshone, being so highly judgmental, is difficult to support—he himself offers only the example of Ralph Nader in evidence—or to refute. Yet his own emphasis on the present ubiquity of the mass media and (as has been noted above) the dependence of the hero upon the effectiveness of a society's publicity-mills allows for the possibility that Monaco's pessimism concerning the present state of heroes is not wholly warranted.

For the first time in human history, thanks to the electronic media, it is possible to receive instant and international publicity. And since the advent of television broadcasting via satellite the power of printed and spoken word has been dramatically enhanced by the power of the "live" picture. "In the future," Andy Warhol has prophesied, "everybody will be famous. For fifteen minutes."[20] The future is not yet now, but more and more of us have seen someone we know on television—in a crowd shot, in a roving reporter interview, or as a witness to or participant in some newsworthy event. The brave cop or firefighter, the rescuer of the drowning child, the citizen who tackles the mugger, all become instant heroes and, equally important, have the capacity for becoming heroes to a greater proportion of a given population than ever before.

In the days before radio even a front-page story about a local act of heroism would not come to the attention of the illiterate, the non-subscribers, and selective readers. Radio required only the ability to own and turn on a set, normal hearing, and a knowledge of the mother tongue, but the absence of a complementary visual image placed more demands upon the imagination and memory than some auditors were willing to meet. Now we not only hear about the scene and circumstances of the heroic deed, we receive the reinforcement of seeing them; now the hero is not only identified but pictured. Thus are both perception and memorial reconstruction of the perception enhanced. Local heroes have never before had such immediate and extensive publicity. Television, then, has transformed what used to be a form of folk culture into popular culture.

But the other side of the television picture is the medium's well-known voraciousness. In a folk society yesterday's hero was less likely to become yesterday's news, for day in and day out there *was* little that was new. The local hero was continually recreated as natives met in the village square or at the church or the tavern and subsequently, whenever occasion would spur reminiscence about local events. It has not been the same for the era of the global village. Television producers seem to lack confidence in the attention-spans and memories of their audiences and thus tend to regard heroes as disposable. Hence their zeal to discover and celebrate new heroes. Monaco may then be half right: contemporary society has witnessed a proliferation of heroes rather than a decline, but their shelf-life has been much reduced. Most of them are driven out, not so much by mere celebrities, as by more current heroes.

The phenomenon of the Hero-for-a-Day may be due to the skepticism, cynicism or ignorance of those who program television news or to the latter's judicious insight into modern life. Heroes have always had to compete for popular attention with the weather, with social, economic and political events, and with personal concerns, but in a folk society, if not the slower pace and simpler nature of its life-style, then its very limited communications network allowed a hero more time on a more limited stage.

The mass media, of course, have changed all that. They bring to our attention not only more heroes, including national and international ones, but more information generally. Information overload is rarely a problem of the folk society. Indeed its more typical information deprivation is what gives its local heroes their durability: their past exploits and their presence help fill the gaps left by the paucity of news. In contemporary society, however, media coverage of regional, national and international events inundates the mass audience with information. Organizing so much information can be difficult even for well-informed viewers. Consequently, because hero-figures (and villains) are, among other things, useful organizing principles—as television producers, like culture creators since time immemorial, understand—news frequently tends to be presented in terms of the newsmakers as heroes or villains. This is particularly true of international news, where fairness doctrines and equal-time provisions do not obtain with as much force as they do in the case of national and regional news. Mother Theresa and Fidel Castro are fair game, the mayor or the President, much less so.

Also contributing to the transitoriness of the modern hero-figure is television's capacity for intensity of focus, relative objectivity of presentation, and comprehensiveness of treatment. Both oral and printed accounts of a hero's exploits can be readily embellished by the communicator's tendency to dramatize and the communicatee's imagination. Seen through the eye of the hand-held video camera, however, the burning home is observed to be a tarpaper shack, the rescuer of the infant from its bedroom a skinny kid with a weak jaw and a limited vocabulary.

There is a high correlation between the potentiality of a hero-figure for serving the psychological needs of hero-worshippers and the vagueness of the hero's image. Archetypes and stereotypes are functional *because* they are one-dimensional—"cool" in McLuhanese. They allow audiences to fill in the blanks on their own, to recreate the hero best suited to their individual fantasies. The hero who can be both seen and heard, in living color (or colorlessness), can thus be at a disadvantage. An individual's very uniqueness serves as a bar towards the evocation of archetypal and stereotypical reponses. Sir Phillip Sidney was a hero to many sixteeth-century Britons, but Ben Jonson knew him to be "no pleasant man in countenance, his face being spoilled with Pimples and of high blood and Long ...."[22]

Not only television but also modern newspapers and weekly and monthly magazines, with their capacities for sharpness of focus and depth and breadth of coverage, have also contributed to the reduced longevity of the hero. If no man can be a hero to his valet, few male or female heroes can stand up to the kind of intensive and extensive scrutiny of which the modern media are capable.—Or to continue to measure up as heroes, over time, as their deeds become ancient history. More so than most, heroes pay the price of being human, and the price comes high in a mass media society. Even the most benign attentions of the journalistic crew almost invariably uncover the flesh and blood behind the instant legend; the suspension from college, the arrest for DUI, the fling with the stripper, the suborning to perjury. Like Alice, the mere human can in one moment become a giant, the next a pygmy; all that is required is to sip from the magical mass media bottle. As Reynolds Price puts it, "It's the merciless flood of *information* that has made living heroes apparently so rare, if not invisible, and so perilous on their heights."[22]

Thus is the real-life romance of the hero re-scripted into real-life tragedy. The ultimate tragedy, however, comes with media murder. Not the attacks launched by critical columnists or investigative reporters, but those mounted by the alienated, the frustrated, the paranoid, who see no hope of becoming famous even for fifteen minutes except by striking down the hero. Death is the best publicity. Basking in reflected gore. It is the very celebrity of heroes that makes them superior targets-of-opportunity for media murderers. Sniping at anonymous passers-by can yield an impressive body-count, but since quantity counts for something there can be no guarantees for any but the most highly skilled marksmen. A single shot at a hero-figure, however, will do nicely. One can even miss and still be all over the front pages and the six o'clock news. John Hinckley, Jr. is assured of as much attention as Sirhan Sirhan, and Lee Harvey Oswald, though dead, is a living legend.

One macabre form of evidence that celebrities are essentially different from heroes is that they rarely draw fire. They do not even rate highly as symbols, like Archduke Francis Ferdinand. It is as if the media murderer senses that terminating one who is celebrated only for *being* is not really *doing* anything or, at any rate, anything sufficient to become truly famous. (This same would be true for gunning down the hypothetical hero-without-publicity.) Only the attempt on the hero, the doer, guarantees that one will become a famous villain. And, given the vagaries of the human mind, the famous villain will inevitably become a hero to some.

The only safe hero then is the fictional hero. They can even be brought back, Lazarus-like, from the grave: Sherlock Holmes resurrected by Conan Doyle (by public demand) after his tragic death in Reichenbach Falls, James Bond being transfigured by Ian Fleming after the popular success of *From Russia with Love.*

Fictional heroes have obvious advantages over real-life ones and popular culture has exploited every one of them. Indeed, contrary to James Monaco, if the real-life hero has been driven into the shade, it is not so much by celebrities as by that other creation of the mass media, the fictional hero of popular culture. What percentage of the population, after all, can identify "Captain Kirk" and "Mr. Spock," and what percentage the first two astronuats to walk on the moon?

iii. Popular Culture and Heropoeia

That the most satisfactory heroes are fictional heroes is as arguable as the assertion that art is superior to life. But in spite of the manifold ironies of "Ode on a Grecian Urn" Keats does give the urn the last word: "Beauty is truth, truth beauty—that is all / Ye know on earth, and all ye need to know." The beauty of fictional heroes is that they are wholly mythic, not like real-life heroes who are historical figures elevated to the mythic. Fictional heroes are— or can be—beauty as truth, truth as beauty; real-life heroes will always be in part facts, which are not necessarily either beautiful or true. Real-life heroes can be enigmas, a General Lee or a General Marshall, for example, but it is fictional heroes like Hamlet who tease us out of thought. If a hero is, as Edgar Morin claims, "A kind of mortal avant-garde ... a human being in the process of becoming divine,"[23] divinity, at least as emotion rather than as idea, is more readily assigned to a fictional hero than to a human one. Divinities lack warts. And of all the fictional heroes, from those of folk culture to those of elite culture, popular culture heroes may have the best claim to divinity: they are the most widely known, the most unreservedly celebrated, and they offer the greatest potential good for the greatest number.

Not all popular culture heroes, of course, are fictional. So long as it is assumed that commercialized play constitutes a kind of reality, athletes, movie stars (even some movie directors), musicians, dancers, popular artists and writers, television-personalities, and other entertainment-industry types can be and are perceived as hero-figures by multitudes. But all of the limitations imposed upon real-life heroes (as explained in the preceding section) impinge as well upon real-life popular culture heroes. Their humanity is their vulnerability. Transiency is their reality.

There is irony in the fact that a Joe Dimaggio, a Clint Eastwood, a Frank Sinatra can exhibit more durability as hero-figure than individuals who have become famous through great deeds. Yet the hold on the popular imagination of real-life popular culture heroes is usually brief. They too are subject to the merciless scannings of the mass media and often they do not hold up. For them as for more traditional real-life heroes, the mass media giveth and the mass media taketh away. Although the hero-status of a Mickey Mantle may be as dependent upon his entertainment value as is that of Mickey Mouse, the real-life popular culture hero exists in time and space, and that is usually his or her undoing. Fictional popular culture heroes, on the other hand, are transcendent beings. So too are the fictional heroes of elite culture, of course, though this is not the place to consider them. The suggestions that follow concerning fictional popular culture heroes—hereafter called only "popular culture heroes"—apply as well to their elite brethren. Milton's Samson and Supermen are brothers under the skin.

Popular culture heroes illustrate some of the advantages life has over art. For example, unlike real-life heroes they are, in theory and in most practice, totally under the control of their creators, who shape what they say and do and what they look like. (The last is not an unimportant consideration for, as shall be explained below, appearance is important to a hero's image.) From another perspective, because popular culture is more responsive to its audience than any other form of culture, there is a sense in which popular culture heroes are also under the maximum control of their audiences. This proposition and that which affirms the control of the heroes' creators are not necessarily contradictory. Superman was the result of the vision of Schuster and Siegel, created wholly in their image and imaginations. The time and space he occupied and the ways in which he occupied them were of their own design, a design that clearly met the needs of the audiences of the 1930s. Yet over the years, years in which neither he nor his supporting cast have aged (another advantage of fiction), throughout the various media he and his world have been changed by his creators to meet the changing world of his audience and that audience's changing nature. A case in point is his celibacy, seemingly a requirement of the superhero: after more than forty years in which the sexual aspect of his relationship with Lois Lane has been variously toyed with in the comics and on television, the consummation devoutly to be wished for finally took place in the movie *Superman II*. There was no appreciable outcry. By convert and mutual agreement of creators and audience, through a kind of reciprocal control over the artifact, the hero is virgin no more.

Because popular culture heroes then, like fictional folk heroes, are more *communal* creations than fictional elite heroes, they bring about a kind of community, one whose citizens are the fans and whose popularly supported leaders are the heroes' creators.

Real-life heroes, on the other hand, can sometimes divide the very communities that celebrate them. Initially a Charles Lindbergh, for example, bonded not only the United States but the world. But that bond did not last: other nations sought to promote their own aviator heroes; other American aviators sought shares in Lindbergh's glory; and finally Lindbergh himself alienated many former worshippers with his pro-German pronouncements of the late 1930s. Being human, Lindbergh could not be controlled, and being Lindbergh, he actively resisted control. Steve Canyon never posed such problems. Or not until Milton Caniff, his creator, seemingly lost touch with his audience, increasingly politicized his comic strip, and alienated numbers of previously loyal fans.

Because popular culture is commercial culture produced by professionals the control wielded by its consumers, though indirect, is considerable. Along with many others, Dr. Johnson himself was distressed beyond measure at the deaths of the king and his daughter, so Richard Burbage arranged a happy ending for *King Lear*. On the other hand, the popular culture audience is also extremely flexible. It can, for example, embrace a score of actors in the role of Sherlock Holmes and at least four playing James Bond. The hero's the thing. And it is in pure myth, "an ensemble of imaginary situations and behaviors"[24] that the hero lives, moves and has his being, endures, ageless and immortal. The increasing decrepitude of the real-life hero, on the other hand, reminds even the most worshipful of their own mortality; the bad marriage or the unheroic job calls to mind the vicissitudes of everyday life; the hero's political ineptitude or foolish investments calls attention to the errors of our own ways. Despite McLuhan, neither we nor real-life heroes can live mythically for more than moments. History and nature have their ways with us. But myth is the *reality* of the popular culture hero and myth defines its own time and space.

A myth, Northrop Frye reminds us, is a story about a god, a godlike being, or a hero, and frequently all three.[25] To be found in every culture, in every historical period, such figures seem infinite in their variety. But Frye sets forth a typology by which they can be conveniently classified, described and related to the particular cultural forms in which they appear. This classification is based upon these mythic figures' "power of action," which "may be greater than ours, less, or roughly the same," as determined by the extent to which they can control the space and time in which they operate and whatever may occupy that time and space.

Type 1: The Super Hero. Super Heroes are "superior in kind" to human beings, to those who populate their mythic world and who comprise their audience. Super Heroes then are not only superior, they are different: if they are not alien beings like Superman, visitors from another planet, they are "semi-aliens" like Captain Marvel and Wonderwoman, or part-alien, part human like The Incredible Hulk. They are with us but not of us. Their weaknesses, if they have any (e.g. Kryptonite) are not our weaknesses. Their powers are ours but extraordinarily enhanced (able to leap tall buildings in a single bound) or of a different order from ours (imperviousness to projectiles). Super Heroes then are superior to the laws of nature as the makers of nature, the gods, are. Stories whose protagonists are Super Heroes are fundamentally mythic whether they take the form of epic (the quest of Banner / Hulk), or romance (Superman comic books), or satire (television's *The World's Greatest Hero*) or comedy (*Mork and Mindy*). In the main, however, Super Heroes are *serious* characters in works of entertainment that are as serious themselves as sacred texts. They are works that trade in truths rather than in facts—tertiary myths (as opposed to elite art myths like *The Faerie Queene* and primary / primitive myths like the Book of Genesis).

Type 2. The Supreme Hero. Whereas "Clark Kent" is only the *nom de guerre* of the "real" Superman, "Batman's" real name is "Bruce Wayne." Both Kent, the bumbling journalist, and Wayne, the millionaire layabout, are all too human, like us and most of the characters they encounter. Batman is also presented as human: he is mortal and vulnerable. If you cut him, he bleeds. But Batman bleeds only rarely, if ever, and given the multiplicity of certain-death situations from which he has escaped, he has about him the aura of immortality. Supreme Heroes then are only "superior in degree" to other humans, but so great is that degree of superiority that they function as demi-gods. They are not beyond natural law, able to leap tall buildings in a single bound, but they scale tall buildings rather readily. As Frye remarks, such heroes move "in a world in which ordinary laws of nature are slightly suspended."

Supreme Heroes can err but seldom do. An interesting exception is Spiderman, the highly successful product of adding one unit of Anti-hero to two units of Super Hero, yielding a Supreme Hero. *Spiderman* comics are popular culture romances—episodic stories of high adventure and love—the typical literary form for the Supreme Hero, though their elements of satire, comedy and even realism set them apart from more traditional tertiary romances like *Batman*.

Type 3: The Leader-Hero. "If superior in degree to other men, but not to his physical environment, the hero is a leader. He has authority, passions, and powers of expression far greater than ours ... but is subject both to social criticism and to the order of nature." Although such hero-figures abound in popular culture, it is possible that there are fewer of them, proportionately, than in either elite or folk culture. Of stories involving Super Heroes Frye has observed that, while they have an important place in literature, they are "as a rule found outside the normal literary categories." If by "normal literary categories" Frye is thinking of elite and folk literature he is doubtless correct: The Leader-Hero is their usual stock-in-trade. It is in twentieth-century popular culture, especially in comic books and comic strips, in movies, and in science fiction that Super Heroes have come into their own. This is true to a much lesser extent in television, whether because the medium's production values tend to be lower, thus limiting the kind of special effects required to dramatize Super Heroes, or because the true hero of television programming is The Family—and Super Heroes tend to be loners.[26]

Leader-Heroes are in several senses much closer to their fellow characters and to their audiences than are Super and Supreme Heroes. They tend to be represented as thoroughly human even though they are usually the best the species *homo sapiens* can produce. An Emma Peel or a John Steed (*The Avengers*) is a constellation of physical attractiveness and physical prowess, intelligence, knowledge, personality and skills to which ordinary mortals can only aspire, but individual members of their audience could conceivably excel them in a given area (such as expertise in the martial arts). Leader-Heroes usually operate in worlds which are presented as close approximations of our own, where time and space must be dealt with, as must society, nature and chance. This can give the works of which they are protagonists the appearance of realism (e.g., the James Bond novels) but on closer inspection they are closer to romance (e.g., the James Bond movies), but can be comic or even satiric (*M*A*S*H* as a television series). If Captain James Kirk of the Starship "Enterprise" can be classified as a Leader-Hero, the type can also figure in the popular culture epic. And if *The Godfather* films constitute popular tragedy, Leader-Heroes can be found in this form as well.

Type 4: The Everyman-Hero. Audience-identification with Everyman-Heroes might seem to be far easier than with types 113, for unlike these figures they have no natural endowments for the heroic. They are men and women whose powers, like ours, are limited, who are noteworthy neither for their virtues nor their acquirements. They tend to be ordinary mortals thrust by chance or circumstances into extraordinary situations. Unlike most mortals, however, they do not back off: they accept the challenge, rise to the occasion, and thereby raise themselves above the legions of the average. Thus, they embody and evoke everybody's daydream. Thus also they should logically be the most popular and populous heroes in popular culture. But this may not be the case. In the movies it has been the male stars—the Fairbanks, the Gables, the Waynes and the Reynolds, leader-figures all—who have dominated the silver screen. In television it has been the leader-type characters— the Paladins, the Matt Dillons, the Rockfords and the Hawkeyes— who have met with the widest and most prolonged approval. In comics it has been the Super Heroes. Logic would seem to favor the Everyman-Hero in everyman's culture, but psychology may offer the best explanation of why such logic breaks down. All culture is a form of play and much play takes the form of wish-fulfillment fantasy, a process in which we create an alternate reality more gratifying than existing reality. Therefore, audience-identification with a "better" object (like Hero-types 1-3) will likely afford a greater yield of satisfaction and ego-reinforcement than identification with an Everyman-Hero, who is in most respects what we are rather than what we might be. Peer-heroes then may offer more psychological gratification in forms like television comedy (Andy Griffith, Mary Tyler Moore) where our dreams are not so much at stake, nor our idealized self-images.

Type 5: The Subordinate Hero. A variety of factors can make a hero-figure subordinate both to other characters and to an audience: age (children and the elderly), economic or social status (women, members of non-dominant races, the handicapped). Initially audiences are more likely to have sympathy for such characters than they are to identify with them. Or they may look down upon figures so obviously deficient. It is only when Subordinate Heroes are put to the test and struggle mightily to meet it that wish-fulfillment again insinuates itself into the transaction with the text and the possibilities for identification are enhanced. As in the case of Everyman-Heroes, Subordinate Heroes are more likely to figure in popular comedy and satire (Charlie Chaplin, Dennis the Menace, Archie Bunker) than in more mythic forms.

—Addendum. Although the foregoing analysis has confined itself to human characters, popular culture is particularly generous in presenting to its audiences heroes who are not of the species *homo sapiens* or its inter-galactic equivalents. Animal heroes abound, of course, in popular fictions targeted upon the children's market—though they often become the guilty pleasures of many adults as well. Who would not weep for Lassie? Benji? Such hero-figures pose some interesting problems in classification—is The Roadrunner an Everyman or Subordinate Hero?—but the tendency of popular culture to Disneyfy or anthropomorphize animal-characters facilitates their accommodation in the hero-typology.

Anthropomorphosis is also very much involved in one of the more interesting and important developments in popular culture of the twentieth century—the transformation of the machine into archetypal hero ("Herbie" the Disney Volkswagen), archetypal villain ("Hal" the computer of *2001: A Space Odyssey*), as helper-archetype ("3CPO" in *Star Wars*), among others. Elsewhere I have suggested that popular culture, more extensively and effectively than elite culture, while mainly seeking merely to entertain, has come to grips with one of the fundamental problems of modern times, the relationship between man and machine.[27] Science fiction novels, television series like *Star Trek*, innumerable movies and comic books dealing with future shock, not to mention scores of films about such familiar but critically important machines like cars, trucks, trains and airplanes—all have explored and exploited our development of, dependence upon, love and fear of, machines.

In the process there has emerged a complex, wide-ranging Myth of the Machine which goes further toward analyzing the natures and functions of machines, setting forth their implications for human development, and suggesting the problems and possibilities they present for society, than have any of our age's thinkers or informational or educational institutions. More important to this popular culture myth than the facts of technology have been the social, pysochological and moral dimensions of the man-machine relationship, and in this regard machine-heroes and villains, like their human archetypal equivalents, have played key roles. For a new perspective on human values, for example, is gained when virtue is incarnated ("inmechanized"?) into an R2D2; a new appreciation and apprehension of evil are attainable when one is faced with the possibility that the Devil may have returned to earth as a sentient black sedan (the movie *The Car*).

Joseph Campbell has called myths "public dreams,"[28] and human beings are, of course, inveterate dreamers, individually and collectively. Which is why "mythopoeia," myth-making, is as antique as the race. Since the arrival of the electric and electronic mass media, mythopoeia has been proceeding at a pace and to an extent never before seen in human history. And since, as we have seen, myths are lies that tell the truth, illusions to live by which impact upon us chiefly through their protagonists, their gods and heroes, "heropoeia"—the creation of hero-figures—is and always has been central to the myth-making process.

iv. Logos and the Popular Culture Hero

Mythos, the story, is the vehicle for *Logos*, the Word. For believers, who perceive both the myth and the word as history (the way things were), as social criticism (the way things should be), and prophecy (the way things shall be), myths are not, of course, fictions. They are chronicles that embody the Truth. Even among believers credence in such stories and truths will vary, and this kind of suspension of belief will be even more frequent in the case of myths made and promulgated by popular culture. Advanced as entertainments rather than as sacred texts, experienced in the home or in theatres rather than in sacred places, the myths of popular culture are bound to be consciously perceived, even by their most avid consumers, only as "escape," as ways of passing time agreeably, as mere diversions of daily routine. Yet, from the perspective of psychology, more is happening in all those transactions between audiences and artifacts than meets the audiences' eyes—and minds.

Escape, time-passing, and diversion do not adequately explain why audiences *care* about popular culture, why they become so involved in it, why they spend so much time, effort and money in seeking it out. The pleasure-principle, obviously, is one answer: human beings are pleasure-seeking animals; the purpose of play is pleasure; humans play in the expectation of pleasure. Man is the only creature who constructs fictions chiefly to play in—play for the sake of play. (Animal play is heavily adaptive, functional.) The play that is culture yields pleasures that are more complex than eating pizza or loafing. Fictions, in addition to offering psychosomatic gratification (e.g., the XXX-movie), also provide audiences with materials for creating wish-fulfillment fantasies (e.g., Harlequin romances) but also anxiety-fantasies (e.g., horror movies). Moreover, fictions afford audiences opportunities for having their attitudes, beliefs and values reinforced (most popular culture), expanded (some popular culture) or challenged (little popular culture). Such "intellectual" experiences can be pleasurable even though popular culture audiences may not be quite conscious that their transaction with a "text" is at all cerebral. All that we usually sense is that we "liked" the movie, the TV show, the best seller.

It is only when a popular culture form departs from what we sense to be The Word that the truth-telling function of the secular myth behind the entertainment becomes apparent. A much publicized example was the death of the loveable "Colonel Henry Blake" in an episode of *M.A.S.H.* For the audiences there is, first, the shock, then disbelief, followed by involuntary and varying degrees of regret. For some members of the *M.A.S.H.* audience there is outrage; for a few there are calls or letters to the network. None of this is due to the program's revelation that people die. Nor to avoidance of the subject of death by popular culture—like many other popular culture fictions, *M.A.S.H.* trades in death all the time. Rather, the extraordinary reaction is more likely due to the subversion of a myth by the violation of a convention which reinforces it. This particular convention is that characters whom audiences have come to know and value (know better and value more, sometimes, than real friends, acquaintances and relatives), do not *die* in the course of a popular culture sequence, are not *supposed* to die. Even when they are shown to be as wholly human as the Maclain Stevenson character—and therefore vulnerable, mortal— they are felt at some level beneath consciousness to be immortal. The immortality of the principals is a convention of television and of much other popular culture.

The psychological truth which the convention reinforces is expressed in our own repression of the fact of our mortality, in our normal tendency to operate as if we will never die. One step removed from this is the *logos* of the *mythos*, that death has no sting, the grave no victory. It is what we want to hear, whether we hear it directly, from the pulpit, or indirectly, in repeated exposure to the secular myths of popular culture. To embody and sometimes express such truths is a primary function of popular culture heroes. They figure forth those attitudes, beliefs and values which comprise the usually haphazard network through which we pass our experience, classify it, comprehend it and judge it.—The Hero as the superego made flesh. In the testing of the hero the superego is itself vicariously tested, and in his or her victory or ennobling defeat the integrity of the superego is reaffirmed. It is no accident that Superman "fights for truth, justice, and the American way."

Popular culture experiences then are in one sense rituals of reinforcement (though to put it thus smacks of redundancy, all rituals being reinforcing). In this light popular culture itself can function as a kind of handbook for the mass audience, promising delight but also delivering instruction. As Joseph Campbell has shown, moral, ethical and religious guidance is one of the main purposes served by myth.[29] The gods and heroes of myth serve as role models for the young—the Imitation of Christ in the middle ages, for the modern period, perhaps, the imitation of that other god incarnated as mere mortal, Superman. For adults myth offers guidance regarding appropriate attitudes and behaviors for conducting their relationships with others and with the gods throughout life's pilgrimage—Holy Living and Holy Dying for the Renaissance, the Good Life for the twentieth century. Here too it is the heroes of myth in particular who show the way—from the courage of David and the pluck of Disney kids to the wisdom of Solomon and the caffein-savvy of Robert Young. The hero thus acts as a stabilizing force, as a supporter of the social order. Popular Culture heroes are rarely anti-establishment. Even when they appear to be, as in the case of the typical Burt Reynolds character, it is the corruption of the establishment that provokes their heroism. At bottom they are secular protestants and reformation is the result if not the motivation of their actions.

According to Campbell myth also has descriptive and informational functions, offering a picture of the universe and of nature which approximates that of current scientific knowledge. Sacred myth undertakes then to explain to its adherents not only the human condition but the cosmic condition, and as a consequence is ultimately more concerned with metaphysics than with physics. Metaphysics, by its very nature, implies stasis more than flux, and it is set forth in sacred texts, which also derive much of their authority from being fixed, absolute. Thus sacred myth tends to resist change; a radical revision of scientific knowledge such as the displacement of the Ptolemaic picture of the universe by the Copernican during the Renaissance can have cataclysmic effects. Secular myth, because its claims are less transcendental, is more adaptable. Indeed the secular myths promulgated by popular culture constantly undergo revision in accordance with the expansion of scientific knowledge, in part because popular culture itself thrives upon new ideas. The universe according to Einstein becomes a new and exciting setting in which the popular culture hero can operate. Relativity affords more plots for the creators of *Star Trek* and *Star Wars* than are dreamt of in the anthropocentric philosophy of the authors of the Bible. As electronic prosthesis becomes more and more commonplace, the *Six Million Dollar Man* takes on a kind of relevance for the popular audience that Samson no longer has.

Whether it is regarded as a "mirror" of life or as a "refractor" of it,[30] popular culture's sensitivity to change and its tendency to use change as grist for its mythopoeic mill makes it an ideal vehicle not only for The Word but for The Latest Word. Science fiction is the most obvious example; indeed the genre so often tends to move beyond even the most current scientific knowledge that there is some justification in relabeling it "speculative fiction." The record shows that there is a mass audience for science fiction, but particularly for its more conservative representations in television series like *Lost in Space* and movies such as *E.T.* Science fiction novels and short stories, though widely popular, are more of a cult phenomenon, like the current interest in fantasy fiction. Because the popular audience is predominantly middle-class and moderate-to-conservative on political and ethical issues in particular, its creators approach the raising of mass consciousness with considerable care. As a result, in the *logos* of popular culture *mythos*, Einstein is O.K., Marx and Freud are still non-O.K., and Darwin fluctuates according to the temper of the times.

Nonetheless, popular culture is second only to institutionalized education in the dissemination of information concerning the nature of nature and of the cosmos, and for many it is the primary source and the favored one. Here again the role of the popular culture hero-figure is pivotal. Although scientists, mad and otherwise, are familiar popular culture stereotypes, modern incarnations of archetypal magicians and wizards, popular culture heroes are sometimes scientists themselves (e.g., Quincy) or at least scientifically or technologically *au curraunt* (e.g., James Bond). Thus they not only become vehicles for information-transfer but their hero-status lends credibility to the information transferred.

As information-retrieval, processing and transfer assume more and more importance in modern society, it is likely that popular culture will respond by offering its audiences more heroes who rely less on physical prowess and more on information-storage and application. (The hero of the 1982 movie *Tron* is a computer programmer.) Powerful but hardly cerebral heroes like Conan the Barbarian and Rocky Balboa will doubtless always have their atavistic place in popular culture, but Mr. Spock (even without the Ph.D.) may be the shape of heroes to come. Once the Six Million Dollar Man and the Bionic Woman are fully wired into computers, cyborg-heroes may begin to make the Man of Steel look like an anachronism.

One other function of myth, the evocation of an ecstatic response to the mystery of the universe mankind inhabits, is carried out more effectively by popular culture than by any other institution in history. Until the mid-19th century, sacred institutions could only promulgate their myths by oral transmission, by means of the printed word, through various forms of iconography (stained glass windows, paintings and sculpture, engraved illustrations), and in musical and theatrical performances. The invention of the camera was not, apparently, perceived by the church as presenting new iconographic possibilities, and even to this day the uses to which the church puts still photography are quite limited.

The institution of popular culture, on the other hand, being dependent upon technology, has usually taken maximum advantage of it. So long as the technology is commercially feasible and potentially profitable, the producers, creators and distributors of popular culture take a chance on it. As a result, the popular audience enjoys: talking pictures and color television, neither of which the churches were quick to exploit; phonographic records and stereophonic sound, still the devil's instruments to some; comic books, slick magazines, the short story and the popular novel, all of which have been utilized by the church only sporadically and haphazardly.

One reason for the church's failure to make full use of technological advances is undoubtedly financial: popular culture is far better capitalized. But insufficient insight and imagination are factors as well. As a consequence, in the twentieth century the secular myths of popular culture have captured and captivated the mass audience to the extent that they have come to rival sacred myths in terms of popular awareness. There *was* a sense in which the Beatles were, as John Lennon claimed, "bigger than Jesus." Modern technology not only disseminates secular myths more quickly and widely than the media upon which the sacred institutions have traditionally had to rely but makes fewer demands upon the perceptual skills of their audiences. Audiences must make pilgrimages to the Sistine Chapel, but the Wild West of television series from *Have Gun, Will Travel* to *Gunsmoke* and *Bonanza* came into millions of homes the world over for decades. A full appreciation of Boticelli's madonnas doubtless required some degree of painterly sophistication even in the fifteenth century, but getting involved in an episode of *Wonderwoman* demands only minimal visual and aural literacy.

Hero-figures by their very nature are larger-than-life, and rare is the static depiction, no matter how artful, that can communicate the hero's power and glory more effectively than the movie screen. Even the reduction in scale that takes place on the 21-inch television tube is no more than that which appears on all but monumental canvases and, just as in portraiture in oils, the hero can be seen at an impressive angle or be depicted in a revealing closeup. And on television the hero not only talks but moves—and movement, action, is basic to the dynamics of the hero-figure. It would seem to be a part of the phenomenology of movies and television that they "heroize"—not only depict the hero in the most vivid way possible but make heroes out of the depictors themselves, the stars. The hero's impact then is doubled: in a reading of the book of Exodus, Moses is only Moses, leader-hero of the children of Israel; on the wide screen Moses is also Charlton Heston.

To fulfill their functions myths must be both accessible and compelling. It is the technology involved in the production and distribution of popular culture as much (or more) than its forms and contents that makes its myths and heroes so available and so capable of involving the mass audience. Whether as Moses or as Ben Hur Charlton Heston defines the hero for the popular imagination, demonstrates for young and old alike what manhood is held to be in Western culture, and what the Judeo-Christian tradition understands virtue and piety to be. Whether contrived by special effects or captured by an astronaut's camera, the majesty of the universe and its mystery are brought home to the ignorant and the learned, the many and the mighty. No longer is the rapture of the cosmic deep an experience accessible primarily to mystics. "Space, the final frontier," or "The heavens declare the glory of god"—either response is possible and valid, and even both simultaneously, for although the secular myths and heroes of popular culture can be seen as competing with those of sacred institutions, the human mind has an infinite capacity for and inclination toward reconciling them. With cognitive dissonance we choose not to live: it is far more satisfactory to utilize *2001* to reinforce Genesis I.

v. Popular Culture Heroes, the Denial of Death and the Affirmation of Life

"**Where** Have All the Heroes Gone?"—The question serves as the title of a 1974 article by Edward Hoagland and a continuing theme of commentators in the 1980s.[31] At times it seems more plaintive cry than question, the nostalgia of intellectual herophiles for their lost youth. At other times the question becomes the jumping-off point for a full frontal assault on the shallowness of present civilization, the skepticism of the age, or the moral bankruptcy of modern art and literature. So the proclamation goes forth—"The hero is dead; Long live the hero!"—and the only survivors are the anti-hero and the existential hero (when the two can be distinguished at all). Even so incisive and profound a thinker as Ernest Becker can claim that we are undergoing nothing less than a "crisis in heroism."[32]

But the hero's obituary notice is perhaps premature. "Where have all the heroes gone?" One answer is: "To popular culture, nor have they ever left it." The hero is alive and well in sports, comic books, bestsellers, television and movies. Reggie Jackson is not Babe Ruth, of course, but the main difference between them may well be that the kind of benign conspiracy among the sports journalists that preserved the public's presumed innocence from the real Ruth is no longer in force. Now we get Jackson and his colleagues, warts, salary squabbles and all.

What is of special interest here is the concern behind the overriding question. The hero? Gone?—It is as if serious and enlightened observers perceive the hero as somehow being essential to human life or to society. And this is, in fact, the main argument of Becker's Pulitzer-Prize-winning book, *The Denial of Death*. His main concern is this work, at once scholarly analysis and wide-ranging meditation, is the real-life hero, but with allowances for the differences between our responses to life and to art, much of which he has to say is of relevance to the fictional hero. We have, Becker claims, "a constant hunger for heroes" (p. 184) and that hunger is not being satisfied in our time:

> What characterizes modern life is the failure of all traditional ideologies to absorb and quicken man's hunger for self-perpetuation and heroism. Neurosis today is a widespread problem because of the disappearance of convincing dramas of [the] heroic apotheosis of man (p. 190).

It is a large claim: the therapy for The Age of Anxiety is apotheosis, the transformation of a human being into a heavenly being, a star, a hero, a god, a symbol of human potential maximized and realized.

"Lives of great men and women," says Reynold Price, "have always reminded us we can make our lives quite literally sublime—lifted up, raised above the customary trails nature has cut for itself through eons."[33] Though few ultimately are chosen for apotheosis, all are called. As Becker puts it, "Our central calling, or main task on this planet, is the heroic" (p. 1). Mankind endures as animal, but prevails as hero. *Realpolitik* has been tried, and found wanting. It may well be then that civilization, progress, the fate of the planet itself, depend upon a new idealism. Mere abstractions will not, however, suffice: the plea for idealism is constantly being issued from pulpits and commencement platforms, with disappointing results. Ideals, "God-terms," as Philip Rieff calls them, "have to be exemplified .... Men crave their principles incarnate in enactable characters ...."[34] Those characters may be real-life heroes, as John F. Kennedy seemed to be to all those who thrilled to his call, "Ask not what your country can do for you, but what you can do for your country." Or they may be fictional characters like "Hawkeye" Pierce, who over the eleven years of *M*A*S*H.*'s popularity may have indirectly, even unconsciously, persuaded individual viewers that humanity, service, compassion, love, kindness and gentleness are the marks of the true hero.

These individual transactions we make with hero-figures (as has been suggested above) are potentially therapeutic. If identification (which is most often unconscious) takes place our self-image is strenthened, our identities are further crystallized, and in general our sense of autonomy and power is bolstered. Heroes then can be ego-reinforcing for non-heroes. As David Riesman has explained, from the point of view of Freudian psychology, "the ego of the hero is in unquestioned command, and [the] conflict between the conscious and unconscious levels of the personality is at a minimum."[35] The neurosis which Becker claims is endemic to our age is, of course, the result of such conflicts between the conscious and unconscious levels of the personality. Therefore, identification with an appropriate hero-figure can make us feel more content with ourselves and more capable of dealing with external reality. Winston Churchill during World War II illustrates the phenomenon on a national scale—as does Adolph Hitler, who seemed at the time to represent an appropriate hero-figure to the German masses.

Identification with a hero-figure can also raise consciousness and extend the ego as well as reinforce it. This possibility is particularly open to the young. When the hero is psychologically processed as not only a gratifying addition to one's fantasy life, but as a role model as well, personal development is facilitated. Mentors of the young have long known the importance of calling their attention to figures exemplary of society's values, attitudes and appropriate behavior. As Otto Rank has said, "the hero should always be interpreted ... as a collective ego."[36]

Freud called attention to the modeling behavior exhibited by children, for whom parents are the initial hero-figures, and later, parent-surrogates such as teachers.[37] Studies by developmental psychologists have confirmed the extent to which role-models help direct the evolution of the personality. It is on the basis of such phenomena that Becker portrays society as a "codified hero system" (p. 7), a "machine" for producing heroes who, it is intended, will be replicated in the rising generations. Real-life heroes can function in this way but so also can fictional heroes, which is why the guardians of the social order periodically view with alarm the heroes fashioned by the creators of society's culture. It is in the interest of society that heroes be establishment figures, but not all artists are of the establishment and not a few of them are critics of it. But the creators of popular culture, who must have access to the establishment's production-and-distribution system, and who must avoid alienating the mass audience and the establishment which controls it, are far more likely to adhere to the society's code of the hero than are elite artists. Hence, the periodic expressions of concern regarding the heroes of movies, television and the comics in particular is frequently off the mark. The alarmists often simply have not done their homework, having based their attacks on superficial and selective readings of popular culture texts.

Moreover, as Freud long ago pointed out,[38] children soon learn the difference between art and life—it is a miniscule minority that fashions Superman capes of blankets and jumps off the roof. Even in their earlier, more impressionable years, the fictional role-models of children receive considerable competition from the real-life role models who surround them and from societal pressures imposed upon them by various authority figures. Common experience indicates that normal children, exposed from infancy through adolescence to real-life and fictional role-models, will in the main encounter real-life and fictional hero-figures bearing the stamp of social approval. For without society's imprimatur heroes will not long receive nor long retain the publicity that enables them to have an impact upon the mass consciousness. It is for good and sufficient reasons that Lincoln, Marshal Dillon, Florence Nightingale, Little Orphan Annie, Dr. Martin Luther King, Jr., and Captain James Kirk have retained their places in the popular imagination. And that reason is not their radicalism.

As a result of their transactions with hero-figures then it is possible for the young to seek to develop new skills, rearrange their priorities, or even refashion their identities, but almost invariably within limitations dictated by practicality and the ideational paradigms established by society. Adults, on the other hand, though some may seek to modify their personal styles or their life-styles as a result of incorporating hero-figures into their psychic economy, are more likely to use heroes, real or fictional, as materials for the generation of wish-fulfillment fantasies. The hero as text for daydreams.

John L. Caughey has pointed out that most of us live in two worlds, one real, one artificial, and the latter consists of "beings known to [us] through some form of the media—through television, radio, books, magazines, and newspapers."[39] In our "real" social world, Caughey suggests, most of us actually *know* only two to three hundred persons. But we are familiar with—sometimes more familiar with and more approving of—"the lives and personalities of a swarm of celebrities—politicians, talk-show hosts, authors, athletes, religious spokesmen, disc jockeys—as well as fictional figures for novels, plays, sitcoms, and soap operas." Most of these engage our attention no more than slight acquaintances do, but a few may become important to us, even more important than some of our relatives and friends. The death of a John Lennon, for example, can leave a vacancy in a fan's life that is considerably more affecting than the death of a seldom-seen uncle. And though we know that actress Jean Stapleton is very much alive, the "death" of "Edith Bunker" may be felt more strongly and more frequently (as we tune in on new episodes of *All in the Family*) than the loss of an old friend.

This is not necessarily a sign of our insensitivity but rather of our special psychological relationship with hero-figures. As one social analyst has suggested, our relationships with friends and acquaintances are "contractual" and reciprocal: we implicitly agree that I will treat you as a friend so long as you treat me as one. But with our heroes we allocate prestige and other social benefits (and sometimes financial benefits) without any expectation of reciprocity in kind.[40]

Caughey's study suggests that such vicarious relationships with popular culture figures are not uncommon among normal adults. These relationships can take the form of adolescent-type infatuations, of fantasizing real relationships, of addressing comments to images of such figures (appearing on the TV screen, for example) and of role modeling. Many of Caughey's subjects "could describe long and conscious histories of patterning some overt behavior on the qualities of people, real *and* fictional, whom they admired.[41] Such interactions can be positive—whites idolizing Muhammad Ali—or negative—blacks expressing hostility toward Archie Bunker. The very nature of the mass media, particularly films and television, encourage such interactions: if the medium cannot get the viewer's attention, maintain it, and deepen it into a form of involvement, it will fail to communicate its messages. In-depth involvement at its most successful has carry-over effects: the experience is remembered and re-lived, becomes material for fantasizing, or even leads to overt behaviors, ranging from purchasing a Polaroid camera because it is associated with Rockford/Maverick/James Garner to making a pilgrimage to Elvis's Graceland.

Popular culture figures then quite commonly become what Caughey labels "media mentors"—role models and heroes. His findings support those of Murray and Kluckholm:

> Ego ideals run all the way from the Master Criminal to the Serene Sage. They are imaginatively created in the course of development in response to patterns offered by the environment—mythological, historical, or living examplars.[42]

If society is, as Ernest Becker argues, a codified hero-system, it is obvious that in the twentieth century the mass media are that system's primary presenters of hero-figures, and that popular culture heroes figure more importantly in the lives of more people than do any other kinds. Whether they be real-life heroes or fictional ones does not seem to be particularly important. Indeed, distinguishing between the two can be difficult. Who is it, after all that the admirer of a Mary Tyler Moore or a Jane Fonda is devoted to—the actress? the roles the actress plays? or a complex synthesis of the actress as person, as performer, and as the roles she typically plays?

The importance of the hero-figure is not confined to our private lives. In their analysis of what they call "corporate cultures," Terrence E. Deal and Allan A. Kennedy explain that a company's goals, promotion patterns and slogans serve to explain to employees what the company stands for. Moreover,

> Successful corporations also have pantheons of heroes, who serve as role models. Like Henry Ford of Ford Motor Co., Thomas Watson of IBM or Ray Kroc of McDonald's, they "have

great symbolic and mythic value within the culture of their companies." Employees are proud to be connected with these magical figures ... and draw strength and courage from them. ... Though exceptional individuals such as Ford, Watson and Kroc are rare, companies continually create new heroes. The members of IBM's "Hundred Percent Club," who have met their annual sales quotas, become office stars.[43]

It is Ernest Becker, however, for whom heroes have ultimate, transcendental importance—as agents who embody and evoke our most profound anxieties, such as our sense of our vulnerability and mortality—but also our most profound desires, such as for immortality. Heroes are by definition risk-takers, which sets them apart from the majority of the race, and what they frequently risk is their very lives, which sets them apart from almost everyone. To witness their deeds, Becker says, is "to rehearse the greatest victory we can imagine. And so the hero had been the center ... of honor and acclaim since ... the beginning of specifically human evolution" (p. 12). For Becker the hero's deed is in effect a denial of death. The theory upon which this hypothesis is based is summarized by Alan Lacey:

> We humans are born tiny in a world of people with larger bodies and sometimes ambiguous intents. We die without ever quite having gotten over things that happen to us in early childhood. Between birth and death we live largely by symbols, the most urgent of which deal with the nasty little human secret separating us from the rest of animal creation. We will die, *and we know it*. We are contingent beings, and we have such uncomfortable knowledge of our contingency that we develop a panoply of cultural symbols, rituals, and institutions offering the illusion of perpetuity .... For each of us our own mortality is the greatest of personal evils .... Not daring to peer into the Abyss, we have invented culture, comforting mechanisms giving meaning and significance to our existence.[44]

And in the last two hundred years we have developed popular culture, the most efficient method the world has ever seen for providing us with heroes whom we may use to give meaning and significance to our lives. As Otto Rank has said of real-life heroes, "we participate in their immortality and so we create immortals."[45] It is ironic, then, and a surprising omission in his book, that Becker entirely overlooks popular culture, the chief source today for the very kinds of hero-figures for whom he calls. Preoccupied with what he sees as the age's sense of "global helplessness" (p. 53), Becker fails to see that the " 'second' reality or better world" than the one given to us "by nature," the world we "must always imagine and believe in" (p. 188) has been created by popular culture. Nor is this creation always unconscious, unintentional, or accidental, the chance result of the desire to market a saleable cultural commodity. As the sophistication of popular culture creators has increased, some of them have embarked upon mythopeia deliberately: Stan Lee devises a new comic book, *Genesis II*; George Miller, creator of the series of "Mad Max" adventure films studies mythology and concludes that "audiences were hungering for mythic heroes who could triumph over evil."[46]

Another problem with Becker's analysis of the "crisis in heroism" is that, in accordance with a Freudian theory no longer widely accepted, he makes a psychologically simplistic distinction between real-life and fictional heroes. A distinction which (as we have already noted) is not necessarily made by ordinary people and not necessarily important to the ways in which they use heroes. Becker maintains that identification with fictional heroes is substitute gratification (as if identification with real-life heroes is not), a withdrawal from life, a counter-productive form of regression. Yet at the same time he concurs with Rank's statement, "With the truth one cannot live. To be able to live one needs illusions" (p. 188). Becker seems to forget that real-life heroes can be as much illusions as fictional ones, but that both can serve as lies to live by, indeed to grow and develop by. Either kind of hero can be used in the creation of "the living myth of the significance of human life," to the "defiant creation of meaning," to the establishment of what is, in effect, a "religion" (p. 7).

The idea is in fact a commonplace of popular culture thought: as established religions continually undergo sectarianization, as new religions multiply, and as society becomes increasingly secularized, the role of religion in reinforcing communal values and providing role models, heroes, who are the repositories of those values, these functions are being taken over by popular culture. What John Leonard has said of television in particular is true of the mass media and popular culture in general: it has become "our common language, our ceremony, our style, our entertainment and anxiety, our sympathetic magic, or way of celebrating, mourning, worshipping."[47] Religion has been efficacious because it is *not* theology, because it makes abstract principles concrete, incarnating Evil and Good, Satan as villain, Christ as hero. Heroes not only mediate between heaven and earth, ideal and reality, but in a sense between the lobes of the bicameral mind: out of the speeches of the gods they help to create consciousness.[48]

Popular culture heroes are *gestalts* of the popular mind, symbolic figures whose totality is greater than the sum of their parts. Though they are often death-dealers themselves and defined and deified amidst death, they are ultimately life-affirming. Life is what they are out to preserve, even at the risk of their own lives. And their victories over death, either through their survival or their transfiguration, are our intimations of immortality.

Lenny Skutnik? In the aftermath of the crash of the Air Florida jetliner in Washington, D.C. early in 1982, Lenny Skutnik, a minor government employee, dived into the freezing waters of the Potomac River to rescue an injured and drowning crash survivor. His deed was recorded by television cameras and he was, for fifteen minutes, famous.[49]

The Lone Ranger? But you *know* who he is.

Notes

[1] *Varieties of Religious Experience: A Study in Human Nature* (New York: Mentor Edition, 1958), p. 281.

[2] "Ode on the Death of the Duke of Wellington," *Poems and Plays* (London: Oxford, 1973), 205.

[3] "Celebration," *Celebrity: The Media as Image Makers*, ed. James Monaco (New York: Dell, 1978), 6. I should note here that while this essay records some of my disagreements with Monaco, he and I have arrived independently at some of the same conclusions about celebrities and heroes. (See my unpublished paper, "Stars / Heroes / Actors / Characters" presented at the 1979 meeting of the Popular Culture Association.)

[4] "Where Have All the Heroes Gone," *The New York Times Magazine* (March 10, 1974).

[5] *The Image; Or What Happened to the American Dream* (New York: Atheneum, 1962), pp. 48, 49, 74. Considerably more accurate is the observation of Marshall W. Fishwick: "Behind every hero is a group of skillful and faithful maniupulators," *American Heroes: Myth and Reality*(1955; rpt. Westport, Conn.: Greenwood Press, 1972), p. 228.

[6] Ibid., p. 56.

[7] Ibid., pp. 45 ff. In *Common Culture and the Great Tradition: The Case for Renewal* (Westport, Conn.: Greenwood Press, 1982), p. 105, Marshall W. Fishwick points out that the mass media can "confer celebrity, not just on people, but also on art objects, places, ways of life."

[8] "Celebration," 6.

[9] *The Image*, p. 59. Also *contra* Boorstin, Fishwick asserts that "Some become celebrities merely by being born..."(*Common Culture*, p. 108).

[10] "Celebration," 14.   [11] Ibid., p. 11.

[12] "Preface" to *Celebrity*, xi.   [13] Idem.

[14] "Popular People," *American Film* 4 (Nov., 1978), 71.

[15] *The Image, p. 61.*   [16] Ibid., p. 58.

[17] *The Anatomy of Melancholy*, ed. Floyd Dell and Paul Jordan-Smith (New York: Tudor, 1927), pp. 46, 48, 49-50.

[18] "Celebration," 9.   [19] Ibid., pp. 5, 10-11.

[20] Quoted in "Celebration," 8.

[21] *Ben Jonson*, ed. C.H. Herford and Percy Simpson (Oxford: Oxford Univ. Press, 1925), I, 138-

139.

[22]"The Heroes of Our Times," *Saturday Review* (Dec., 1978), 16.

[23]*The Stars*, trans. Richard Howard (New York: Evergreen, 1961), p. 39.

[24]Idem. Myth, as Marshall T. Fishwick has put it, is a "charter of society" and "heroes are the personification of its ethos," *The Hero: American Style* (New York: David McKay, 1969), p. 116.

[25]See *Anatomy of Criticism: Four Essays* (Princeton: Princeton Univ. Press, 1957), especially pp. 33-34. Some of the terminology and description which follows has been borrowed from my own paraphrasing of Frye's text in *Hero / Anti-Hero* (New York: McGraw-Hill, 1973), pp. xiii-xxi.

[26]For a more detailed discussion of television characters, see my essays, "In the Family: Television's Reformation of Comedy," *Psychocultural Review*, 2 (Fall 1978), 275-286 and "TV Heroes and the Denial of Death," *Prospects*, ed. Jack Salzman, 5 (New York: Burt Franklin, 1980), 457-466.

[27]Roger B. Rollin, *"Deus in Machina*: Popular Culture's Myth of the Machine," *Journal of American Culture* 2 (Summer 1978), 297-308. See also William Blake Tyrrell, *Star Trek*'s Myth of Science," *Journal of American Culture*, 2 (Summer 1978), 288-296.

[28]Quoted in Gerald Clark, "The Need for New Myths," *Time* (Jan. 17, 1972), 50-51. Ray B. Browne has observed that "myth and the urge to heroize seem to be profoundly a part of man's nature...," "Epilogue," *Heroes of Popular Culture*, ed. Ray B. Browne, Marshall Fishwick, and Michael T. Marsden (Bowling Green, Ohio: Bowling Green Popular Press, 1972), 186.

[29]Idem.

[30]The metaphor of the mirror is from David Manning White and John Pendleton, *Popular Culture: Mirror of American Life* (Del Mar, CA: Publishers, Inc., 1977); for the metaphor of the refractor I am indebted to Professor Michael Marsden of Bowling Green State University.

[31]"Where Have All the Heroes Gone?" (fn. 7). See also John Gardner's review of Paul Zweig's *The Adventurer* in *The New York Times Book Review* (Dec. 22, 1974), 7; Pauline Kael, "After Innocence," *The New Yorker* (Oct. 1, 1973), 113-118 (a review of the film *The Last American Hero*); "The Heroes of Our Times" (fn. 22); Wilfred Sheed, "In Search of Heroes," *Family Weekly* (June 28, 1981), 4, 6-7.

[32]*The Denial of Death*, (New York: Free Press, 1973), p. 6.

[33]"The Heroes of Our Times," 17.

[34]"The Impossible Culture: Oscar Wilde and the Charisma of the Artist," *Encounter*, 35 (Sept. 1970), 41.

[35]*Individualism Reconsidered and Other Essays* (Glencoe: Free Press, 1954), p. 369.

[36]*The Myth of the Birth of the Hero* (New York: Robert Brunner, 1957), p. 68.

[37]"The Dissection of the Psychical Personality," *The Complete Psychological Works of Sigmund Freud*, ed. and trans. James Strachey et al (London: Hogarth Press, 1965), XII, 57-89.

[38]See "Creative Writers and Day-Dreaming," *The Complete Works of Sigmund Freud*, ed. and trans. James Strachey et al (London: Hogarth Press, 1959), IX, 143-153.

[39]"Media Mentors," *Psychology Today*, 12 (Sept., 1978), 45.

[40]William J. Goode, as cited in David White, "Tight Little Island," *Psychology Today*, 16 (June, 1982), 11.

[41]"Media Mentors," 48 (italics added).

[42]Cited in "Media Mentors," 45.

[43]" 'Cultured' Corporate Winners," *Time* (July 5, 1982), 46 an account of Deal and Kennedy's *Corporate Cultures* (Addison-Wesley, 1982).

[44]"Ernest Becker: A Cultural Historian Who Explored the Intellectual Landscape," *Chronicle of Higher Education*, 13 (Feb. 15, 1976), 40.

[45]*Art and Artist: Creative Urge and Personality Development* (New York: Knopf, 1932), p. 407.

[46]Dale Pollock, "Hot Wheels: His Road to Success," *The Los Angeles Times* (March 24, 1982).

[47]"And a Picture Tube Shall Lead Them," *Playboy* 23 (June 1976), 204.

[48]See Julian Jaynes, *The Origins of Consciousness in the Breakdown of the Bicameral Mind* (Boston: Houghton Mifflin, 1976), particularly the section on the contrast between *The Iliad* and *The Odyssey*, pp. 272-277.

[49]For a moving essay on the heroism of what I have here called the Everyman Hero, see Roger Rosenblatt, "The Man in the Water," *Time* (Jan. 25, 1982), 86, a piece inspired by the Air Florida crash.

The Myth of the Hero: From *Mission: Impossible* to Magdalenian Caves

Bruce A. Beatie

*T*he contours of the typical hero-tale are by now as well-known to the general reader as they are to specialists: the "lone wolf" who sets off in quest of "the impossible dream" or faces an enemy apparently beyond his powers, who overcomes in spite of all obstacles and becomes an important figure to his community—this pattern has become a stock reference for media commentators[1] and television comics. Specific details of the pattern have been described and the pattern itself refined repeatedly since Otto Rank's work in 1909,[2] and by now it has become the trademark of the Jungian mythographer Joseph Campbell.[3]

Fictions in television employ an equally limited repertory of images and plots, and probably the most patterned of all television series was *Mission Impossible*, which ran for some hundred episodes more than a decade ago, and is still seen in re-runs.[4] Although the "impossible" problems the team faced seemed infinite in their variety, the sequence was consistent from episode to episode:

In each episode we first saw Jim Phelps, the team leader, in a normal situation: walking down a street, or shopping, or driving a car (*Initial situation*); but the normality was broken by the statement of a problem (*Villainy*), the self-destructing tape: "If the team accepts this assignment, the bureau will disavow any knowledge of its actions." The next scene was always a council-session of the team in Jim Phelp's apartment, where the problem

46

was described in detail (*Mediation*) and the team decided, as it had to do if the show was to continue, to accept the assignment (*Counteraction*). The problem to be solved was never in the next apartment or the next street, but somewhere far away; the next stage of the narrative was always a journey, explicit or implicit (*Departure*). The main body of the story always consisted in a series of sub-tasks which tested the resources of the various members of the team (*Testing, Reaction*), but there always came a point where all their efforts seemed to fail (*Near-failure*)—a point immediately followed, of course, by the successful resolution of the initial problem (*Solution*). The final scene of each episode invariably showed the team bundling into some vehicle which was to take them home (*Escape*).

This pattern is not, however, simply and only the "formula" of that particular variant of the hero-tale represented by *Mission: Impossible*. It is part of a more complex pattern that was first recognized by the Russian folklorist Vladimir Propp in 1928.[5] A product of the Russian formalist tradition, Propp had perceived that, in spite of their surface variety, European fairy tales showed a similarity in narrative pattern that went beyond the formulaic "Once upon a time ... And they lived happily ever after" of their beginnings and endings. He set out to determine, much more precisely than Rank, Raglan or Campbell, how extensive these similarities were, by analyzing 100 tales from the Afanas'ev collection, the Russian equivalent of the Grimms' tales. He discovered that *all* the tales could be described by using only 33 action-descriptors he called "functions," nine of them belonging to the "Preliminary section" of a tale, and 24 belonging to the tale proper. He noted that while any particular tale might not show all functions, there was a strong tendency for the functions that did occur usually to occur in the same sequence.[6] Although the list of functions has been reprinted frequently, it is difficult to understand their interrelationships except in the context of an actual tale;[7] there is one tale occurring in both the Russian and German traditions that illustrates all but three of the 24 main-tale functions. We shall, therefore, follow the sequence of functions in "The Golden Bird":[8]

Once upon a time there was a king who had three sons and a beautiful castle, in the courtyard of which grew a tree that bore golden apples (*Initial situation*). One day he discovered that an apple was missing, so he told his eldest son to watch that night; but the eldest son fell asleep by midnight and the next morning another apple was gone. The king asked the second son to watch, with the same result. The youngest son asked his chance and, against his father's will, watched too; avoiding sleep he saw, shortly after midnight, a beautiful bird approach the tree, alight and take an apple in its beak. Amazed, he was slow to raise his crossbow and, when he shot, succeeded only in knocking a golden feather from the bird (*Preliminary section*).

When the youngest son took the feather to his father and explained, the king was at once inflamed with desire to own the bird (*Lack*), and ordered his eldest son to seek it (*Mediation*). The son agreed (*Counteraction*), and set out (*Departure*). After travelling for some time, he came to a field where he saw a fox sitting up, and raised his bow. "Stop!" said the fox, "I know your task, and can help you. Tonight you will come to a village where there are two inns, one attractive and one ugly. Only if you sleep at the ugly inn will your quest succeed." (*Test*) The eldest son laughed, shot at the fox, missed, went his way, slept at the attractive inn, and so enjoyed himself that he forgot his quest (*Reaction negative*).

When the eldest son did not return, the king sent his second son, with precisely the same results. (*Test, Reaction negative*). And when *he* did not return, the youngest asked his chance. "How can *you* succeed when your brothers could not?" asked his father, but finally agreed. The youngest son also met the fox (*Test*) but listened to his advice (*Reaction positive*). "Hop on my tail," said the fox, "and I'll take you to the village faster than the wind." (*Reward, Transference*). That night at the ugly inn, the fox told the prince what he had to do. "The golden bird lives in a castle in the next valley. At night, when everyone sleeps, you must creep in. In the room with the bird you'll find a golden cage and an old wooden cage. Be sure to put the bird into the wooden cage and you'll escape with the prize" (*Task*). The next day the fox took the prince on his tail to the castle, and he crept in. But when he saw how beautiful the bird was, he could not bear to put it into the ugly wooden cage. When he tried to use the golden cage, however, the bird awoke and screamed, and the prince was captured (*Solution negative*). "The penalty for trying to steal the bird is death," said the ruler of the castle, "but I'll forgive you *and* give you the bird on one condition. In a castle in the next valley lives a horse that runs faster than the wind. Get him for me and you'll get the bird" (*Task*).

The prince set out again and soon met the fox, who first reproached and then advised him. The new situation was similar (golden harness vs. old leather harness), and so was the outcome (*Solution negative*). This time the prince would be forgiven and earn the horse if he would get for the horse-ruler the princess who lived in the next valley's castle. *(Task)*. The fox agreed to help a third time, this time his special advice was "Don't let her say goodbye to her parents!" but the prince failed a third time to obey. *(Solution negative)*. The task he had set this time, however, was different: "Outside my west window is a mountain that blocks my view of the sea. Remove it in one night and you can have the princess." *(Task)*. The fox magically did so and the prince got his princess *(Solution positive, Liquidation)*. The fox then helped the prince to keep all his prizes—princess, horse *and* bird—and they started home *(Escape)*.

As they got under way, the fox said, "I've helped you, now do what *I* ask. Shoot me!" "I can't!" said the prince. "Well then," said the fox, "I must leave you. But here are two final pieces of advice: don't buy gallows flesh, and don't sit on the edge of a well."[9] The fox disappeared, and the prince continued. Coming to the village with two inns, he discovered his brothers about to be hanged and bought their freedom. As they rode on, the brothers said "It's hot! Let's stop and drink at that well." *(Pursuit)*. Unthinkingly the prince did so, sat on the edge, and his brothers threw him in; returning home, they claimed that *they'd* won the prizes *(Fraude)*. But the bird would not sing, the horse would not eat, and the princess cried unceasingly.

Just as the young prince despaired of his life, the fox peered over the edge of the well, dropped his tail and helped him out *(Rescue)*. They returned, and as the prince entered his father's castle the bird began to sing, the horse to eat and the princess ran to the king to tell him the truth *(Recognition, Exposure)*. The older brothers were sent into exile *(Punishment)*, the prince married the princess and became king *(Wedding)*. Some time later, the fox reappeared, repeated his odd request and, at his wife's urging, the new king shot the fox, who at once changed into a handsome prince, the enchanted brother of the golden princess[9]—and *now* they lived happily ever after.

The three main-tale functions which do not occur in "The Golden Bird," *Branding, Disguise* and *Transfiguration*, belong to the cluster in which recognition occurs. One of the clearest examples of the Branding-Disguise-Recognition cluster is the medieval romance of *King Horn*, where Rymenhild, as her beloved Horn leaves, gives him a ring; he later returns disguised as a beggar at her forced wedding, drops the ring into the wine-cup she is about to drink from, and so is recognized.[10] A clear example of Transfiguration is the ritual bath given to Tristan by Isolde, her mother and the chambermaid after Tristan has killed the dragon;[11] here he has branded himself by cutting out and retaining the dragon's tongue, which later serves both as Tristan's recognition-token and to expose the fraud of the steward.

These last examples serve also as reminders of the general prevalence of this pattern in medieval romance, Arthurian and otherwise,[12] but its range is hardly restricted to folk tale and romance. Many critics and interpreters have discussed aspects of its presence in popular fictions from *Star Wars*[13] through Tolkien's *Hobbit* and *Lord of the Rings*,[14] the modern detective novel, and the multiforms of traditional ballad, epic and tale back to the beginnings of recorded literature. Homer's *Odyssey* has been studied with particular frequency as an example of this pattern,[15] and over a thousand variations of modern Hispanic ballads have recently been published as "romances de tema odiseico" (Beatie RT, pp. 40-45). The narrative pattern of these ballads focuses on that aspect of Homer's poem which led Albert B. Lord to call it generically (along with a large number of modern Yugoslav epic multiforms of it) the "Return Song."[16] One needs, therefore, little reminder of how precisely the *Odyssey* follows the Proppian pattern, from Odysseus's escape from the wreck of Troy, his pursuit by Poseidon and Hera, his rescue by Athena, the fraud of Penelope's suitors, Odysseus' return in disguise and his stepwise recognition by Eumaeus, Telemachus, his dog, Eurycleia and finally Penelope, his exposure and extreme punishment of the villainous suitors, and his transfiguration in a ritual bath before the resumption of his wedding with Penelope.

What one is less prone to remember, however, is that the *Odyssey* forms part of a much longer complex of traditional narrative, the Tale of Troy,[17] which like "The Golden Bird" shows the whole of the Proppian pattern rather than just its return portion. The abduction of Helen is the villainy initiating the action. It leads to a council (*Mediation*) in which the Greeks agree to get her back for Menelaus (*Counteraction*). They depart for Troy, and are tested in Aulis: Agamemnon's reaction, his sacrifice of Iphigeneia, earns the reward of successful transference across the sea to Troy, where a long struggle and a near-failure take place before the Greeks are able to liquidate the villainy by rescuing Helen. The remainder of the pattern survives most clearly in the *Odyssey*, but we know from classical sources that the tradition knew many other Return Songs.[18]

In other tales from the ancient epic tradition of the Balkan peninsula we see some of the additional elements which are part of the Rank-Raglan-Campbell monomythic pattern: the *Miraculous birth* of the hero, his *Exile* and *Return*. In such tales as the ones of Jason, Theseus and Oedipus, however, it is clear that these are not functions of a single tale, but represent rather a reduction of what Propp called a whole Move: a tale-segment which itself moves from

Lack to Liquidation. The pattern of exile and return in the cases of Theseus and Oedipus, for example, is set off by the lack of a father; and their trajectories toward recognition follow the Proppian pattern exactly before a second move begins in Theseus's journey to defeat the Minotaur and in Oedipus' tragic quest for his father's murderer.

This pattern did not originate, however, in classical Greek mythology. Its earliest known version comes, as we suggested, from the dawn of recorded literature; and it is remarkable that this earliest version, the *Epic of Gilgamesh* (whose tradition may have begun as early as around 3,000 B.C.),[19] is not the simplest but one of the more complex examples of the pattern. In the Gilgamesh-tale, the elements of miraculous birth, exile and return do not form part of a separate move but, in a sense, make up the introductory section of the two-move Proppian tale. Gilgamesh is two-thirds god and one-third man, miraculous enough in itself; but the clearer "miraculous birth" is the creation of Gilgamesh's surrogate Enkidu, who is exiled to live among the animals before sex, in the form of a temple prostitute, brings him to the city of Uruk where he becomes Gilgamesh's friend, magical helper and substitute hero. Their joint journey to defeat the beast of the Cedar Forest, Humbaba, follows the Proppian pattern exactly,[20] with the added function of near-failure; and in a very interesting book just published, David Bynum has shown that the small motif of the cedars hewn down by the heroes is part of a very widespread traditional complex with perhaps still more ancient roots.

The Gilgamesh-tale does not end, however, with the conquest of Humbaba. The heroes have angered the gods (as Odysseus had angered Poseidon and Hera), Enkidu is killed, and Gilgamesh, feeling the lack of immortality caused by his man-third, sets off on a second Proppian quest even more remarkable in its functional sequence and with an even more marked near-failure. And indeed, though Gilgamesh does through grace rather than force obtain the herb of immortality, he loses it during his return journey and so his second move, like Beowulf's against the dragon, is unsuccessful. His return to Uruk is shadowed in some variations by anticipations of his death.[21]

With *Gilgamesh* we have moved back through some five thousand years of recorded history to its dim dawn, and before we move further backward into the darkness of time, we need to take stock. The story-pattern we are considering is a familiar one, but people seldom recognize with what consistency of detail it recurs. It is not simply a matter of a very generalized theme that is often repeated, but of a sequence of very specific details that interrelate in equally specific clusters. That specificity becomes most apparent when one looks at the pattern in the form of a chart: an expanded list of the action-descriptions that belong to the pattern of the hero tale. In the following list, X or — indicate presence or absence of a function; the brackets indicate clusters that are interrelated either in the general pattern or in a specific tale-tradition; and the abbreviated column-heads stand for *E*pic *T*radition, *P*ropp, *G*olden *B*ird, *M*ission: *I*mpossible.

If the chart were extended to show the pattern of other specific texts like "The Golden Bird," and if one were to include information allowing us to see the sequence and textual extent of particular functions, both the complexity and consistency of this pattern would become still more obvious: suffice it to note that for the frequent recurrence even of a randomly-ordered 30-element set to be coincidental, much less for that of a partially-sequenced set, would strain the odds-makers' art. There must be a reason for the pattern's existence and recurrence.

But recurrence alone is not its only point of significance. Even those who have accepted the fact that this pattern recurs with almost unbelievable frequency throughout the last five millenia of Near Eastern and European cultural tradition have seldom noticed that the pattern is extremely rare *outside* of that tradition. Indeed, to the extent that available evidence allows us to generalize, its frequency seems to decrease in direct relationship to geocultural distance from that tradition: we find some examples in modern North and Central African folk-narrative traditions and in Chinese tales, where one can at least suppose the possibility of cultural contact; but in the non-Indo-European traditions of the western hemisphere it seems (in spite of Alan Dundes' efforts to prove the contrary) to be totally absent.[32] In other words, this extremely complex pattern of narrative seems to be culture-specific.

II

What is the meaning, therefore, of this story pattern that is so central to, and perhaps so characteristic of, our western tradition?

Frazer and his descendants explained it on the basis of cults and rituals, and as we shall see, their intuition may be correct. But the information about ritual patterns which they use to explain the origins of myth derives solely from classical and modern sources. As *Gilgamesh* proves, however, the pattern existed in full-blown form long before the usually-cited evidence of such cults and rituals.[33] The explanation must lie somewhere in time's darkness before *Gilgamesh*; and as a sign-post for the next stage of our journey, let us take a brief poem by Barbara R. de Michele published recently in *The National Observer*:[34]

> Cavemen lived in dark black holes,
> Devising pictures with bits of coals,
> Retelling stories of hunts and fights
> Around the campfires' flickering lights.
> Evolution has brought us here:
> Modern man sits with his beer
> Within a pitch-black living room—
> And inside that cozy womb
> Watches TV, with its flickering lights,
> Retelling stories of hunts and fights.

In 1953 Gertrude Rachel Levy published an unusual study of the pattern we are considering here that has received too little critical attention,[35] in which she identified three phases through which the hero-pattern and especially its modality are progressively transformed: 1) the narrative of creation (her example is the Babylonian *Enuma elish*, but others could be adduced), 2) the narrative of search (the strict Proppian quest-pattern, for which she takes the *Odyssey* and the *Ramayana* as examples), and 3) the narrative of fraternal conflict (the *Iliad* and the *Mahabharata*). Her point of departure, however, is an ancient Hittite wall-carving whose iconography[36] reaches not only forward at least to King Arthur and his "sword in the stone" but back to a much older tradition of imagery which Levy had described in 1948 in a still more important book called *The Gate of Horn*, subtitled "A Study of the Religious Conceptions of the Stone Age, and their Influence upon European Thought."[37] With imagination, insight and solid scholarship Levy demonstrated that a clear pattern of thought could be deduced from the archeological evidences of paleolithic culture, and that the complex of symbols which constituted this pattern persisted through at least 20,000 years of European cultural development, even though the meaning attributed to the symbols changed, to emerge in the first millenium before Christ as the central symbols of western thought and literature. In the present context, we can use her argument as a bridge to move in the opposite direction, from Gilgamesh back to the world of the paleolithic caves.

Most of us are familiar with the magnificent painted and engraved animals of paleolithic caves like Lascaux and Altamira. But we know them, as Kenneth Clarke recently reminded us, mainly "through reconstructions of anthropologists that give an entirely false impression of them. In fact, they are little more than blots and scratches, among which we may recognize undeniable likenesses of bison and other animals."[38] We have often seen, for example, a picture of the Abbe Breuil's reconstruction of the "Horned God" or "Sorcerer" of Trois Freres, but a photograph of the actual surviving painting shows only a pattern of smudges:[39] we can recognize the legs and torso, and little else. And when we move back to observe its larger context, we see the smudge partly hidden in a rock crevice some fourteen feet off the floor of the cave.[40]

But such reconstructions are not the only problem. We see these images reproduced neatly and in glorious Technicolor on the accessible pages of art books and popular magazines, but we know little of the actual circumstances of their survival. To correct the false impressions of popular journalism, let us make a journey into one of these caves. The journey will be artificial to the extent that no satisfactory description or set of photographs of a single cave has yet been published. But the journey will be as authentic as one can make it on the basis of published sources.[41]

The first false impression that needs correction is that paleolithic man *lived* in caves.[42] He lived, in fact, in rock shelters or overhangs within which, in some cases, there was an entrance to a deeper cave. At Font-de-Gaume, for example, we look from a river-valley up a loose shale slope to a sheer cliff with an umbrella-like overhang covering a depression at its base; after we've climbed the slope we find inside the depression a smooth-floored room at whose rear a waist-high opening leads back into the deeper cave.[43] In the layers of habitation which archeologists have excavated in these rock shelters and cave-mouths, we find abundant evidence of everyday life over millenia: hearths and animal bones, the shards of tool-making and the tools themselves, and the graves of the tool-makers. The only cave-mouth objects with apparent symbolic significance are the carved and sculpted steatopygic female figures that have been popularly called "Venuses,"[44], though as Levy points out, they "are only found in a domestic context," "not in the separated recesses presumably devoted to cave rites" "and not at this time directly connected with cave ritual" (Levy *Gate*, pp. 27, 56, 7).

Indeed, it is possible that their arrow-like extremities allowed them to be stuck in the ground simply as casual and ever-present companions of the campfire. To repeat: at the cave mouth there is little evidence of symbol, ritual or myth, but much evidence of abundant life in its cyclic movement: T.S. Eliot's triad of birth, copulation and death.

As soon as one moves into the darkness of the cave proper, however, one is struck by the *lack* of signs of life. Even the footprints frozen into the clay floors of Niaux (Graziosi, pl. 112a) and other caves show this lack by their very presence, for had there been much traffic into the depths, such signs would have been worn away. We are struck too by how deep one must penetrate into the caves before we find the paintings so accessible to us in the art books: at Niaux (Levy, *Gate*, p. 12, fig. 7), over half a mile through narrow passages past many blank and smooth walls that would be, to a modern *graffitiste*, open invitations to stop and draw; at Trois Freres and Tuc d'Audoubert, along the bed of an underground stream that sometimes rises to close off all entrances (Begouen-Breuil, end-paper map). In other caves, the animal images are still more difficult of access. The plans of the caves alone, says Levy (*Gate*, pp. 11, 13),

give little indication of the formidable nature of these defenses of twisting, often very narrow, always slippery corridors, along which the intruders groped their way, clinging to curtains of stalactite, descending into chasms, negotiating waterfalls or chimneys, into the gigantic darkness of halls ... whose dimensions their tiny lamps could never have revealed ... where ... the dripping of distant water was terribly magnified to ears alert for the cave-lion or bear .... The entry to Pech-Merle has such narrows, such abysses, such sliding cataracts of stalactite, [and] the chamber of Clotilde must be approached on hands and knees. Font-de-Gaume ... once straitens to a tunnel through which a broad figure can only with difficulty be pressed, before advancing to the halls of frescoes. La Pasiega is reached through a man-hole below which a subterranean river hurls itself against precipices above whose most perilous ascents are painted signs and animals. It leads by "a labyrinth of sometimes dangerous, always narrow galleries, above an inaccessible rock-face," to the painted hall with its rock-cut "throne," "a mystery desired and sought," as its discoverer﹃ describe it, "in an arcanum forbidden to the profane." At Montespan three hours are required to overcome the obstacles of "un dedale de galeries superposees," whose only signs of previous occupation are the tracks of great beasts in the clay, to a natural stairway leading up to one small gallery, where the moulded figures remain above a floor covered with ruined reliefs. Tuc d'Audoubert, approached like Montespan by means of a sunken river, requires a climb by ladders and pegs, then a crawl through corridors to the prints of dancing feet and the modelled bisons beyond. Les Trois Freres needs half an hour's walk through a succession of corridors to the chamber whose principal figure is wholly visible only after the crawl through a pipe-like tunnel and negotiation of a rock-chimney, with a foot on either side of the chasm. The descent to Labastide is a vertical pit. The cave opens from its side, a hundred feet down, into another pit that leaves only a narrow ledge by which passage can be made to vast corridors.

Near the entrances to the deeper galleries one finds, not animal paintings but other symbols such as the negative image of a hand of El Castillo (Graziosi, pl. 262), or claviforms, or patterned dots like those on the ceiling of the entry-passage at Pech-Merle (Leroi-Gourhan, p. 67), or meander-patterns that some have interpreted, on the analogy of similar usages in modern stone-tool cultures like the Australian aborigines as symbolic maps by which the initiate may find his way into the darkness.

Once we have, with great difficulty, reached the chambers where the paintings and engravings are located, we are surprised by two things: first, especially if we have noticed the enticingly blank walls along the way, by the fact that the artists have often chosen the most unlikely surfaces for their work. At La Pasiega, for example, we find frescoes and engravings from six to fourteen feet off the floor of a high passageway little more than twelve inches wide and curved sharply on both horizontal and vertical axes (Graziosi, pl. 266c). As the count Henri Begouen wrote in 1929,[45]

One ... must perform veritable contortions in order to be able to admire these splendid creatures.... They are drawn on every side, but the variety of positions one must assume in order to see them emphasizes the fact that the original artist must have been through just the same contortions while he was designing them.

And Levy (*Gate*, p. 15) notes that

> Long rods must have been used for the painting of signs on
> the overhanging walls of Santian or Pech-Merle, or on the roof at
> Bolao Llanes, arched above one of those sunless lakes whose
> prehistoric existence may be presumed from the absence of
> stalagmites in their beds. It is difficult to imagine that certain of
> these signs could ever have been visible from below.

The second surprise lies in the incredible quantity of visual material
that is present. Leroi-Gourhan's schematic map of the sanctuary at
Niaux (p. 362) gives only a limited idea of the ways in which, over
millennia, drawings overlap drawings to create a veritable
kaleidoscope of images. At Lascaux, for example, we see in one
reproduction[46] a middle-sized black-and-ochre antelope
superimposed on the back of a large black-outlined aurochs; below,
and painted over both, is a train of small running horses. Below the
nose of the aurochs appears what seems an ochre bush; but another,
more enlarged reproduction[47] shows this to be the antlers of the
foremost of a herd of reindeer. On one rock face at Trois Freres, we
see what seems a maze of randomly-engraved lines across which
runs a hump-curved painted smudge; only in the interpretive
drawing by the Abbe Breuil can we recognize the hundreds of
engraved horses, complete and incomplete, over which a bison has
been painted (Begouen-Breuil, pl. 116 and fig. 19). The artists often
made use of the natural contours and formations of the rock in
creating their figures, such as at Niaux, where four nascent
stalagmites become the eye and three wounds in the side of an
engraved bison (Leroi-Gourhan, pl. 89). Such practices suggest,
according to Levy, "that the cave itself was considered the
repository of magic influence, that the animal 'souls' were conceived
to exist already in such localities" (Levy, *Gate*, p. 22). Human figures
are rare, and when they do occur are clearly subordinate to the
animals: as our final example, consider the ambiguous and oft-
discussed "Man in the Well" at Lascaux (Leroi-Gourhan, p. 74),
where we see a large bison facing left, horns lowered, a broken spear
through his loin; falling back to the left before and under the bison's
horn is a spindly, small bird-headed human being.

III

We have reached not only the depths of the caves but the end-point of our temporal journey, and must endeavor to escape, or at least to return, more quickly than we came. What is the meaning of the paleolithic situation described above, and how is it related to the hero-tale? First, as the count Begouen had recognized already in 1929, it is clear that the cave paintings are *not* "art" in our sense of that word but rather the products of actions which we can only see as magical or sacred. The creators of the paintings were rare individuals who, because of the tribe's need for food, chose (or were selected) to make a difficult journey from the lively cave-mouth into the realm of darkness and death, a journey involving symbolic tests of identity. At the farthest point of their journey they undertook a task of painful difficulty: the creation in near-darkness and under deliberately unfavorable circumstances, of an animal-image by which, one may suppose, the hero-artist and thereby the tribe gained power over or a sense of identity with the animals that were their source of life and sustenance.

The archeological evidence shows us that, as millenia passed, these journeys moved deeper and deeper into the caves until, with the end of the Magdalenian era, human behavior changed and the cave-sanctuaries were abandoned to silence and darkness. Why? The glaciers had finally disappeared into the distant north, and we know that the hunting cultures were turning slowly to the more secure sustenance of agriculture. What is significant is that, here in the cave-culture of at least 20 millenia before us, we find the Proppian quest-pattern, the central portion of Campbell's monomyth, not just as a fiction but as a *pattern of behavior*: not as a fiction told to explain a ritual but as a reflection of something actually done by living people, in the geographical area that still houses our western civilization. And while such journeys were by definition no everyday occurrences, neither were they isolated phenomena. There are over a hundred caves known from southern France to northern Spain with such images;[48] particular caves contain a vast number of them (the sanctuary at Trois Freres, for example, shows nearly 200 animal figures); and they were not done in a brief span of time (at Trois Freres again, the execution of the figures covers a period of some 10,000 years).[49]

Thus this pattern of human experience was repeated by our European ancestors over a span of time that we, restricted to threescore years and ten, can scarcely comprehend: a span sufficient, if recent biochemical theories of the molecular basis of long-term memory have any validity,[50] to imprint the pattern into our genetic code. The etymological roots of the words "cult" and "ritual" all imply repeated actions; and the suggestion that millenial repetition of a journey to the cave-depths lies at the roots of the quest-pattern provides a theory of the "ritual origins of myth" that goes well beyond the evidence that Frazer and his followers could adduce. But there are two problems inherent in this theory that merit at least mention, though I can provide no solutions without beginning a quest myself at least as lengthy as the one I've described here.

One lies in the suggestion of "genetic imprint." In psychobiological areas I am only an eclectic layman: I have taken the notion of "imprinting" from the ethological studies of Konrad Lorenz and grafted it to admittedly controversial theories of molecular-code memory (with a side-glance to Chomsky's equally controversial idea of genetically-coded linguistic universals). The product is indefensible as science; but as a speculative proto-hypothesis it may at least suggest directions for further study. Some older work on molecular transfer of memory[51] as well as some very recent experiments on the relationship between patterning and memory[52] indicate that my proto-hypothesis may not be quite so "far out" as it might have seemed a decade ago. In any case, my concern has been not so much to find a point of origin as to show that the well-known quest-pattern is far older than is usually assumed.

The other problem, raised all too justly by one of the readers of this paper, is endemic in all origins-studies: the "chicken or the egg" question. Even if one assumes the possible validity of my suggestion, all it does is to push the origins-question back a stage or two; but "what motivated primitive man to begin with?" Why did paleolithic man, between 30,000 and 20,000 B.C., begin to make this mythical journey? To that question I have no answer, at least in this context. For my original question was rather: why is the quest-pattern still popular today? and to that question I have at least given a tentative answer. If indeed the pattern is more than twenty millennia old, then perhaps we should not be surprised that our popular fictions still retain the structural shell of this pattern of behavior, nor that we still seem to prefer it to others even if its meaning has long disappeared.

But has that meaning in fact disappeared? The meaning of the pattern was, if my suggestion was correct, a sacred one; and the pattern survives to our day not *only* in popular literature. Let us listen again to a *sacred* story that is still recited each Sunday by millions of members of our western culture as part of a ritual ceremony, just as, three millennia ago, the Babylonian *Enuma elish* was recited on the fourth day of the festival of the New Year by the *urigallu*-priest:[53]

> I believe in God the Father Almighty, maker of Heaven and Earth, and in Jesus Christ His only son, our Lord, who was conceived of the Holy Spirit, born of the Virgin Mary (*Miraculous Birth of the Hero*), suffered under Pontius Pilate (*Testing, Reaction*), was crucified, dead and buried (*Struggle*). On the third day he rose again from the dead (*Escape*) and ascended into heaven (*Transfiguration*), from whence he shall come to judge the quick and the dead.

Here, in a text that is not a theological abstraction but rather a *story* that forms a core of religious belief,[54] ends this essay's metaphoric journey, whose shape is thus not only its content but its message or argument: that myths are *not* just "stories someone believed in once upon a time." They are story-patterns so much a part of our whole way of perceiving the world that, while we take them for granted and seldom attend to them seriously, we like (to understate the case) to hear them reiterated. In our preference for fictions like *Mission: Impossible* or *Star Wars* there lies a dim, unconscious perception of their mythic meaning, a faint shadow of the spiritual quest that Magdalenian man imprinted in our blood and which now writes itself in the characters of our heroes.

Notes

[1]See most recently Reynolds Price, "The heroes of our times," and Paul Zweig, "The hero in literature," *Saturday Review* 5 (Dec. 1978), 16-17, 30, 35.

[2]*The Myth of the Birth of the Hero. A Psychological Interpretation of Mythology.* Tr. F. Robbins and S.E. Jelliffe, New York: Bruner, 1957. It was further defined by Lord Raglan in *The Hero: A Study in Tradition, Myth and Dreams.* London: Methuen, 1936. Bruce A. Rosenberg has more recently shown how the pattern refined by Raglan has influenced popular perception of American history: *Custer and the Epic of Defeat*, University Park, PA: Pennsylvania State Univ. Press, 1974; his argument is more easily accessible in an article of the same title in *Journal of American Folklore* 88 (April-June 1975), 165-177. See also the monograph by Alan Dundes cited in note 54.

[3]*The Hero with a Thousand Faces*, Princeton, NJ: Princeton Univ. Press, 1973 (Bollingen Series, 17), originally published in 1949. Dolores S.B. Rodi recently studied the whole tradition in which Campbell's work stands: "A study of the contributions of Carl Jung and James Frazer and their followers to the hero archetype with suggestions for teaching literature," Ph.D. dissertation, University of Texas, 1977, abstracted in *Olifant* 5 (May 1978) 378-380. For a look at Campbell's popular influence see Eugene Kennedy, "Earthrise: The Dawning of a new spiritual awareness," New York *Times Magazine* 128 (April 15, 1979), 14-15, 51-56.

[4]See Jose M. Ferrer III, "Brains and Action—with no jokes," *Life* 62 (Jan. 13, 1967) 15; and "Mission Impossible," *Time* 91 (March 1, 1968) 53. In the show's first season (1966-67) the team leader was named Dan Briggs, played by Stephen Hill; from 1967-68 on it was Jim Phelps, played by Peter Graves.

[5]An excellent review of Propp's work in the light of subsequent structuralist studies appears in the "Introduction" to *Patterns in Oral Literature*, ed. Heda Jason and Dimitri Segal, The Hague: Mouton, 1977 (World Anthology). See also my " 'Romances tradicionales' and Spanish traditional ballads: Menendez Pidal vs. Vladimir Propp," *Journal of the Folklore Institute* 13 (No. 1, 1976) 37-55 [hereafter cited parenthetically in text and notes as "Beatie RT"], and "Saint Katherine of Alexandria: traditional themes and the themes and the development of medieval German hagiographic narrative," *Speculum* 52 (Oct. 1977) 785-800. An earlier comment by Claude Levi-Strauss with a reply by Propp appears in the Italian translation: *Morfologia della fiaba*, con un interventio di Claude Levi-Strauss e una replica dell'autore, a cura di G.L. Bravo, Turin: Einaudi, 1966 (Nuova Biblioteca Scientifica Einaudi, 13).

[6]Propp in fact asserted that the sequence was invariable: *Morphology of the Folktale*, 2nd. ed. rev. and ed. with a preface by Louis A. Wagner, Austin: Univ. of Texas Press, 1971 (Publications of the American Folklore Society, Bibliographical and Special Series, 9), pp. 22-23. This assertion has been one of the points most often criticized: see most recently David E. Bynum, *The Daemon in the Wood: A Study of Oral Narrative Patterns*, Cambridge: Harvard Univ. Center for Study of Oral Literature, 1978 (Publications of the Milman Parry Collection, Monograph Series, 1), page 296 [hereafter cited parenthetically as "Bynum"].

[7]Propp insists that a particular narrative segment can be identified as a particular function only by its relationship to other functional segments of the tale, and not by its apparent content, just as, in generative grammar, it is not the surface form of a token, but its relationship in phrase structure to other tokens that defines its type. The problem with many supposedly Proppian analyses is that they forget this part of the definition. If analysis of this sort is to have any lasting value, it is necessary constantly to keep referring back and forth from deduced deep structure to the particular surface structure (text) one is working with.

[8]Since my concern here is with traditional tales, I am retelling "The Golden Bird" from memory without reference to any published variant; it may be checked, for example, against tale no. 75: "Der goldene Vogel," in any full edition of the Grimm's *Kinder- und Hausmarchen*. The Russian version is called "Prince Ivan, the Firebird, and the Grey Wolf" in *Russian Fairy Tales* by Aleksander Afanasev, tr. N. Guterman, 2nd ed., New York: Pantheon, 1973, pp. 612-624. Johannes Bolte and George Polivka (*Anmerkungen zu den Kinder- und Hausmarchen der Bruder Grimm* 1 [Leipzig: Dieterich, 1913] 503-515) refer to a great many versions and analogues in most European languages.

[9]These two sections, which have no function-designations in the text, are more complex, but still analyzable in Proppian terms. The fox's two pieces of advice are *Interdictions* of which the prince's kindnesses to his brothers are the *Violations*; functions occurring most frequently in the "Preliminary sections" of tales (see note 24). The shooting and transformation of the fox are relict-functions of a separate tale or move in which the fox was a victim-hero: donor-figures like the fox frequently seem to come into a tale from tales of their own.

[10]See John McLaughlin, "The return song in medieval romance and ballad: King Horn and King Orfeo," *Journal of American Folklore* 88 (July-Sept., 1975), 305-307; for another example see Beatie RT, p. 44.

[11]E.g., Gottfried von Strassburg, *Tristan*, vv. 9983-10499.

[12]See Eugene Dorman, *The Narreme in the Medieval Romance Epic: An Introduction to Narrative Structures*, Univ. of Toronto Press, 1969; and Bruce A. Beatie, "Patterns of myth in medieval narrative," *Symposium* 25 (Summer 1971), 101-122. For a more recent and detailed look at the pattern in one romance see Pierre Gallais, "L'hexagone logique et le roman medievale," *Cahiers de Civilisation Medievale* 18 (1975) 1-15,133-148.

[13]Daniel F. Melia ("A definitive analysis of 'Star Wars'," *Harvard Magazine* 80 [March-April, 1978] relates the film not only to Propp but to traditional romance.

[14]Bruce A. Beatie, "Folk tale, fiction and saga in J.R.R. Tolkien's 'Lord of the Rings'," *Mankato Studies in English* 2 (Feb. 1967), 1-17.

[15]Rhys Carpenter, *Folk Tale, Fiction, and Saga in the Homeric Epics*, Berkeley: Univ. of California Press, 1958 (Sather Classical Lectures, 20: originally published in 1946).

[16]*The Singer of Tales*, Cambridge: Harvard Univ. Press, 1960 (Harvard Studies in Comparative Literature, 24), pp. 120-121 and Appendix III, pp. 242-259.

[17]William F. Hansen is one of the few Homeric scholars to emphasize this point: "The Homeric epics and oral poetry," in *Heroic Epic and Saga: An Introduction to the World's Great Folk Epics*, ed. F.J. Oinas, Bloomington: Indiana Univ. Press, 1978), pp. 7-26.

[18]See, e.g., Apollogorus, *Epitome*, VI, 1-30: *The Library*, with an English translation by Sir James G. Frazer, Cambridge: Harvard Univ. Press, 1970, vol. II pp. 242-279 (Loeb Classical Library, 122).

[19]The main surviving texts are from the seventh to the fourteenth centuries B.C., though some fragmentary tablets date from the nineteenth through the sixteenth centuries B.C.; but two epics concerning figures who are close to Gilgamesh in the Sumerian King list reflect, according to Johannes M. Renger, "the relations between lower Mesopotamia and the Iranian plateau during the fourth and third millennia B.C." See his "Mesopotamian epic literature," in *Heroic Epic* (note 17), p. 27.

[20]For a related analysis, see Joseph Blenkinsopp, "The search for the prickly plant: structure and function in the Gilgamesh epic," *Soundings* 58 (Summer 1975), 200-220.

[21]Ragland and Campbell (notes 2 and 3) identify a series of actions and motifs pertaining to the death of the hero, but that section of the pattern has not been studied sufficiently for its shape to be as unambiguous as that of the parts I've considered here. I have suggested elsewhere (Beatie RT, pp. 47048) that "the functional difference between a romantic and a tragic narrative . . . is . . . not a matter of different functions, but of transvalued functions . . . ."

[22]In some cases I have renamed Proppian functions to clarify the action they describe.

[23]Propp does not consider these as functions, but he does include them as "Materials for a tabulation of the tale": *Morphology* (note 6), pp. 119-127. See my "St. Katherine . . ." (note 5), pp. 791-796.

[24]In Propp this section involves nine functions; for the sake of simplification and clarity, I have subsumed *Absentation, Interdiction, Violation, Reconnaisance, Information, Deceit, Deception* and *Preliminary misfortune* under a single heading. In "The Golden Bird" one can clearly see the king's ordering his sons to watch the tree as a trebled interdiction which is twice violated, and the stolen apples as a trebled preliminary misfortune; absentation, deceit and deception do not occur, but one may perhaps see the bird's visits as reconnaisence leading to the youngest son's gaining information. See also note 9.

[25]Propp considers *Villainy* and *Lack* as allomorphs of one another (see also note 29), but they are sometimes hard to separate; the abduction of a princess, for example, is a villainy creating a lack. If one looks at this function in the Frazer-Jung-Campbell context, it is tempting to consider "Lack" (the "wasteland" motif) as the primary function, from which "Villainy" is derived by projecting the perceived lack onto an "other" whose maliciousness has caused it.

[26]In "The Golden Bird" this set of functions is trebled.

[27]In "The Golden Bird," *Testing* is trebled, "Reaction" also with changing valences (-, -, +) and "Reward" occurs only once. In "Mission: Impossible," since the role Propp calls "Donor" (more clearly "Magical Helper") is absent, there is no reward *per se* save that the action moves closer to solution and liquidation.

[28]"Transference" is trebled, as are the other three for the youngest son, with "Solution (-) in all cases; the fourth "Task" (getting rid of the mountain) is solved by the fox, the prince's magical helper.

[29]Propp considers "Difficult Task"/"Solution" as one pair of functions, and "Struggle"/"Victory" as a different pair; but in fact the latter is simply a special case of the former. See note 25.

[30]This function has been given its name by Lord (*Singer* [note 16[, pp. 196-197), who points to Beowulf's near-failure in the cave of Grendel's mother, to Charlemagne's in the battle with Baligant and to Achilles' in the battle with the river; it also occurs in Gilgamesh, as we saw. Why it is present in the older epics and in the very recent "Mission: Impossible" and absent in the folk tale and romance traditions is a question whose answer goes beyond what I can consider here.

[31]"Liquidation" is also trebled, although there is only a single initial lack.

[32]See his *The Morphology of North American Indian Folktales*, Helsinki: Academia Scientiarum Fennica, 1964 (Folklore Fellows Communications, 195); Claude Bremond provided a very detailed critique: "Posterite americaine de Propp," *Communications* 11 (1968), 148-164. The absence of the hero-tale pattern in the Western hemisphere is perhaps most tellingly underlined by those few cases where a European folktale has entered Amerind oral tradition. The "Cinderella" tale, for example, has entered Zuni tradition as "Turkey Girl" (*Tales of the North American Indians*, sel. and annot. by Stith Thompson, Bloomington: Indiana University Press,

1971, no. lxxxiii, pp. 225-231), which seems initially to follow the Proppian patterning of its European original clearly enough, certainly, that one can identify its source; the action of the tale from the middle on, however, shows that its teller had not perceived the Proppian pattern *as* pattern, and he shifts it into an action-mode more familiar to him. Some recent new-world archeological research suggests that emigration across the Bering-Straits "bridge" to North America did not take place until after the formation of an ideational system which Gertrude Levy (see note 37) identifies as late Neolithic: see Walter Sullivan, "Early America found swayed by view of sky," New York *Times*, 128 (June 17, 1979), section 1, p. 20.

[33]David Bynum, for different reasons, calls this "the ritual fallacy," and his argument is worth considering. See his chapter four, pp. 147-254.

[34]"Dauntless doggerel," *National Observer*, April 23, 1977, p. 10.

[35]*The Sword from the Rock: An Investigation into the Origins of Epic Literature and the Development of the Hero*, Westport, CT: Greenwood Press, 1976 (orig. London: Faber & Faber, 1953).

[36]The "two trees" image studied by Bynum is closely related to this carving; though he refers to many examples of Near Eastern art (pp. 172 ff.) he misses this connection.

[37]London: Faber & Faber, 1963 [hereafter cited as "Levy *Gate*"]. I have dealt at some length with the interrelationships of Propp, Levy and Bynum and the problems their works raise with respect to the study of traditional narrative in a paper at the Rocky Mountain Modern Language Association in October 1979.

[38]"Animals and men: love, admiration and outright war," *Smithsonian* 8 (Sept. 1977) 52. For a recent journalistic account see Boyce Rensberger, "The world's oldest works of art," New York *Times Magazine* 177 (May 21, 1978) 26-29 ff. Such misconceptions are unfortunately perpetuated by scholars as well as journalists: see the totally unrealistic scenes created by the Abbe Henri Breuil, the virtual founder of the study of cave art, in his *Beyond the Bounds of History: Scenes from the Old Stone Age*, tr. M.E. Boyle, London: Gawthorn, 1949; and Max Raphael, *Prehistoric Cave Painting*, tr. N. Gutermann, New York: Pantheon, 1945 (Bollingen Series, 4).

[39]Henri Begouen and l'Abbe H. Breuil, *Les Cavernes du Volp: Trois Freres-Tuc d'Audoubert a Montesquieu-Avantes (Ariege). Paris: Arts et Metiers Graphiques, 1958 (Travaux de l'Institute de Paleontologie Humaine)*, plates XX and XIX [hereafter cited as "Begouen-Breuil"].

[40]Begouen-Breuil, plate XVIIIa. See also Begeuen, "Un dessin releve dans la caverne des Trois Freres, a Montesquieu-Avantes (Ariege)," *Academie des Inscriptions et Belles Lettres, Comptes Rendus*, September-October, 1920, pp. 303-310, for an early discussion of this figure.

[41]Older publications concerning individual caves and sites concentrated on presenting and interpreting the "works of art," and provided little by way of description of physical circumstances. More recent studies offer only a little improvement. See, for example, Martin Almagro Bosch, *El Covacho con Pincturas Repustres de Cogul (Lerida)*, Lerida: Instituto de Estudios Ilerdense, 1952 [no description of caves]; Lous Meroc and Jean Mazet, *Cougnac, Grotte Peinte*, Stuttgart: Kohlhammer, 1956 [only a very brief though clear description]; Begouen-Breuil (the best study of an individual cave that I've found); Simeon Gimenez Reyna, *La Cueva de La Pileta (Monumento Nacional)* Malaga: Dardo, 1958 [brief description, excellent "map" of the cave]; Eduardo Ripoll Perello, *Pinturas Rupestres de La Gasulla (Castellon)*, Barcelona: Monografias de Arte Rupestre, 1963 [little description]; and Antonion Beltran *et al.*, *La Cuvea de Le Portel*, Zaragoza: Seminario de Prehistoria y Protohistoria, 1966 [little description]. The best available descriptions of individual caves (except for Lascaux: see note 42) can be found in Andre Leroi-Gourhan's superb *Treasures of Prehistoric Art*, tr. N. Guterman, New York: Abrams, 1967 [hereafter cited as "Leroi-Gourhan"], thus far the most substantial synthetic study of paleolithic art; its original title (*Prehistoire de l'Art Occidental*, 1965) was more accurately descriptive. Next best in terms of descriptive usefulness is a tourist guide: Ann and Gale Sieveking, *The Caves of France and Northern Spain: A Guide*, London: Vista, 1962, which offers very good descriptions, with maps of the major caves. For a graphic account of what it's like to discover caves, see Norbert Casteret, *The Descent of Pierre Saint-Martin*, tr. J. Warrington, London: Dent, 1955, pp. 102-107.

[42]The following account is based mainly on Levy *Gate*, pp. 3-28. When she was writing in the early 1940s there were few synthetic studies of paleolithic culture available, such as Hermann Muller-Karpe's *Geschichte der Steinzeit* (Munich: Beck, 1974); Louis Capitan's *La Prehistorie* (Paris: Payot, 1922) and M.C. Burkitt's *The Old Stone Age: A Study of Paleolithic Times* (Cambridge Univ. Press, 1933) were superficial, and only Hugo Obermaier's *Fossil Man in Spain* (New Haven, CT: Hispanic Society of America, 1924; originally published in Madrid, 1916) offered anything like an overview. Therefore, her only sources were published accounts of individual archeological sites. Lascaux, which offers some problems in terms of her themes, had

only just been discovered when she was writing: see Fernand Windels, *The Lascaux Cave Paintings* (New York: Viking Press, 1950; originally published in France in 1948) and Georges Bataille, *Lascaux, or the Birth of Painting* (Lausanne: Skira, 1955). It is remarkable, therefore, to find that her insights have been largely confirmed by recent scholarship, though few recent scholars seem to be aware of her work. See the Abbe H. Breuil, *Four Hundred Centuries of Cave Art*, tr. M.G. Boyle, Montignac: Centrte d'Etudes et de Documentation Prehistorique, 1952 [the most detailed, though not the most reliable, dating of monuments]; Christian Zervos, *L'Art de l'Epoque du Renne en France*, Paris: Quarante Millenaires d'Art Parietale, Paris: Michel, 1960 [includes African and Australian monuments, but mainly a description of sites, little synethsis]; A. Laming-Emperaire, *La Signification de L'Art Rupestre Paleolithique: Methods et Application*, Paris: Picard, 1962 [good review of theories, only tentative new conclusions which, based mainly on atypical Lascaux, are perhaps doubtful]; Herbert Kuhn, *Eiszeitkunst: Die Geschichte ihrer Erforschung*, Gottingen: Musterschmidt, 1965 [describes, decade by decade, the discoveries since about 1830]; and Leroi-Gourhan, whose "Analysis of cave-art sites by style and topographical character" (chart xx,p. 507) shows that while Levy's account is not representative of all sites, it becomes progressively more valid as one moves chronologically from his style I (32,000-23,000 B.C.), where *all* art is in open air, through styles II (25,000-17,000 B.C.—75% in open air), III (17,000-14,000 B.C.—32% open air, 9% difficult access), and IV (14,000-9,000—only 20% in open air, 31% difficult access). It should be noted that he obviously defines difficulty of access far more stringently than does Levy; on the basis of available descriptions, including some of his own, his evaluations of difficulty seem understated.

[43]Paolo Graziosi, *Palaeolithic Art*, London: Faber & Faber, 1960, Plates and 214b [hereafter cited as "Graziosi"].

[44]Rudolf Drossler, *Die Venus der Eiszeit: Entdeckung und Erforschung altsteinzeitlicher Kunst*, Leipzig: Prisma, 1967. For excellent photographs in color of the Laussel and Lespugue "Venuses," see Leroi-Gourhan, plates 55 and 52.

[45]"The magic origin of prehistoric art" (tr. S. Seeley), *Antiquity* 3 (March 1929) 7.

[46]Luis Pericot-Garcia *et al.*, *Prehistoric and Primitive Art*, New York: Abrams, 1967, plate 61.

[47]Pericot-Garcia, plate 62.

[48]Leroi-Gourhan lists, in charts XVII and XVIII, 110 sites of cave-art and 130 sites where decorated objects have been found: 213 different sites in all, and he does not list all the sites mentioned by other scholars.

[49]See Breuil, *Four Hundred Centuries* (note 42), page 406 and Begouen-Breuil, p. 84.

[50]See Wesley Dingman and Michael B. Sporn, "Molecular theories of memory," *Science* 144 (April 3, 1964), 26-29; the disagreements between the molecular and the electrophysiological theorists was recently described by Joan Arehart-Treichel, "The biology of memory." *Science News* 104 (Oct. 6, 1973), 218-219. A related hypothesis on holographic memory-structuring may help to explain, more clearly than does the Jungian notion of "archetypal memory," the very long-term survival of story-patterns and symbol-complexes: see Karl H. Pribram, "The neurophysiology of remembering," *Scientific American* 220 (Jan. 1969), 73-86, with responses in the March (p. 6) and June issues (pp. 6-7), and Paul A. Kolers, "Pattern-analyzing memory," *Science* 191 (March 26, 1976) 1280-1281. Some of the people who have heard this paper (see note 54) have inquired about the effect of the emotions involved in "mythic" experience on the long-term memory I postulate here; there seems to be little theoretical work done in this area, but a very recent article suggests that it may not continue to be ignored: see Joel Greenberg, "Memory research: an era of 'good feeling'," *Science News* 114 (Nov. 25, 1978), 364-365.

[51]See James V. McConnell *et al.*, "Attempts to transfer approach and avoidance responses by RNA injections in rats," and Holger Hyden, "The question of a molecular basis for the memory trace," both in *Biology of Memory*, ed. Karl H. Pribram and Donald E. Broadbent, New York: Academic Press, 1970, pp. 129-159 and 101-119.

[52]See especially *The Use of Schemata in the Acquitition and Transfer of Knowledge*, by Perry W. Thorndike and Barbara Hayes-Roth, Santa Monica, CA: Rand Corporation, Nov. 1977 (Rand Paper Series 6046). Other relevant papers in this series, by Dr. Hayes-Roth and others, are nos. 5806, 6045, 6054, 6065 and 6193.

[53]*Ancient Near Eastern Texts Relating to the Old Testament*, ed. by James B. Pritchard. Princeton Univ. Press, 1950, p. 332.

[54]The parallel I've made briefly here was recently elaborated in detail by Alan Dundes, *The Hero Pattern in the Life of Jesus: Protocol of the 25th Colloquy 12 December 1976*, Berkeley, CA: Center for Hermeneutical Studies in Hellenistic and Modern Culture, 1977. I first began expressing the ideas in this paper in lectures to classes and general audiences in 1971; the first

formal delivery of the paper was at the Ohio Modern Language Teachers Association Conference in Columbus, April 7, 1978; it was given in its present form at the Third Annual Conference on Literature and Myth, Stockton State College, Pomona, NJ, March 30, 1979; and for the Department of German, University of Massachusetts, Boston, April 11, 1979. I am grateful to all these audiences for much provocative discussion, and especially to Dr. Joseph Campbell, who commented in detail on the paper at the New Jersey conference.

The Superhero's Two Worlds

Robert Inchausti

*L*iterary critics have seen comic book superheroes as archetypal figures.[1] This fascination with the mythic elements in superhero narratives has identified specific motifs—such as secret identity—as parts of larger proto-mythic structures. As a result, these motifs have seldom been the subject of poetic analyses in their own right. Using Kenneth Burke's notion of narrative as symbolic action, I shall consider the motif of secret identity—not simply in terms of mythic significance but aesthetic function. This function will vary from hero to hero and from story to story. But in the way this motif is perpetually redrawn lies a key to the aesthetics of the entire superhero genre. The aesthetics of the genre is the key to the symbolic significance of the superhero as a mythic archetype.

Secret identities establish a tension within superhero narratives that represent the antinomy each of us finds within ourselves between the finite and infinite poles of existence, between the world of quotidian reality and the pure possibility of our existentially free selves. The hero never resolves these tensions; he lives within them. And though various events threaten to expose him and collapse the contradictions of his life, he always escapes. These escapes teach us through images how to live in two worlds, how to keep our lives balanced, how to be productive schizophrenics.

We know who we are by how we name our states and create who we become by the choices we make based upon those interpretations. Our search for identity is our search for images and symbols capable of giving shape, significance and value to our lives. In order to know who we are, we need to be able to say what we are like. The equations we draw between ourselves and images and words make up our cultural identities.

Finding our true identity means finding the one image, myth or icon that mirrors the self better than any other. But this is impossible because the self is not any one single thing. There are acts of identification, but no final set of images for who or what we are. To borrow a few metaphors from the post-structuralist psychoanalyst Jacques Lacan, the self is a gap, an absence, a fantasy of language. Even to call it these things is to risk advancing a new idolatrous monomyth.

But if there cannot be any single identity which is our *true* one, we can nevertheless lend meaning to our present lives by inhabiting momentary incarnations, disguises and roles. And this is, in fact, what we do. The self inhabits a role for a while, finds its momentary identity, then dissolves again into pure possibility. As this process recurs, its logic becomes the style of our life, and we evolve our own personal mythologies to account for the people we pretend to be. There will always be a gap between our existential lives and the names we use to characterize them.

Lacan contends that this alienation is universal.[2] As children our ascent into language generates a splitting between our biological nature (what we feel ourselves to be) and our role in the family world (our cultural identity). All our lives we will sense a disunity between what others call us and what we sense ourselves to be. So we will seek our lost unity in our own speech, in dreams, in myths, stories, icons and heroes—even in the image of our own bodies before a mirror. But none of these representations will ever heal the split or synthesize our existential and social selves into one true identity.

In comic book adventure stories the legendary origins of the superhero often focus upon how his or her life was split in two.[3] This splitting is analogous to the split every individual undergoes in his movement into language and culture. Typically, at the hero's origin, he will dedicate himself to some purpose and choose a new name and image. By so doing, he acquires a consciously held personal mythology for the very first time. The old identifications remain intact as private, secret, self-descriptions. But they acquire a subordinate status—living alongside the mythic self.

Of course neither set of identifications is the hero's true self. He is more truly the gap between them. But unlike Lacan's neurotic individual who seeks to fill this gap and fails, the hero does not seek oneness. He celebrates his duality and seeks to remain undefined, a mystery, an anonymous force.

This is not an easy thing to do; the mind of man hates undefined forces. There is always the temptation to identity with some final set of images—whether it be the symbols in one's private life or those of the public myth. But if the adventures are to continue, the hero must resist collapsing his identity one way or the other. He must possess examplary negative capability and live perpetually in two worlds at once. His dual-self, thus, represents a perpetual inward tension which is best left unresolved.

The two worlds of the superhero are the two poles of human experience. On the one hand there is the world of power and pure possibility depicted by the surrealistic iconography of bizarre villains, time warps, interpenetrating dimensions, invisible forces, magic allies and sacred objects such as Kryptonite. It is a mythological world whose imagery inspires our spiritual aspirations and desires. On the other hand, the world of everyday life is represented by a stick-figure realism. This is not a world of archetypes and heroic deeds but of cliches and social misunderstandings. It is a comedic world whose only contact with the fantastic comes in the forms of villainous threats from super-criminals who attempt to remake everyday life over to suit their own larger than life conceptions of themselves.[4] The superhero protects the mundane world—not by redeeming it, but by protecting it from these magical intrusions. His public quest is essentially the same as his private one: to keep the sacred and the profane, the mythic and the literal, in proper balance. Keeping that proper balance means keeping these worlds distinct, linked only by a necessary tension.

This tension is not the aesthetic ambiguity praised by the New Critics in the 1950s. Superhero narratives do not aspire to the static purity of a Grecian urn. The balance the hero achieves between these two worlds and between contending sides of himself is merely a temporary solution to a perpetual narrative instability. It reflects our own attempts to keep our lives together after our fall into culture. But the superhero does not see his dual-life simply as an affliction; it is also a tactic, a way of getting on in the world with a minimum of personal compromise. It is a way of organizing inward complexity, a psychological division of labor like the one used by schizophrenics. Only, superheroes consciously subordinate one set of personal identifications within a larger one, know why they are doing it, and unite the two identities within the same moral purpose: the pursuit of justice, order and balance.

The exact nature of the superhero's two worlds varies with each particular superhero and with the specific events surrounding his or her ascent into culture. This is why the reader must know the legend of origins in order to appreciate the symbology of particular heroic adventures. Superman is a case in point.[5] As Superboy he identified with his adopted parents before he was awakened to the larger system of symbols from Krypton capable of more fully explaining his experience. Once he learned of his extra-wordly identity, his old self as "Clark" becomes less real to him. He does not cease being Clark (the identity still holds important associations for him)— rather he learns to wear that social self lightly, using it as a role, a disguise. It is, thus, no accident that Superman pledges to serve humanity over the graves of Ma and Pa Kent, for they were his link to the human world of social roles and pretend identities. As his archetypal human parents, they initiated him into the deception called culture while also teaching him that culture was not where his ultimate identity was to be found.

Clark Kent is Superman's real human identity: his true phoniness. Superman is Clark Kent's creative potential, that part of him that supercedes all the things of this world. Clark is everyman; Superman an icon for genius. Superman without Clark would be a man without human relationships. Clark without Superman would be a man who turned his back on his destiny. To be authentic Superman must live in both worlds. But this creates problems and is the source of narrative instabilities.

These instabilities dramatize the tension between the finite and infinite realms of human experience, between domestic and public roles, and between sacred and profane existence. The superhero is the proverbial man in the middle. But he is not seeking a way out of his quandary; he is attempting to live within it. In our quests for personal identity, the best we can do—according to the superhero myth—is achieve a creative, internal balance.

Batman is a superhero whose origin is quite different from that of Superman, so the symbolic meaning of his dual identity is also quite different.[6] Batman did not receive his mythic identity from his father by birthright. He invented it himself. He chose his public disguise as a rhetorical device to strike terror into the hearts of criminals; Superman chose to remain "Clark Kent" so as "not to scare people." Batman is the "existential" superhero—Bruce Wayne's total re-creation of himself. This new identity was spawned in his mind shortly after the death of his parents and nurtured into being through years of work, study and dedication. The conflict Batman faces when his secret identity is threatened is how to keep a balance between his invented self, based upon his own choices and commitments, and his "given" self, based upon those identifications given him by fate. Where the tension in Superman's life is between sacred and profane existence, infinite and finite capacities, the tension in Batman's life is between the created self and the accidental self—the for-itself and the in-itself. Whenever Batman triumphs over an adversary attempting to expose him, we see the victory of human will and ingenuity cheating the caprices of destiny. Whenever Superman triumphs over an adversary, we see the victory of transcendant creativity over the reductive ways of the world. In each case what is affirmed is a balance, a proper subordination of matter to spirit so as not to deny the importance of either.

In the *Encyclopedia of Comic Book Heroes*, Michael Fleisher cites over seventy instances in which Batman's secret identity is nearly revealed. Each escape provides us with an object lesson in the fine art of preserving a sacred space within us that exists outside public definition. For example, Batman was once captured by the Penguin and tied up. But before the Penguin could remove his mask, Batman smudged a bit of stage make-up on his face.[7] The Penguin removed Batman's mask and saw his secret identity—Bruce Wayne. But upon closer inspection of Batman's face, the Penguin notices the make-up and assumes that Bruce Wayne's face must have been yet another disguise hiding Batman's true identity. Before he can look for the face beneath the make-up, Batman escapes. Here we see Batman using the logic of those seeking to demystify the secret at the center of existence to preserve the integrity of his own multiple self. He does this by pretending to play a role when there are no roles left to play. The lesson seems to be that even the most seemingly inconsequential semiotic smudge is enough to turn a literal truth into a metaphor and clothe a naked man with the cover of an idea.

In looking over the seventy threats to Batman's secret identity catalogued in Fleisher's encyclopedia, it is clear that super-villains like the Penguin are less dangerous to Batman's dual life than the more traditional criminals. The super-villains recognize the need for myth, and so there is a kind of tacit code of honor to respect Batman's private life as of little consequence in their cosmic battles. Super-villains prefer to beat Batman on his own terms, toe to toe, myth to myth. They do not want to demystify Batman's mythic stature; they want to overcome it with their own. The Joker, for example, once tied Batman up in an episode much like the one just mentioned. He ruminates for a while over whether or not to remove Batman's mask, then remarks, "Ha, Ha! No! It's too simple—

unworthy of my intelligence. And I like these battles of wits! The hunt ... the chase! ... that's the breath of life to me!"[8]

The real danger to Batman's secret identity comes from crafty con-men, down-and-out detectives, confidence men, corrupt computer experts, authors out to make a name for themselves, crooked lawyers—the brains of the comic book underworld. Many of these people have been able to deduce Batman's secret identity, but he is usually able to subvert their logic through brilliant ruses that confound them. In one instance, he hired a double (who is blind, deaf and dumb, and therefore incapable of ever revealing the ruse) to stand in for him as Batman, and then he appeared beside the hired imposter as Bruce Wayne. When dealing with the profane criminal mind, the superhero's best defense seems to be an act which is logically impossible given the debunking criminal's assumptions. Like an artist, Batman's best weapons against a killing literalism out to strip away his personal mythology are magical images, visual paradoxes and seemingly miraculous deeds.

Those few who do find out who Batman really is and remain convinced are either part of Batman's inner circle or they die, get amnesia or travel somewhere else in time. The message here is that you cannot know how the two can be one unless you live within the myth or die to the world. The other possibility, that you reveal the secret and thereby kill the myth, cannot happen so long as Batman remains the cowled crusader.

The search is for a life in which the multiple spheres of one's existence do not impinge on one another but achieve a kind of harmonious give-and-take, like the changing images on a crackerbox toy. Life seldom allows for such pristine dualities, however, and there is always some villain out to characterize our duality as duplicity or some task requiring us to be two places at the same time. Again and again we are forced to deal with contradictions between who we are and who we pretend to be. The superhero lives out these conflicts through the motif of the secret identity, and shows us through his action and ingenuity how to outwit those wishing to define us. He does not just live in two worlds; he lives between them in transit, "not resting heavily in a single spot but gaily, lightly turning and leaping from one position to another."[9] This is the cosmic dance choreographed by the secret identity motif, and it reinforces the serial nature of the form. The superhero is the composite Self forever in between identities and adventures—never achieving the aesthetic wholeness of a completed life and never wanting to. He wants "to be continued."

And this continuity in diversity, this oneness through the many, makes up the underlying thematic of most superhero adventures.

Now throughout this analysis, I too have been masked in the rhetorical garb of the literary analyst. The critic is very much like the comic book heroine Lois Lane—in love with the hero, professionally exploiting his powers through writing, and yet secretly longing to domesticate him through a kind of marriage. As a reporter, Lois will do anything to "get the story," but secretly longs for transcendence through a sacred marriage with the supernatural. Critics also want to "get the story," but also long to break free from narrative particulars to an absolute identification with the values those narratives depict. But, like Lois, we cannot imagine how such a marriage is possible, so we settle for a professional relationship with the ones we love. We write about them.

But a marriage *is* possible. And the answer lies right before us in the figure of Clark Kent—our peer, our competitor, our fellow phony. Like Lois we are fooled by appearances to assume that the boy next door cannot be the man of steel. But we are wrong. Mythic powers always live in obscurity, and the way into the sacred realm of the hero is through the images of the profane.

This union between critic and story may seem to imply a dangerous confusion between the real world and the fictive. But our common separation of these two realms is actually more a symptom of the fact that in our contemporary world the commonplace no longer mirrors the archetypal. Without a symbolic sense, everyday life flattens out into adventureless moments in the ledger of time. And we only see genius in the flight of exceptional individuals across the horizon of world history—totally ignoring its quiet underside in the humble images of everyday life. As a result we never do find out who Superman is. We miss the surprising truth that transcendance is incarnate, and that it is incarnate in others.

Superhero narratives are one way to reveal this secret, for they provide us with the image of the two in one. Little wonder then that when I saw the film *Superman II*, grown adults cheered Superman's flight across the screen. He represents the irrepressible force of human spiritual resistance. He is the part of us the world refuses to acknowledge because it cannot believe such a reality exists. The Superhero confirms our inward suspicions that we are more than we ever dared dream ourselves to be, and that it is best to keep this knowledge secret, to play along, to bide our time, to wait until we are really needed. For what is most human in human affairs is our capacity to remake ourselves again and again—outstripping any and all identities that society or anyone else uses to define us.

Notes

[1] See for example, Maurice Horn's *Women in Comics* (New York: Chelsea House, 1977).

[2] Jacques Lacan, *The Language of the Self*, A. Wilden, trans. (New York: Dell, 1968).

[3] Stan Lee, *Son of Origins of Marvel Comics* (New York: Simon & Schuster, 1975).

[4] Stan Lee, *Bring on the Bad Guys: Origins of Marvel Villains* (New York: Simon & Schuster, 1976).

[5] George Lowther, *Superman* (Los Angeles: Kassel Books, 1979).

[6] Michael Fleisher, *The Encyclopedia of Comic Book Heroes* Vol. I "Batman" (New York: Macmillan, 1976).

[7] Fleisher, p. 303.

[8] Fleisher, p. 235.

[9] Joseph Campbell, *Hero with a Thousand Faces* (Princeton, N.J.: Princeton University Press, 1968), p. 229.

The Shrinking of Psychiatry: A Broken Image

Linda B. Martin

'You have been in treatment long enough to know there is no overnight cure. After all, I'm an analyst, not a magician.'

'Then perhaps what I need is a magician,' Kugelmass said, rising from his chair. And with that he terminated his therapy.

—from Woody Allen's *Side Effects*

*T*his revealing dialogue from the short story, "Kugelmass," aptly epitomizes the growing cultural disenchantment with psychiatry. Toppling the psychiatrist from his pedestal-shrinking him down to size, so to speak—has become a national pastime. Unlike the Aristotelian hero, elevated to grandiose proportions the farther to fall, the psychiatrist in American society today has already fallen from his accustomed heights.

Inflationary times breed deflated images. As dollars shrink, there is a growing tendency to dismiss analysis as unnecessarily expensive and time consuming. Breaking the myth of the psychiatrist's powerful authority provides a convenient catharsis. This attitude reflects on our political and economic troubles as the American Dream transforms into a nightmare of instability and uncertainty. No longer is the psychiatrist worshipped unconditionally as a rational, omniscient superbeing, a hero; losing his divinity, he becomes a humanly vulnerable figure, at the very least, or more critically a scientist who has misused his power.

Dr. Robert Jay Lifton has described how we generally "live on images and the images shift." The psychiatrist's altered image is especially apparent in the increasing frequency and severity of society's attacks on him. Heroes, it would seem, cannot be revered and reviled concurrently. As mythologist Joseph Campbell has observed, "a god outgrown becomes immediately a life-destroying demon." What we are witnessing today is the breaking of the psychiatrist's image, as the heroic myth is tempered by mortal fallibility.

The psychiatrist is especially vulnerable to criticism because of his unique position in society. In his professional role as a secular father-confessor, he is privy to unspeakable intimacies. This creates an uncomfortable tension between trust and suspicion. As surgeon of the psyche, cutting deep into the unconscious, he is perceived as both powerful and frightening. Operating in a world which has grown intolerant of *all* authority figures, the "headshrinker" becomes a natural target for the attacks of a society whose values have shifted from unqualified optimism to paranoid mistrust.

Even within the profession itself, all is not well. From the President's Commission on Mental Health comes a prediction that by 1990 there will be a critical shortage of over 13,000 psychiatrists. Reflecting a marked imbalance in the availability of mental health services, already two thirds of the counties in the United States do not have even a single psychiatrist. Dr. William E. Mayer, of the Alcohol, Drug Abuse and Mental Health Administration, has responded to decreased Government grants by noting a disheartening trend toward the "trivialization" of the field.

Psychiatry, it would seem, is literally a shrinking profession. A recent Conference on Career Choice in Psychiatry reveals that increasing numbers of medical students are turning away from this specialty, actually the lowest paying branch of medicine despite popular misconceptions to the contrary. But the reasons for this dwindling interest are not economic. Some students feel that psychiatry is "unscientific" and "not a real medical specialty." Others point to the "instability" of psychiatrists themselves (divorce and suicide rates for would-be psychiatrists are significantly higher than for other doctors-in-training). And, not surprisingly, many potential candidates are deterred by the negative image of psychiatrists in our culture—the unfavorable stigma attached to the profession as well as the generally unflattering portrayal by the media.

Viewed historically, it is fortuitous that the analyst in Allen's "Kugelmass" story should compare his role to that of a magician. In the earlier years of this century, when telephones and cars were still considered modern marvels, faith-filled Americans welcomed psychoanalysis as yet another manifestation of human progress. At last acknowledging repressed desires, Freud's theories coincided with the wish for increased moral freedom. There appeared a new faith in the miracles of science. Max Eastman wrote in 1915 that Freud's processes were indeed "a kind of magic." A 1917 *Ladies Home Journal* dubbed the psychiatrist "a priest of the new order." Revered as a spiritual leader, the psychiatrist was thus invested with that power ascribed to the shaman or tribal medicine man: the magic gift of healing.

But being a magician is no easy role to sustain; though his tricks may seem marvelous at first, the magician's illusions pale before critical inspection. So did the psychiatrist's image tarnish as the unquestioning optimism of The Gilded Age gave way to the disenchantment and increased hostility of our own Age of Anxiety.

Freud unwittingly anticipated this shift in attitudes when, in a 1910 address on "The Future Prospects of Psychoanalytic Therapy," he commented: "There is hardly anything like this in medicine, though in fairy tales you hear of evil spirits whose power is broken as soon as you can tell them their name." With analysts increasingly being put on the couch by society, it was not long before the spell of their golden image was irretrievably broken. Now it's Freud himself who is undergoing analysis, emerging "no longer the majestic prophet of the legend, but more like one of the neurotic egoists who might have frequented his own couch."

Thus gradually but inevitably has the pyschiatrist as hero become a cultural underdog to be stereotyped, satirized and derided. Pitting good against evil has always been a universally shared delight. Everyone loves to boo the villain, whether it be by throwing rotten tomatoes from the rogues' gallery or by exaggerating the psychiatrist's foibles in popular culture. Fickle as hemlines, the targets of any society respond to fashions of morality. According to the messages being received from the media, this season it's stylish to debunk the psychiarist.

*   *   *

Back in 1905, Freud ironically foresaw the fate now befalling psychiatrists. In *Jokes and Their Relation to the Unconscious*, he might have been speaking today of negative allusions and overstatements about psychiatrists, their representation by opposites and overblown details, the displacement jokes made at their expense. Since all joking is a socially acceptable way of channeling hostility, in the case of the psychiatrist it offers a perfect vehicle for sublimated attack. The whole process of analysis is based on a struggle between instinct and intellect, as the patient resists recovery, fearful of insight and change. Jokes about the profession help people to feel less threatened as they decrease the doctor's position of omnipotent authority. Demeaning the psychiatrist becomes the group defense mechanism of an ambivalent, fearful and mistrustful society.

Merely to be labeled a "headshrinker" carries an inescapable burden of social ridicule and mistrust. Fated, it seems, to be the perennial butt of jokes, the psychiatrist is often derided for sitting and listening—and getting paid for it. One wiseguy defines the psychiatrist as someone "who asks a lot of expensive questions which your wife asks for nothing." Or, he is glibly described as "a person who convinces you that your parents were failures because you turned out to be such a louse."

For the psychiatrist at leisure, there is a penalty too. Often he risks losing potential friends if he tells his true profession. Faced with the inevitable question, "What kind of doctor are you?" the honest psychiatrist must resign himself to the possibility of nervous smiles and the never-to-be-seen-again syndrome. After all, being friends with a "mind stripper" is no fun!

This is not just a problem for psychiatrists. Psychologist Joyce Brothers relates how a party guest, afraid that she was "reading his thoughts," confessed to feeling strangely naked, as if "standing in his underwear." People somehow get the foolish notion that their mind is being instantaneously x-rayed. A suburban psychiatrist who revealed his profession to a tennis partner now finds that once-friendly neighbor deliberately crossing the street when he walks the dog. Even when seeking relaxation at the movies, mental health professionals are often confronted with oversized screen images of their chosen profession, finding themselves as one doctor puts it, "in session after hours."

The less-than-perfect psychiatrist is everywhere. It becomes a daily occurrence to open a magazine or turn on the TV and find pejorative references to practitioners of this "impossible profession." As the sands filter through the hourglass of time, the "soaps" use breakdowns as a convenient excuse to get rid of unwanted characters in the script. Mental illness is a disease to be spoken of in hushed and solemn tones. The psychiatrist is often personally weak, tormented by problems, perhaps in the throes of divorce. Worse, the doctor may suggest the use of electric shock. Under the influence of television's persuasive mind control, gullible audiences get firsthand reinforcement of their fears that the psychiatrist is an evil scientist who puts electrodes on people's heads to tamper with the brain.

Radio follows television's example. In one commercial, Harold the elevator operator is referred by his female therapist for primary therapy at the Amalgamated Bank ("But first get off my lap!" she advises). Julius Caesar's shrink asks his patient to bring him an extra bottle of Fontana Candida. Even Public Radio offers us the character of Sigmund Matchit, psychiatrist, who is being divorced from wife Sybil because he can't "make it."

Newspapers also help shape negative public attitudes. In a *New York Times* column William Safire tells the joke about how Sigmund Freud is called in to analyze God's depression ("He has delusions of grandeur .... He thinks He's Al Haig"). More far-reaching is the announcement of "the largest psychological injury award granted in the country," $4.6 million to a woman whose psychiatrist had abused her sexually.

National magazines, too, fill innumerable readers with doubts about psychiatry. *Newsweek*'s cover story on "The Hidden Freud: His Secret Life, His Theories Under Attack" is hardly intended to impart a positive image to the profession. Nor is *Life* Magazine's "new series on psychotherapy" which begins by boldly suggesting the folly of "spending months or years on a couch, confiding in a mysterious and aloof figure...."

As seen satirically, the psychiatrist becomes the foolish "expert." Usually he has a mock-German accent or is caricatured as dozing behind the patient's couch. Often he is absent-minded, his thoughts off in the Caribbean while he urges the patient to remember. His expensive leather couch reflects unfavorably on rising fees in times when money is scarce. Always, the office walls are hung with lots of diplomas, as if to certify his position of authority. "And what does that mean to you?" he interjects between nods and "uh-huh's," offering external proof of his concentration and involvement.

Imagine the endless cartoon possibilities. A clock with only fifty minutes on it. An office full of swollen heads waiting to be shrunk. Or a too-small head, already shrunken, resulting from over-analysis. Perhaps the doctor might be putting himself to sleep as he swings a watch to hypnotize his patient. Why not have him puffing smoke from his ever-present pipe under a "thank you for not smoking" sign? Or have his fertility goddess displaying prominent breasts to a blushing adolescent? A sectional couch to treat split personalities? At the very least, his profession can be added to the familiar "How-many-does-it-take-to-change-a-lightbulb" joke: one psychiatrist to change it, one to analyze the situation! The themes and variations are endless.

"Psychiatrist abuse" filters into the media at even the simplest levels. Several years ago, it was enough for Linus to carry around his security blanket, or for Lucy to give pyschiatric advice for a nickel. More recently, there is the satire of cartoonist Tom Wilson, whose popular bulbous-nosed "Ziggy" finds his way into millions of households. In a good-natured but still critical way, Wilson takes advantage of the current trend to de-mythify the psychiatrist. Ziggy, it seems, requires the services of "Dr. Shrink" (alternately spelled "Schrink" to add the ethnic touch). In one instance, Ziggy is seen sitting in the waiting room; next to him, symbolically for those who catch it, is the image of a cracked pot.

On that most plebian of messages, the birthday card, Ziggy again appears in a waiting room, this time under a black hat sporting a prominent "N" (for nut?). While Ziggy is on the couch, Dr. Schrink is shown blowing bubbles, keeping time to a radio after admonishing his client for watching too much television, lighting a match to a stick clenched in Ziggy's toes, jumping up and down because the patient refuses to follow his advice. Here, on the simplest level, accessible to children as well as adults, is a vision of the psychiatrist as silly, immature and failing to practice what he preaches. Even a ten-year-old knows not to nominate the psychiatrist for cultural hero.

It is always easier to take advice from an equal rather than from a superior. Turning the psychiatrist into a "common man" by satirizing his faults, breaks the myth that he is without feeling and emotion himself. And, to point up his human vulnerability lessens the fear felt in the presence of this distant authority.

So, in a cartoon spotted in one issue of a medical journal, the psychiatrist—with obligatory beard and diploma—attempts to form a bond with his anxious patient. He reassures his client that his problem is not unique: "We have *all* gone through it. *Everyone's* birth was traumatic." Or, in *The New Yorker*, W. Miller portrays the shrink—balding but bearded and under two diplomas—sobbing tearfully into his handkerchief on hearing the sad tale of his patient. These are visual images deliberately designed to manipulate the public picture of the psychiatrist and decrease the awesomeness of his profession. He is, after all, as human as the Freud in Ralph Steadman's cartoon who laments, "And to think I could have been a simple brain surgeon!"

Attacks extend to books as well. Implying that the old ways of treatment are no longer valid are treatises on alternative techniques, from shower therapy to how colors can help you live a better life. Casually checked out from the local public library, *Night Vision* is Frank King's perverse novel about Dr. Helene Roth, the psychiatrist who has repeated sex with a hospitalized psychotic killer. Dr. Roth discovers a dream process to transmit evil and destroy her former lover, Dr. Stanislas, also a psychiatrist. Under her influence, Dr. S. steals, brutalizes, rapes his patient, violates his daughter—and then must "go home and practice psychoanalysis." Need we say more?

Reflecting current tendencies is the new twist in "how-to" books. A quick check reveals such suggestive titles as *Instant Shrink: How to Become an Expert Psychiatrist in 10 Easy Lessons,* or *How to be Analyzed by a Neurotic Psychoanalyst.* There's even one called *Shrink Lits,* billed as "seventy of the world's towering classics cut down to size." The application to psychiatry is obvious, as seen in this jargon-filled interpretation of the Dr. Jekyll/Mr. Hyde schism:

Had he been a
  Smarter doc
He'd have scooted
  Round the block
To the Mental
  Health Assoc.

They'd have had him
  Analyzed
"Schizoid type,
  Externalized."
Then, his psyche
  Normalized.

Traumas would be
  Transitory.
Gone would be the
  Details gory!
And loused up
  A nifty story.

Not to be outdone by other media forms, plays, too, jump on the critical bandwagon. Jean Kerr's "The Lunch Hour" gives us Oliver, the Park Avenue psychiatrist who specializes in marriage counseling but cannot stop his wife from having an affair—the hypocrisy of the detached professional who can analyze others but fails to heal himself.

Again, in "Beyond Therapy," one therapist hugs her Snoopy and calls her clients "porpoises"; another shouts to his patient, "You pay me to listen. Talk!" Obviously, they have their problems, as does Dina Merrill, the Germanic child psychiatrist with a boot fetish in husband Cliff Robertson's one-actor, "The V.I.P.'s " And Mendel the psychiatrist in William Finn's "March of the Falsettos" could use a few lessons in restraint. On hearing that his friend has gone homosexual, Mendel wastes no time in wooing and marrying the wife, while poor son Jason is advised: "Get thee to a psychiatrist." Enter the psychiatrist, on a house call, jumping wildly up and down and singing, "Why don't you feel alright/For the rest of your life!" With Jason, we wonder, "Is that therapy?"

Perhaps of all the media, movies allow for the widest and most dramatic range of attacks against psychiatry. Cinematic techniques create larger-than-life screen images which rebellious audiences can scorn in anonymous safety. This capacity of films to concentrate on and magnify details makes even minor criticism appear prominent. Even in "Ordinary People," where the psychiatrist is for once perceived as decent, the cinematographer pans the office of Dr. Berger, consciously lingering on his messy tabletops and rusty radiator to create the desired negative effect. The camera can also focus momentarily on a bit-part character, like "Jerome the psychiatrist" in "It's My Turn," to make him instantly unpopular with the audience. Or, it can dwell in harsh detail on the facial expressions and nervous hand movements of Dr. Mogens-Jensen, the hypocritical psychiatrist of Ingmar Bergman's "From the Life of the Marionettes."

Sometimes, the doctor does not even have to appear on the screen to take the rap. In "Private Benjamin," for example, Goldie Hawn blames the failure of her first marriage on her unseen therapist who advised her to find a "father figure." Similarly, in "Absence of Malice," there is the situation of a poor girl who commits suicide when her abortion is made public—even though "she was seeing a psychiatrist."

Even given cameo roles, the therapist fares poorly. The two inept psychiatrists in "Willie and Phil" are no more capable of making intelligent psychological evaluations than the aloof, hostile and expensive shrink in "Ten," or the "seven learned psychiatrists" who totally miss the therapeutic boat in the film, "Oh God! Book II." Then, there's the brief appearance of the psychiatrist ("OK, let's wheel in the shrink!") in "Whose Life is it Anyway?"—a nervous, hypochondriacal fellow obsessed with folding napkins ("You've got a nasty little tidiness compulsion," chides patient Richard Dreyfuss).

For images of professional perversion and sickness, the movies offer equal richness. There's Michael Caine as the successful but sexually mixed-up psychiatrist/murderer who disguises himself as a woman in "Dressed to Kill." In "Twinkle, Twinkle, Killer Kane," Stacey Keach is a murderer play-acting at being a hospital psychiatrist. And what of "Bad Timing: A Sensual Obsession," the tale of a masochistic psychoanalyst who compromises his professionalism by performing sexual "ravishment" on the comatose body of his Viennese playmate?

Unlike one-dimensional jokes and cartoons, the cinema can create a convincing illusion of depth with its ability to shift back and forth in time and place. Revealing thoughts by such devices as dream sequences, flashbacks and premonitions of the future, movies are capable of self-conscious vision. In this way, many film directors—themselves the products of analysis—use their medium to explore their own ambivalent attitudes.

One effective example appears in Woody Allen's "Stardust Memories," where even the title alludes to the recall process so crucial in therapy. There is the dream scene where, trusty pipe in hand, Victor Truro as the "hostility psychoanalyst" pursues a hairy "rage" creature who is carrying off Mr. Allen's mother. Or, there is Mr. Allen imagining himself dead, projecting a vision of analysts growing famous by writing scholarly papers about his misfortunes. Involved in therapy for more than half his life, Woody Allen hides behind the safety of films and stories to express his love-hate relationship with psychiatry. Eager for scapegoats, their appetites whetted by popular culture, audiences do likewise.

*   *   *

Why have the tables turned against psychiatry? Not long ago, psychiatric theories criticized social customs; people took note for instance, it was shown that smothering a child with too much affection might be as damaging as neglect. Now, social customs revert to criticizing psychiatry. The mass media depict the psychiatrist as a public scapegoat for the ills of society which his profession has failed to cure.

According to Dr. Herbert Pardes, head of the National Institute of Mental Health, there are several reasons for this image reversal. He notes a "mainstreaming of psychiatry" which has increased society's general awareness of the mental health field at the same time as it has evoked strong reactions against it. There is, too, a greater tendency for people to criticize *any* authority, especially a professional group which sets itself up as "ostensibly perfect" ("When they see you on television, think you must be God," says psychiatrist Mary Ann Bartusis, a talk show regular). Dr. Pardes also feels that there is a "halo effect from stigmatized patients," whereby the psychiatrist is thought to absorb some of his clients' negative attributes. In popular terms, it's as if "craziness" were contagious.

There is a disquieting mystique about entering into the mind that is at once compelling and frightening. Feeling hypnotically drawn to "confess," one grows vulnerable and suggestible. Going to a psychiatrist involves probing explosive human forces: placing trust in the strength of a stranger, penetrating unconscious motivations, being able to alter established patterns of behavior. A deep and intimate bond is formed with a person who, it is hoped, will help and heal. The psychiatrist thus becomes a mythical talisman capable of dispelling evil and restoring order.

However, as in the myth where only a "white blackbird" can cure the king's misfortunes, the precise solution is difficult to find. Put to the test of reality, the psychiatrist often falls short of being a magic god. Perhaps the process requires more time, honesty and pain than anticipated; perhaps the concept of scientific healing of the mind is just not feasible. As a slip of the knife in surgery can kill, the slightest deviation by the psychiatrist is misinterpreted as neglect or incompetence. With increasing disillusionment and mistrust, with money tighter and anxiety-relieving cynicism on the rise, it becomes more comforting to denounce the psychiatrist as a charlatan who takes your money but doesn't deliver the promised goods.

Our media simply reflect the general loss of faith which has seeped into all levels of society, a world where "exact change after dark" and "watch your valuables" are daily passwords. The disintegration of the psychiatrist's once-elevated position of authority, the lessening of his alleged powerfulness, coincides with growing economic, social and political doubts. Sometimes, it's purely a matter of dollars and cents that makes his services superfluous. Other critics harp on the doctor's inability to cure his own hang-ups, thereby rendering him ineffective as a professional problem-solver. The psychiatrist's image is clouded by pessimism. Everything about him—the cut of his clothes, the length of his hair, his office decor, his preoccupation with time—becomes a potential target for public attack.

Society has gradually grown more wary in matters of trust. As patent medicines are now passe, blind-buying is going out of style. With the emphasis on educated consumerism, people now scrutinize those who offer mental health care as cautiously as they read the ingredients on labels. Promises are fine, but results are more convincing.

People always opt for the quick and easy cure. In the days of uninhibited advertising, attaining health seemed as simple as buying miracle drugs which promised to work while you slept. Wouldn't it be wonderful if it were so? Maybe if psychiatry could be similarly bottled, it would be more palatable. Clearly in a world grown impatient and angry, alternatives like popping pills or submerging one's consciousness in a tank of water can seem more immediately appealing than long-term therapy. There is a wish to find an "instant shrink," a wonder doctor who can somehow manage the mind with the speed of a radar oven or the convenience of dehydrated soup.

Even in Shakespeare's time, the necessity for patience thwarted the cure. When Macbeth pleads for "some sweet oblivious antidote" to restore his lady's "mind diseased," the doctor responds that the patient "must minister to himself." "Throw physic to the dogs, I'll none of it," retorts the intolerant Macbeth, wanting immediate results or none at all. Today he might as well be telling off a psychiatrist—or involved in a malpractice suit after his dependent wife solved her own problem by committing suicide!

Nearly four hundred years later, in the movie "Ordinary People," the public is invited to witness how a potential suicide can be averted by a sympathetic if eccentric psychiatrist. Perhaps of all the recent cultural offerings, this film most appears to raise psychiatry's broken image. Reminiscent of Greek tragedy, the movie depicts the eventual wisdom won through suffering. Conrad endures his brother's death and his mother's scorn; he has tolerated electric shock and the taunts of his classmates who call him "crazy." The key to his therapeutic triumph is pain. As the movie shows, wisdom comes only when positive action transcends that pain.

But along with the challenge comes the doubt of failure. Even the basic optimism of "Ordinary People" is tempered by a mistrust in the efficacy of psychiatry. Conrad's father expresses society's growing disbelief in this science which is "precise and clear and honest." Venturing initially into therapy himself, Mr. Jarrett remarks, "I just don't believe in psychiatry as a panacea for everybody."

To our surprise, the psychiatrist doesn't rush to defend his profession. Rather, he responds with candor and even a sad touch of resignation: "Neither do I."

Neither, it seems, do most people these days.

Searching for Heroes

David Manning White

L ying restlessly in his bed, Jacob Davost heard the hall clock strike two slightly atonal clangs. That damnable clock had been making such jarring cacophonies for 100 years or more, even when it had been his grandfather's in a cold, gloomy house on outskirts of Portland, Maine. The hollow discordance of the chimes made him wonder whether the ghost of some long forgotten hero had somehow become caught in the clock's innards.

In those quiet hours between midnight and dawn each ticking second seemed to be carrying a load that strained credulity itself. Zounds! It was going to be yet another one of those nights when Jacob Davost and insomnia would joust until daybreak! To what avail would his slender shield embossed with a Rosicrucian mandala be against the savage blows of that terribly awake Black Knight who carried the moon-emblazoned shield?

Often during these nocturnal forays Davost's thoughts turned to his more than 60 years' quest to identify those individuals who might fulfill his need for authentic heroes.

When he was a very little boy his hero had been "Black Jack" Pershing, that no-nonsense general who led the A.E.F. into France in the war that surely would end all wars. An apocryphal family legend had it that the two-year-old Davost would eat porridge only when his mother prefaced each spoonful with, "Now, General Pershing is leading his men into the Meuse-Argonne!"

In 1920 when the triumphant General of the Armies waved from a resplendent Pierce-Arrow landau on Chicago's Michigan Avenue in yet one more triumphal parade, Davost was there, perched on his father's shoulders, a tiny voice screaming in concert with the thousands who crowded the streets.

Within a few years Pershing had to share Davost's adulation with Tom Mix, the paragon of cowboys (who, strangely had served in real life with Pershing's troops during 1916 in a not so heroic attempt to capture Pancho Villa in Mexico). About that same time Davost went through his Douglas Fairbanks period, and each afternoon as soon as school was over he and his two best chums hied themselves to their version of Sherwood Forest, where Fairbanks was Robin and they the zealous members of his band. Davost always yearned to be Little John, but inevitably was given the persona of Friar Tuck.

Later they were Athos, Porthos and Aramis to Fairbank's D'Artagnan, as the Three Musketeers tried to foil the Machiavellian antics of Cardinal Richelieu's cohorts. When he was 10 young Davost had a recurring dream in which he flew across the skies on a magic carpet, with the redoubtable Fairbanks as the Thief of Baghdad guiding the way.

Davost's father, whose love he sought with no palpable return, maintained an inordinate admiration for Theodore Roosevelt, even though the bitter acrimony of the Bull Moose campaign had somewhat tarnished Teddy's aura. So, Davost admitted the colorful Rough Rider into his galaxy of heroes, which by the time he was eleven included, along with Tom Mix and Doug Fairbanks, Ulysses S. Grant, Joan of Arc, El Cid, Hercules, Hannibal and such kings as Charlemagne, Alfred, Arthur and Theseus. One of the neighboring hills became the sceme of Colonel Teddy's assault of San Juan Hill, as Davost's cry of "Bully, lads, let's show these Spanish tyrants what we are made of!" inspired his charging horse soldiers.

After the winters of discontent which followed the stock market crash of October 1929, Davost sublimated his mythological, folk and movie-engendered heroes and began to look for some real-life, contemporary ego-ideals who could help him *and* America find its *elan vital*.

In 1932, a jaunty, confident man with a silver voice told 16-year old Jacob and his younger brothers, Jeremiah and Amos, that they had nothing to fear but fear itself. There they were all huddled around the little radio in their kitchen. And for the rest of his adolescence Davost never had the slightest doubt that this distant cousin of the great Teddy would subdue the San Juan Hill of the Depression with the same Roosevelt spirit.

Now on this sleepless night 50 years later, this Davost, just recently retired from the English department at Wesleyan, was reminiscing over the *fallen* heroes of his life. When these bouts of insomnia overtook him he found it far more rewarding than counting sheep in a feckless quest for sleep.

There on the proscenium of his memory he relived the April day in 1945 when he awoke in Manila, a skinny corporal in MacArthur's army, and heard the radio announcement of F.D.R.'s death. Especially, he recalled the tears it brought to his eyes. And then there was that terrible Friday in 1963 when one of his graduate students burst into his office crying, "Dr. Davost!—have you heard the terrible news—someone in Dallas has just shot President Kennedy?" Oh, the lost promises that began that bitter, snowy day in Washington with Robert Frost at the side of the beguiling master of the new Camelot.

But now his memories of F.D.R. and Jack Kennedy were besmirched with the stories that had surfaced after their deaths. One biographer after another in an apparent compulsion to "let it all hang out" vied to unearth demeaning anecdotes about his heroes' lives.

Nothing seemed to stimulate sales of such books as much as a release to the press about some alleged sexual affair involving Roosevelt, Kennedy or whoever the latest target of the new muckrakers' research might be. Maybe I am damned old fashioned or simply naive, Davost thought, but I liked the times better when we didn't feel we had to know every jot and tittle of a man's personal life. Hadn't even one popular historian or adversary journalist ever considered the Roman maxim, "De mortuis nil nisi bonum?" Maybe Scott Fitzgerald was right when he said, "Show me a hero and I'll show you a tragedy."

As a matter of fact, why had mankind been denigrating its heroes for at least 3000 years, if not from the earliest days of civilization itself.

He thought about the youthful David whose incredible courage in facing Goliath elevated him into the pantheon of the greatest of Old Testament heroes. And yet the scribe of the Book of Samuel II felt compelled to include the baser aspects of King David's moral character. Did he really need to know that a lust-driven David planned the death of Uriah the Hittite in order to marry Bathsheba? And there probably are still some academic bounty hunters who would like to make a splash by "proving" that young David and Jonathan were lovers before it was stylish to be gay. Did the Bible really have to include all the other soap-operatic troubles of poor old David, the man who started out such a hero?

Nor had it been better in America, even from the earliest years of our republic. From the time when a bitter, disaffected journalist named Callender in Richmond started the apocryphal, scurrilous canard about Thomas Jefferson and Sally Hemmings to the latest prurient twaddle about Marilyn Monroe and the Kennedy brothers in yesterday's gossip press it had never ceased.

Whatever the motivation, the exhumers of his heroes' lives had left Davost with few, if any, 20th century heroes, and it seemed they were just as intent in destroying those he had esteemed from earlier centuries. Having survived the disillusionment of learning about the apple that William Tell never shot, the ride that Paul Revere never finished and the flag that Barbara Fritchie never waved, Davost wondered how many more heroes there were left to decimate. Thank God they hadn't turned old Barbara into a superannuated camp follower who yearned for the body of Stonewall Jackson!

Maybe it was simply a mass enactment of what Freud had termed the primal scene, wherein the little kid in his trundle bed is awakened during the night by mama and papa's orgasmic moans in the secret room down the hall—awakened, confused, titillated, aroused. Perhaps the heroes we sought to endow with bigger-than-life qualities were merely extensions of what we wished our fathers to be. If this were so, small wonder that our heroes must inevitably come under the curious scrutiny of the peep-eyed youngster who has merely changed into the body of the peep-eyed oldster.

Why this accursed salacious itch, Davost thought, from which few Americans (including, alas, occasionally himself) had escaped. Is it because we are pervaded by an all-encompassing, corrosive, venal and virtually amoral mass culture which thrives on sex and violence? Considering the lowest merchants of sleaze in our media, publications such as America's most widely read weekly, *The National Enquirer*, it's clearly evident that we are being immersed in the primal scene from all sides.

Even if he had all but given up in his quest to find the heroes and heroines who brought hope and zest to *le comedie humaine*, Davost wondered to whom the youth of the 1980s would turn. Would it be Archbishop Glemp in Poland making a heroic confrontation with the Soviet puppet, Jarulzelski? Lech Walesa, alas, had been virtually declawed by the NKVD when they slipped a mickey into his coffee during his detention and then propped him in bed to take photos of him with some doxie "performing" sexual acrobatics. Lousy antics, but not much worse than what a gigantic American corporation tried to do to Ralph Nader when he was getting too obstreperous in his earlier crusades. Maybe, *mirable dictu*, it would be Ronald Reagan, who in a moment of supreme inspiration would call the new Russian power-boy, Andropov, and arrange a quick summit wherein they would decide, for the very future of humanity, to dismantle their atomic arsenals. If there were ever a time in mankind's history that begged for the emergence of great heroes it was now, this very night, Davost thought.

But what if our media-speckled, hyped-up age is no longer able to produce authentic heroes? What if this very moment some paranoid lieutenant in Svedlovsk or his drunk, overwrought counterpart in Huron, South Dakota, has "accidentally" unleashed the first ICBM's speeding their merry way across the skies to Chicago or Leningrad? Then, thought Davost, I must at last become my own "hero," and in that terrible hour of *dies irae* I shall go back to my childhood prayers and beseech the Lord, my soul to keep. And on that somber note he fell asleep.

Hero with 2000 Faces*

Ray B. Browne

*H*eroes serve as models and leaders of people and nations because they reflect the projection of the consensus of the dreams, fantasies, self-evaluations and needs of individuals and of society itself. Heroes like a lens concentrate the power of people, of a nation and serve as the muscle for the movement and development of a people, which they epitomize. In a simple society such as that reflected in the *Epic of Gilgamesh* (3000 B.C.) or the Greeks' Odysseus, they are simple and straightforward, tending, in the words of Joseph Campbell, to be "monomyths," serving definite and clear purposes in society.

In more complicated societies, however, heroes wear many faces because of their many responses to the numerous needs of individuals, groups of people and national purposes. As the needs get more complicated, so too do the heroes; as people get more sophisticated the heroes become less modeled on the conventional demi-gods of the past, less clear-cut and obvious. In a volatile and swiftly moving society like the present, heroes undergo rapid transformation, frequently developing in ways and for purposes not immediately apparent. Twentieth-century American heroes, existing in a highly technological society and driven by the electronics of mass communication, change quickly. But they are no less genuine and serve no less an important purpose than their counterparts of old.

In our day the hero still has the conventional body and soul of his predecessors, still serves the mythological purpose of helping to explain ourselves to ourselves and helps us maintain a stability and national purpose, but appears in different guises. The hero, as outlined by Northrup Frye, Freud, Jung, Lord Raglan, and dozens of others, has developed the thousand faces, as recorded by Joseph Campbell, into *thousands* of faces, and the number is growing. These are genuine heroes, as useful as those of old. They are not so stable, so formulaic, so stereotyped as those of conventional mythologic proportions of old, but they are essentially the old heroes tailored to suit different peoples. Gods can live only by filling the needs of the society they serve; otherwise they become relics, useful only in studies of origins and the past. They cannot serve living purposes for the living.

To a large extent, naturally, modern heroes are developments, though not inventions, of the technological media simply because the media are our present-day means of communication. To many observers the media create *celebrities* not *heroes*. Daniel Boorstin, an elitist negative evaluator of the media, feels the hero was a being who achieved something, the celebrity merely a name. As he cleverly phrases it: "The hero was a big man; the celebrity is a big name." Elaborating on the celebrity, Boorstin says: *The celebrity is a person who is known for his well-knownness.*"[1] The tense in Boorstin's verb is significant. Apparently he feels that, as the Bible says, there were giants in the earth in the old days but there can be none in our time.

There is, of course, some validity in the observation, but it has its limitations. The hero-celebrity schism is more the tool of the phrase-maker than of actuality. It is something like the unfortunate term "fake-lore" that folklorist Richard M. Dorson coined early in his career to try to distinguish between genuine and "specious" folklore (folklore being of the people, "fakelore" a commercialization of the genuine article) and remained trapped by the term for most of his academic life though in his later years he admitted that the difference, insofar as there is one, is not similar to his distinction and far more subtle. The difference between the hero and the celebrity is largely artificial except in definition. Both exist on a continuum, and there is much of both in each. True, most heroes have done something, something perhaps even "heroic" in the old sense of the word. But not all. Contrary to Boorstin's assertion not all heroes have done something, or even exist. Paul Bunyan, for instance, patron saint of loggers, and especially of people who are not loggers, has been for over half a century the hero of woodsmen. Giant in size, boisterous, independent, generally indifferent to the niceties of logging, Bunyan epitomized what people think is the spirit of the logger. But he never existed. Created by a logging company in Westwood, California, because the management needed a logo, Bunyan, because he was needed by the folklore of the loggers, assumed mythological proportions, no matter what his origins. Other heroes have their proportions puffed by the popular media. Abraham Lincoln, surely one of our greatest heroes, was created partially through the "mass media" of his day: the dime songsters, the joke books, the burlesque books, newspapers, every form of popular culture. The hero almost always stands on a platform, of his own making or that created by others, of dissembling and deceit. Most heroes, it goes without saying, have done less than they have received credit for—regardless of their time of action. An excellent case in point was Johnny Appleseed, patron saint and hero of the Ohio Valley in the nineteenth century. Johnny was heroized for having walked from one end of the Ohio Valley to the other distributing what the people needed most—material to read, conversation and gossip and apple trees. Born and raised in Fort Wayne, Indiana, Johnny worked in a fruit nursery and apparently did sell apple trees. But he hardly planted the Valley by tossing apple seeds hither and yon as he wandered about like a scholar-benefactor of old since apple trees are not planted from seed. Johnny Appleseed did not quite fill the role that mythologizers created for him. All heroes are more the product of their "press agents" than of their own actions. Likewise, many celebrities have accomplished *more* than their press agents and negative commentators will allow them to get credit for. Nineteenth-century Davy Crockett is a good illustration. Despite the fact that he was largely a product of slick East Coast puffery he was a real hero to Tennesseans and frontiersmen and to the millions who have known the story of the fall of the Alamo. In our day, Alan Alda is a celebrity for his role in the television show *M*A*S*H* but a hero to many individuals because of his stand against the insanity of war. Billie Newman (Linda Kelsey), very modest and quiet female star reporter of the television production *The Lou Grant Show*, assumed heroic proportions to many people who saw her as a leader in women's fight to attain equal rights.

In the argument over the proper media for the development of the hero, it is hardly realistic to ask that heroes be self-developed. The *true* hero is, presumably, too much interested in being heroic to publicize himself, and often his acts of heroism are too private and unnoticed ever to be known by anyone. There are, to paraphrase the English poet Thomas Grey, many heroes "born to blush unseen and waste their sweetness on the desert air." For example, Lenny Skutnik, the Government worker who happened along in January 1982 when the Air Florida airplane which had just taken off from the Washington National airport plunged into the Potomac and dived in to save a woman who was obviously drowning, would have gone unnoticed had not television cameras been there and wanted to turn him into a celebrity; Skutnik was embarrassed and felt that the media were making too much of his somewhat involuntary act of heroism. Chances are had the media not been present Skutnik would have received a brief and evanescent recognition by the people present, would probably have been discussed for a few days by the witnessing people, might even possibly have had a song written about him or a tale told about him, but his exploit would have received limited circulation. The media, however, made him known to everyone and in so doing, although they may have burned out the hero himself, made his heroic deed a part of American life, re-stating one of the fundamental principles of American mythology—that Americans are unselfish, willing to give to, or even to die for, other people.

Romantics and folklorists (especially library romantics and folklorists) think that heroism is circulated exclusively by word of mouth. Such an attitude is hardly tenable. Heroes have always been created by the media available at the time. If the operating medium is the bard around the campfire talking or singing of the deeds of someone on the hunt, that is the existing form of mass communcation. If it is the illustrated manuscript of pre-movable type days, that is the means of communication. If it is the newspaper or the dime novel—or the TV camera—that is the means of mass communication. If it is today's gossip, that is the means of communication. The main difference among all the media is one of intensity. Some burn cool and relaxed; some are hot and hurried. In the cool media the hero takes a long time developing and therefore can last a long time because his fire, never very hot, remains banked and can be drawn forth when needed. In the hotter media the life expectancy is much shorter. The hero serves his purpose and is then passed over, being left in the minds and hearts of the populace if he merits it, for a newer model. The media do not destroy so much as they just pass over. Like the eighteenth century deistic belief of God as creator who wound a cosmic clock and then sat back to see it unwind, they create and then move on.

Conventional definitions of the hero as necessarily demi-god are based on very little faith in the people the hero serves. They assume that the hero cannot survive in the light of reality in a democratic and technological society. There is, of course, a lot of hocus-pocus and mystery about the role of the hero. It is axiomatic that the more ignorant the society, the more heroic the hero. The needs of society demand and often want less than full revelation of the facts about the hero. No doubt had there been news media present when Odysseus returned to Ithaca from his odyssey, newsmen would have told him that it was poor navigating to spend ten years wandering around in the small lake of the eastern Mediterranean, and they would have suspected that his adventures among the unnatural creatures and gods and goddesses for ten years were merely an excuse to stay away from home. But had they searched around for background and in-depth interpretation they would have been able to confirm that the voyage, meaning more than it seemed, was symbolic and mythological and therefore *true*. More actuality about the voyage would not have destroyed its meaning but it would have made it less elevated, and greater circulation might have terminated its importance sooner, though it would not have negated its importance. In our own history, for example, Thomas Jefferson's stature as American hero has not been diminished, except among the Jefferson-cultists, by Fawn Brodie's revelation that he had a long-time affair with Sally Hemings, his slave, and had several children by her. America's Camelot of the early 1960s may have been strenthened not weakened in the long run by more closely associating it with the mythological world of King Arthur, through the revelations that John F. Kennedy, like Lancelot of old, had his Guineveres traipsing up and down the backstairs of the White House. And probably the late President Lyndon B. Johnson will withstand the revelations of his biographer, Robert Caro, that he was far less than a perfect man.

To assume that the people of a modern, technologized nation are too simple minded, too thoughtless to be able to appreciate a hero, warts and all, is to underestimate both the importance of the hero and the intelligence of the people. In an advanced civilization there is less room for and patience with the misty, part fake-phony hero, the anthropological culture hero of the past, because there is less dependence placed on him. People have less need for demi-gods. The kind of hero that is still needed—the down-to-earth, realistic role-model—still serves contemporary society. To serve society, the individual needs to be known. The people in their slow but ultimate wisdom will recognize the difference between the heroic and the well-knownness and distinguish between the hero and the mere celebrity. And the hero will benefit.

Sometimes the media instead of casting too much light, cast too little, instead of over-exploiting, they underexploit. For example, Henry Ford, who along with Charles A. Edison was the hero of the first half of the twentieth century, suffered from underexposure on at least one point. In explaining what he thought was the proper presentation of history, Ford said that if history were not a record of the common, instead of the elite, aspects of life, it was incorrect and therefore, in the words that were picked up by everyone, "history is bunk." Quoted out of context, he was thought an ignoramus, when in fact had his full attitude and statement been publicized he would have been celebrated and become more heroic because he was merely stating what was felt by many people and groups (the Italian Futurists, for example, who believed that art ought to brought out of the museums and given back to the people). Annoyed with the exclusive and therefore false interpretation of elite historians, Ford created Greenfield Village in Dearborn, Michigan, and demonstrated his (now recognized as a proper and useful) view of a enlightened way to record and study history.

Heroes, somewhat like fads though of longer life, come and go. They are "in" and they are "out." They are "national" in influence or local. The Puritans of New England are not much revered these days; sometimes one has to remind the untutored of the greatness of Benjamin Franklin; and only the specialist knows of the heroic exploits of Israel Potter during the Revolutionary War.

But the hero, even the transient heroes of the last quarter of the twentieth century, still represent on a passing or eternal scale, a star in the distance, bigger than life and bright enough to attract imitation. They still serve as chinning bars on which are exercised the hopes and aspirations of individuals, groups and nations.

Heroes can by nature be either conservative or radical, can serve as havens of refuge or as sharp swords to draw the blood of progress. As stereotype and formula they have two edges, the drag edge and the cutting edge. Both serve useful purposes as counterbalancing weights to keep the pendulum of society from running amok and swinging too far either way.

Therefore in the 1980s, although they might be somewhat obscured by the glare of different types, there still exist many of the old heroes—Lincoln, Kennedy, FDR, Walter Reuther, and the like. But especially in the 1960s and 70s new heroes were created by a people tired of the old: Elvis Presley, the Beatles, Jane Fonda, and particularly Martin Luther King, Jr., and many others. They were the new image of the role of America in the world at a time when people, goaded by the frustration of the war in Vietnam and fired by a genuine feeling of outrage at the immorality of war, demanded change. The old heroes tended to represent invalid ways of looking at things, of models for behavior.

These new heroes of change have tended to become less important in the 80s than they had been in more rebellious times. Heroes, as well as celebrities, suffer the vagaries of becoming anachronistic, and the energies that drove those in the 60s and 70s and the people supporting them, for better or worse, are burned out and banked. Society in 1982 was more indifferent to the supposed injustices which articulated the heroes of those two earlier decades. Now, instead, people seem to have other purposes, other goals, and the heroes must correspondingly change. In the early 80s there was a rebirth of political, economic and religious conservatism of the right wing, more pragmatic and less idealistic than of old.

Heroes come in different sizes at different stages in a nation's development. When a nation is admittedly young and naive, heroes stand ten feet tall. But when the people are more advanced, more sophisticated, more cynical, they like their heroes more of their own size—at times even the dwarfs of anti-heroism. In the more sophisticated societies the heroes serve more as only role-models.

Of all the media undoubtedly television has been the most instantly important in shaping or reflecting the changed faces of the heroes of the 80s. This medium reveals individuals little more "heroic" than ourselves, but with greater abundance. This attitude is well exemplified in the apocryphal joke about the husband (wife) who asked his wife (husband) what her lover (mistress) had that he (she) didn't have and was told "Nothing"; she (he) just had it "better developed." Or the one always told by the woman in the country occupied by American soldiers who has abandoned her former boy friend and taken up with one of the soldiers, he "has it here."

What we see in television is a direct reflection of the changed heroic role: this changed hero is aptly exemplified by soap operas. Soap operas are the Big Rock Candy Mountain of present-day American dreams, the lotus-land of body's desire. They reflect the contemporary pragmatism, the new materialistic bent. They represent wealth, power, beauty, self-indulgence, all the things that people now think are the real goals in life. Prime-time soaps, like *Dallas*, and its numerous spinoffs like *Flamingo Road, Knots Landing* (a direct take-off), *Dynasty* and *Falcon Crest* intensify the philosophy of the day-time soaps. *Dallas*'s J.R., for example, is a full-fledged hero of many Americans because he is wealthy, cunning, ruthless, powerful. There are Satanic heroes in our lives as well as angelic. J.R. is Faustian, lusting for power as did Satan, Hitler, the mafia, and willing to pay the price to get it.

In the print-medium, bestselling fiction represents one of the most obvious forms of our heroes. Bestsellers must be timely, must give desired information, must be readable, must present some appeal just beyond our fingertips. Heroes in these bestsellers are only slightly distanced from ourselves. In our narcissistic age when TV commercials say that we deserve only the best, we are inclined to be self-indulgent. We are therefore caught up in the various best-selling diet and self-help books because they insist that our rainbow is just over the hill and easily attainable.

Another best-selling genre, detective fiction, can be all things to all people, supplying heroes and heroines for all demands. The Golden Age, Classic detective fiction is selling at an unprecedented pace. Agatha Christie's Hercule Poirot is still number two or three on the best-selling charts, having sold so many copies that not even the publishers can estimate the number. Scores of other Classic detective stories are selling widely: Mary Robert Rinehart, Dorothy L. Sayers, P.D. James, Catherine Aird, to name only a few.

Perhaps no one character in the Classic detective mode so reveals this bent in the present-day readers as the return of Sherlock Holmes. The genuine works of A. Conan Doyle are being reissued in numerous editions, there are numerous "continuations" of Holmes' adventures by other authors (such as Michael Dibdin, *The Last Sherlock Holmes Story*, with Holmes as Jack the Ripper; *The West End Horror* and *The Seven-Per-Cent Solution*, by Nicholas Meyer, *The Return of Moriarty* and *The Revenge of Moriarty* by John Gardner; *Sherlock Holmes in New York*, from the TV film written by Alvin Sapinsley adapted by D.R. Bensen; various psychological studies of all aspects of Holmes' life; and various collections, and television shows, about Doyle's contemporaries who wrote Victorian detective stories).

At the other extreme, the hard-boiled detective writers were satisfying the needs for heroes for millions of other readers. John D. MacDonald's Travis McGee (the private eye in about half of MacDonald's works) was the center of many people's dreams, as was Ross Macdonald's Lew Archer. There were literally hundreds of other such writers.

Raymond Chandler's call in "The Simple Art of Murder" (1934) for a democratization of detective fiction was being met in the 1980s in various other ways. Michael Collins, for example, had resurrected the tradition of the pulp heroes of the 1930s and 1940s of the defective detective, the hero with physical defects or malformations—a missing leg or hand, one-eye—and written about Dan Fortune, a hero with only one arm, who because of this deficiency was always being physically abused but was apparently always successful with women. Another defective detective in this line is provided by George C. Chesbro in the person of Mongo, a dwarf.

Mongo apparently represents another needed dimension of the hero. Mongo's real name is Dr. Robert Frederickson. He is a professor of criminology at a New York City university. He is also, as the blurb on one jacket cries, "a former circus headliner, a black-belt karate adept." As university professor he illustrates a growing hero/heroine development in detective fiction in the early 1980s— such fiction being written by so-called intellectuals and university professors. Ross Macdonald has a Ph.D. in English literature from the University of Michigan (with a dissertation on Samuel Taylor Coleridge). Helen Hull, author of *A Tapping on the Wall*, was a University of Chicago Ph.D., and her work concerned a university professor and his female assistant. Peter Lovesey is a former British academic. Amanda Cross is a Columbia University professor, and her detective heroine, Kate Fansler, searches out crimes on university campuses. Martha Grimes, one of the brightest of the new Classic detective authors, is a professor of English at Montgomery County Community College in Maryland. Robert Parker, author of the Spenser series, was until recently a professor of English at Northeastern State University. And Stuart Kaminsky, whose detective Toby Peters relives the crimes that were attendant to the stars of the great days of Hollywood, is a professor at Northwestern University.

Obviously the needs of the readers have led to the creation of university-placed detectives who satisfy many needs. Increasingly university people are cutting detectives out of the cloth they are familiar with, and placing their crimes on campuses and among university and college personnel. In so doing, perhaps they are demonstrating that the traditional town-gown schism has pretty much disappeared, as readers would like, or perhaps revealing, to the delight of the readers, that even academia is not safe from crime.

Nor is the religious establishment. G.K. Chesterton's popular Father Brown series, which began the type, was carried on in the 60s by Leonard Holton's similar but not so popular Father Bredder (as in *A Pact with Satan,* 1960), and by such writers as Harry Kemelman and William Kienzle, among others. Charles Merrill Smith's success series about Father Randollph, ex-football player and successful businessman, perhaps pleases the reading public by demonstrating that not even the holy places are immune to the crimes of the outside world, but the cleric can handle the situation.

In the last three decades, despite the gradual development of what someone has called the "Americanization of the South," or perhaps because of the pressures put upon some Southerners as they have evolved from the protective cloth of the myth of the old South, there has grown up a resurgence of another myth, that of the sexual lust of blacks for whites and whites for blacks, a subject pretty much taboo until recently. This feeling was fed in 1957 by publication of Kyle Onstott's novel *Mandingo.* Traditional in all ways except for the reintroduction of an inordinate amount of violence, this book unearthed the old bogie of the irresistible lust of white men for black women and vice versa. A national bestseller, it was made into a successful movie. Founding the so-called Mandingo or Falconhurst series, this approach to life in the antebellum South was developed through at least a dozen other novels by Onstott and others. Advertised as savage, shocking and tumultuous, all obviously were appealing to the old myth. But fear, and insecurity can dust off old heroes and make them viable again. Disguise it as one might, such an attitude toward the antebellum South thrives throughout the country in the moral majority philosophy of the 1980s, whose heroes represent the dark under belly of American life.

Another new manifestation of the heroic, with many faces, has evidenced itself in the form of the Romances. Romances are, of course, not new. Dating at least from the eighteenth century in England and America, in the Gothics of the Bronte sisters and Charles Brockden Brown, romances flowered in the seventies and eighties in the United States with a future that no one can predict. They came in numerous bindings and story lines, all portraying particular kinds of heroes and heroines. The Harlequins, popularized in the 1950s, spawned other series by other authors and publishers: Silhouette Books, Ecstasy, Second Chance at Love, Circle of Love, Regemcoes, Rendezvous, Desire, and so on. It is estimated that by September 1982 there would be sixty contemporary romance books published each month, with sales running into the millions, perhaps some 10 every second of every day of the week.

Each series in order to distinguish itself from other series has to have its own type of hero and heroine. In Silhouette's, a typical kind, the heroine is young, not beautiful, but fragile looking, independent, high-spirited. She is a vocational comer. The hero is ruthless, domineering and arrogant. He is 8-12 years older than the heroine, self-assured, masterful and hot-tempered.

Success in the field demanded growth and development, and the changes in one type were over exploited and new grounds and needs generated others. In Silhouette, for example, the plot guidelines state that the heroine is between 26-40, and one who tries to juggle the demands of woman who favors the ERA and the more conventional woman; she is a mature young woman who has already had a serious love relationship. She should be attractive, appealing and spirited yet vulnerable. She should have either a profession or a great interest (sports, the arts, etc.). She should not be a typing-pool secretary. If she does not work she must have a serious interest that shows her to be a well-rounded person. The *Second Chance at Love* heroine rarely crumbles in a confrontation, blushes, cries or runs away.

The *Second Chance at Love* hero is virile, masterful and attractive.... tender and sensitive.... while he need not be rich, he must be successful.... he need not be "brooding," the "strong, silent type," or any of the other stereotypes found in traditional romances. He may be open, honest and amusing. But regardless of the maturity and success of the hero, and the realistic approach to life of the hero, the readers of the various kinds of romances insist on the woman finally accepting the traditional role of women. The women do this gladly, as a natural thing.

Who are the readers who demand this apparent "liberation" of women and yet the final foldback into the traditional role? If market research is to be trusted, the readers are generally rather traditional-minded women who find life somewhat boring and who therefore want to escape into the make-believe. These are middle-class matrons.

But there is also another kind of woman—often underpriviliged poor, blacks and Chicanos, who, especially the Chicanos, learn to read or to improve their reading skills on these books, and who use them not so much in the conventional escape pattern as in the form of surrogate psychologists. There is considerable proof to back up the assertion that these books serve as a kind of peace-maker in the troubled world these underpriviliged people inhabit: after a hard day, filled with anxiety and troubles, the book makes everything right or bearable. By the early 80s the demands for such books, for all their various purposes, was almost unfillable.

Perhaps one of the most startling new faces in the literary

heroes of the early 1980s was that worn by western literature, in which a new mythology and hero and heroine are emerging. The change is almost nation-shaking.

The mythology of the west is at least as old as America. From the first year when the earliest settlers saw the sun sinking over the horizon, wanderlust and wondering about what lay beyond the horizon drove the settlers to move toward the setting sun. The freedom, the pressure-valve, the magic of the West created a mythology and peopled it with attendant heroes and heroines who stood apart from the rest of the nation's people, ten feet tall, mysterious, powerful and unselfish.

The myth took its written expression from the beginning and animated the works of Eastern transcendentalists like Thoreau, Emerson, Melville and others. As people began to move to the West the myth was furthered by such writers as Teddy Roosevelt, Owen Wister, Zane Grey and a legion of others. Always the West was a magic land, where men stood straighter and taller. It was a land where men were *men*. Unrealistic as the picture of men that emerged was, that of women was even more peculiar. The men generally sat tall in the saddle, were naive, gun-prone and sometimes not gentlemen; but the women were always ladies—schoolmarms, straight-laced, "superior" creatures; there were, of course, whores, but the respectable women were super respectable. The heroic woman has saved the West from its inferior creatures throughout literature. Even the realistic best-selling Western writer Louis L'Amour gave only a modified version of the stereotypes.

In the 1980s, however, a major overhaul of the myth, the stereotype, was intruded into the Garden of Eden. Apparently spurred by the realism of various other kinds of popular writing, perhaps by the growing realism of the so-called romances and the popularity of soft-core pornography in general, the authors of the western novels began what they called "Adult Westerns," with results that shattered the stereotype. In these new novels the women of the West moved out of the whore houses and the school buildings and into the little white cottages along main street. There they were allowed the freedom of natural life in the West, with the normal desires of women, and the freedom to ask for and demand satisfaction in money and sex. The new trend developed along two or more lines differing somewhat in approach and markedly in degree.

One line of development perhaps can be described simply as greater freedom of sexual statement among the women and the men.

Luck of the Draw, by Zeke Masters (Pocket West, 1980) is a good example. Here we are not dealing with a whore. Linda Dorrance, one of the women who seduce Faro Blake, the hero, is from Philadelphia and "just served [her] time in Finishing School." As the author graphically describes, her clothes reveal all her sexual attractions, and she is more than willing to take them off at the hint of an invitation. Another of the women is a lady jailer with unquenchable sexual appetite. And so on.

Another line of development can be illustrated in a somewhat more risque type, Brick Killerman's *Hell's Half Acre* (Tower, 1981), in which the heroine is likewise far from a whore. She is a pioneer type who rides the wagons with the men, fights alongside them, and acts sexually free and easy. Chance, the hero, is the typical bad-man hero, and, according to the blurb on the jacket is "quick on the draw, fast with his fists, and hell on women."

The cover art of both these volumes is significant. On both the women are pictured with their breasts almost completely exposed. On *Hell's Half Acre's,* the girl is sitting with legs spread and mouth open with eyes filled with desire. The hero is standing above her with his legs spread, gun at his hip, obviously symbolizing the macho male. All women in the books are more than ready to drop their blouses and raise their skirts. But the parallel between these women and those of the Romances although obvious is not altogether complete. The women of the Romances are much nicer, though not necessarily any more chaste, and determined to fill their role as women. The roles of the "adult Western" women is not quite so clearly outlined. Though, as one blurb reads, "willing to use their hot bodies," these women are no longer stereotypical, except in their earthiness. They are more nearly from Erskine Caldwell's *God's Little Acre* and *Tobacco Road* than the Romance, and inasmuch as Caldwell's treatment of the Southern woman introduced a new kind of realism, the women of these new adult westerns seem to be opening up new vistas.

But what they demonstrate is a new set of heroes and heroines, especially the latter. Readers of Westerns (not to mention readers of sexual explicity, even soft-core pornography and violence books) are demanding, and responding to, a new set of models and their wishes are clearly being fed. By the winter of 1982-83 there were at least sixty titles a month being published in these new Westerns.

Of all the new heroic faces introduced to America by 1983, perhaps the most significant was that in the 1982 movie *E.T.*. Directed by Steven Spielberg, the popularity of the movie was astounding. Floating to a large extent on the popularity of the director, *E.T.* got off to a running start, and on the strength of its merit, during its first few weeks it made more money at the box office than any other movie in history. And the popularity continued. By December of 1982 it had grossed more than $300 million, more than any other movie. Though touted as a major cinematic aesthetic achievement, the movie was rather badly edited and somewhat jerkily directed. But with or without flaws, its attraction to the general public was unparalleled, especially to kids. Children, from the mid-teens down, saw the movie 6 to 8 times. It was not unusual to see a movie house filled with hundreds of people, 90% of them kids, all noisy and having a splendid time, identifying with the star of the movie one hundred percent.

What was this marvelous movie and what was it telling the audience and what was it revealing about American society?

E.T. is a tale of the Christ child, coming to earth, being loved by children and hassled by adults, and then ascending back to the sky from whence it came.

Into a crowded California countryside comes a flying saucer from another planet. It lands on a mountain top, amidst a cathedral of giant trees. Attracted by the eerie lights, a massive array of adults, with screeching cars and blinking lights and flashlights, rushes to protect themselves and society from any foreign invaders. Forced to leave hurriedly, the flying saucer gets away leaving one of its children on the ground. The child manages somehow (method not revealed) to get to a toolshed of a typical family, a group of kids, and a mother whose husband has just abandoned her. There the extra-terrestrial kid (E.T.) is discovered in the family's "manger" (the toolshed) by the youngest of the kids. He is brought into the house, and secreted by the kids in their room. When he gets out and goes to the kitchen and plays around with the refrigerator, the mother, although she looks almost directly at him, cannot see E.T. The kids love him, teach him to cope with U.S. life (he is remarkably precocious). He learns to talk, he has magical powers that can cure wounds, and as events show can in fact resurrect himself. Kids understand him best, and he loves kids most. Seeing a comic strip Buck Rogers, E.T. begins to voice the movie's leitmotif, "Home." He wants to go home.

He rigs up his own form of wireless communication in order to get word through to the flying saucer to get it to return to save him. Taken back to the mountain-top cathedral of trees one night E.T. sends his message. Then because the saucer does not return for him,

E.T. "dies" of exposure, spreadeagled alongside a stream of running water. At first abandoned by the kids he is found "dead" and is placed in a coffin. As the kids and the adults work on this obvious corpse, he is revived, and the revival is declared "a miracle" by one of the adults. Revived, E.T. is again taken back to the mountain top cathedral, where the flying saucer returns to pick him up. At this point there occurs a poignant scene in which the Earthkid tries to get E.T. not to leave and go "home," and E.T. would like to take the Earthkid to his planet but realizes that everybody needs and deserves a "Home." So as the movie ends E.T. is taken back on the saucer and goes back to his home. The Earthkid remains here.

In directing this movie Spielberg said that he was unleashing all his childhood fantasies. *E.T.* is a combination of Huck Finn and Tom Sawyer, *Mary Poppins*, *Wizard of Oz*, and old-time witchcraft (which is very popular in 1982 especially in the various best-selling occult works of Stephen King). This movie is a free ranging fantasy.

But it is more. It is a very significant statement about present-day concepts of and need for heroes. There is no doubt that it is another version of the Christ child savior. It demonstrates a clear-cut desire to return to the world of Huck Finn. But it probably more mythologically reveals a deep child-centered hero that we might not want to admit. It is saying that "Except ye become as little children, ye cannot enter the Kingdom of Heaven." And apparently we feel sufficiently vulnerable to want to enter. Our woes are stacked on a pile of frightening realities such as technology shock, topped by unemployment, covered by financial anxiety, flooded over with the syrup of old-time religion. It is a strangely old-fashioned concept.

America's needs however were apparently not quite the same, or not fraught with the same emotion, as the British's.*E.T.* opened in London in December 1982 to SRO audiences, but with a different reaction. In America the adults and kids had been happy, laughing, talking, wanting to cuddle E.T. In England, however, the audience's reaction was tears. Everybody was bathed in tears, even Prince Charles and his Princess. The same mythology plays to different reactions with different peoples.

Of all heroes of 1982 undoubtedly E.T. was the most powerful in America. Spin-offs came in every conceivable form—dolls, balloons, gloves, buttons, T-shirts, everything—saturating society, and thus revealing the depth to which the pictured hero affected society.

In the world today different societies still have various mythologies and heroes, all very strange to people of other groups. If it is true in the present world, where, despite the obvious vast differences among societies, there are fewer major differences than there have been in the history of mankind, try to imagine how vastly and unrecognizably different the mythologies and heroes have been throughout history.   The wonders that Marco Polo saw on his trip to Cathay pale into sameness when one considers the differences throughout history. Obviously heroes had many faces.

It is unrealistic then to imagine that the heroes and mythologies of old have not had to be stretched mightily and completely modernized, to make them serve the needs of the present, when technology has made the world more different now from anything of the past than at any other time in history. Heroes and heroines in the early 1980s have thousands of faces. With the obvious changes in the function and appearances of heroes and heroines, it seems clear that it is time to change and modernize definitions. Failure to do is being unrealistic and blind to the function of the form in society.

Notes

*Professor Roger Rollin and I independently arrived at virtually the same conclusions about the status and development of the modern hero.

[1]Daniel J. Boorstin, *The Image: A Guide to Pseudo-Events in America* (New York: Atheneum, 1977), pp. 57, 61.

Heroes Don't Need Zip Codes
Lenny Skutnik—Accidental Hero

Richard Shereikis

*L*enny Skutnik. It's a name you think you remember. Maybe a
utility infielder for the Cubs or Phillies back in the '50s.
Scrappy little guy. Got his uniform dirty a lot. Batted maybe
.230 lifetime in a short career. Or maybe a guy from your old high
school. Kind of an average student. Wrestled at one of the lighter
weight divisions and worked hard to keep in shape. Even when
people hear the name for the first time, they furrow their brows and
rummage in their memories. "Lenny Skutnik. Lenny Skutnik. I'm
sure I know the guy, but I just can't place him." It's that kind of
name.

But however unromantic the name may sound, Martin Leonard
Skutnik III is an American hero. He's been toasted by governors,
lionized by legislators and proclaimed a savior by our President.
Millions have seen him on television, short and sturdy with dark
brown hair that is cut most unromantically. For a hero, he's quiet
and modest and really very shy, which makes his appearances
before large and distinguished groups a bit of a trial for him. "In
school," he remembers, "I'd go up to do an oral report and hide
behind the paper and just start reading it without any punctuation.
And the teacher would tell me to sit down because I was making a
fool of myself." But recently he's talked to huge audiences that have
included politicians and other public figures. "Sometimes I'll say to
myself afterwards, 'How am I doing this? I just talked to 800 people.
How am I doing this?' " But the audiences, big and important, hang
on his few and simple words, and Lenny has grown easier in the
mantle of fame which has been thrust upon him willy-nilly.

If the name sounds familiar, it's because, like one of those subliminal messages that hidden persuaders can put into movies, Lenny blipped his way into the national consciousness for one brief shining moment on a dismal day in January 1982. On Wednesday, January 13, Lenny was the one who leaped into the freezing Potomac River to save a sinking victim of the crash of Air Florida Flight 90. The 737 had gone down soon after take-off at 4:00 p.m. from Washington's National Airport, ripping into the 14th Street bridge and crashing into the Potomac. Seventy-four passengers and four people on the bridge were killed in the disaster, and Priscilla Tirado, 23, would have been among them had it not been for Lenny's quick and decisive act.

Along with other commuters who were snarled in the traffic caused by the crash and the swirling snowstorm that hit Washington that day, Lenny and the others in his carpool had gone down to the shore to see what the problem was. Lenny and the others had watched as a U.S. Park Police helicopter had first lowered a ring to Priscilla and another man who were somehow, miraculously, afloat on the ice. They had watched as Priscilla had let go soon after the lift, her frozen hands unable to hold on. She had fallen back to the ice while the helicopter had dropped the man safely ashore. The copter tried again, and again Priscilla had grabbed, but this time, too, she had slipped off, now splashing into the freezing water about 20 feet from shore.

Lenny didn't think about what he ought to do, about the cold or about his lack of lifesaving skills. He kicked off his boots, shed his jacket, and dived in, swimming surely as he'd learned to do in his youth in Upper Michigan, where his father, an army man, had been stationed for a while. "I just did what I had to do," Lenny says quietly, as is his way. "I got out behind her and then I kinda pushed and stroked, pushed and stroked, until we got to shore. Her eyes were rolling back in her head, and she looked real bad." When they got Priscilla to the hospital, her body temperature was 81 degrees, Lenny recalls. If he had hesitated even slightly, she might have perished with her husband, Jose, 23, and her two-month-old son Jason, both of whom were lost in the crash.

It was a noble and courageous act. Lenny had risked his life to save a life. He had responded like a hero. A hero, as opposed to the mere celebrity, as outlined by Daniel Boorstin, is "a human figure— real or imaginary or both—who has shown greatness in some achievement. He is a man or woman of great deeds.[11]

But Lenny's deed alone, as selfless as it was, would not have been enough to change his life as it has been changed since that awful winter afternoon. There was another force involved, and that was what pushed Lenny so vigorously into the spotlight of celebrity he endured in the months following his heroic act. There was a television camera on the shore that day, and Lenny's deed was beamed across the country. That made all the difference. "The hero created himself," says Boorstin. "The celebrity is created by the media" (p. 61).

As Lenny himself says, these kinds of things are not rare. "You hear of firemen who go into burning buildings and come out with a kid under each arm. It happens daily. It's just that the cameras aren't there all the time. It was just that that day, that place, everything was so dramatic and unexpected, it was a big deal."

But that day, because it was in the nation's capital and the cameras were there, Lenny Skutnik, 28, a $14,000-a-year service assistant at the Congressional Budget Office, a family man and a former painter and super market porter and Burger Chef cook and worker in a meat packing plant and furniture factory, became a national figure. Because the cameras were there, Lenny Skutnik the hero, also became Lenny Skutnik the celebrity—a "person who is known for his well-knownness," as Boorstin expresses it. On that bleak and tragic day, Lenny had seized the moment, given the country something to cheer about, something to admire; but because the cameras were there, he was also threatened by the danger of celebrity—what Boorstin calls "the congested traffic of pseudo-events" (p. 54).

He got nearly 1600 pieces of mail in the first few weeks, some of it addressed to "Lenny Skutnik, Hero of the Potomac." Heroes don't need zip codes. The letters came from everywhere, according to Skutnik, mostly "short, real personal notes, telling how it made them feel. How they were watching TV and saw the girl and started screaming, 'Somebody save that girl!' They came from young, old, elementary school kids, classrooms, from all walks of life. Anybody and everybody."

Other, more public tributes came quickly over those same weeks. The state of Mississippi, where Lenny was born, celebrated "Lenny Skutnik Day" on February 10, and Lenny was flown there in the governor's private plane. Columbia, Mississippi, the home town of Lenny's mother, had used February 9 to celebrate another "Lenny Skutnik Day." He was honored by the Virginia legislature and had lunch with Governor Charles Robb.

The walls of his living room in Lorton, Virginia, are lined with over 20 handsome plaques and framed testimonials and citations.

There's one from the Japan Volunteer Firemen's Association, signed by Ryoichi Sasakawa. There's one from the 110,000 members of the International Airline Passengers Association, and others from the Polish American Police Associations of Philadelphia and New York, as well as one from the Chicago chapter, in which Skutnik's cousin is an officer. There's a Liberty Bell replica from Mayor William Green of Philadelphia, and from Senator John W. Warner of Virginia an American flag that had flown over the Capitol. American Legion Post 162 and Auxiliary Unit 162 of Lorton gave its 1982 Citizenship Award to Lenny, "Whose heroizm (sic) will long remain as a guideline to those who follow." There are awards from the Rotary Club of the District of Columbia and the Arlington, Virginia, Chamber of Commerce, and a framed Webelos Activity Badge for efforts as an aquanaut, from Cub Scout Pack 1900 of Lorton, one of whose members is Skutnik's 8-year-old stepson, Mitchell.

He's had other honors and gifts, too. An anonymous check for $7000 came from somewhere in Virginia, telling Lenny to pay his rent or buy a car or whatever he wanted with the money. A Washington, D.C. auto dealer offered him the use of a car for a year. He has taken trips to Mississippi, Chicago, Ohio, Philadelphia to receive honors, and turned down trips to Hawaii, Germany and Canada for reasons that tell us much about the values of the man. He was scheduled to throw out the first ball at the home opener of the Chicago White Sox, and he has been featured on "Real People." The recreation building in the housing complex where he lives in Lorton has been officially named "The Lenny Skutnik Center." Through the works of syndicated columnists, stories and columns about him have appeared in hundreds of American newspapers, in every cranny of the land.

But most prominent and suggestive in his collection of awards and tributes is a picture that hangs in the middle of the living room wall above his television set. It's a large framed color photograph of Lenny and his wife Linda, standing with Nancy Reagan during the President's State of the Union message. During the speech on national television, the President had paid special tribute to Lenny, who had stood to acknowledge the generous applause which the distinguished audience had given him. The picture in the living room captures that moment, and it is inscribed, "To Lenny and Linda Skutnik—With Great Appreciation and Warm Regards. Nancy and Ronald Reagan." For the second time in a month, Lenny Skutnik was pressed into the national consciousness, and he began to understand more about the business of being a celebrity, which had, he learned, little to do with his legitimate heroism.

"What I think I'm getting now is publicity on top of publicity— like that State of the Union thing," he says. "That made 'em forget. It put what I actually did on a lower level and put that [the appearance with Nancy Reagan] on top. A few people said to me afterward, 'Hey, aren't you the guy who was on the State of the Union?' That kind of thing. Not, 'Hey, aren't you the guy who jumped in the river and saved that lady?' " After that night, Lenny moved toward becoming one of those people "known for their well-knownness." And he may be a harbinger of that future that Andy Warhol forecast, when "everyone will be famous for 15 minutes."

That kind of fleeting fame, however, may be a blessing, given what happens today from overexposure to the spotlight of celebrity. Lenny Skutnik will be lucky, because he'll fade before he's tarnished by the very cameras and attention that put him center stage to begin with. His act was decisive and unambiguous. It cannot be second-guessed. No amount of revisionism or investigative reporting can diminish what Lenny did for Priscilla Tirado in the Potomac on that miserable January day. He's become perhaps the only kind of hero we will know from now on—the quick-fix kind that doesn't tax our attention spans but does satisfy our needs to admire something, especially when our lives seem stifled by forces we cannot control or even understand.

As a nation, we've grown ever more impatient with complexities and nuances and ever more insistent on instant gratifications. We prefer the clear and obvious stories of popular movies and television to the subtleties and ambiguities of serious literature and other art forms. Impatient with the leisurely pace and subtle strategies of baseball, we have made American football, with its quick strikes and violent finality, our national sport. Too restless for the subtle ebbs and flows of outdoor soccer, we've invented our own peculiar indoor game, with a faster pace and more frequent scores, analogous to the movie version of a Dickens novel: similar to the original in its larger outlines, but sparse and less rich in its details and flourishes. While symphony orchestras languish from lack of patrons, we buy millions of copies of "Hooked on Classics," in which 30-second segments of classical melodies are strung together to a disco beat. A quick fix for the ear. Our children are mesmerized by Pac Man, which eliminates subtlety or ambiguity, even in their play. (Think, as contrast, of the endless negotiations and debates and compromises that were essential to the sandlot baseball games that have all but disappeared from our national experience. And think of Pac Man foreign policy, in which quick, ferocious actions will take the place of delicate discussions and compromises.)

So Lenny Skutnik may well be all we can handle in the way of heroes today. He flashed across our consciousness, giving us a little lift, at least, at a time when it felt like nobody could do even a little about anything. It wasn't his fault that celebrity was also thrust at him, and he has acted nobly and wisely in resisting it. Most people who get in the news eventually get hurt by the very attention their celebrity brings. George Brett has never been the same in the public eye since we learned about his hemorrhoids. Steve Garvey, who would have been cultivated as an All-American man by yesterday's journalists, is victimized by voyeuristic peeks at his divorce. And look at what happened to Marva Collins, the Chicago educator whose image as a miracle-worker has been diminished by the very media forces which built it in the first place.

So even if the Bretts and Garveys and Collinses can't hold up, we'll still need something to admire, and maybe what we need is a succession of Lenny Skutniks, who can give us a sense that something can be done, even in the face of the worst disasters. However fleeting celebrity may be, we'll always need the heroic as an inspiration, that rare act of human courage that reminds us of our potential to do good by being decisive.

But with Lenny Skutnik we should also remind ourselves of another kind of heroism, which may be more precious and more rare than the courage he showed in the Potomac. It isn't really embodied in the act of saving another human life, as important as that act was. Lenny's real heroism lies in how he's handled the mantle of celebrity that was flung at him so unexpectedly. It lies, too, in his ability to realize the real significance of his act. It lies in his ability to maintain his sense of basic human decency even while those around him, starting with the journalists, are losing theirs.

A few days after the crash, for example, he was called by CBS News and asked if he would be interested in meeting Priscilla's father, Beirne Keefer, of Clearwater, Florida. The man had just lost his grandson and son-in-law, and Lenny had misgivings about the appropriateness of such a meeting. "I had a weird feeling about that," Lenny recalls. "I thought, 'Well this is too soon.' But I finally said, 'Well, if it's alright with him, OK'."

Ike Pappas, the CBS newsman, warned Lenny not to tell any other reporters about the meeting, or else he'd have a hundred of them invading his house, as they had on another occasion, a day or two earlier. Lenny didn't want any more disruptions of his life or his living room, so he agreed, and only the CBS camera crew waited outside his town house, preparing to capture the meeting between the hero and the father of the person he saved. Later, Lenny learned that Mr. Keefer had not expected any cameras there, that he was expecting only a simple, personal meeting arranged by Pappas, who was an acquaintance of his from their days in the service. In any case, Lenny knew it was all wrong as soon as he saw Mr. Keefer. "The minute I laid eyes on him, I could tell he was in no condition, that he shouldn't even be there," Lenny says.

And then, after they were all seated, and the cameras were rolling, Pappas asked the time-honored tasteless question: "Mr. Skutnik, how do you feel about meeting Priscilla's father?"

Lenny recalls his shock at the banality of the question. "Here's the man, his eyes all swelled up, he's all emotional. How can you answer something stupid like that? What can you say? And I told him [Pappas], I said, 'What kind of question is that?' I said that. And I just gave him short snappy answers to the rest of the questions he asked." That act alone should make Lenny a hero, a defender of some little nook of privacy against the ravages of the media.

There's something heroic and very telling, too, about Lenny's criteria for accepting the trips and vacations he's been offered over the months which followed his deed. "If there's family there, I'll go," he says quite simply. "If there isn't, I won't." Hence his acceptance of those trips to Mississippi, to Chicago, and Philadelphia, and his rejection of the ones to Hawaii, Germany and Canada, where he wouldn't feel comfortable because he wouldn't know anyone. The heroic restraint seems refreshing, in these times when "Where's mine?" has become all but a national motto.

Finally, there's his heroically sensible and modest perspective on the act he performed and the subsequent handling of it by the press and other media. "They embarrassed me," he says, "because what they were doing is they were bragging on me, which I never did and don't do. I just did what I had to do. And they're trying to make a macho man out of me." They tried to turn a hero into a mere celebrity, in other words, and Lenny has been Olympian in his resistance to "the congested traffic of pseudo-events."

He pauses, sorting through his thoughts and feelings about all the fuss and attention. "It's a big deal to me personally that I saved someone's life. That's important," he says softly. "Other than that, all this that's come about is mostly ..." and his voice trails off before he can say anything too negative or nasty, which would be against his nature. He's justly proud of his heroism, but he recognizes mere celebrity for the specious and fleeting thing it is.

Other words of Boorstin's come to mind. "In our world of big names, curiously, our true heroes tend to be anonymous. In this life of illusion and quasi-illusion, the person with solid virtues who can be admired for something more substantial than his well-knownness often proves to be the unsung hero ..." (p. 76).

So it is with Lenny Skutnik, now that the blinding light of his celebrity has dimmed, and we can see his virtues clear.

Note

[1]Daniel Boorstin, *The Image: or What Happened to the American Dream* (New York: Atheneum, 1974), p. 49. Subsequent references to this work will be made parenthetically in the body of the text.

Tarzan and Columbo, Heroic Mediators

Gary L. Harmon

*H*eroes function in many ways. Heroes may be "mirrors of the times."[1] They may be role models reinforcing widespread beliefs and attitudes for a time—black is beautiful, live within nature, small is better—or simplify complex issues. They may even provide a guilt-free release of our repressed aggressions, or put us in touch with our repressed selves. And they may even provide a means to criticize or put in perspective various patterns of behavior or attitudes.[2] At their best, they make strong contributions to the lives of the public that admires them—inspiring feelings, beautifying life, or magnifying the issues of life.

Our most popular hero myths, according to the anthropologist Claude Levi-Strauss, serve to resolve unwelcome contradictions, to avoid what a people finds arbitrary, incoherent or alien so that a meaningful harmonious whole be re-established.[3] By extension this is the purpose of all myths in which the archetypal figure of the hero, as quester, healer, deliverer, savior, scapegoat or whatever, is involved. Heroes thereby act as mediators in the complex issues that boggle the collective mind. This dimension of the hero as mediating agency may seem unusual because of the modern terminology used, but whatever the name we give it—mediation, task, quest—its function is always the same: to help man get rid of the uneasiness, sometimes the fear, that chaotic, unintelligible or even hostile circumstances produce in him. This heroic dimension is evident not only in the god-like characters of old, but also in our most popular figures, as in Tarzan and Columbo, two excellent and prototypical examples.

The stories of Tarzan and Columbo, repeated in various forms and circulated widely, form a complex language, like that used by Levi-Strauss' primitive peoples in their myths. Indeed, they rise to the level of the mythic—a "system of communication"[4] in the structuralist way of examining such a subject. If the stories of Tarzan, transmogrified into numerous forms, as well as the stories of Columbo, repeated over a five-year period and rising to the foremost popular detective program among thirty such television shows, provide a banquet of mythic heroes for millions upon millions of persons over a period of time, then it should be important to find a means of exposing the way in which they generate their special powers. We shall find that Tarzan and Columbo are, in fact, heroic mediators for their audiences.

Decoding Heroes a la Levi-Straus

Since Levi-Strauss or the work of Roland Barthes, among others, myths are no longer understood as the random constructions of a primitive and backward mentality. Instead, they contain an underlying order that helps the mythic analyst arrive at the fundamental structure of the unconscious—the collective—mind. Our hunt for patterns should furnish us with a "logical" model the human uses to evade unwelcome contradictions—in the social context and in the individual psyche—which is a fundamental premise underlying Levi-Strauss' concept of the structural study of myth.[5] "Levi-Strauss' concern is ultimately with the extent to which the structures of myths prove actually formative as well as reflective of men's minds: the degree to which they dissolve the distinction between nature and culture. And so his aim, he says, is not to show men think in myths, but 'how myths think in men, unbeknown to them'."[6]

This is no mean goal. To show how the mythic language of the Tarzan and Columbo stories "think in men" is within our grasp using the structuralist approach to analysis. A simple example may illustrate how the identification of the mediating function works with a popular joke—the traveling salesman joke, in which the farmer is always naive and generous and the farmer's daughter is always beautiful and willing to fulfill the desires of the traveling salesman. These jokes serve their tellers and listeners by helping them to evade the unwelcome contradiction between the wish and need for free and uncomplicated sex and the denial of such freedom by harsh sexual taboos in the broad society. The jokes—call them "myth bundles" here—function to mediate such contradictions, to make them appear less oppressive than they really are. We in society make up our reality as we go along, to resolve what are in fact unresolvable "oppositions," and so make our experiences adequate to our theoretical presuppositions. As Levi-Straus puts it, "mythical thought always progresses from the awareness of oppositions toward their resolution."[7]

We are, as Susan Sontag observes, in the company of the anthropologist as hero.[8] Levi-Strauss wants to do no less than to reveal the logic of thought systems which guide us all through the chaos of social turbulence. He wishes to help us find how we cope with unpleasant contradictions in our lives and how we are guided by orderly value systems, whether these are so-called primitive systems or civilized, scientific ones. His analysis of certain Pueblo Indian myths, for instance, shows that the central problem that the myth cluster (several forms of the same myth) seeks to resolve is the opposition between life and death—unpleasant contradiction. He finds a three-fold category distinction: agriculture, hunting and war. Agriculture is a means to life for man but entails the death of animals. Agriculture is thus a mediating middle category that helps the Pueblo Indians reconcile unpleasant contradictions in their social system[9]—so they survive as a healthy, thriving people, united in this "mental construct."

We can now explain more completely the premises on which we are depending. They will cause difficulty if one thinks about myth in a conceptual frame provided by Sir James George Frazer, Ernest Cassirer or Carl Jung who regard myth as a set of symbols pieced together into a non-rational story, much as in a fantasy or a dream. For Levi-Strauss, on the contrary, one must accept a thicket of important premises about mankind and about mythic language:

> *First, the human mind is programmed* by the structure of language as well as by the structure of cultural phenomena; in other words, myth and ritual are social activities that contain value constructs which program the individual mind and hence his behavior.

*   *   *

> *Second, form is more important than content*; indeed, form *is* the content that the structuralist seeks. (*Levi-Strauss* is not so concerned with the story a myth tells as with the way the

symbols used in different versions of the same myth reveal the
same "contrastive relationships" and the same resolution of the
main oppositions.)

*   *   *

*Third, myth furnishes a "logical"—that is, structured—model
by which the human mind can evade unwelcome contradictions.*

*   *   *

*Fourth, there is no essential difference between the primitive
and the civilized minds.* They are the same mind, but the myths
and rites they use to order the chaos of the natural and the social
worlds may be different. Western civilization is thus *not*
privileged and unique among human kind; it is *not* "superior" to
primitive culture. It works the same way; only the structure of its
mythic language and its activities betray value differences.
Primitive myth and modern art have the same mediating
functions.

*   *   *

Finally, humanistic premises and history are *not* useful means
of inquiring into this "search for unsuspected harmonies" of the
human mind.

We are after a mind system, a "logic," a mythically represented
way of reconciling or justifying contradictions in reality.[10] To
accomplish this, Levi-Strauss proceeds to "decode" a myth by first
assembling variant forms in which it has been recorded, regardless
of date and source. Then, one must search for the fundamental
essence, the logical structure that persists throughout all the forms
of the myth. Taken to its ultimate, this means that investigating
stories and their structures is similar to atom smashing. The
structure of the myth—the atom—is split and then reconstructed
according to a system of logic which is supposedly inherent in the
myth, but *not accessible to its narrative content.* The narrative
content, after all, is but a container, and we would be misled as to the
true mental construct of a myth form if we spent time with the
narrative alone. Once a pattern is perceived, Levi-Strauss
maintains that a really thorough application of the method would
require the use of punched cards and the services of an electronic
computer. Such intellectual complication may arouse suspicion

from those who think myths are meaningful in a rather straightforward way. In any case, the variant forms of the Tarzan or Columbo myths are so familiar and formulaic that they need not be detailed here.

We are looking for a number of expressed or unexpressed principles of opposition constructed on a "multiplicity of axes"—for example, honey/tobacco, male/female, raw/cooked, original/conventional, paradise/real world, dry/wet, moving (living) creatures/static creatures, life/death, rational/irrational, order/chaos. Once found, these dialectically expressed constructs must relate to the social context of the myth if we have identified them properly. Binary oppositions populate Levi-Strauss' findings—they *are* the *sine qua non* of structuralist analysis—and they are recreated in the popular series of Tarzan novels and Columbo shows.

Where does Levi-Strauss obtain his idea of "binary oppositions"? Certainly they are fundamental to our analysis. Drawing from Ferdinand de Saussure's linguistic theory, Levi-Strauss applies to the analysis of culture the same method the French linguist applies to the analysis of language. The central question he raises is "whether the different aspects of social life (including even art and religion) cannot be studied by the methods of, and with the help of concepts similar to those employed in linguistics, but also whether they do not constitute phenomena whose inmost nature is the same as that of language."[11] In other words, language is a form of "encoding" by means of which nature and culture come to terms, and culture in all its aspects, including myth, is a gigantic act of "encoding" on the model of language— that is, it *is* itself a language. This "encoding" is based not on individual items of the language or of the culture but on the relations between them, and its "decoding" should reveal a full pattern of systematized relationships which the individual items only point at. These relationships are "recognized" because they are contrastive[12] and it is precisely this opposition between them that renders them meaningful, as is evident in the following Tarzan and Columbo explanations.

Tarzan Decoded
1983 marks Tarzan's seventy-first anniversary, and his stories are as popular as ever. Perhaps *Tarzan of the Apes*, the first novel, is a world novel, spreading the Tarzan myth around the globe with Edgar Rice Burroughs' twenty-three other Tarzan novels and with

other forms of literature. Tarzan has been featured in thirty-eight American films, in animated cartoon films for Saturday morning children's shows, in the television series with Ron Ely (1966) and the occasional late afternoon reruns, in comic books, in the 1953 Bob Lubben and Dick Van Buren comic strip series that is often reprinted around the world, in big little books, and in advertisements and figurines.

In the scholarly world, an article on Tarzan in contemporary Arabia identifies the legion of ways the Tarzan stories and heroic figure (most often a loin-clothed, knife-raised figure giving the victory yell) have penetrated Yemen culture.[13] Appealing to children there through gum wrapper pictures, filmstrips, comics, films and the like, the Tarzan hero may well be entering traditional Arabic culture as an unconscious means of shifting traditional attitudes toward an accommodation to modernization.

Anyone curious about the power of popular literature must wonder why the Tarzan of *Tarzan of the Apes* and the novels and films that repeat the original adventure story in various ways has echoed so endlessly for millions upon millions of persons—for perhaps as many as fifty million readers of that novel alone ... in English and fifty-eight other languages.[14] One scholar of popular culture history has observed that "Tarzan remains the greatest popular character creation of all time" and that, "except for Mickey Mouse, Tarzan is undoubtedly the best-known fictional character in the world."[15]

Burroughs most certainly derived his Tarzan from good mythic stock—from the Romulus and Remus legend, from Kipling's *The Jungle Book*, from H. Rider Haggard's romances using the lost race motif, and even from Thomas Love Peacock's *Melincourt* (1817) which, like the Tarzan books, tells of a wild man who, lost in the woods and suckled by a lioness, ends up in Parliament.[16] So powerful is the mythic appeal of the Tarzan hero that a scholar, Erling B. Holtsmark, has produced a book, *Tarzan and Tradition: Classical Myth in Popular literature* (1981),[17] explaining how the Tarzan novels, especially the first six books, constitute an artful and sophisticated modern epic. Certainly, Tarzan is a Myth of the Hero, a recurring narrative that provides a large, controlling image that expresses our collective fears and anxieties, hopes and dreams. To those who admire him, he inspires awe and gratitude about the mystery of man's existence in this life. He does this by resolving some difficult contradictions of our lives.

We may examine the narrative, the linear story which is the

container for the more important, repeated structure of the binary oppositions. Though the birth and growing up phase of the story is unique to *Tarzan of the Apes*, among all the Tarzan stories, the rest of the story is basically the pattern for adventure narratives in its depiction of Tarzan performing remarkable feats and achieving victory over death.

I. The Voyage Out and the Young Tarzan

Lord and Lady Greystoke sail to West Africa, but on the way are stranded on the coast because of a mutiny. Tarzan is born, loses his parents to death, and is adopted by Kala, who mothers him to youth. At ten, he returns to the cabin Greystoke built, finds books and his father's knife, and kills the ape Bolgani, using the knife.

II. Tarzan Grows Up.

Very much an "ape-man," Tarzan participates in the ape death dance of the Dum-Dum, but he visits the cabin often to learn to read and write. And he begins to wear the loin cloth. Kulonga, a black warrior, kills Kala; Tarzan kills Kulonga but cannot eat him. The villagers "adopt" Tarzan as a god. Tarzan kills Kerchak to become king of the apes and then creates his victory yell. He feels the growing gap between him and the apes.

III. Encounters with Civilized People

The Arrow, with Jane, her father, Clayton and others arrives. Tarzan saves Clayton from a lion, kills a lion that threatens Jane and Esmerelda, and saves Dr. Porter and Dr. Philander from a lion. He removes to rebury the treasure chest he has seen sailors bury. And he writes to Jane telling her he loves her.

IV. Remarkable Adventures and Triumphs

Tarzan saves Jane from rape by the ape Terkoz and kills him, taking Jane into the jungle. *The Arrow* leaves the Clayton party ashore, and a French cruiser rescues the survivors of *The Arrow*. Jane realizes she loves Tarzan. The rescue party for Jane is attacked by fifty black warriors, seizing Lieutenant D'Arnot. Tarzan rescues him and takes him into the jungle, nursing him back to health. D'Arnot teaches Tarzan French. The French cruiser leaves for home with the Clayton party (and Jane)—but without the treasure Tarzan has reburied. Tarzan learns civilized manners and more French from D'Arnot.

V. The Journey to Civilization

Tarzan and D'Arnot travel a month through the jungle to outposts of civilization. Tarzan becomes "Monsieur Tarzan." D'Arnot reads the Greystoke diary, finds the young Tarzan's fingerprints, and takes Tarzan's fingerprints to compare them. Tarzan travels to the United States, gives Dr. Porter (Jane's father) a check representing the value of the treasure, finds Jane who is about to be married to Robert Canler, rescues Jane from a

forest fire, and almost kills Canler. Jane stalls the wedding.
D'Arnot informs Tarzan he is Lord Greystoke. Tarzan
withholds this information from everyone, so as not to deprive
Clayton, Jane's presumed future husband and Tarzan's cousin,
of his possessions.

One may study this narrative to advantage for its similarity to other
adventure stories or hero myths. Still, a structuralist approach will
help us find a set of binary oppositions that never interfere with the
linear formula that frames the story. Even the racial and sexual
stereotyping which Burroughs uses, much in the character of the
day, does not distract us from getting to the underlying structure.
Throughout the story, Tarzan as hero is linked both to nature and to
our western civilization. That basic dialectic is the armature for the
many Tarzan stories, with Tarzan mediating between the opposing
elements.

The Nature/Civilization Opposition: These contradictory
elements are the primary ones, subsuming other polarities. Their
prominence in the story may explain why the Tarzan books and
films appeal to the young and to people in cultures moving from an
agrarian life to a modern one. Tarzan is a natural man, joining the
pantheon of other natural American heroes such as Davy Crockett,
Daniel Boone, Natty Bumppo, Kit Carson, Bill Williams,
Huckleberry Finn and Jeremiah Johnson. All these heroes mediate
between the civilization (comprising complication) they left behind
and the nature (simplicity) they cope with. Tarzan, however,
outdoes them all, with his genetically superior, upper class origins
from Lord and Lady Greystoke, and his birth, growth to manhood
and incredible accomplishments amid raw nature. Tarzan also joins
the classic minotaur myth that expresses one way of reconciling the
barbarity of one's animal nature and one's human (civilized)
identity. His successful bridging of the timeless confrontation
between the forces of nature and culture places him in a great
tradition, ancient and modern.

The Tarzan stories' nature/civilization polarity first arises in
the behavior of Lord Greystoke, who is the archetype of civilized
erudition, learning and control, with his equally civilized bride Lady
Greystoke. His Appolonian cool courage during the mutiny
emphasizes his self-control, order and stoic courage that epitomize
British civilization's ideals. He stands successfully against the
forces of Dionysian chaos, the dark side of nature represented by the
crew. In a clash between the captain and his crew, he mediates
between the rule of such ships and the impassioned and brute-like

force of the sailor. As such, he is a model of what Tarzan is to become in his mediation between the world of the unruly apes and natives and the forces of civilization. Tarzan's first kill depicts him as using his father's knife, a hand-me-down from civilization, to establish his supremacy over nature, represented by the ape, who is otherwise stronger than Tarzan. He is stronger than a normal civilized man but weaker than an ape, so the use of the knife (culture) and his strength (nature) helps him save his life. His donning of the loin cloth covers his natural nakedness with enough civilization to be acceptable in both worlds. Other examples occur throughout the Tarzan series of novels and films.

The Tarzan hero forms a harmonic coupling with the most primal tension between nature and culture that each human must somehow resolve within the self. Burroughs is aware of the archetypal connotations of his hero, as in this passage: "Tarzan of the apes, little primitive man, presented a picture filled, at once, with pathos and promise—an allegorical figure of the primordial groping through the black night of ignorance toward the light of learning."[18] That the Tarzan archetype seems corny to many should not bother us if we recall Carl Jung's observation (in *Memories, Dreams, and Reflections*) that the archetypes of our collective dreams *are* corny, exaggerated and often two-dimensional. Tarzan and his fellow characters, including the animals, help a society bridge contradictions at the base of both public and private lives.

The Heredity/Environment Opposition: This polarity echoes a century-long controversy reminding us that the Tarzan hero portrays a compressed archetypal history of human evolution. From the moment Lord and Lady Greystoke are cast ashore, they establish "civilization" in the form of their house, supposedly made impregnable to resist the invasion of the brutes of jungle nature. When both die, their baby, Tarzan, illustrates how a hero with the proper heredity can, in a proper environment, evolve into a likable and strong man. Gentle Kala, marvelous natural mother, nurtures Tarzan to strength and independence. His ape diet and exercise must help his size—bigger than an English lord, smaller than a jungle ape—another compensation (or mediation). His environment had taught him that one eats the "meat of the kill." Burroughs suggests, in the scene in which Tarzan has killed Kulonga, that his "hereditary instinct" prevented him from eating human flesh. Tarzan's gift to Jane of the diamond locket is also a successful mediation. Burroughs writes,

It [the giving] was the hall-mark of his aristocratic birth, the

natural outcropping of many generations of fine breeding, an
hereditary instinct of graciousness which a lifetime of uncouth
and savage training and environment could not eradicate.[19]

Tarzan's heroic mediation between jungle ways and civilized ways
is one more method of assuaging or collective anxieties, if not
puzzlements, about human evolution.

The Chaos/Order Opposition: White men in the Tarzan stories
come from civilization without an understanding of nature's ways.
Their ignorance introduces chaos into their lives in the midst of the
jungle. At one point, Professor Porter and Mr. Philander are lost in
the jungle, oblivious to their danger. They are speaking of some fine
points in history when they see a lion. They flee, thinking that it is a
lion that has escaped from the zoo and unrealistically decide they
must "proceed with more decorum." Finally, Mr.Philander "broke
into a mad orgy of speed," and "Professor Archimedes Q. Porter
fled" with "streaming coat tails and shiny silk hat." Tarzan
interrupts to save these misplaced and quixotic types to restore
order to this jungle scene.

The apes, with their Dum-Dum dance and their proclivity
toward acting out their instincts and passions, express the
libidinous, chaotic side of nature. The black cannibals represent the
downward path of evolution to disorder, in sharp contrast to the
Greystoke heritage of order, devotion to duty, controlled emotions
and sense of decency. Tarzan's rescue of Jane from a fate worse than
death, about to be perpetrated on her by an impassioned ape out of
control, is one more example of Tarzan's bringing law and order to
the chaotic situation of the jungle.

Once more, readers and viewers participate through Tarzan in a
collective resolution of our anxieties about being plunged into the pit
of life's victims and being rescued by one who represents our hopes
for the human race. Tarzan is a figure operating at the level of
primal needs—to live freely and to mate successfully, using the best
of society's rules to counter the lawless licence of jungle life. As
Tarzan ponders his attitudes toward Jane and compares them with
those of Terkoz who was about to rape her, Burroughs writes,

> True, it was the order of the jungle for the male to take his
> mate by force; but could Tarzan be guided by the laws of the
> beasts? Was not Tarzan a Man? But what did men do? He was
> puzzled; for he did not know.[20]

In Tarzan films, viewers are familiar with Tarzan and Jane's living
together without the benefit of marriage. (Not so in the books, for

they marry in the sequel to *Tarzan of the Apes*.) One might say that they avoid the "order" of a proper marriage, but they are saved from the chaos of sin by the mediating bond of love and mutual respect.

This sampling of value polarities that the Tarzan hero mediates between shows how Tarzan successfully resolves the contradictions of our collective primal concerns. This fact may well explain the immense, long-lasting appeal to the millions of us who find Tarzan's loin-clothed figure an appealing wish fulfillment for our own psychic needs. His main function as mediator is to resolve our own nature/culture contradiction, in which all other contradictions, as those named here, are subsumed.

Columbo, Myth Televised

Myth analysts need go no further than their living rooms to examine certain powerful, popular stories that appear weekly on their television sets. "Myth bundles," as Levi-Strauss has called repeated stories in variant versions, enter our consciousness with swift succession over TV. The television corporation functions in much the same way as the Bard of medieval Europe did with the minstrels and jongleurs, who had to learn five hundred or so tales by heart so they could reproduce them accurately among the homes and hearths of the countryside. While literary historians can be relatively certain of their conclusions about medieval culture, owing to the stability and slow spread of change within the myth bundles scattered by the workmen of the network—minstrels or jongleurs—the rapid changes in mind constructs offered to the American public also deserve attention. We must, as it were, strip the televised images bare on occasion to reveal the myth structure in the raw. That is what myth analysis is about.

After watching *Columbo* in numerous stories, it becomes clear that there is but one story. It reads:

I. The Opening Situation
   A. Setting, atmosphere, principal characters
   B. The crime, a homicide
II. Solving the Crime
   A. Accumulation of clues, especially from something "bothering" Columbo about the case
   B. Finding the hard evidence, trapping the criminal
III. The Solution and Finale
   A. The villain, arrested and taken away
   B. Columbo can go home to wife, but does not
   C. Final Image: Sense of "things are ok again"

This sequence, with its variations, contains oppositions which form the basic components of a code that warns against violations of taboos or acts as positive moral instructions. These paired oppositions, subsumed in the nature/culture contradiction, should be constant elements in a metasystem of values. The linear structure gives way to a set of binary opposites. These oppositions do not interfere with the linear formula that frames the story.

It is important to see that Columbo's style as a hero is inextricably linked to our particular period of history: One that is urban, complex, capitalistic, consumer-oriented, industrial, machine-supported—and one that espouses individuality, independence, logical reasoning, originality, staying within the law, status-achieving and money-making as desirable ideals. Does *Columbo* sustain these ideals? The events of the linear structure do seem to promote these ideals, in general, but the binary oppositions within the narrative do not.

The following discussion reveals five sets of binary oppositions in the Columbo stories. The "culture" element is represented, successively, by conspicuous consumption, order and cleanliness, technology, rationalism and logic, and law and order. These elements are explicit in the *Columbo* imagery, while the "nature" element is represented by implicit possibilities. They are implicit because of their contextual association in American culture with the named "culture" elements. These "nature" elements include, respectively, impoverishment, chaos and "mess," life without technology, intuition and "feeling," and society as "jungle." Columbo serves to mediate between these contradictions in our own culture.

The Conspicuous Consumption/Impoverishment Opposition: The villain's usual lair is a posh suburban home with all the trappings of wealth and privilege. Material wealth is exhibited in vast expanses of well-appointed interior design, with space and privacy, and in the luxury cars—all representing the spoils of a capitalistic system for the successful competitor. Counterposed against this imagery, which expresses American ideals, is Columbo the plainsclothes detective, whose self-denying, working-class values are represented in his soiled raincoat, his general looks, his language and his unpolished aging chariot, a much-used car. He appears to be living within his $11,000 salary, and he even contrasts with the other, neater police who assist him. He succeeds as a healthy social specimen despite the fact that he is not a conspicuous consumer. Further, he has not skidded into poverty or loss of dignity, though his salary indicates that he is on the borderline. He mediates, in other words, between our fondest dreams, which we see as tainted capitalistic success, and our unconsciously held worst fears, such as wretchedness, poverty, misery, loss of dignity.

The Order and Cleanliness/Chaos and "Mess" Opposition: The villain is characterized as a tidy, orderly, neat person. One retired captain, played by the white-haired, refined Eddy Albert, had a large cruiser whose motors needed breaking in by such a precise method that the captain had to do it himself. Even the crimes are characterized as exquisite taste and tidiness. Murders are not bloody messes but efficient, well-timed rituals of order and cleanliness that the villain has mastered. The villains stand straight, walk rhythmically and appear neatly dressed. In other crime series, it is impossible to distinguish the villain and the sleuth on the basis of consumption or order and cleanliness oppositions; Mannix, Cannon, Barnaby Jones, Ironsides, Banachek—all these seem to be part of the same system, only one is evil and one is good. Columbo, by contrast, is anything but neat. He even walks bent over a bit, tilts when he stands, with rumpled raincoat and rumpled hair. His conversation proceeds in jerks, he is a poor driver of his messy car, and he can never seem to organize life so as to join his wife at home. Out of his seemingly chaotic, "messy" lifestyle, there emerges the idea that he has enough order, enough neatness to do the job without submerging his personality to the demands of a conventional status-seeking society. And yet he has managed to avoid the chaos which middle America seems to fear the most.

The Technology/Life Without Technology Opposition: Perhaps this contradiction is the most unwelcome one for contemporary Americans. Imagine a life without the benefits of technology and we are plunged into the wildest nightmares. Columbo's villains are proved masters of the technology; they have lived by the system, and they have been rewarded by it. Each one in turn is a master of some technology—photography, telephones, chemicals in cosmetics, computers or the like. If the villain stands to lose his rewards—as in the case of the business executive whose partner was trying to deal him out of their empire or in the case of a lady who wished to take over a cosmetics firm without a surviving person who could testify that she had developed a poisonous facial cosmetic—he or she uses the technology in unusually brilliant ways to stay at the top and to vanquish the opposition. But Columbo comes along, and as a loner without the technological aids of car radios, computers, walkie talkies, laser beams, or what not, he finds a flaw in the criminal's management of the technology and pins him with the crime. He uses just enough of the technology to help him on occasion, but the series does not seem to assure one's faith in technology as the basis for the dream life represented by the villain. Columbo represents an individual adaptation of the technology to particular circumstances when using it as a necessity.

The Rationalism and Logic/Intuition and "Feeling" Opposition: Columbo's villains are always highly rational; they have, after all, achieved their present status of wealth and power through an extremely intelligent use of logical reasoning. Columbo, on the other hand, does not necessarily proceed by reason alone; intuition plays an important part. For instance, when Columbo is searching for clues and finds that a murder victim's car radio was turned to a classical music station at the time of his death, he *feels* that something is wrong. The victim hated classical music and loved only country music. Because he is typically bothered by some such small discrepancy that leads him to question the story of the actual criminal, he then invokes his more rational self to search for other clues that catch the criminal. Even his halting, jump-to-one-subject-and-then-to-another manner suggests a seemingly disorderly mental process. "Say, where were you at 3:00 o'clock yesterday?" "Yeah? Well, Say, where did you get those shoes. I always wanted a pair like that." "Oh, good. Thanks. I'll check that out." "By the way, I almost forgot. I found your calling card stuffed in a chair at the scene of the crime. How do you suppose it got there?" Again, without appearing to succumb to the totally "reasonable" and logical thinking processes that we identify with the criminal, he is not all just "feeling" either. There's enough rational method to his halting, jumbled style to lead him to depose a social kingpin whose existence depends almost solely on rationality, keeping cool and logical in the midst of managing great numbers of details. Columbo mediates intuition and reason to solve crimes.

The Law and Order/Society as "Jungle" Opposition: This key issue of our society is not omitted in the Columbo myth. Sometimes the villain *is* a lawyer; in all cases the criminals are people who know the law. On the surface they have led law-abiding lives. Without strict adherence to law, most of us are led to believe that society would be a jungle, chaotic and uncivilized. *Columbo* and some other detective series portray detectives who bend laws and rules and conventions in order to bring about stability, albeit temporary, in the society. These programs do not exactly support a strict constructionist interpretation of the nation's laws. Columbo sometimes resorts to bending rules, once even bugging a phone, to collect mainly circumstantial evidence to convince himself that the suspect is guilty. His evidence would not be admissible in court. While he is not totally "legal," in this sense, he is not lawless either, for his circumstantial evidence leads him to a key piece of information or enables him to trap the villain into exposing himself as the killer. Columbo and other sleuths often use "jungle" tactics to help find the legally proper evidence that will place the killer behind bars.

As a hero, he does not give credence to traditional notions of success, individuality, consumption, logic, the system, the law, though he does reinforce our traditional virtues of work and duty. He does not support the success-seeking hero and its associated values that predominate in an oil-based, industrial society. He is perhaps an inadvertant attack on the excesses of capitalism and individualism, on success and conspicuous consumption, on rigid laws, on a mindless bowing to authority and order. He works within the police system, but just barely. He does his selfless, downbeat bit with health and pleasure in his work, for the good of society, helping those whose lives are pinched by the scheming capitalists of high-finance society. Just as Sherlock Holmes took cocaine and other crime fighters have their weaknesses (women, usually), Columbo's main fault is that he is a social clod and a slob, which turns out to be a virtue, for his opponents underestimate him because of his appearance. While he is sloppy in dress and boorish in manner, though never discourteous, he does not reject status symbols and manners so much as he is oblivious to them for himself. He steers a course between the "culture" represented by the lifestyle of the villains and the "natural," raw life possibilities we might face were our culture supports removed. Such mediation makes him our culture hero.

As a kind of analysis, structuralism may be very useful to apply to the popular arts and literature, for the heroes appearing in their many stories invite the methodology Levi-Strauss uses with myths. Tarzan and Columbo, as very popular heroes, may be typical of our popular culture, for they mediate the culture and nature contradiction in several important ways this essay has examined. Their mediating capacity links them with other heroes, ancient and modern. They become timeless, linking present with past and future. Tarzan's popularity may be with the world for some time, for he shares an epic stature with the classical hero. He resolves the timeless contradictions discussed here in a manner that a reader or viewer of the Tarzan stories never forgets. The Tarzan myth "thinks in men, unbeknown to them." Tarzan appeals to us in several ways—through the grandness of his acts against the background of an epic environment. Columbo, by contrast, *seems* unheroic. He is small, clumsy, unattractive, plain—and he is placed in an anti-heroic environment. His mediation is small: it cannot "set [the] lands in order"[21] permanently, as we expected the ancient mythic heroes to do. Perhaps because adults know our culture is a modern waste land, a Columbo can appeal to us quite powerfully. The waste land, after all, determines the characteristics of the hero, his tasks, and the extent of his mediation. That leaves Tarzan with the young, many of whom can still believe that the lands can be set "in order."

Notes

[1]Marshall Fishwick, *The Hero, American Style* (New York: David McKay, 1969), p. 2.

[2]For a fuller treatment of functions of popular culture, which includes myth, see Gary L. Harmon, "On the Nature and Functions of Popular Culture," *Studies in Popular Culture* 6 (1983), 1-12.

[3]Claude Levi-Strauss, *Structural Anthropology* (New York: Basic Books, 1963), p. 197.

[4]Roland Barthes, *Mythologies* (New York: Hill & Wang, 1972), p. 109.

[5]See the chapter, "The Structural Study of Myth" in Levi-Strauss.

[6]Terence Hawkes, *Structuralism and Semiotics* (London: Methuen, 1978), p. 41.

[7]Claude Levi-Strauss, p. 224.

[8]Susan Sontag, "The Anthropologist as Hero," *Against Interpretation* (New York: Farrar, Straus & Giroux,1966), pp. 69-81.

[9]Edmund Leach, "Levi-Strauss in the Garden of Eden: An Examination of Some Recent Developments in the Analysis of Myth," *Transactions of the New York Academy of Science*, Ser. II, 23: 4 (Feb., 1961), pp. 386-396.

[10]An early example of searching for such a logic in popular stories is in Bruce Lohof's "A Morphology of the Modern Fable," *Journal of Popular Culture* 8: 1 (Summer, 1974), pp. 15-27.

[11]Claude Levi-Strauss, p. 62.

[12]In language, as Saussure points out, only the phonemic opposition is the one that the speaker recognizes as meaningful; other differences—phonetic—go by "unrecognized" because they do not affect meaning. Levi-Strauss' method implies the application of the same principles of what he himself calls "the phonological revolution" to the whole cultural experience. The constituent units of cultural behavior—marriage, rites, cooking, totems, *myth*—are seen again in their contrastive relations, as binary oppositions similar to those of the phonemic structure of language.

[13]James R. Nesteby, "Tarzan of Arabia: American Popular Culture Permeates Yemen," *Journal of Popular Culture* 13: 1 (Summer, 1981), 39-45.

[14]Richard J. Hurley, "Tarzan of the Apes, Newest Folk Hero," in Edgar Rice Burroughs, *Tarzan of the Apes* (New York: Ballantine, 1963).

[15]Russel B. Nye, *The Unembarrassed Muse: The Popular Arts in America* (New York: Dial, 1970).

[16]James R. Nesteby, "The Tenuous Vine of *Tarzan of the Apes,*" *Journal of Popular Culture* 13:3 (Winter, 1981), 483-487.

[17]Erling B. Holtsmark, *Tarzan and Tradition: Classical Myth and Popular Literature* (Westport, CT: Greenwood Press, 1981).

[18]Edgar Rice Burroughs, *Tarzan of the Apes* (New York: Ballantine, 1963).

[19]Ibid., p. 168.

[20]Ibid., p. 163.

[21]T.S. Eliot, *The Waste Land.*

Quixote Rides Again: The Popularity of the Thriller

Peter Rickman

The kind of hero an age looks up to reflects its aspirations and values. Characteristic for our own time is the emergence of the thriller hero. It is, therefore, illuminating to consider his literary antecedents, contrast him to his "relative" the detective story hero and compare him to other contemporary manifestations of the hero.

It is possible to approach this exploration by social surveys and psychological probing. We might thus discover such interesting information as to how the popularity of the thriller differs between the old and the young, the rich and the poor, men and women and the more and less educated. We might also learn what people give as their reason for reading or watching thrillers. Few theoretical problems stand in the way of such inquiries, but they are so costly and time-taking that one may wonder if they can be justified by the probable results.

However the subject can be approached in another way, namely by analysing this particular form of literature itself and so focussing attention on its dominant themes and typical plots. Individual works cannot always be placed neatly into such pigeonholes. Very often the lines which I am going to draw between thriller and detective story are—like many other conventional demarcation lines—smudged. However, singling out different "ideal types" of fiction and analysing their dominant characteristics can help us to understand the untidy range of mixed forms between the relatively pure extremes. Such an analysis is

131

also, one may add, an essential preliminary to the kind of empirical inquiry I have mentioned, because it can help us to ask the right questions and make the most appropriate distinctions.

*   *   *

The most common types of thrillers are the spy story, the political thriller dealing with assassination plots, revolutions or the liberation of political prisoners, the tale of organised crime often with a master criminal plotting an assault on society, and, more occasionally, the narration of an individual crime, personal revenge or other adventures. The genre ranges from realistic accounts of international intrigue, the description of the sleazy world of espionage and the grim reality of police states, the cold war or dope traffic to cheerful fantasies often embroirdered with pseudo-technological magic. Particularly characteristic is the recent emergence of the spoof thriller in which the art form parodies itself with hilarious effects.

Thrillers are essentially stories of crime and violence (usually including killing) featuring the clash between "goodies" and "baddies." Because it shares these characteristics with the classical detective story which in England it is supplanting in public esteem, an analysis of the differences is instructive.

The classical detective story, in spite of having conflict and violence for its theme, presupposes and portrays an ordered, stable and meaningful world. Part of this orderliness is the fixed, pre-ordained role of the detective who is also the hero. He is a police officer, private detective or gifted amateur and the task of solving a crime—the theme, by definition, of the detective story—lands on his plate because of his status or reputation. This status assures him organised help; if he is a police officer he is supported by a whole complex system: sergeants follow him, experts respond to his bidding and police forces of other countries respond to his telephone calls. Private detectives—Lord Peter Wimsey, A. Campion and Ellery Queen are examples—are consulted and helped by the police, others, such as Perry Mason and Nero Wolf, have their own investigators. The case of the lonely detective with everyone's hand against him is relatively rare and even then the solution of the crime brings the superior forces of law and order to his side.

As fixed and securely established as the hero's status and role is the scene of his operation and the cast of characters. Because the detective story presents—by a well established convention—a process of investigation number of suspects within a self-contained and, therefore, adequately describable setting. This is why we get all these murders, in schools, colleges, isolated villages, country houses, theatres and hotels, or on trains or ships.

Over and above such orderly and intelligible social situations something which could be described as a metaphysical order is also required. Nothing that happens can be accepted as accidental and irrelevant. The twitch on the suspect's face or the cigarette stub in the shrubbery *is* a clue to be evaluated and the final solution must make sense of all such clues. In an almost Hegelian sense the real is the rational and the rational the real.

The salient features of the thriller are virtually the opposites of these characteristics of the detective story. The hero is, usually, not pre-ordained, he is not doing his normal, freely chosen job. In many stories (such as *The 39 Steps* or many E. Ambler novels) he blunders into the plot of the story through the accident of being on the spot or being mistaken for somebody else. In other cases he is picked out because he happens to have some special qualification, he is the only accessible person who knows the geography of Montenegro, can attend the brain surgeons' congress in Moscow without arousing suspicion, or knows a particular person by sight. Even where we are presented by professional agents it is noteworthy how often they are not just there to do their own jobs but are, like Le Carré's Smiley, brought back from retirement, or, like Bond, snatched from holiday, because an agent has been killed. Plunged into a new commitment he faces a strange world without support from a stable, reliable organisation. As a spy abroad, or a stool-pigeon infiltrated into a gang of criminals he is cut off his base and disowned by his employers. Even the contacts assigned to him are likely to fail him, either from being found dead or turning out to be unreliable. The thriller hero is alone in an alien and unfriendly world.

This lonely hero finds himself in anything but a stable, well circumscribed setting. Usually he has to travel into the unknown. Unlike the hero of the detective story, he cannot go home to his wife or manservant after a day's detecting. He is cut off from his background and either moves from place to place or is confronted with successive new aspects of the unfamiliar scene into which he has been dropped. Nor is there a limited set of characters he can gradually come to know. Those he encounters are only of temporary interest and, in any case, fade out or are killed. There is always someone else in the shadows whom it is more important to find and the most important encounter may mark the end of the story. This applies as much to his enemies as to the shadowy organisation he represents.

All this is connected with the nature and purpose of these two literary forms. The detective story is a reconstruction of the past. The book begins with the crime, usually, or even with the report of a crime which has taken place earlier. The aim of the story—like that of history—is to make sense of what has happened and this presupposes an intelligible order among the facts and an intellectual achievement on the part of the investigator.

The thriller, as an adventure story, takes the reader on a journey into an unknown and unstructured future in which new, unsuspected possibilities will open up. So the thriller writer, unlike the writer of detective stories, need not make his hero as intelligent as he can. Of course we like our heroes to be intelligent and able to outwit their opponents but in the thriller this is no more essential to the plot than being handsome. In fact the plot often hinges on their stupidity, their falling into every trap set for them or failing to protect vital secrets with the care the average person would give to looking after his purse. Instead they must be brave, determined and skilled and these qualities will, eventually, carry them to success. Often these qualities are described as virtually or literally superhuman, ranging from exceptional boxing skills to the use of "miraculous" tools and the possession of fairy-like capacities, like those of Superman or Spiderman.

Both forms of literature have their literary precedents. The detective story with its ritual form with which it proceeds cogently from the initial deed to the final solution has its model in classical tragedy where everything follows from an original act or flaw in the hero's character. The thriller has its precedents in the epic and medieval stories of knight errantry where the hero sets out to accomplish a mission, to capture Troy, bring back the Golden Fleece, liberate Gudrun, kill a monster or discover the Holy Grail. Even the modern hero's superhuman characteristics have their counterpart in, for example, the near invulnerability of Achilles and Siegfried. There are also the same kind of ordeals which test his manhood and establish him a knight or hero.

So the thriller appeal to unchanging human interests by putting perennial themes into modern dress. However, this cannot wholly account for its appeal because epics and knightly tales have long gone out of fashion while the thriller achieved its spectacular success only in the last few decades. We can ask therefore quite specifically what there is in our time which makes the thriller so popular. Why does Don Quixote ride again?

A further look at what fundamentally distinguishes the thriller from the detective story which it has overtaken in popularity may be illuminating. The latter presents and presupposes not only a rational and therefore intelligible order but also an essentially stable and just social order in which the law is ultimately vindicated and sporadic outbreaks of violence subdued and punished. We can be sure that the rightful heir will be restored, unwarranted suspicion, dispelled and loyalty rewarded. The purpose and meaning of the closed and limited world on which the process of detection casts its search light is restored and reaffirmed. The detective himself merely re-plays his accustomed role and reasserts his well established mastery.

In the thriller there is no such presupposition of a meaningful world, of a fixed order in which one can play one's accustomed role. The normal life from which the prospective hero is snatched by accidents or someone's mysterious choice, is a meaningless humdrum routine which behind its deceptive surface hides violent forces which may destroy that normality once and for all. Meaning, not present either in the life of the hero or the society around him, is bestowed or created by the act of election. Circumstances or individuals in authority pick him for a mission, just as the bestowing of knighthood gave a medieval man a role, duty and purpose. This mission is intensely personal. Without the detective's resources of organised help and a system of law enforcement, the thriller hero must put his own courage and ingenuity against elusive and powerful forces. The journey into the unknown is an ordeal which tests his manhood because the meaning to be realised is as much what is "in him" as the objective attainment of the mission. This is why a series of "tests" is usually built into the plot. There is the threat "lay off, or else." There are temptations: the beautiful enemy agent slipping out of her clothes, or the offer of money ("we would like to hire a resourceful chap like you"). Finally there is the actual ordeal, being beaten up and carrying on in pain, being tortured and not cracking up, being imprisoned and clawing one's way out.

These features of the thriller—the continuous violence, the rapidly changing scene, the struggle against organised forces which may be within a hair's breadth of disrupting an increasingly fragile order, and the search for personal meaning in excitement and adventure—all reflect features of the modern world. It is not only that violence is pervasive in the form of mugging, rapes, violent demonstrations, riots and terrorism but that such violence is increasingly defended as, at least, understandable and perhaps even justifiable. Only violence—so it is felt and argued—can draw attention to the injustice suffered by ethnic minorities or the unemployed, only terrorism can change unacceptable situations, be it the existence of capitalism or of Ulster and Israel. It is necessary because other means of change such as rational debate, or appeal to institutional arrangements, such as the ballot box or the court, are supposed to have failed or contain a bias against desirable change. The existing order can only be destroyed—or defended—by force.

Modern youth culture mirrors this trend. Rapid technological and social change have broken the continuity in which sons followed in the footsteps of their fathers, thus creating a cultural gap between the generations. Because deepening crises have made the economic future and place in society of the young uncertain they do not feel part of, and rebel against, the crumbling order which confronts them.

Both the politics of violence and the reaction of the young against their social environment exhibit a (sometimes spurious) individualism which easily spills over into a cult of personality. This phenomenon is fairly pervasive because it represents a reaction against the impersonal and oppressive forces of society. Leading sportsmen, entertainers, actors, called "stars," colourful politicians, television announcers and pundits become much photographed and talked about "personalities." They, together with some eccentrics and criminals (such as members of strange cults or the train robbers) become our heroes. What is "spurious" about this development is that so often these people become heroes mainly because they are "visible," as Daniel Boorstin cogently argued in his book *The Image,* and not because they significantly differ from the rest of us or even others of their profession. The boy who can sing no better than the rest of us is more likely than an operatic tenor to be hailed as a star. These stars are not predestined to success by status or ability but achieve it—like the thriller hero—by chance or the almost arbitrary choice of others. This allows their audiences to dream of being similarly lifted from their humdrum existence and this is their main attraction.

Seeing things in terms of personalities has a further advantage; it helps us to feel that we can understand the world around us. The interplay of social and economic forces, the clash of ideologies and the weighing of political options is infinitely confusing. Michael attacking Margaret or Tony fighting it out with Denis reduces all this to a familiar human scale.

The cult of personality is as much a response to features of our age as is the resurgence of violence or the accent on youth. We have lost the belief that life has a secure meaning because everything has become complex and impersonal, everything is constantly changed by forces beyond our control. We are confused by and trapped in this world and the thriller reflects these feelings because the fictional escape it offers is an inverted image of our unease.

One of the reasons why the thriller does not provide the intellectual challenge and rational satisfaction of the detective story is that its audience, swollen by film and television, extends beyond the well educated which constituted the main, at least British, readership of detective fiction. But it also reflects a loss of faith in the intelligibility of the world among the thoughtful. The thriller caters largely to a less sophisticated taste than the classical detective story but provides more excitement, adventure—in fact "thrills"—to an audience which seeks absorbing fantasies to compensate for a life of dull and unfulfilling work and distraction from uncontrollable anxieties. Some thrillers, like those of Le Carré, are, of course, highly sophisticated and intellectually demanding, but even these, far from making the world intelligible, often deliberately obstruct the reader's comprehension.

To those who can no longer believe that the social world around them is sound, stable and even reasonably just, the thriller offers a vision of a universe in tension where evenly matched forces of good and evil are locked in constant, or even renewed, combat. Though the right triumphs, success is temporary and the fight has to be constantly renewed. The hero—like the knight errant—fights for an ideal order, a utopia which could never be solidly established on earth.

The thriller offers not only meaning and purpose through quest and ordeal but also liberation. One of the reasons why life is boring and frustrating for so many is the multitude of restraints which confine them in a narrow compass. Work is controlled by bosses or supervisors and sometimes the requirements of a machine, home life by a nagging spouse or mother-in-law and all their lives are hedged in by regulations about parking, drinking hours, smokeless fuel, tax payments and the like. Identification with the hero affords escape and this is made easier by his ordinariness. Not only is he picked almost by accident but even his extraordinary qualities are externally and temporarily super-added (as in the Incredible Hulk and Superwoman) to an inconspicuous personality, or provided like a toolkit as in the Six Million Dollar Man and—even more literally—James Bond. To facilitate such identification further many thrillers take the form of the hero's first person narration.

The range of activities licensed by such imaginative identification is highly significant. All escapist literature offers some license as does for example the detective story by justifying violence on the part of those defending the law and so allowing the reader vicariously to enjoy such violence, including the ultimate violence of the death sentence. Prying curiosity also is licensed. A lot of people like poking their noses into the private affairs of others but either suffer rebukes or feel a little shamefaced about it. The detective's snooping is justified by the highest motives—as is frequently stressed in this form of literature. These detectives who are often described as scholarly and gentlemanly have chosen—we are assured—to investigate private affairs as a career or hobby for the highest motives—to bring the guilty to justice and life suspicion from the innocent.

The hero of the thriller enjoys a much wider license. He is free though man may everywhere else be in chains. The constraints, rules and conventions which bind others do not apply to him. With false papers he crosses frontiers closed to others. No boss can look over his shoulder as he roams freely tied to neither desk nor workbench. No wife or steady girlfriend can watch his steps and no one can check his expense account. What instructions he has received may have to be modified in the light of his own judgment and he is even freed, by means of technological devices, from the constraints of natural laws. Most significant though is the freedom from moral restraints. In the course of his mission he may lie, cheat and burgle. His freedom to engage in personal violence finds its sharpest expression in the "license to kill." A little torture may be part of his stock in trade. Sexual promiscuity is not only permitted but may become part of his duty.

At the very least this breaking of conventions and violations of moral and civic duties is excused by all taking place "in another country." They have no lasting consequences because they are parts of isolated episodes remote from his normal life. His misdeeds will not be reported to his local police station; his wife will not meet his mistress at the office party. It is all encapsulated, as it were, in a dream from which the hero awakes on completion of his mission. But it may also be justified by the great world-saving mission it serves. This is an alluring fantasy escape for all those who find external restraints or even their own conscience irksome.

The function of conjuring up effortless satisfactions which elude readers in ordinary life, the thriller shares with all entertainment literature. It offers freedom to those confined in narrow channels, excitement to those frustrated by the complexities of modern life, and heroes in personal combat in a drab anonymous world. It also opens vistas on a wider world not accessible to most of us. Even the detective story's appeal lies partly in its satisfying curiosity about spheres unknown to most readers, such as the inside of a nunnery, an advertising agency or a public school. The thriller takes us beyond our own world to such esoteric places as countries behind the Iron Curtain, to the Far East or into the sphere of organised crime and international conspiracy.

More important and central, than all these various reasons by which people are attracted to thrillers is the quest for meaning. The thriller deals with a fleeting present and an open future and not, like the detective story, a completed past which can be rationally explained. What we need to know about the past as we follow the action of a thriller is provided by a concise briefing at the beginning. It is casually presented and usually does not contain a hint of how that information was obtained. Almost immediately we follow the hero into an unpredictable future in which a process which serves no agreed on purpose and reflects no understandable meaning will unfold. If the philosophy underpinning the detective story is a Hegelian belief in ultimate order and rationality that of the thriller is something like existentialism, which abandons faith in a preordained meaning and purpose of life and insists that any meaning must be created by the choices and acts of individuals. The mission thrust upon the hero bestows meaning on his life which lacked significance before. This meaning can only be fully realised by the personal choices, the committed actions and exertions of the individual. The objective success of the mission may only be temporary: a battle is won against the espionage network of a foreign power, or the Mafia, a prisoner is freed or a plot foiled, but foreign espionage and international crime are not eliminated. There will be more plots to foil and more prisoners to free. The hero's actions alone are really meaningful for through them he discovers or even creates qualities of character unrevealed and even unrealised before. To make life meaningful in this way is the real point of the mission, the ordeals and the breakthrough into an extraordinary freedom from social and even physical constraints.

We have made the assumption that the thriller, precisely

because it is not a realistic art form trying to describe what things are like, reflects what readers think, need and want. It looks, therefore, as if these readers had lost their faith in a meaningful order of life and in an intelligible past which makes sense of the present. Instead of being able to rely on any continuity of traditions and trends they entertain the rather desperate hope that personality, created by personal choice and courageous participation in a perennial and never finally decided struggle will project a glimmer of meaning on the darkening chaos of our world. The final twist toward nihilism comes from the spoof thriller which makes us laugh at, and so negate, this faint hope in a heroically achieved meaning.

Am I making too much of what people read on trains, in their spare time or as a steady diet? We cannot lightly dismiss the suggestion that for many readers or watchers of thrillers this genre provides a superficial, temporary and casual satisfaction, isolated mental episodes of dwelling for a brief but refreshing moment in a fantasy world which is left behind when they put down the book or switch off the set. Yet the line between what flits through the mind and becomes a fixed conviction, between a fantasy and a motive for action or the germ of an idea is not irrevocably and unchangeably fixed. The popularity of the thriller may be only a straw in the wind, but it may be more important than it seems.

Pulp Vigilante Heroes, the Moral Majority and the Apocalypse

Gary Hoppenstand

"The Time is Short"

—Hal Lindsey

"There is Hope For America, But We Must Act Quickly."

Jerry Falwell

"The Four Horsemen Of The Apocalypse Laughed In Their Saddles As They Thundered Their Mocking Call of Doom."

—Operator #5

*L*ethal, relentless, savage, the fictional vigilantes of the pulp magazines, comic books and paperbacks offer some penetrating insights into the nature of formula construction. Characters like The Shadow, the Executioner and Edge appear, at first glance, to be hopelessly pathological and homicidal. They seem to be literary deviants, packaged and sold by paunchy, cigar-puffing hucksters in cheap, pulp-ladened publications. Schools and libraries have condemned their adventures ever since the first adolescent was caught reading them instead of reading the proscribed history and math assignments. Proper bookstores refuse to stock their novels, while newsstands, grocery stores, drug stores and other traffickers of the commodities of daily existence nestle stacks of their books and magazines next to the latest issues of *True Confessions* and *Screen World*. The odor of splattered blood forces away from the pulp, and yet both are interconnected to the same

141

social forces that shape and mold the nature of reality. Like the father who refuses to acknowledge his bastard offspring, charismatic Christianity pledges campaigns to purge violence from the mass media. No doubt, part of the problem is that the features of the child too closely resemble those of the parent. Self-recognition, for many, is difficult, especially if the image reflects the specter of Death. The pulp vigilantes and the Moral Majority both embrace that specter, and their preferred Angel is the one who carries the sycthe.

The Moral Majority's dark prophecies of the future, and their solution to those prophecies serve the same social function, in ritual and myth, that the fictional adventures of the pulp vigilante-heroes served, in formula. Cawelti suggests that there are "four interrelated hypotheses about the dialectic between formulaic literature and culture that produces and enjoys it."[1] The second of these is medicinal in nature: "Formulas resolve tensions and ambiguities resulting from the conflicting interests of different groups within the culture or from ambiguous attitudes toward particular values."[2] For Cawelti, formula acts to structure cultural ambiguities, as ritual does for its practitioners, and then to resolve those ambiguities in highly predictable fashion. Formula gives form to the formless and meaning to the meaningless, heroic outline to a society's heroes. Formula is a cheap physician who is able to soothe the blisters of the human condition. It offers a commonality, on a societal level, for people of diverse backgrounds and experiences. And, ultimately, it offers security. It is the great national teat. Formula, by its defintion, mirrors the past and predicts the future. It makes vital a tradition. Fictional motifs that are combined to create formulas archetypically remain constant inconclusively in the past, the present, and the future. In American society, for example, during periods of great crisis, formula fiction has dusted off its vigilante-heroes and offered them as grim-faced saviors of the day.

One of the most popular hero-creations in pulp literature during the Great Depression was The Shadow. In mid-1930, a radio program entitled *Detective Story Program* featured an announcer known mysteriously as "The Shadow," who dramatized material from a magazine. Street and Smith publishers, who possessed a strong tradition of marketing heroes during the dime novel era, recognized a potential commercial property and decided, in 1931, to launch *The Shadow Magazine*.[3] Walter Gibson was contracted to write the first Shadow adventure, more to secure the copyright of the radio personality than anything else, and writing under the pseudonym of Maxwell Grant, Gibson produced *The Living Shadow* (Vol. 1, No. 1, April 1931), though not without some difficulties. Gibson remarks that after writing the early chapters of *The Living Shadow* he was asked to rewrite them, introducing a "Chinese angle," somehow tying in a man in Chinese costume," clutching an upraised hand that cast a hugh shadow on the wall behind him."[4] When *The Shadow* hit the newsstands, it touched the Depression demands and sold out. A second and a third novel nearly sold out, and Street and Smith decided the demand was great enough to warrant the magazine becoming a monthly rather than a quarterly. Even with a novel a month, readers still clamored for more stories. With the October 1, 1932 issue, *The Shadow Magazine* was released as a bi-weekly and remained that way through March 1, 1943. The magazine continued publication to the Summer of 1949, eventually totaling 325 Shadow adventures, most of which were written by Gibson. Concurrently The Shadow continued his presence on the radio, becoming one of the most popular detective/adventure radio heroes of the Depression. What had begun as a simple copyright practice quickly blossomed into a media event because it supplied something heroic that the reading public needed, the extent of this need being reflected in the speed with which the public bought the issues.

Street and Smith decided to duplicate their luck and in March 1933 published the first *Doc Savage Magazine* (entitled *The Man of Bronze*). Though not as successful as The Shadow, the *Doc Savage Magazine* continued publication through the Summer of 1949, tallying some 181 adventures. With the near-instant success of The Shadow and Doc Savage, other publishers released their own hero pulp magazines—with dollar signs gleaming in their eyes—and between 1931 and 1949 some fifty-six different character titles appeared.[5] The heroes of these magazines included men like The Avenger, Captain Satan, The Moon Man, Operator No. 5, The Phantom Detective, Secret Agent X and The Spider.

After 1931 dozens of pulp vigilante-heroes laughed, whispered, blasted, battled and killed their way through the fictional "mean streets" of Depression America. Their heroes offered for their magazine reading audience simple solutions to complex problems. The Depression, its causes and effects, were not clearly understood by Americans who lived through it. Rather than seeing the Depression as a social problem, it was viewed as a personal problem. The Depression was not perceived as the result of a failed capitalistic system but as individual failure, which is why, in part, American capitalism survived the 1930s. Thus, rather than developing radical answers for the Depression's problems (e.g. social revolution) Americans rededicated themselves to the traditional Puritan Work Ethic and tried to work their way out of the economic morass. Americans groped for the familiar, and the familiar was the paradigm of the White Anglo-Saxon Protestant.

One aspect of the Depression WASP mindset was the radically conservative—even reactionary—attitude toward criminals and crime in the hero pulp magazine formulas. In these formulas, traditional law enforcement agencies were unable to deal with crime; thus the pulp hero adopted vigilantism to deal with the problem. If the crook was menacing society and threatening destruction of law and order, the pulp vigilante-hero offered a simple, conservative solution: kill the enemy.

Most of the villains of the hero pulps represented the bottom rung of the social ladder. They were the foreigners, the ethnics, and the hardened unemployed. The supervillains of the hero pulps were symbolic socialists and communists who literally adopted the "share the wealth" worldview of their Marxist predecessors. Though they undeniably craved personal wealth and power, they nonetheless employed that element of society that was shunned. The supervillain offered, formulaically, a type of liberal social reform that was distasteful for the Depression readership. The pulp vigilante-hero, as the fictional agent of extreme conservatism, inexorably "got his man," before the devil of economic insanity overthrew the virtuous capitalistic power structure. The supervillain, as reformer, offered an unsure, an insecure future, while the pulp vigilante-hero offered the promise of a secure WASP conservatism, the same "stuff" (mythically) that made America great.

Naturally this vigilante-villain dialectic suggests a great deal more than an economic or political romance. Moral issues are involved. The plot structure of the typical hero pulp defines the Christian dilemma. Forces easily identified as Good in a Christian sense are pitted against demonic forces of Evil in an Apocalyptic struggle in which the very soul of humanity is at stake. The pulp hero adventure is an epic *Pilgrim's Progress* in which the road to salvation is led and guarded by the pulp vigilante-hero. The alternative to this road is damnation.

Metaphorically, the vigilante-hero's quest in the supervillain's underworld lair, which occurs with such formulaic regularity in the hero pulps that it becomes a motif, is akin to a descent into hell. In The Shadow's adventures, a favorite den of villainy is New York's Chinatown. The following excerpt from *The Teeth of the Dragon* (Nov. 15, 1937) illustates a scene which could easily exist in Dante's *Inferno*:

> The underground headquarters of the Jeho Fan was the most grotesque meeting place that The Shadow had ever seen. Secreted among forgotten catacombs of Chinatown, its location was untraceable. Confident that the stronghold would ever be secure, the Jeho fan had spent a fortune in its embellishment.
>
> The result was a garish, hideous medley that resembled an opium smoker's nightmare.
>
> The square room was illuminated by a sickly, greenish glow. In that olive-tinged light, The Shadow saw monstrous faces peering down from every corner. They were hugh statues, each of a Chinese joss, that stood as ten-foot guardians over the meetings of the Jeho Fan.
>
> ...From that floor, more statues were visible, set between the giant images that stood in the corners. Some were figures of Chinese devils, slightly larger than lifesize. Others were dwarfish idols, squatted upon taborets.[6]

Naturally the inhabitants of such a place call Satan friend:

> Two of the demons stepped from the side walls. They clamped hands upon The Shadow's shoulders, hauled him to his feet. Their hands were covered with heavy gauntlets, spiked with metal that dug through the prisoner's cloak. With a forward sweep, the pair sprawled The Shadow at the feet of the Tao Fan.
>
> The leader delivered an ugly, basso laugh. It brought a response from the devil-members. Their harsh mirth was loudened with the domed room, giving it a demoniac fury.[7]

The Shadow's escape from hell necessitates a heroic re-birth, a type of regeneration through violence:

> The Shadow ran his doubled hand to his forehead. His forefinger dipped into the blood that still oozed slowly from the gash. The forefinger joined the others. The whole move of The Shadow's hand looked as he intended it. He had apparently reached to press a painful wound.
>
> Captors swung The Shadow to his feet. They were dragging him away, while the Tao and Ming Dwan watched as scorners. Then, from a pitiful, sagging sight, The Shadow became a power. His whole body whipped to action.
>
> His right forearm sliced upward; cracked the chin of a big

false head and sent it flying, to reveal a wizened, baldish Chinaman instead. Twisting from the grip of those on the left, he drove in a hard punch toward the other captor on the right.[8]

The American Depression was a moral depression. The primary cause of the fall was the consumeristic excesses of the 1920s, and the price of failure for many Americans was economic insecurity, and, more importantly, moral insecurity. The Depression was a "real life" enactment of the Apocalypse. The Devil stood laughing in every bread line, and the country, as a whole, fell one notch deeper in the fiery pit each time a bank closed. America craved a Christ-figure to combat this insidious moral decline. The pulp magazine publishers, sensing a market, produced dozens of titles totaling millions of copies, featuring the bloodthirsty avenger who could battle his way out of hell every issue. It was an allegory of its day which later proved to be the allegory of any day in which there was perceived a moral crisis.

The December 1934 issue of Operator 5 perhaps best illustrates the allegory of the Apocalypse during America's "dark decade." Even the cover of the pulp magazine is fraught with conflict as titanic forces wage their war. A nattily dressed Operator 5 places himself between an angry mob of blue-collar farm workers and a small group of cowering men and women. There is an older, distinguished looking man in the small group who could very well be any American banker or businessman. A young boy, no doubt Operator 5's dedicated assistant, Tim Donovan, stands at attention, ready to sacrifice his life if needed. Two attractive women, a blonde and a brunette, cringe behind Operator 5, representing in their own way the flower of WASP American womanhood. The threatened group stands on what appears to be the steps of a Washington monument, while in the distance, well behind the angry mob of farmers, a swirl of dust rises from a desolated farm, forming a black funnel cloud in which there ride the Four Horsemen of the Apocalypse.

The story details the attempts of a madman named Apocryphos to achieve political domination in the United States. He develops a super strain of deadly insects which devour the food reserves of the nation. He also employs a dark legion of fanatic followers who destroy warehouses and shipments of food. His ultimate goal is the starvation of the American people, which, of course, leads to political and social anarchy. Only the courage, strength and intelligence of America's secret service ace, Operator 5, halts the

plans of Apocryphos, and as the magazine's blurb forecasts: "...
only one man—Operator 5—realized the ghastly extent of the
diabolical plot. And only he ... could hope to bring the canny
schemer to the justice he deserved—death."[9]

Those monthly fictional Apocalypses—pounded into that pulp
paper, covered with garish chrome-stock illustrations, and selling
for that thin dime—always ended happily ever after. Though cities
fell and governments toppled, the vigilante-hero never failed to save
the day. The allegory suggested that with the proper heroic
dimensions, the real-life Apocalypse of the Depression, too, could be
licked. Satan was overcome every issue in the hero pulps, and there
was never any actual fear within the formula that the King of
Darkness would have the last laugh.

However, Lois Parkinson Zamora suggests that:

> In the past two or three decades and in fact during much of this
> century ... America's sense of its apocalyptic historical destiny
> has become almost universally pessimistic in outlook. In our
> time, millennial optimism seems to have been transformed into
> a foreboding suspicion of the imminence of great cosmic disaster
> in which the world may be annihilated, with no possibility of
> anything beyond the cataclysm.[10]

This transformation of the Apocalypse from a positive allegory to
an entropy nightmare was solicited by the various emerging
charismatic Christian organizations in the 1970s and 1980s.

Drawing upon the Apocalyptic tradition in American culture,[11]
author-evangelist Hal Lindsey has written a series of bestselling
publications, including *The Terminal Generation, Satan Is Alive
and Well on Planet Earth* and *The 1980's: Countdown to
Armageddon*, in which he applies ancient Biblical Apocalyptic
prophecies to current world social and economic strife. Perhaps the
best-known of his work is *The Late Planet Earth*, which is
advertised on the cover as being a 15 million copy bestseller.

Throughout the book, Lindsey describes his personal vision of
the nation's Apocalyptic turmoil, citing as examples America's
fascination with astrology (the text of the Devil), with "false"
prophesy (as epitomized by Edgar Cayce and Jeane Dixon), with
spiritualism and mysticism, and with other growing cult concerns.
Lindsay states that Christian people should put their faith in the
Bible and its teachings, and if these people desire to know their
future, they should turn to The Book of Revelations and other
Biblical texts. Lindsey's cookbook of the future contains current

social ingredients:

> Look for the present sociological problems such as crime,
> riots, lack of employment, poverty, illiteracy, mental illness,
> illegitimacy, etc., to increase as the population explosion begins
> to multiply geometrically in the late 1970's.
> Look for the beginning of the widest spread famines in the
> history of the world.
> Look for drug addiction to further permeate the U.S. and
> other free world countries. Drug addicts will run for high
> political offices and win through support of the young adults.
> Look for drugs and forms of religion to be merged together.
> There will be a great general increase of belief in extrasensory
> phenomena, which will not be related to the true God, but to
> Satan.
> Astrology, witchcraft, and Oriental religions will become
> predominant in the western world.[12]

Stir these ingredients well, bake and then serve a generous portion
of Armageddon.

Interestingly, all of the points of impending doom that Lindsey
illustrates in his book are the same formulaic motifs that appear
time and again in the hero pulps. In fact, one of his chapters
concerns "The Yellow Peril,"[13] which also happens to have been one
of the most popular plot formulas during both the dime novel and
pulp eras. The implication here is that the social troubles that
plagued America in the 1930s also plague America in the 1980s, but
what the hero pulps worked out formulaically in positive fashion,
the charismatic Christians of today, in negative fashion, fail to
resolve. The current Christian Apocalypse is fated to happen. The
only recourse for the true Christian is an unswerving adherence to
religious doctrine. For the pulp magazine reader in America during
the 1930s, the Apocalypse could be averted. Today, for the
charismatic Christian, the Apocalypse is inevitable.

One of the leaders of America's conservative political
movements in the late 1970s and early 80s, Jerry Falwell, heads a
religious political action group, the Moral Majority,which professes
to consist of 60 million born-again Christians, 60 million religious
"promoralists," and 50 million "idealistic moralists."[14] Whether
Falwell's numbers are accurate or whether they are heroically
exaggerated can be a point of debate. What cannot be debated is the
fact that Falwell and his Moral Majority during the first few years
of the 80s decade were a well-financed, well-organized and highly
effective lobbying group. In the 1980 national elections, they had a

noticeable impact in American politics, aiding in the defeat of a number of "liberal" politicians and the election of a number of "conservatives."

In his book *Listen, America*, advertised as "the conservative blue-print for America's moral rebirth," Falwell restates Lindsey's Apocalyptic forecasts, with an essential difference. Whereas Lindsey's solution to the perceived "moral decline" of the American lifestyle is a personal rededication to charismatic Christian views, Falwell's solution comprises political and social action. Falwell desires to legislate morality, and he has established himself as the "hero" of the new right and the champion of the nation's moral rebirth. He has become a type of real life pulp vigilante-hero, utilizing reactionary methods to achieve a simple end. As the hero pulps of the 1930s formulaically offered uncomplicated answers to complex questions, Falwell's Moral Majority of the 1980s does virtually the same thing. For Falwell, the "nation's sins" can be boiled down to five major areas: abortion, homosexuality, pornography, humanism and the fractured family.[15] And, as Falwell states: "To change America we must be involved, and this includes three areas of political action: 1) registration ... 2) information ... 3) mobilization."[16]

Falwell's new direction for charismatic Christianity coincides with the recent renascence of the vigilante in most forms of the mass media. Three of the top five grossing films of all time, *Star Wars, The Empire Strikes Back* and *Raiders of the Lost Ark*, feature the pulp vigilante-hero character. All three were released after 1977. On television, the action-detective show, like *Magnum P.I.,* is challenging the dominance of the situation comedy. Comic book superheroes enjoy a multi-media popularity, and paperback genres, including the adult western, the adult science fiction adventure, the adult romance and the adult war adventure, have become increasingly reactionary with their treatment of social injustice while featuring the hero as savior.

All this seems to indicate that some types of formula and religion are flip sides of the same insecurity. Man, the myth-maker, the explainer, the sometimes rational creature residing in an always irrational world, requires a sane building plan for his life. He craves a sense of order in his existence. He yearns for a purpose in life. The framework of formula is the superstructure of Man's building plan. Fabricated from the sturdy wood of myth, formula explains, in a repeated, comfortable way, where Man has been and where he is going. Formula offers the cultural tradition that is necessary for social stability during times of actual or perceived collective crisis. Laying their planks on the superstructure of the formula vigilante-hero, consciously or unconsciously charismatic Christians like Hal Lindsey and Jerry Falwell have framed their particular worldviews on the already established Apocalyptic literary institution in American culture.

Using this institution, they have established themselves as our moral saviors, indeed as the gun-toting, death-dealing opponents of Satan. One can perhaps say that in formula, there is a little bit of reality, and in reality a little bit of formula-fantasy. Formula and ritual, after all, make an excellent structure for withstanding the winds of social insecurity.

The muscle of this particular formula is the hero—the larger-than-life individual who solves the problems and makes the world safe for the timid and frightened. Not so much has changed in American culture in the last fifty years. Though we call them somewhat different names, the old vigilante-heroes have been resurrected and are forced to serve our purposes today.

Notes

[1] John G. Cawelti, *Adventure, Mystery, and Romance* (Chicago: Univ. of Chicago Press, 1976), pp. 35-36.
[2] Ibid.
[3] Robert Sampson, *The Night Master* (Chicago: The Pulp Press, 1982), pp. 25-30.
[4] Maxwell Grant (Walter B. Gibson), *The Crime Oracle and The Teeth of the Dragon* (New York: Dover Publications, 1975), p. IX.
[5] Robert Weinberg and Lohr McKinstry, *The Hero Pulp Index* (Evergreen: Opar Press, 1971), pp. 1-48.
[6] Maxwell Grant (Walter B. Gibson), *The Crime Oracle and The Teeth of the Dragon* (New York: Dover Publications, 1975), p. 121.
[7] Ibid., p. 122.   [8] Ibid., p. 125.
[9] *Operator 5*, "The Legions of Starvation," (Dec., 1934), Vol. 3, No. 1).
[10] Lois P. Zamora, *The Apocalyptic Vision in America* (Bowling Green, OH: The Popular Press, 1982), p. 1.
[11] Ibid.
[12] Hal Lindsey, *The Late Great Planet Earth* (New York: Bantam Books, 1973), p. 174.
[13] The "Yellow Peril" was the ritualized fear that Western civilization could be overcome by the Orientals. In American and British formula literature, it was a very popular plot motif. Perhaps the most famous of this type of story is Sax Rohmer's Fu Manchu novels.
[14] Jerry Falwell, *Listen, America* (New York: Bantam Books, 1981). Author's note.
[15] Ibid., pp. 221-223.   [16] Ibid., pp. 226-234.

The Catalytic Child Hero in the Contemporary Gothic Novel

Hanna B. Lewis

Catalyst: A substance that causes activity between two or more persons without itself being affected.

*T*he catalytic child hero in the contemporary gothic novel causes events to happen and people to interact. The effect of actions upon himself is far less important than the total resolution of the plot.

My definition restricts such a child to a truly human one, who may perhaps have some extra mental or physical abilities, which are within the realm of possibility. We must immediately discard those "children" who are half demonic or divine, of which there have been many in recent years: Jerome Bixby's monstrous baby in "It's a Wonderful Life"; the devil's spawn in Ira Levin's *Rosemary's Baby* or David Seltzer's *The Omen*; the fetal Anti-Christ or Messiah in James Patterson's *Virgin* (where the Second Coming is female, in a bow to women's lib); or children possessed by the devil like Megan in William Blatty's *The Exorcist*. And children who have only evil and no good aspects like the parricidal children of Ray Bradbury's "The Veldt" or William Murch's *The Bad Seed* are too one-dimensional to fit the pattern.

The true catalytic child hero is basically innocent and his impact upon the plot frequently arises from his desire for family stability, happiness and a normal life in a stable society. One of the archetypal catalytic children of the previous generation of writers is the hero of D.H. Lawrence's 1933 short story "The Rocking-Horse Winner." This story has all the elements we will find in our catalytic children: an only or lonely prepubescent child who does not relate to his/her siblings, a family with problems, financial or psychological or both, and a special sensitivity or psi ability which enables him to influence events about him.

Paul has two sisters, but they have no place in the story. His mother is a cold woman and his father a charming ne'er-do-well. The only adults to whom Paul relates at all are his Uncle Oscar and Bassett, the young gardener, and they see only what Paul does, not what he feels. We are immediately made aware of both the family's problems and Paul's psi ability by his perception of the house's repeated whispering demands for money: "There must be more money."[1] Paul satisfies these demands by riding his rocking horse and putting himself into a trance in which he can predict the winners of horse races. A modern psychologist would probably find many of the characteristics of the autistic child in Paul's behavior and mental state. Basically, however, Paul is still a human child, not infallible or inexhaustible. His psi ability comes and goes, and only a mortally debilitating effort finally brings enough money for the family. But the catalyst is used up and no longer necessary. Death (or total autism) must remove him from the family.

More prototypes appear in Henry James' *The Turn of the Screw*.[2] Here the role of the children is ambiguous and their catalytic action depends largely on the interpretation of the novella. There has been considerable argument among critics about the focus of the story, although James himself insisted that the ghosts were actual and had really corrupted the children. But, since the point of view is that of the governess, Freudian interpretation is certainly possible. Are the happenings of the story, the ill-fated love affair of the previous governess, Miss Jessel, and the evil Peter Quint, the machinations of the children, only the figments of the new governess' sick, sex-starved imagination, or are the children truly evil, irreversibly corrupted by Quint and actually bent on her destruction? If the children are the latter demons, they are not catalytic in our sense, but if they are innocent, and the evil is only in the governess' fervid imagination, they are truly catalytic in causing her final breakdown and the death of the boy, Miles. Flora, the girl, is "saved," but Miles' heart, like Paul's, has stopped. He is also "used up."

At least three contemporary American writers have used the

device of the catalytic child hero in recent novels. The most prolific in it use is Stephen King. Almost all of his novels have as their protagonists catalytic children or adolescents. King has a Wordsworthian respect for the innocence of childhood and his characters seem to become more and more corrupt as they reach adolescence and young manhood or womanhood. King's children thus become catalysts for evil as they grow older. The best example for this is his first novel, *Carrie* (New York: Doubleday, 1974), in which the heroine eventually deliberately uses her catalytic abilities to destroy her enemies. Another used-up catalyst is discarded; she dies, but her destructive spirit has a half-life, perhaps indefinitely.

So it is only the very young people in King's novels who truly fit our heroic pattern. The best known of these is Danny in *The Shining* (New York: Doubleday, 1977). Unfortunately the film made from this book has changed the focus from Danny to his father. And King, himself, does not see Danny as the central figure of the book. In his *Dance Macabre* (New York: Everest House, 1981), a book about horror in fiction and film, he insists that *The Shining* centers around the evil still existing in the old Colorado hotel rather than the characters themselves. This is perhaps evident to King, but to the reader, Danny is a small heroic fighter against the almost overwhelming forces activated by the arrival of his family. Jack, Wendy and Danny Torrance come as winter caretakers to a summer resort, where Jack is planning to complete the play he has desultorily been working on for the seven years of his marriage. There is real cause for concern for the future of Danny's family without any introduction of supernatural events.

The Torrances' marriage is already on the verge of breaking up. Jack has an explosive temper. He has been fired from his previous job as English teacher at a prep school in Vermont for drinking and beating a student. He had, two years earlier, broken Danny's arm in punishing him for a minor infraction. He is a human time bomb.

And, if the isolation and claustrophobic winter atmosphere of the hotel were not enough, the man hiring Jack tells of the previous caretaker, whose personality and problems were similar to Jack's, and who finally had killed his wife and two daughters and himself in a drunken rage. Another woman has also recently committed suicide in the hotel. In all, forty to fifty have died in the Overlook in the last sixty years.

Danny, as a typical catalytic child, is well aware of the problems of his parents and the evil of the hotel. He can sense "bad things" because of a limited psi ability, which an old black friend,

Hallorann, calls "the shining," telling him

> "...you've got a large thing in your head, Danny. You'll have to
> do a lot of growin' yet before you catch up to it, I guess. You got to
> be brave about it."
>   "But I don't *understand* things!" Danny burst out. "I *do* but
> I *don't!*" People ... they feel things and I feel them, but I don't
> know what I'm feeling!" (p. 83).

It is Danny's problem that he really cannot understand his
visions or communicate them adequately. He considers his psi
ability to be thoughts spoken to him and visions shown to him by an
imaginary friend, Tony.

> "Who's Tony?" Hallorann asked again.
>   "Mommy and Daddy call him my 'invisible playmate',"
> Danny said, reciting the words carefully. "But he's really real.
> At least, I think he is. Sometimes, when I try real hard to
> understand things, he comes. He says, 'Danny, I want to show
> you something.' And it's like I pass out. Only ... there are
> dreams, like you said." He looked at Hallorann and swallowed.
> "They used to be nice. But now ... I can't remember the word for
> dreams that scare you and make you cry" (p. 83).

Danny cannot read or interpret the word REDRUM he "sees" in
the mirror of a hotel room which contains a murdered body in a
bathtub and it is not till the end of the novel that the reader is
informed that this is MURDER. But Danny is immediately aware of
the danger to his family, and since the point of view is constantly
shifting from one character to another, the reader is also aware of
this danger.

At first, the "shining" is only a perceptive quality, but we are
made aware by a small incident in which Danny demonstrates his
ability to Hallorann that Danny's power can have physical
consequences.

> "Give me a blast. Think at me. I want to know if you got as much
> as I think you do."
>   "What do you want me to think?"
>   "Anything. Just think it *hard.*
>   "Okay," said Danny. He considered it for a moment, then
> gathered his concentration and flung it out at Hallorann. He
> had never done anything precisely like this before, and at the
> last instant some instinctive part of him rose up and blunted

some of his thought's raw force—he didn't want to hurt Mr. Hallorann. Still the thought arrowed out of him with a force he never would have believed. It went like a Nolan Ryan fastball with a litle extra on it.

(Gee I hope I don't hurt him)

And the thought was:

(!!! HI, DICK !!!)

Hallorann winced and jerked backward on the seat. His teeth came together with a hard click, drawing blood from his lower lip in a thin trickle. His hands flew up involuntarily from his lap to the level of his chest and then settled back again. For a moment his eyelids fluttered limply, with no conscious control, and Danny was frightened (pp. 80-81).

As the novel progresses, Danny's "shining" gives the reader more and more glimpses of the dangers of the hotel—not only the supernatural elements, but the overaged boiler, which is overheating, although the gauge does not show it. Danny, in his ignorance and innocence, cannot interpret the signal, but his flashes of insight provide an omniscient point of view, which is King's major plot device. Finally, all Danny's premonitions are realized. Jack becomes, or tries to become, the ax-murderer his predecessor was and stalks his family through the deserted hotel. As Danny sees it, Jack is no longer his "daddy"; he is the creature of the hotel. And Danny's innocence penetrates his father's madness and saves his own life, just as his "shining" realization that the boiler is about to blow up saves his mother and Hallorann.

Everything that occurs in *The Shining* can be explained on a natural level—almost. The seeds of Jack's madness are already there when the Torrances move into the Overlook. Danny's communication via the "shining" with Hallorann could be an instinctive bond between the two that allows them to understand each other non-verbally. Danny's informant, Tony, is the imaginary playmate many children have. But King postulates that the hotel reacts to Danny's innocence in a particularly vicious way and that he is passively responsible for all that happens for bad and, finally, actively for good. King also hints in the epilogue that Danny's ability will fade as he grows older and, in a non-stressful environment, will no longer be needed. From a child hero, Danny will fade into a nondescript adult.

In King's *Firestarter* (New York: Viking, 1980), the heroine is slightly older, but still prepubescent and named Charlie to emphasize her androgynous state. There is an actual physical cause for Charlie's pyrokinesis (ability to start fires by psychic power). Charlie's parents had been unwittingly involved in an illegal government experiment with hallucinatory drugs, which killed some of the participants and caused a genetic change in others—thus creating her unusual talent.

This is the only novel in which the catalytic child is deliberately manipulated by opposing forces for their own benefit. "The Shop," a CIA-type covert operation, that conducted the original drug experiment, has discovered the effect upon Vicky, Charlie's mother and her. The government men kill Vicky and try to gain control of Charlie and her talent. Andy, the father, who has always discouraged the use of her talent, because he realizes its destructive potential, tries to protect her and is killed in the process.

Danny and Charlie have another factor in common. In both children, the catalytic psi ability is activated by a desire to protect a threatened and beloved parent (Danny's mother from his father and the hotel, Charlie's father from the "Shop.")

As Charlie becomes older and more cynical, she becomes less catalytic and more actively heroic. She learns to control her ability and avenges the death of her father by destroying the evil geniuses in the "Shop." But the "Shop" itself will go on and it is only by revealing her power to the country (thereby restricting its secret use) that Charlie can save herself. Eventually, King indicates the loss of her youthful innocence and her growing awareness of her own awesome power will make her a force to be reckoned with, a true superwoman. There is no guarantee that she will be benevolent. Her last lines are ominous:

> "I need to see someone who writes for your magazine," Charlie said. Her voice was low, but it was clear and firm. "I have a story I want to tell. And something to show."
> "Just like show-and-tell in school, huh?" The receptionist asked.
> Charlie smiled. It was the smile that had so dazzled the librarian. "Yes," she said. "I've been waiting for a long time." (p. 371).

The catalytic child heroine has become a possible world dictator.

In King's latest novel, *Cujo* (New York: Viking, 1981), there are two children, both with some psi ability. True to the law of the catalytic child (diminishing innocence equalling diminishing psi ability), Tad the four-year old is more prescient than the older Brett, but also less able to communicate his knowledge and therefore more vulnerable. The central plot device is a large St. Bernard dog, Cujo, who apparently becomes possessed by the persona of a dead "mad strangler," Frank Dodd, and turns rabid. Through a series of unfortunate events, Tad and his mother are trapped in their stalled car at the house of Cujo's owners and Tad dies of heat exhaustion and dehydration, while his mother tries to keep the maddened dog from breaking into the car.

Tad has always had a premonition of disaster, but unlike Danny or Charlie, is too young to avert the problem of his even lesser ability to communicate clearly. From the beginning, he senses the spirit of Frank Dodd, who had earlier terrorized Castle Rock,[3] the locale of the novel. Dodd committed suicide before being captured and his vengeful uneasy spirit first seems to appear in Tad's closet. Tad senses that, but Tad's parents rationally consider his fear as a typical "night terror" or nightmare. They almost convince Tad; at least he learns not to try to show his fears to them anymore, because his mother and father will not take him seriously. Tad's father has given him a magic verse (the "Monster Words") to use against the unknown evil which seems somewhat efficacious, but at the crucial moment, Tad is too weak and too exhausted to use them.

The older boy, Brett, fortuitously (for the plot) on a trip with his mother, when Cujo becomes ill (or possessed by Dodd's spirit), sleepwalks at his aunt's house, muttering, "Cujo's not hungry no more, not no more" (p. 245). He senses psychically that something is wrong with his dog. But neither boy has the intensive psi ability of Danny or Charlie. Tad's closet monster could be his overactive imagination. Many four-year-olds fear the dark and see "boogeymen" in closets and under beds. There is even a certain attractiveness for the children in this idea (a delicious shudder). In an interview with David Letterman (April 1, 1982), King tells of his own fears of dark cellars and closets as a small child. Only in Stephen King's novels are the visions taken at face value. Tad's parents may sense the monster, but because their adult world precludes admission of supernatural beings or events, do not accept its reality.

Brett's mother knows he has sleepwalked before. He has been worrying about his dog and who will feed it, since he does not trust his father to do so. It is therefore quite natural that he should act out and speak of this feeding in his dream.

Cujo is a much more poorly structured book than King's previous ones. Its main problem is that it is basically a short story, stretched beyond its limits to make a novel, and that the trio of Tad, Brett and Tad's mother, Donna, dilute the heroic focus. There are too many points-of-view and no single true protagonist, too many extraneous plot lines that do not advance the main plot. For half the book, Tad and his mother are trapped in their disabled Pinto at Cujo's house. The reader knows that rescue will eventually come, so King's attempts to delay it are more annoying than suspenseful. Tad's death is an unnecessary and unpleasant surprise. Flashes of King's perceptive understanding of young children still occur, and he recognizes the weakness of their vocabulary to articulate all their understanding.

King has abandoned much of his use of the catalytic child in this novel. He does not clarify his own point-of-view—are Tad's and Brett's premonitive flashes real or accidental; does the spirit of the dead murderer really inhabit Cujo or does the dog only have a clinical case of rabies? In his previous books, the catalytic children have psi abilities and heroic qualities which are actual in the mind of reader and author, even if other novel characters cannot understand them. In losing his catalytic child as the heroic focus in the novel, King loses his own focus and weakens the impact upon his audience. *Carrie* was an outstanding novel-into-film sui generis; *The Shining* had to be cut in length to fit a theater film format; *Firestarter* like *Carrie* would adapt excellently to a two-hour film format. *Cujo* will never serve for more than a one-hour television feature.

Thomas Tryon's *The Other* (New York: Knopf, 1971), has a title, which describes the problem of choosing the catalytic child hero in his novel. The plot delineates the course of action of a surviving twin boy, Niles Perry, in regard to his family and neighborhood. Originally, the family consisted of a mother, father, two grandmothers, twin sons, Holland and Niles, and an adopted daughter. The novel has a dual point-of-view: that of a first person, obviously writing from a mental hospital and that of a quasi-limited author's view—although third person, it is primarily through Niles' eyes that we see the world. Now the family has been altered by the mysterious accidental death of the father and the madness of the paternal grandmother and has added an aunt and uncle and an unprepossessing male cousin of the twin's age.

What Tryon subtly introduces gradually into the novel and which is not apparent until two-thirds of the novel is that one of the twins has also met an early accidental death. The two boys— Holland, the bad, psychopathic twin, and Niles, the good sensitive, perceptive twin—have now become two aspects of one personality, when earlier they had been one aspect of two.

> ... As twins should, they had been inseparable to begin with. Why, they had shared the same cradle, head to foot—that old wicker cradle, still in the storeroom—until they outgrew it, and then they slept in the same crib. You would have thought they were Siamese twins, so close they were; one being housed in two forms (p. 58).

Niles is a real sensitive, an ability inherited from his Russian grandmother, Ada, who was able to empathize with all of nature.

It is this sensitivity, receptivity, that makes him particularly vulnerable. Niles becomes the physical catalyst for the sins that Holland has not yet committed and which he now unwittingly perpetrates in the dead brother's persona. So Holland is supposedly responsible for the deaths of his father, mother, grandmother, baby niece and cousin, as well as assorted animals. (Holland actually loses his life, drowning his grandmother's cat in the well.)

The spirit of Holland is passed on to the "good" brother in the form of the family seal ring. Niles, urged by Holland's "voice" cuts off the dead boy's finger with the ring and keeps it in a tobacco can. Like Stephen King, Tryon explains his plot on a purely realistic basis—Niles comes from an unstable family and the traumas of the quickly succeeding deaths of his father and dominant twin brother drive him into an extreme form of criminal schizophrenia. Niles finally loses his own identity completely and believes he *is* Holland.

But artistically, Niles-Holland is a catalytic child hero, used by his inner turmoil to perform actions of which he is not aware and for which he has no real responsibility. These actions, which the reader at first assumes are accidental, then comes to believe, are caused by Holland, and finally, in an understanding of the prologue and the epilogue, realizes are the acts of Niles, are excellent novellistic devices.

Joyce Carol Oates has written so prolifically in the modern Gothic mode and with so many characters, that it seems that her children would include several examples of catalytic heroes. But Oates' characters are frequently passive rabbits waiting for the snake of fate or death to strike. They do not cause the plot to progress. The child murderer of *Expensive People* (New York: Vanguard, 1968), appears, at first, to be an ideal candidate for our thesis of the child as catalyst, but he ends the plot, such as it is, rather than advancing it. But in *Bellefleur* (New York: Dutton, 1980), Oates has created the figure of the ultimate catalytic child hero. Germaine Bellefleur is our heroine, and she is conceived at the beginning of the lengthy novel, born well into the novel, and is only four years old at its conclusion.

Bellefleur (Oates said in an interview with Dick Cavett after publication of the novel that she intended the title to be an ironic play of words on Baudelaire's "Fleurs de Mal,") is an extremely complex Gothic-cum-family-cum historical sage. It can best be compared to a mixture of Garcia Marques' *One Hundred Years of Solitude* and Sherwood Anderson's *Winesburg, Ohio.* As in the latter bok, most of the characters are "grotesques"—a characteristic of Oates' characters that adds a dimension not encountered in King's or Tryon's novels.

Oates' novel combines actual historical events of American history with the telling of the story of seven generations of the Bellefleur family of up-State New York, living in a huge castle-like mansion on the shores of the appropriately named Lake Noir. The number of major characters (there is a much-needed geneological chart in the front of the book) and their bizarre lives (a mountain man who spends his whole life seeking God, a boy genius, the inamorata of a vampire, a boy who can turn into a dog, to list only a few) would be even more confusing if it were not for the short life of Germaine holding it together.

Germaine is literally larger than life-size, a semi-divinity who contains both male and female elements. Even before her birth, Leah, her Demeter-like mother, senses her strength: ". . . nothing was so real to her now as certain flashes of sensation—taste, colors, odors, vague impulses and premonitions—which she interpreted as the baby's continuous dreaming deep in *her* body" (pp. 78-79).

Leah's pregnancy lasts more than ten months and she is in labor for three days to produce a female child with the bottom parts of a half-formed twin brother attached to her at the abdomen. (Oates is not concerned with the biological improbability of this monster.) Della, Leah's mother, disposes of the unwanted parts with three chops of her knife and Germaine starts immediately demonstrating her powers on her mother. As she becomes a toddler, more people are influenced by her psi abilities, though she remains a regular child in many ways: she was a baby, yet "intermittently and unpredictably precocious." But as she reaches the eve of her fourth birthday, her "powers" (Oates' quotation marks, p. 512) seem to diminish.

On her birthday, her father breaks his promise to take her for a long-desired ride in his airplane. She senses disaster, but can only watch as he crashes his airplane into the castle, destroying it and killing most of the other Bellefleurs.

But Oates implies that Germaine is just at the beginning of her career as a "femina superior." It is indicated in the novel (and stated by Oates in the Cavett interview), that she will be a true heroine, not just a catalyst used to unify the varying strands of the novel and forward the plot. She is different from most other catalytic children in that her maturity will presumably bring positive fulfillment, not a loss of potency.

The catalytic child can also be found in non-English language novels, for example, in (Gunther Grass' *The Tin Drum*) it may be debatable whether Oskar Mazerath, the hero, is a "child" for the whole Nazi period. But he consciously makes the choice to stunt his own growth at the age of three, so that he may never be an adult, a feat he accomplishes for eighteen years. He is certainly a catalyst, when he plays his drum and shrieks, for he is able to cause reactions, without being himself affected. His drumming and piercing cry causes glass to break and rallies to be disrupted. Though technically only an observer of Hitler's Germany, he represents to a large extent feelings of the many Germans, who did not support the Nazis and who went through an inner emigration. For these people, the Nazi period was a hibernation period, in which spiritual and intellectual growth was stunted, like Oskar's physical growth, until 1945 when Oskar begins to grow again and to find his way into the adult world. Again the close relationships to his mother, grandmother, stepmother and fathers (real and legal) influence his behavior strongly.

Ultimately, all catalytic child heroes share certain characteristics: they are prepubescent and not able to communicate all their cognitions verbally to the adult world; they have psychic abilities beyond that of the average human being; and unfortunately, their powers, though they themselves are innocent, frequently result in the destruction of the world around them or much of it. They provide a marvelous plot device for an author to unite diverse elements and give coherence to his/her novel or to make political and social statements.

More important, perhaps, the popularity of such statements of heroism in our present-day society points toward a deep underlying belief in (to one extent or another) the validity of such characters and readers' interest in them.

Notes

[1] D.H. Lawrence, "The Rocking Horse Winner," in *The Portable D.H. Lawrence* (New York: Viking, 1954), p. 148.

[2] Henry James, "The Turn of the Screw," in the short novels of Henry James, New York: Dodd Meade, 1961, p. 407 ff.

[3] Frank Dodd is the villain of an earlier Stephen King novel, *The Dead Zone* (New York: Viking, 1979).

Unlikely Heroes:
The Central Figures in
The World According to Garp,
Even Cowgirls Get the Blues, and
A Confederacy of Dunces

William Nelson

*T*he *World According to Garp, Even Cowgirls Get the Blues,* and *A Confederacy of Dunces* constitute three highly popular comic-tragic novels. Pocket Books brought out its edition of *The World According to Gary* with covers in six different colors; it remained on the *New York Times* bestseller list for twenty-five weeks. There were Garp T-shirts, hats, headbands, and posters. One critic went so far as to call it a "return of the 'serious' novel to its popular heritage." *Even Cowgirls Get the Blues* was also a best seller, both in hard cover and in a subsequent paper-back issued by Houghton Mifflin. *A Confederacy of Dunces* was a Book-of-the-Month selection, a best-seller, and winner of the Pulitzer Prize for 1981. The hard cover edition published by Louisiana State University Press was followed by a paper-back from Grove Press. Even a brief account of publication data on the three books suggests the wide spread readership of these novels which, because each protagonist is a bizarre individual and each novel a venture into the grotesque, leads to the question: Why such interest in the unusual comic-tragic mode that results? An examination of each of the unlikely heroes is one way of seeking an answer to this question.

Ignatius J. Reilly, the hero of *A Confederacy of Dunces*, is an obese slob with a gluttonous appetite; he wears a wild assortment of clothes, including a green hunter's cap, and being too lazy to work, relies on his mother for support. He has a Master's degree in English from Louisiana State University, writes obscurely about his 'worldview' in Big Chief tablets, and masturbates. This is not the stuff of which heroes are made. Reilly has adopted Boethius's *The Consolation of Philosophy* as a guide; we may presume that it is from Boethius that Reilly's 'worldview' takes its shape. It is clear that Ignatius J. Reilly is a self-indulgent predator on his mother until she herself is ready to have him committed. We are never told exactly what his 'worldview' is but it clearly has little to do with anything that has happened in the world since the 15th century. Reilly wishes for a king and for unreformed churchmen. He finds almost everything in his world lacking in taste and decency although his bringing it to our attention amidst the shambles of his own life is the kind of humor generated when a tramp exaggeratedly imitates the manners of high life in the style of Charlie Chaplin. While prattling of taste and decency, Reilly pushes a cart through the streets of New Orleans from which he consumes far more of the poisonous hot-dogs than he sells. When Fielding refers to Tom Jones as "this rogue, whom we have unfortunately made our hero" (*Tom Jones*, bk. 17, ch. 1) we recognize the irony from the fact that Jones appears to be a rogue but actually will emerge superior to the people around him who are getting by with astounding hypocrisy. Reilly is difficult to fit into a similar pattern although the epigraph to the novel supplies a clue or perhaps an ironic misdirection. "When a true genius appears in the world, you may know him by this sign, that the dunces are all in confederacy against him." (Jonathan Swift, "Thoughts on Various Subjects, Moral and Diverting.) The irony of this statement in relation to Reilly cuts both ways, but Reilly is still the 'true genius' and his tormentors in the book are the dunces. Ignatius J. Reilly's views about the nature of the universe, whatever they may be, are not clearly stated in the novel; however, we do get a sharp definition of his political philosophy. Accused by his mother of being a 'communiss,' Ignatius responds: "What I want is a good, strong monarchy with a tasteful and decent king who has some knowledge of theology and geometry and to cultivate a Rich Inner Life" (p. 232). By implication Reilly rejects much more of contemporary culture than those items which he does condemn specifically with one of his favorite words, "abominations." If his is 'true genius' its manifestations remain a puzzle to the 'dunces.'

Sissy Hankshaw is the unlikely heroine of *Even Cowgirls Get the Blues*; she has been born with outsized thumbs, which, by the time she is eleven, constitute 4% of her body weight. Otherwise she is a tall slim pretty girl of 'model proportions.' Her childhood consists largely of trying to cope with misguided would-be helpers who see her as handicapped and the consciously and unconsciously cruel who call attention to her thumbs by pointedly ignoring them or by making jokes about them. Sissy, attempting to make the best of what she has, adopts a career of hitch-hiking in which the point is not a potential destination but the process itself. Among her other attributes is complete acceptance of her own sexuality and that of everybody else. Sissy is not the American sweetheart, a glorified version of the girl-next-door, or the one who married dear old dad.

As a consequence of her hitch-hiking she is often warned that she may be picked up by an evil man who will take advantage of her. The implication is a world in which evil quite possibly exists so that young women must guard themselves against its occasional manifestation. In her experience, however, every man who picks her up makes some sort of sexual advance. It is hinted that her abnormal thumbs enhance her sexual attractiveness. Sissy permits them to fondle her as they please so long as they keep driving; she simply looks upon it as a fringe benefit of her hitch-hiking hobby. Conventional responses to the situation are inadequate in two regards. They misjudge the sexual nature of the young girl in assuming that she would automatically reject such stimulation and they underestimate the extent of potential child molesters. The result is comic exaggeration, but it also asserts that conventional wisdom fails to understand the true nature of the world. Instead of innocence corrupted by a failure of the norm, there is lack of innocence experiencing the perverse sexuality as a norm and yet refusing to be contaminated by it. Thus Sissy's responses to the circumstances are seen to be more desirable than those of the society which has so far only succeeded in making her virtually an isolate.

Along the way, Sissy meets Julian Gitche, a Mohawk Indian with a Yale degree in Fine Arts; in a comic reversal he is anything but the 'natural' man that he might conventionally be supposed to represent. He has no interest in Indian culture; in fact, he considers it hopelessly archaic even to think about. He also has asthma and is often incapacitated in critical moments by psychosomatic attacks. Their subsequent marriage seems doomed from the start. A trip to the Cowgirls' ranch brings her to a character known as 'The Chink' who is actually a Japanese-American interned during World War II and a continuing refugee from civilized society. Sissy becomes pregnant as a result of a sexual debauch with the Chink and we then learn the symbolism of her gigantic thumbs:

> In a post catastrophic world, your offspring of necessity intermarry, forming in time a tribe .... A tribe of Big Thumbs would relate to the environment in very special ways. It could not use weapons or produce sophisticated tools. It would have to rely on its wits and its senses. It would have to live with animals—and plants!—as virtual equals (p. 357).

Sissy Hankshaw's thumbs provide the key to her destiny as well as to her character and personality. She is forced to find salvation in herself or, as the Chink says: "Be your own master! Be your own Jesus! Be your own flying saucer! Rescue yourself. Be your own valentine!" (p. 227). What this sunny philosophy amounts to in practical application is difficult to say, but the Chink adds, "Each individual must work it out for himself ... gather about him his integrity, his imagination and his individuality and ... leap into the dance of experience" (p. 227). Sissy's thumbs have made it necessary for her to do just that or perish. It is characteristic of all of the cowgirls, who stand for the non-conforming cutting edge of the future in the book, that they are outcasts from the present or at least have the courage of their lack of conviction. The novel implies that only those like Sissy who are among the alienated are likely to be redeemed through the enjoyment of polymorphous sexuality and other attributes of a more natural life style. The world which they experience as insensitive and unsupportive is a world of destruction of the environment, of hypocrisy and sexual perversion, of false values, and a general lack of meaningful interpersonal relationships. Sissy and the other cowgirls comprise fictional representatives of the young of the 60s who referred to themselvs as 'freaks' in contrast to 'straight' society.

T.S. Garp is an even more difficult instance of the unlikely hero; details of his birth and death compare with those of Jesus in a comic-grotesque parody. His conception is the only sexual experience of his mother, Jenny Fields, a nurse who is uninterested in either sex or marriage but who does want a child. The time is 1942. Jenny chooses for her child's father Technical Sergeant Garp, whose shrapnel wounds to the head have left him a vegetable; even then, she waits until she is certain he is soon to die. She is referred to as "Old Virgin Mary Jenny." As Jenny slips into his bed, another wounded soldier in a nearby hospital bed, exclaims, "Christ." The events suggest a comic parallel to the Annunciation. The result of this quasi virgin birth is named T.S.—the initials stand for nothing—Garp. He performs no miracles, but at age thirty-three he is killed by a fanatic feminist. He is intended to be seen as a mutated spiritual hero. His uneasy career illustrates something of the way in which the grotesque functions as a literary device. Garp is a writer who writes of grotesque horrors in order to assuage the horrors of the 'real' world. The narrator says of his death,

> It was a death ... which in its random, stupid and unnecessary qualities—comic and ugly and bizarre—underlined everything Garp had ever written about how the world works (p. 576).

By implication the way the world works requires the comic grotesque to do it justice in literary form and an unlikely hero hovering between the tragic and the absurd to be its chronicler.

The personal relationships in *The World According to Garp* are strained by controversy and catastrophe, but they are also threatened by the UnderToad, a child's erroneous interpretation of 'undertow' about which he had been warned and which has become a family code word for any apprehension of disaster. Garp poured his sense of the horror of events after a crisis in his own life into a book called *The World According to Belsenhaver,* a ghastly story of rape and killing. It is not a narrative parallel to the family tragedy that has happened to the Garps, but it does parallel the way in which Garp feels the world actually works. It is but a short step to assume that John Irving's book is intended to reflect this philosophy, that is, that only the grotesque accommodates to the sense of absurd horror that events in the modern world engender, including the terrible punishments for trivial transgressions and the lack of cosmic justice. According to Philip Thomson in his book *The Grotesque*

> the grotesque ... is an appropriate expression of the problematical nature of existence. It is no accident that the grotesque mode in art and literature tends to be prevalent in societies and eras marked by strife, radical change or disorientation (p. 11).

Just as Ignatius Reilly has Boethius and Sissy Hankshaw has The Chink so Garp has his favorite mentor. One of the chapters in *The World According to Garp* is entitled "The World According to Marcus Aurelius"; the following quotation from the Stoic philosopher is emphasized by repetition:

> In the life of a man, his time is but a moment, his being an
> incessant flux, his sense a dim rushlight, his body a prey of
> worms, his soul an unquiet eddy, his fortune hard, his fame
> doubtful. In short, all that is body is as coursing waters, all that
> is of the soul as dreams and vapors (p. 126 *Garp*).

The outlook of Marcus Aurelius, which clearly has profoundly
affected Garp, leads him to develop a sense of the comic grotesque to
enable him to continue to sustain a little simple dignity in the world.

The world, according to Garp, is an X-rated soap opera; the book
is an illustration of this theme. His best friend is not only a
transsexual, but a transsexual who was formerly a tight-end for the
Philadelphia Eagles. His mother is asexual except for the one
deliberate fertilizing experience which resulted in the birth of Garp.
Garp, after his marriage to Helen, has several sexual entanglements
with baby-sitters, a swapping arrangement with another couple
which began in an effort to keep the other husband from having
affairs with his students, plus a pre-marital affair with Cushy
Percy, the daughter of one of the professors at Steering School where
Garp grew up. There are too many disturbing horrors to recount in
this context, but one especially horrendous sequence is an
automobile accident in which one of Garp's children is killed,
another loses an eye, and Garp's face is shattered. In the other car
involved in the accident his wife is performing fellatio on one of her
students and the impact causes him to lose two-thirds of his penis.
Recounted quickly, the horrors become grotesquely comic; even in
the longer context of the book, they remain a grim reminder that
ghastly events do not occur in the dignified surroundings of
classical tragedy. In the generation after freedom and dignity, what
remains but the grotesque for the tragic writer who cannot, or
doesn't care to, proclaim at the end of his piece that the cosmic order
has been restored or that some transcendent grace has been
established over the human sacrifices?

Yet there is a sense of harmony at the close of the book. The
narrator extrapolates on the lives of the characters, giving brief
synopses of the remainder of their lives, carrying some far beyond
present time. Garp is conceived in 1942; the lives of some characters
are delineated by implication well into the 21st century. Thus the
ending, while it is non-dramatic, restores a sense of perspective over
all the events in the book. If there is no evidence of a cosmic order,
there is a coming to terms with the world as it exists. That Garp is

the major prophet of whatever system of belief is involved in the final harmony is clear from the time structure of the novel. Garp's mother has classifed her World War II patients as Externals (burn victims), Vital Organs (internal injuries), Absentees (head injuries causing mental aberrations) and Goners (some combination of the others). Her granddaughter, Jenny Garp, the one survivor at the close of the book, remembers the classification and adds the corollary, "in the world according to Garp, we are all terminal cases."

All three of these novels contain attitudes or reflections of attitudes that were prevalent during the 1960s. The works extol individualism and excoriate the ways in which ordinary people spend their time—that is, by being well-behaved members of institutions and by conforming to social mores. The novels evoke individual life, not how to conform to social and moral norms, but an assertion of the duty of each person to be an individual because that is the only 'good' one can know. Each novel uses the grotesque comic mode to suggest both affirmation of the primacy of the individual and the acceptance of multiple modes of being, the corollary of individualism. The unlikely hero in each is a bizarre character, one who does not have the romantic aura of the 'lone crusader' or any other heroic stance. There is nothing grandly heroic about the figures nor do they project a private code of honor. They are often the objects of ridicule, including self-ridicule. It is largely through contrast with the alternatives and the fact that the reader sees the events through the main characters' points of view that any sympathy can survive, so perverse is their behavior. Each perspective rejects traditional ways of being in the world. The heroes' often non-rational responses are intended to preserve the individual's right to *be* in a chaotic and irrational universe. The terror of this universe and the hypocrisy or falsification of conventional views of it require the comic mode to accommodate for and to humanize the chaos. Other modes, including the tragic, which implies dignity, transcendence or reconciliation, distort the true nature of the situation as seen by the novels.

In each of the novels the depicted world is a chaotic place and none of its goals ultimately defensible by its inhabitants. Much in the society against which each protagonist has to struggle is destructive to the human spirit. It is a world given over to Chance, to unmanageable changes in the human condition; it is a world of forces that are, if not perverse from some malign agency, become perverse through their out-of-proportion effects on the lives of the characters. As the narrator in that book says, "In the world according to Garp, an evening could be hilarious and the next morning could be murderous" (p. 565). Part of the conclusion to *Even Cowgirls Get the Blues* reads, "I believe in everything; nothing is sacred. I believe in nothing; everything is sacred" (p. 365). This cryptic remark is perhaps more pretentious than profound, but it does suggest a world in which individual perception, however different from any other perception, is all that its inhabitants have to cling to. Only the 'freaks' are attuned to the liberating perception of Reality.

What is said of Sissy Hankshaw might be said of all three of the unlikely heroes:

> Sissy Hankshaw, who, following a suggestion from nature, had created herself and then paraded her creation before ye gods and planets that whirl above our daily routine; Sissy Hankshaw, who proved that grandiose ambition need not be Faustian, at least not for a woman in motion .... Sissy had committed herself to motion and learned that one could alter reality by one's perception of it—and it was that discovery, perhaps no less a one than Einstein's, that finally allowed her to smile away humiliation... (p. 71).

Our world is violent and bizarre. Headlines call attention to aberrations that have become the norms of modern life—the attempted and successful assassinations, the operations of secret police, the corruption in high places. There is a soap opera quality in the seamy sexuality which often surrounds our public figures. The form of our response is not that of a comedy in which there is a reconciliation of social differences nor can the actors sustain the dignity of the tragic mode. The consciousness of such contradiction causes popular literay representations to take the form of the grotesque and their most important characters to be unlikely heroes.

The Changing-Unchanging Heroines and Heroes of Harlequin Romances 1950-1979

Rita C. Hubbard

*I*n 1979 Harlequin Romances sold 168 million copies—an average of five books every single second—to become the most successful line of fiction ever published,[1] and sales of these "brand name" novels increased to 200 million in 1980.[2] Written by women for women, the books have a formula plot that is always the same: the Cinderella story with variations that reflect the interests and attitudes of the period in which they are written. A young, innocent woman of modest means meets and falls in love with a "prince" of a man, affluent, sexy, and domineering. After a series of misunderstandings, love triumphs; without losing her virginity, the heroine by acquiescence wins the hero who raises her up and promises to love her for a lifetime.

For over thirty years, Harlequin Romances, leaders in creating the boom of romance literature specifically marketed for women, have used a profitable heroine-hero combination that has exalted the average, nurturing woman who when awakened by love becomes beautiful, fulfilled and submissive to a powerful super-hero.

The purpose and effect of Harlequin Romances can be conceived in several ways. They are popular escape novels written to entertain and transport readers from their own humdrum worlds to exciting fictional worlds of pleasurable romantic fantasy. In addition, however, they recommend and validate a specific social order. They

171

reaffirm traditional values and mores, and extend the hope of conflictless female happiness with privilege offered as more desirable than equality. For thirty years, their heroes have been distinctly macho and successful in breaking the wills of smitten females. The heroines, though increasing in spirit and feistiness over the years, have all rejected feminine liberation, each choosing instead to be her hero's "Other." In this way, then, the novels can be conceived as rhetorically reactionary. Millions of copies per year are circulated, often to more than one reader, and each bears the implicit message: traditional women (Harlequin heroines) merit eternal love; liberated women (the heroines' foils who lose the heroes' love) taste ashes. And a real hero has money, power, brooding sexuality and enough physical strength to subdue the most willful female. He makes the rules and accepts no back-talk.

An analysis of Harlequin Romances, based on a random sample of 30 novels from the decades 1950-1979, the women who write them, the women who read them, plotlines of the novels and, most importantly, the heroines and heroes who populate them, is revealing.

Fred Kerner, Harlequin's Vice President for Publishing, reports that no man has been successful in writing a Harlequin Romance. "Men just can't seem to get the female viewpoint."[3] According to *Duns Review*, the authors are "a factory of 140 women writers."[4] But the term "factory" is misleading. These female authors do not work for a wage or "turn out the pages." Their works are artistic wholes, each written by a single woman. The books are purchased directly from the authors, published first by Mills and Boon Limited of London, and then reissued by Harlequin Books. However, there is a sense in which Harlequin Romances are produced by a stable of writers. Many of the authors do write numerous Harlequin Romances.[5] In fact, in a special 1979 edition celebrating their thirty years of publishing, Harlequin Books printed reflections of twenty-nine of their most prolific authors, women from England, New Zealand, Australia, the United States, Canada, Ireland and South Africa.[6]

Most of the authors are beyond their middle years. Of these twenty-nine, twenty-three report that they are married, sixteen have children, seven speak of moves related to their husbands' occupations, and all twenty-nine concentrate on family information in their copy, mentioning some or all of the following: parents, brothers and sisters, children, children's marriages, grandchildren, family illnesses. Seven indicate that they began writing when the children slept or when the children entered school or when their husbands urged them to turn their "scribbling" into serious writing; three report specifically that their husbands and children approve of their writing "hobby." The authors reflect on their homes, their gardens, their husbands' careers and job-related moves, their children, their extended families and their travels. Except for references to World War II, they do not speak of social, economic, political or philosophical issues. On balance, these twenty-nine prolific authors, with rare exceptions, are traditional women with visions and values derived from the first half of the 20th century. They are not, for the most part, college-educated or trained in journalism, and most held service jobs before their marriages as nurses, teachers, secretaries and clerks. They are not, in fact, very different from their readers.

Harlequin Romances, translated into 18 languages, are read by millions of women in 80 countries. Harlequin Books claims to have 14 to 16 million readers in the United States alone, and these women constitute a broad cross-section of women from 15 through 90, with the average age between 40 and 44. Fred Kerner offers some specifics: "About half the readers are married women. About half are working women. The average educational level is just about or slightly above the U.S. norm—secondary school and a little more. Average income is just about exactly the U.S. norm."[7]

Harlequin Romances may be read by men in various countries, but Kerner considers its male readers to be "just a smattering." For this reason, he says marketing research is done specifically among women with surveys at various levels: an on-going questionnaire for reader monitoring, placement tests such as those given by the National Family Opinion Poll to determine what is read and how much, a vast sampling program with non-related products like Lux Liquid from which a cross-ruff is done with a way of gathering information from a questionnaire in the back of each book, and additional follow-ups with those who respond from the sampling program.[8]

The bottom line is that sufficient research is done so that Harlequin Romances are written by women who are in tune with their readers, and the readers' tastes and responses are carefully monitored so that the books written and published are those the readers want. The Harlequin formula then is a direct response to a particular articulated consumer preference for specific cherished love fantasies.

What is most interesting in the plotlines and in the dimensions of heroes and heroines is that while there are distinct differences in the rendering of the Cinderella formula in each decade, the final outcome in each plot is identical so that there is a consistency of message.

In the 1950s, the Harlequin formula is acted out by a heroine who is truly an unassuming "Cinderella," modest, humble and willing to be dominated by a superior hero. Indeed, she considers it her privilege to serve him; she is grateful when he chooses to make her his adoring and obedient wife. In the 1960s, the Harlequin formula underwent a change. A "feisty Cinderella" emerged. She is as pure as her predecessor of the 1950s, but she lacks humility and must be subdued by the superior hero before she acquiesces to him as ruler. In the 1970s, the Harlequin formula employed a "virgin temptress," articulate and more determined to manage her own life than her sister of the 1960s. She engages in real battles with the hero, but eventually she not only bows to his superior strength of body and will but declares that she likes to be dominated.

So Loved and So Far, for example, an all-time favorite by Elizabeth Hoy, first appeared in 1954 and was issued in its seventh printing in 1980. It is typical of Harlequin Romances of the 1950s with a heroine, a lowly social secretary in England, who falls in love with a handsome, wealthy horseman described as far above her in social status. She loves him from afar and despairs because she thinks he loves another. Her despair turns to bewilderment as from time to time his fingers tighten painfully on her wrist, as he swings her around and kisses her savagely. She wonders if he thinks she is a "cheap little flirt." Finally, she understands that he is in pain from his sexual longing for her and his fear that she loves another. It seems incredible to her, but he wants to marry her. She protests humbly at various times, "I am not of your world. I cannot talk to you as these other women of your acquaintance do of hunting and riding and traveling."[9] And, "I am young, insignificant; I've been nowhere, done nothing. While you are ... famous...."[10] And finally, "I am not nearly ... important enough to ... be your ... wife"[11] Rich color rushes up into her face as she brings out the incredible word and he tells her that miracles have only begun.

The heroine of this novel is typical of the 1950s heroines who are young, small, ordinary, low in self-esteem, isolated from family and friends, and pure but sexually ripe. And she interacts with the typical 1950s hero, invariably tall and handsome, affluent, powerful, arrogantly commanding, sullenly mysterious, passionate and emotionally in need of a woman who will transform his meaningless passion into a complete love relationship.

The heroine who emerges in the 1960s Harlequin Romances has the same traits as the 1950s heroine but some appear in differing measure because she is, additionally, articulate, at times calculating, and temporarily feisty. In *House of the Winds*, by Roumelia Lane, first published in 1968 and issued in a fourth printing in 1980, we can observe the newer heroine, in this case the small, young orphan who admits that she would have gotten a fuller education if she had the brains. She tricks a big game hunter in Tanzania into taking her on safari into the African bush so that she can photograph wild animals and gain stature in her career. He becomes angry and abusive because he is dead set against taking women on such dangerous trips, and he scoffs at her ambitions. Unlike heroines of the 1950s, this one can drive a car, speak her mind and brave dangers. As the plot unfolds in the African bush, however her feistiness and ambition diminish as the strong, gruff hero rescues her six times from wild animals, the elements, and other threats to her life, each time offering insults as he grabs her roughly out of danger. Finally, he adds to the later rescues his hard kisses which kindle frightening sparks in him and in her. They almost "go too far" but she proves her virtue. She abandons camera and career eventually, promises to be his obedient wife, and to follow him to Nyumbaya, even though she doesn't know what their life will be like there. He promises eternal love, to care for her, and to give her children as they walk hand in hand toward the whispering waves, taking their "first steps in this new and wonderful world that was love."[12]

The hero of the 1960s differs from the hero of the 1950s in two respects only: 1) he must prove his power in order to achieve authority over the heroine; and 2) he is more aggressive in testing her self-control and purity. He continues to operate as the rule-maker, as did the 1950s hero, but now he must engage in both verbal and nonverbal persuasion to enforce his rules; he must subdue the heroine before she accepts his superiority.

The plot ends, however, in the same way it ended a decade earlier. Though the heroine must be converted to docility in short skirmishes, she eventually bows to the hero's superiority, and the traditional gender arrangements come into play with the male as provider-protector and rule-maker, and the female as his supportive "Other," happy in her position as his privileged love.

The Cinderella formula undergoes further changes in the 1970s as the heroine becomes a stronger and more confident woman, militant in her demands for equality and aware of her sexual urges. She engages in determined struggles with the hero who must use both argumentation and power displays to subdue her and achieve a dominant position.

The Crescent Moon, by Elizabeth Hunter, published first in 1973 and reissued in a fourth printing in 1980, illustrates the changes. In this Harlequin Romance, a small, dark, young shorthand-typist meets a famous, wealthy, commanding university professor, and though she feels the swift strong stirrings of passion she cannot accept his chauvinistic attitude. "I believe in complete equality," she asserts.[13] And so the male-female sparring begins and continues throughout the novel as he presses his points. "There is no such thing as equality between us," he declares.[14] "I don't like ambitious females."[15] "Wouldn't you rather be the chattel of a man than the equal of a mouse?" he asks.[16] And with confidence, he says: "You'll find yourself a better follower than a leader when we finally do come to terms."[17] And he is right. As he takes an "unhurried toll of her lips" and proposes marriage, she recants:

> In any argument between them he would always win hands down. They both knew that physically he could dominate her any time he chose. If he stopped to ask her, the result would be just the same; he would demand and she would submit and would delight in her own weakness. You could call it chemistry, or the way that things were meant to be, but she wouldn't like it at all if it were the other way about![18]

So we see that the formula changes as do the heroines and heroes. The humble heroine of the 1950s who did not even know the name of the stirrings within her evolves in the 1970s into a woman more easily moved to recognized passion and confident in her aspirations to equality. Her hero as he evolves, moreover, must by both talk and action dispel these notions of equality and establish their love relationship on the traditional base of male-female complementarity with himself as the leader and his surrendering heroine as his pure, persuasible and grateful partner. Of particular note is the heroine's expressed gratitude for her luck in attracting the superior male. As stated by the heroine in *The Crescent Moon*, "I've never done anything to deserve you, and I probably never shall, but I will try to be all you want all my life long."[19]

This analysis of Harlequin Romances[20] confirms the theories of John Cawelti in some measure but not fully. His book *Adventure, Mystery and Romance* advances four inter-related hypotheses about the dialectic between formulaic literature and the culture that produces it.[21] He states that formula stories: 1) affirm existing interests and attitudes of those who read them, 2) resolve tensions and ambiguities arising from conflicting interests and values within a given culture, 3) enable readers to explore in fantasy the boundary between what is permitted and what is forbidden and the possibility of stepping over that line, and 4) assist in the process of assimilating change. Harlequin Romances do these things but within certain definite limits.

First, they affirm the existing interests and attitudes of the readers for whom they are written. They affirm the interests and attitudes of those in society who hold to traditional gender roles, but they do not reflect many gender role changes already accepted by a large group in Western society.

Second, they resolve the tensions and ambiguities arising from conflicting interests and values within a given culture. They do this by reaffirming the "old ways." There is some compromise in them which permits the introduction of the new feminine thrust for equality but then quells it quickly and converts the heroine to traditional postures.

Third, they enable readers to explore in fantasy the boundary between what is permitted and that which is forbidden and the possibility of stepping over the line. They do this by exhibiting heroines who challenge male authority in progressively stronger ways but who stop short of an attempt at real equality because they are incapable of it. Harlequin Romances cast the heroine as so inferior to the hero that her incapacities limit her challenge.

Fourth, they assist in the process of assimilating change but only to a limited extent. Most of the multiple social changes that have occurred over the last 30 years are excluded from their pages. Their heroines have not grown in education or career status as have many real women. Divorce and other threats to the nuclear family are ignored, as are social, economic and political changes. The novels continue to portray a tranquil upper-class world free of conflict except for the skirmishes over gender roles which are won easily by powerful heroes who reject equalitarianism.

Harlequin Romances stop short of recognizing many real changes in society or integrating them into their formulaic plotlines. They reflect cultural shifts by their recognition of greater militancy in female attitudes, but they take a stand against these attitudes and against changes in social mores and social institutions. They argue against changes which they consider dangerous, namely changes in gender roles and changes in the distribution of power.

There are several conclusions which can be drawn. An extraordinarily popular line of "brand name" fiction, the novels have created for all practical purposes a separate business within the paperback industry. Over 2,500 titles have been marketed, and Harlequin Books presently dominates approximately 28 percent of the U.S. paperback market. Though they include travel and occasional adventure, Harlequin Romances provide basically stories of male/female relationships. Their readers are millions of women, most of whom as determined by publisher's research are average in education and income. And these formula novels, written by women for women, are constructed to suit the taste of their readers who are carefully monitored for their opinions and responses.

The Harlequin heroines and heroes are specialized heroines and heroes created for a specific audience. Though each is superficially different, they have stereotypic clusters of characteristics identifying them. The Harlequin heroine is simple, pure and nurturing, the embodiment really of the positive woman extolled by Phyllis Schlafly in *The Power of the Positive Woman*.[22] Her overriding need is to love and to provide a home for her man; she is emotional, intuitive, faithful, monogamous, physically and intellectually inferior to men though superior to them in moral standards. And, just as the Harlequin heroine is uniformly expressive, the Harlequin hero is uniformly instrumental. He is older than the heroine, successful, strong, aggressive, passionate, intelligent, capable of making rules and enforcing them. Though he is sexually experienced, he relies on his virginal bride to transform his meaningless passion into elevated love. And these two, heroine and hero, establish in each novel a female/male complementarity which confines them rigidly to tradiional gender roles.

But though the Harlequin Romances are rhetorically reactionary, their arguments against the changes fostered by the new feminism cannot be laid at the feet of the male establishment. There is something in the romantic fantasies created by women authors which obviously satisfies a relatively large segment of the female population, women who can identify with or who wish to identify with the simple Cinderella who is raised up by a handsome powerful prince of a man and finds happiness as his significant and obedient "Other."

During their three decades of existence, Harlequin Romances

have basically affirmed the existing interests and attitudes of their faithful readers, and beginning in the 1960s they have resolved within their formulas tensions and ambiguities arising from the women's movement, allowing the female readers to explore in fantasy rebelliousness to male domination while at the same time bringing both heroine and reader to the novel's denouement when the heroine acquiesces to carefully structured male superiority. Their message is clear: though male/female relationship style may change, it is a man's world. The woman who accepts this "gets her man," a man who will raise her up and cherish her forever. Ultimately, privilege is better than equality for the Harlequin Woman.

These novels then promote the ideology of heterosexual romantic love which has its roots in the courtly tradition of the Middle Ages, a tradition based on the supreme value of love between the sexes, an overwhelming passionate love that can lead to bliss or misery, a love inspired by the beauty and character of the loved one, and striking suddenly.

While men's fantasy literature reflects their choice of rugged, powerful, aggressive heroes who frequently treat sex as a physical event, the popularity of Harlequin Romances indicates that romance evolving into permanent love and marriage is still a powerful and perhaps primary female fantasy. Elitist literature may treat love cynically, but Harlequin Romances do not. Romantic love is so desirable that Harlequin heroines pay the price of submission to guarantee it.

Notes

[1] "Harlequin: The Fastest-Growing Line of Paperbacks in the World," *Publisher's Weekly*, 29 Aug. 1980, p. 117.
[2] Rebecca Sinkler, "Pop Romances Under Scrutiny," *Philadelphia Inquirer*, 8 Mar. 1981, Sec. 3, p. 47, cols. 2-6.
[3] Telephone interview with Fred Kerner.
[4] "Harlequin Enterprises: Cashing in on 'Hard-Core' Decency," *Duns Review*, Mar 1978, p. 32.
[5] Ibid., p. 33.
[6] *Thirty Years of Harlequin:* (Toronto: Harlequin Books, 1979), pp. 155-253.
[7] Letter received from Fred Kerner, 28 Oct. 1980.
[8] Telephone interview with Fred Kerner.
[9] Elizabeth Hoy, *So Loved and So Far* (Toronto: Harlequin Books, 1980 Seventh Printing), p. 14.
[10] Ibid., p. 15.   [11] Ibid., p. 189.
[12] Roumelia Lane, *House of the Winds* (Toronto: Harlequin Books, 1980 Fourth Printing), p. 190
[13] Elizabeth Hunter, *The Crescent Moon* (Toronto: Harlequin Books, 1980 Fourth Printing), p 13.
[14] Ibid., p. 71.   [15] Ibid., p. 41.   [16] Ibid., p. 126.
[17] Ibid., p. 71.   [18] Ibid., p. 120.   [19] Ibid., p. 186.

Superhero:
The Six Step Progression

Hal Blythe and Charlie Sweet

Amerca is obsessed with heroes and anti-heroes. Naturally this is reflected in that unique American genre, the comic. The staple of the comic book industry is the superhero, who has been developed in three eras: the Golden Age (1938 through World War II), the Cold War Age, and the Marvel Age. For practical purposes we are going to treat only the one with which the majority of us are familiar, the third stage, and mostly the company that lends its name to the age, Marvel Comics.

In September 1961, Stan Lee's *The Fantastic Four* was the big bang of the Marvel Universe. Its echoes signaled that henceforth the plethora of horror titles which reflected the previous decade's Cold War fears of foreign invasion and/or nuclear energy were to be replaced by comics featuring the superhero. With the ascension of King Kennedy to his Camelot on the Potomac, America conquered much of its fear. We began to look forward to the New Frontiers of space and atomic energy, mercurially launching Alan Shepherd into orbit and harnessing the atom to generate electricity at Oak Ridge and to treat cancer at Brookhaven. Marvel Comics mirrored this new hope. In *The Comic-Stripped American,* Asa Berger claims that in Marvel "Despite the violence and terror in the comics they display an underlying optimism about man's possibilities."[1] Gradually the BEMs (Bug Eyed Monsters) were replaced by super-powered figures. Thor took over from Thomgorr, and Antman supplanted the giant anteater. Interestingly, many of Marvel's new heroes debuted in the very titles they would replace: *Journey Into Mystery* became *The Mighty Thor*; *Amazing Fantasy* switched to *The Amazing Spiderman* and *Strange Tales* was supplanted by *Dr. Strange.*

More specifically, Marvel's superheroes appearing on the scene from 1961-1965 demonstrated America's ability in part to deal with both invaders and nuclear energy. The origins of the twenty superheroes created during this period (i.e., heroes who would have their own titles) illustrate that aliens and the atom can be benefactors of mankind. In particular, the Marvel Bullpen (Stan Lee, Jack Kirby and Steve Ditko for the main part) developed two types of superheroes, the Benevolent Alien and the Nuclear-spawned Mutant.

Marvel's shift to the superhero was representative of the entire industry, for DC was reviving the Flash, Green Lantern and the Atom, while Charlton brought out their costumed adventurers like The Blue Beetle. Obviously, then, comic books reflect their culture, but what is needed, as Thomas Inge suggests, is not another cultural exploration but a serious study of the comic medium: "the comics are also of importance unto themselves, as a form of creative expression apart from their relationship to other forms of art. This is the most difficult area to write about because we lack a critical vocabulary and have not even begun to define the structural and stylistic principles behind comic art."[2]

A good place to start is the superhero comic, for it is a highly restricted form. First, comic books are aimed at primarily juvenile audience. Jim Shooter, the general editor of Marvel at the present, is fond of quoting a market study that revealed the median age of his company's readers as 11.8. A recent study found that 90-99% of American children read comic books. And, while that audience is changing, it is still predominantly male. Furthermore, because of the juvenile audience, the Comic Magazine Association of America created in 1954 the famous Comics Code Authority. While its extremely rigid guidelines have been loosened, the industry still toils under its strictures. No other popfic genre is comparably limited in what it can and can't do. That each story must be told within 17-20 pages (or multiples thereof) provides an additional stricture.

The situation of each superhero story is essentially the same. Society is threatened by a powerful menace. The stakes are high. Only a superpowered hero can stop the threat, and the resultant battle will be simplified into a war between good and evil.

Out of this basic situation, a conventional pattern develops. Generally the superhero plot breaks down into a six-step progression, although the order of the steps may vary and a great deal of latitude for development exists within each step.

The story usually opens *in medias res* (in the middle of things) like in the Classical epic, which was in itself heavily formulaic. A menace attacks. The menace is usually more than a common criminal. It may be a supervillain (Dr. Doom), aliens (the Dire Wraiths), a crime cartel (AIM) or a monster (The Blockbuster). Sometimes the initial attack is delivered by an agent of the larger menace (an android or an underling in Hydra); only later is the superior, guiding force discovered. Like the villains themselves, the motive for the attack is often masked. A seemingly simple bank robbery is actually perpetrated to obtain funds needed to finance the Ultimate Weapon. A seemingly insignificant character's abduction is part of the Dire Wraiths' scheme to replace a key personage. A break-in may be accomplished to obtain plans for an important piece of equipment or the equipment itself. Behind the initial attack always looms a larger plan that threatens no less than the very fabric of society or even the existence of the world (Galactus).

In any case the menace is so powerful it is more than the victim, the authorities or society can handle. The Commissioner Gordons of the world, realizing their impotence in the face of the overwhelming threat, summon the superhero. This call constitutes an admission by society of the strictures of legal or physical laws under which it functions.

So the superhero appears. Although some heroes are called (by the aforementioned authorities, the victim, or even the haughty villain), some happen on the menace. In a city of twelve million or so, isn't it extraordinary how often Spiderman can swing upon a crime in progress? Occasionally Lois Lane or Sue Dibny is threatened, but usually a superhero is not personally involved with the victim (with TV, on the other hand, Simon and Simon or Magnum almost always come to the aid of a coworker, a college chum, etc.). During this involvement, the superhero may foil the menace temporarily or the menace may gain a partial victory but always the ultimate menace remains at large to continue its master plan so that good and evil may continue to struggle.

Like his counterpart in the detective story, the superhero begins an investigation, the pursuit phase. Sometimes this process involves finding and tracing physical evidence (Batman). Sometimes it uses technology (Spidey's tracer). sometimes it necessitates a patrol of a crime area—past, known, or suspected (Captain America). Sometimes surveillance is needed (Green Arrow). Sometimes the investigation is only possible because of the superhero's powers (Superman's x-ray vision, Green Lantern's power ring). Regardless of its methods, though, the investigation is secondary, certainly not as important as in a Holmes or a Miss Marple mystery and certainly not as important as the next stage, the confrontation. Furthermore, the investigation is aimed at discovering the menace, not the menace's motive. That is, the socio-economic forces surrounding the menace (e.g. poverty, industrial responsibility for waste) are either non-existent or tangential, much in the manner that the early nineteenth-century Romances never dealt with man in society. The result of the investigation is ultimately, then, not so much *why* or *who*. The important things are *where* or *when* might the menace strike again and/or how might it be flushed out.

The heart of every story is the confrontation between the superhero and the supervillain. Because comic plots follow the inevitable cycle of pursuit-capture-escape, this meeting may occur in several mounting stages or at the tale's climax (sometimes, as in Captain America's search for his real past or Roy Thomas' tying up of the Thor legend, the adventure may take several issues). This confrontation is often the result of the hero's investigation/pursuit of the villain or vice-versa, as in a story where the villain wants revenge on the hero. The confrontation is primarily physical, and because of the superpowers of the villain the victory is in question. Indeed, the superhero's life can be in jeopardy (e.g. Shiva is as powerful as Thor; Galactus is stronger than the Fantastic Four). If the confrontation is part of a mounting series of encounters, the hero may even be captured. Of course, he then escapes and the cycle continues.

Although the final confrontation, like previous minor skirmishes, is basically physical, the factor that tips the scales in the hero's favor is not. Ultimately the victory over evil is achieved through mental, not physical superiority. Comics place a premium on intelligence, and in the end the hero outthinks the villain. Thor, realizing Shiva's prowess, outwits him by shifting the scene of battle to the Thunder God's familiar universe. The Fantastic Four find an alternate world or source of energy for Galactus. In fact, in this element, the hero's intelligence, the comic plot has the greatest opportunity for innovation, or what Cawelti calls invention. Perhaps the major variant in the entire superhero formula is the mental means by which the hero asserts his superiority, gaining the victory for good over evil.

The final phase of the plot as in all popfic is the restoration of order. With the villain defeated, society returns to its normal functioning—until the next menace appears and the cycle begins anew.

Not only is the plot formulaic, but the superhero is streotypical. In popfic the protagonist is basically an idealized self-image of the typical reader. Representing the optimum development of the reader's positive traits, the hero is someone with whom the reader can readily identify.

Obviously a superhero by definition has super powers. These range from the high development of human skills (Batman's mental and physical prowess), to a single super power (The Flash's speed), to many powers (Superman). Regardless of the development of his powers, the superhero uses them in a positive manner—for good. Interestingly, comic books in which the protagonist(s) used powers for evil—as in *Supervillain Teamup, The Secret Society of Super-villains* and *The Joker*—did not last.

The superhero is human. Readers find it difficult to identify with robots (*Machine Man*), aliens (*Hawkman, Captain Marvel,* J'onn J'onzz), animals (*The Swamp Thing*) gods (Adam Warlock), or spirits (Deadman). The Hulk is an animal, but he constantly reverts to Dr. Bruce Banner. Thor is a god, but because he is a child of Mother Earth, his human identity as Dr.Don Blake comes naturally. Conversely, Submariner and Aquaman, though half-human, have always teetered on the edge of success, for they have no everyday identity. Superman is an alien, but he has adopted an earthly identity complete with parents, education, job and problems. The Thing, possibly an exception, was still once human, expresses very human qualities (e.g. anger, love, sense of humor), is always teamed with human superheroes, and actually returns temporarily to his human form once a year.

Closely related to this humanness is the secret identity of the superhero. This everyday persona makes reader identification possible, and so when Mr. Commonman is transformed into Captain Superhero the reader can follow right along. When the hero has solely a superpowered self, there can be no identification; the reader/hero gap is too great. Interestingly, superheroes without everyday identities have not fared well. Witness the fate of Plasticman, Omega, The Inhumans, Submariner and Aquaman.

The superhero's powers are limited. If the hero were omnipotent, there would be no possibility for conflict since no one could oppose him. Moreover, when a god is pitted against another god the reader can identify with neither. So, as in Kirby's *New Gods, Forever People* and *The Eternals*, the reader loses interest. On the other hand, Thor, a demi-god, is limited by his human self and by Odin. Superman is vulnerable to kryptonite, and, more recently to make him even more limited, magic; even his human emotions (e.g. love for Lois) can place him in jeopardy.

The superhero is also an adult, white male who holds a white-collar job in his secret identity. In this third age of comic book superheroes, the costumed kids who once served as partners have for the most part disappeared. Robin has gone to college, and Speedy has dropped out. Today heroes like Peter Parker and Johnny Storm have grown up. Nova blew out, while Firestorm is part teen, part adult. Perhaps the 11.8 year-old reader wishes like Billy Batson to become a marvelous man capable of controlling his own destiny. Maleness, adulthood, whiteness, and white-collar positions are, after all, what our society reveres. Black heroes (Black Panther, Black Goliath, Black Lightning, the Falcon) don't seem to appeal to a predominantly white readership; they are not role models. Neither are females for this basically male audience. If women are teamed with males (Justice League of America, Avengers, Defenders) or lead subservient roles in their secret identities (Wonder Woman), they seem to be successful. Liberated women don't seem to make it— remember the cancelled Ms. Marvel, SpiderWoman and She-Hulk? White-collar jobs (TV newsmen, corporation heads, lawyers) are to what readers aspire—who wants to grow up and be a junkman (Ragman)?

Just as the superhero is physically strong, he is morally superior. His acts spring from his very nature as a superhero (whose major motive is to do good), and thus these acts are beyond questioning by the reader. Batman, for instance, has such moral carte blanche that when he breaks into the evil psychologist's office no reader thinks of the illegality, of the Watergate, implications. The Avengers can do anything, go anywhere with impunity because they carry a Shield priority A-1 card. The reader does not care how often the superhero transgresses man's petty laws, for the hero operates under a higher law that always has the ultimate good of society at its center.

The superhero functions amid other conventional comic book types—the limited authorities, the sidekick (passe), the super-villain, the victim, and the supporting cast. The supervillain, for instance, is the antithesis of the superhero, his image reflected in a dark mirror. Perhaps another study will center on the supporting characters' tangential role in the superhero formula.

The setting of a superhero comic is likewise stylized. Obviously a reader finds it easier to project himself into a contemporary setting. Comics which treated the past—either the 30s (*Doc Savage, The Avenger, The Shadow*), World War II (*Steel, The Invaders*), or the 50s (*The 3-D Man*)—did not make it. Likewise, future settings as in *Kamandi, War of the Worlds* and *2001* cannot be sustained. The contemporary locale is basically urban America, whether a real city (New York is the favorite) or a fictitious Metropolis. Doubtless, the reader can more readily accept the conflict of good and evil in the Gotham Cities of Comicdom than set against the edenic rural landscape. Even Dracula had his coffin shipped from his native Transylvania to Boston. And The Hulk may wander across America, but he always returns to the city. Interestingly, comic heroes striving in space (*Shade, Starman*) or the sea (Aquaman and Subby) could not stay afloat.

Thus, a distinct comic book superhero formula consisting of conventional situations, plots, characters and settings exists. Importantly, this formula does not constitute a narrow, inflexible list of do's and don'ts for writers nor is it a pejorative statement about comic quality. It is rather a descriptive framework of the general patterns found in the subgenre. When a reader picks up *Captain Superhero*, he has certain expectations, though they may not be consciously spelled out, and if they are not fulfilled he is apt to be disappointed. The reader has not made an innate qualitative value judgment; his taste has simply been thwarted. When we go to McDonald's, we expect a Big Mac. If we are served a filet mignon, no matter how exquisite, we are dissatisfied at not receiving what we expected.

The success or failure, then, of any superhero comic depends more than we have realized not on some nebulous standard of "good" or "bad," but rather on its adherence to the formula. There is, as we have pointed out, room for innovation within the formula. Most certainly, stories can deal with the hero's motivations (*why* he fights for good), his relationship with other characters, and even his concern with moral issues, but innovations can exist only within the framework of convention.

The concept of the superhero formula provides such a framework. The formula, what Inge calls for, is also a doorway to understanding what's going on in the comics. This knowledge gives the reader a foundation which allows him to specify in common terminology what has previously seemed a matter of pure personal taste. Now when he comes to a story that seems different but effective, he has a definite mechanism for analyzing what it is that makes the work innovative and thus appealing.

Notes

[1]New York: Walker Publishing Co., 1973), p. 207.
[2]" 'Introduction' to the Comics as Culture," *Journal of Popular Culture*, 12 (1979), 637.

The Cultural Roots of our Current Infatuation with Television's Befuddled Hero

Elizabeth S. Bell

*T*ime is no longer measured in hours, but into segments such as family hour and prime time. Children today adopt Farah Fawcett or Fonz hairstyles, just as their parents embraced Davy Crockett coonskin caps and Dale Evans fringe. Football, basketball, and baseball are no longer sports, but mega-businesses of proportions that boggle the mind. Dinner time no longer supports conversation, but provides background for the daily news reports. Like it or not, we live with television, and its content affects how we look, act, feel, and think.

Its daily schedule requires a steady stream of new scripts and fresh concepts. Prime time has become so hungry for winners and ratings that it has left little time for behind-the-scenes gestation for programs and characters. Instead it has relied on accepted formulas and stereotypes that have succeeded in the past for its entertainment staples. Traditionally television has found these commodities within the pages of our literary works, and it has adapted in simplistic form the heroes, rascals and scamps created for other genres.

In fact, traditionally television as a medium has oversimplified our national literature, lifting from it two distinct and separate strands of protagonists—the heroes and the clowns—which have until reently remained separate orders of creation. These formulas have entertained us season after season, in different costumes, with different names, but in forms easily recognizable from series to series. Currently, however, television has tampered with its

188

formulas by blending the two, and in so doing has created a fresh and appealing television protagonist who can only be described as the befuddled hero, capable of saving the world, but not quite adept at handling the requirements of everyday life. With this new breed of television hero, the 1982 season has capitalized on a synthesis of two very strong elements of American literary and cultural tradition.

The first of these two strands—the one which gives us the traditional television hero—is based on our nationally avowed respect for the rugged individual who is both self-sufficient and self-reliant. He represents our national self-concept, for he is embodied in the image of the colonists carving a new life from the wilderness and settling a new, unexplored and isolated continent. Willliam Bradford's *History of Plimmoth Plantation* (1650, 1856) describes the perils he faces and the resilience he displays when pitted against overwhelming odds. Puritan diaries document the seriousness with which he undertakes his mission—to set up a new Eden on earth, fulfilling the requirements, as Perry Miller pointed out in his book of the same name, of his "errand into the wilderness." The hero appears again as the patriot formulating a new nation from the symbols of English common law and America's newly formed cultural identity. We see him in Franklin's *Autobiography* (1771, 1788). He cries aloud to us from the pamphlets of Thomas Paine and Phillip Freneau. Thomas Jefferson gave him sustenance and voice in our *Declaration of Independence* and other precedent-shattering documents.

In fictional form the American individualist is immortalized as James Fennimore Cooper's Natty Bumppo—the Deerslayer, Hawkeye, Leatherstocking—who sets the pattern for fictional heroes to come. He sings in Whitman's "Song of Myself" and fights injustice through the personas of Hamlin Garland and Frank Norris. He has appeared consistently in our entertaining media as the staple of adventure drama from the dime novels of last century to the John Wayne movies of mid-century to the Cartwright brothers, Peter Gunn, Marcus Welby and Lou Grant of the television era.

Although these characters share an obvious streak of nonconformity and disregard of the conventional modes of behavior, they also embody a fundamental purity borne of their recognition of the intangible values of life and of their own inherent honesty and sense of duty. They share a belief that they recognize rightness and that their duty lies in correcting the wrongs that confront them. Week after week, season after season, they pursue with single-minded determination justice in its many guises. The Ponderosa and the *Tribune* city room seem very similar and their occupants become as one.

The hero's origins lie deep in our past and owe their relevance to the particular history of America. Sacvan Bercovitch hypothesizes the importance of the Puritan heritage in the development of our national self-image and hence the formulation of the hero. His *Puritan Origins of the American Self* (1975) discusses "the celebration of the representative self as America, and of the American self as the embodiment of a prophetic universal design" (p. 136). His construction posits, among other things, that the American self-image developed from the union of the allegorical with the historical—in other words, with the conjunction of the Puritan sense of mission with the real opportunities involved in settling a wilderness. R.W.B. Lewis goes even further in his analysis, *The American Adam* (1955), to point out that the American was essentially without a national past and, hence, like Adam before the fall faced the future with an innocence and a sense of possibility, again because of the conjunction of symbol and history: "... the American myth saw life and history as just beginning" (p. 5). Lewis contends also that the hero image developed from this, creating "the hero of the new adventure: an individual emancipated from history, happily bereft of ancestry, untouched and undefiled by the usual inheritances of family and race; an individual standing alone, self-reliant and self-propelling, ready to confront whatever awaited him with the aid of his own unique and inherent resources" (p. 5).

This character in fictional form has provided the substance for television protagonists. Over the years they have demonstrated an unswerving dedication to "truth, justice, and the American way." They have captured our admiration, at least in the abstract, while they have provided vicarious adventures for us. They are our serious heroes and represent part of our television fare.

The second literary branch represents a more comic tradition and produces a protagonist with an entirely different personality— the lovable clown. This character begins with the likes of Rip Van Winkle, but reaches full flower in the Southern humor format. As Wade Hall tells us in *The Smiling Phoenix* (1965), the characters in Southern humor draw on nostalgia, on our own wistfulness for what used to be, to become comic stereotypes. Thus in the best of our humor there is a touch of poignancy. Hall finds support for this contention in Max Herzberg's and Leon Mones' *Humor in America* (1945) which labels a great deal of humor as "a gentle playing in our memories" (pp. 398-9). Comic protagonists from this part of the tradition inspire sympathetic laughter instead of ridicule.

Television has from its beginning adopted this stipulation for its formula. Its clowns have been almost to a person gentle souls who touch our hearts as well as our laughter. Recent exceptions are noteworthy because of the attention they receive: Archie Bunker and his spin-off and alter ego George Jefferson. At the birth of the original series, audiences were aghast at Archie's bigotry and insensitivity. Over the years, however, he has mellowed because audiences have demanded it, as Wayne Warga points out in a recent *TV Guide* article, "Make Archie Lovable . . . Give 'Hot Lips' Respect . . . Let Fonzie Cry" (July 24, 1982, 4-8). Ironically, the changes in character are not away from the traditional television formula but toward it. Archie is being brought back into line. Producers seem to understand that television audiences want to like their clowns.

While this reliance on a likable main character certainly comprises only a small element of the comedic heritage, it is, in fact, an important ingredient in the TV formula for successful humor. Thus we have seen a generation of lovable bumblers who retain our sympathy even in the face of their own incompetency or unworthiness. After all, they mean well, and their problems result from mistakes, not malice. TV has given us some masters of this trade: Wally Cox, Ozzie Nelson, Bob Denver, Dick Van Dyke and John Ritter, to name only a few. The comic characters of these men, as nonconforming and pure as their dramatic counterparts, the heroes, display an amazing naivete that leaves them ill-equipped to handle the demands of everyday life.

Unlike the heroes, who are problem solvers *par excellence*, these clowns are plagued with problems—frequently of their own making—which are resolved in spite of their actions. Thus, far more than the heroes they are victims of circumstance and chance, and unlike the heroes, cannot rely on their own actions to save them from unpleasant situations and complicated consequences. They are, then, both exasperated and exasperating.

Throughout our history these two kinds of protagonists have been popular. We have enjoyed and loved them all as stereotypes, and they have remained recognizable as separate kinds of characters. We have expected from our serious heroes nothing short of perfection. They are to know all the answers, make no mistakes, epitomize dignity at all times, choose duty over any of the enticements thrown their way. They are, after all, the only forces capable of defending the defenseless in a hostile world. On the other hand, we expect from our clowns an ineptness of the sort that transcends the ordinary, but nevertheless proves endearing. They face the absurdities of the cosmos, just as we all do, and through luck or grace survive the contest. We have loved both sets of characters, but for different reasons and in distinguishable ways.

Currently, however, we are witnessing a cultural shift which blends these two kinds of protagonists, producing the nonconformist hero who is both macho and vulnerable, wise and befuddled. He is not purely a hero, for he creates his own problems and displays sometimes alarming ineptness. Even his friends recognize the absurdities of his situation. Yet he is not purely a clown either, for he solves the problems with his own resourcefulness and skill. He is, furthermore, unswervingly dedicated to protecting justice, even at great cost to himself.

The following scenarios demonstrate how the new hero differs from the old. The time is the 1950s. Mild-mannered Clark Kent sits at his typewriter working on a story for the *Daily Planet*. Suddenly Lois Lane bursts into his office alerting him to a crime spree that will become his scoop of the year. Making some excuse for his abrupt departure, Kent runs to a broom closet and emerges as Superman, "the Man of Steel." For the remainder of that particular episode, he will bend metal rods, deflect bullets with his chest, peer through buildings and walls with his x-ray vision and save Lois Lane from the criminals in question. No one recognizes Kent as Superman; no one knows his secret identity; everyone, including the criminals, respects and admires Superman.

The scene changes. The time is 1981. Mild-mannered history teacher Ralph Hinkley receives a magic suit from aliens from outer space. He promptly loses the instruction manual and consequently loses control over the suit. His friend, somewhat materialistic FBI agent Bill Maxwell, requests Ralph's aid in solving a case for which Maxwell will get full credit. In due time Ralph must make a lightning change from his everyday clothes to his magic suit and his secret identity as "the Great American Hero." Minutes tick away as he fights the trousers and the shoes. At last wearing the suit, he has no place to stash his regular clothing. Ultimately abandoning it, he leaps into the air only to fly haphazardly into a billboard. People laugh at him and believe him to be crazy. However, he uses his suit as best he can, harnessing its powers slowly. He captures the criminals, foils their crime. He protects "truth, justice, and the

American way" just as surely as his more heroic counterpart did thirty years earlier. The audience has been quick to spot the change. *TV Guide* reported the following exchange which took place during the filming of a recent episode of "The Greatest American Hero": "It's Superman,' one elder observes at last. 'No,' his companion corrects, 'Superman is a great big guy.' A pause, then the first announces decisively, 'This is some kind of funny Superman' " (July 24, 1982, 28). Clearly Ralph Hinkley has added laughter to the respect and admiration his actions demand.

While Hinkley is the most sensationalized of the new heroes, he is not the only one, nor indeed the first. Our befuddled hero appearead successfully, if unspectacularly, for several seasons as ex-con private detective Jim Rockford, who lived in an aged trailor on a public beach and worked for clients who never paid him. His father kept asking Jim when he was going to get a real job, while his friend Angel, also an ex-con, kept trying to gyp him out of money.

But it was during the 1981-82 television season that the inept hero gained stardom and won our collective hearts, for he appeared in several roles. He was in somewhat understated and truncated form "The Fall Guy," a movie stunt person approaching middle age who moonlights as a bounty hunter and finds that as age progresses, he must rely more on his wits than on his physical skills. Periodically he must hock his pickup truck to pay for damages caused by his misguided attempts to capture bail jumpers. In more developed form, he was Bret Maverick—the con-man gambler of the Old West who is trying to retire, but is having little success. His friends distrust him, and strange characters from his past keep appearing to get revenge or at least one last con on the Maverick of old. In most popular form, however, he is Magnum, P.I.—the Vietnam veteran who lives as permanent guest on a plush estate in Hawaii. His war buddies, Rick and T.C., constantly laugh at him and refuse to lend him money or extend credit. Higgins, his host at the estate, constantly exchanges barbs with Magnum and gloats over the fact that his two attack dogs refuse to recognize Magnum as a resident instead of an intruder. These protagonists are all decidedly scoundrels of sorts. Clearly they deserve a measure of the ridicule they receive. Yet just as clearly there is more involved as well. In true heroic fashion, week after week these men solve mysteries, capture criminals, and protect the rights of the downtrodden and victimized.

In these characters the pranks and flippancies of the rogue hero are tempered by the dedication and sense of duty of the conventional hero. The strength, dedication and general "rightness" of the macho hero are humanized by the talent for mistakes and misadventures of the comic counterpart. This very synthesis, however, is important for several reasons. First it reveals a profound change in our cultural self-image, for it presupposes a comfortable, good-natured laugh at the stereotypes of our heritage. Our new befuddled hero is at once more realistic and more fantastic than our tradition has allowed. We still expect honesty and dedication from him, but we accept his comic proclivity for running afoul of the everyday frustrations of contemporary life. He is, in short, more entertaining and more human while he fights the good fight and corrects all wrongs.

Steve Cannell, producer of "The Greatest American Hero," comments on both the reason for and the general appeal of this approach: "For starters, the superhero genre is malarky. Flying through the air, stopping bullets, lifting cars, nonsense. I wanted a nice-looking Everyman, not some guy with eight miles of jaw, and my Everyman, Ralph Hinkley, is saddled with this ridiculous suit, and to make it more fun, I took away the instructions for the suit" (O'Hallaren, p. 30). In the midst of its obvious humor, his answer posits two pertinent ideas. First, from our heroes contemporary audiences require more reality, at least in the elements of plot most closely connected to daily living. Thus, viewers who will accept a magic suit from outer space balk when confronted with a superhero who becomes unrecognizable when he puts on glasses or who never needs to worry about fitting a cape into a pair of trousers. We all know those things are impossible. Second, contemporary viewers appreciate the human nature, the Everyman, in our heroes. This makes them more believable and more like "the rest of us." A scrawny superhero is perhaps good for public morale.

There are other indications as well that the cultural stereotypes are changing. *McCall's Magazine* for August, 1982, published the results of a recent "Thinking Woman's Poll" on male sex appeal, and with just a bit of license we can apply its results to our discussion of heroes. One of the poll's most appealing men is Tom Selleck, the actor behind Magnum, P.I. If ever an actor looked the part of a macho superhero, it is Selleck. He is tall, good looking, rugged. But according to *McCall's*, his appearance is not the most important part of his appeal: "... the intrinsic Selleck dynamite does not (repeat, does *not*) lie in his deep dimples and his Marlboro-country machismo, as undeniably attractive as these may be. While the superstructure, the curly head and the bristly moustache can hardly stand against him, it's not these external attributes but his

attitude toward himself and toward life that warms the female heart
... and mind" (p. 10).

Later, the same poll spotlighted other virtues associated not
only with Selleck but with other men as well. Toughness and
intelligence were paired, as were strength and vulnerability (p. 12).
Yet the most unexpected quality the poll discovered harks back to
the beginning of our discussion when we were describing the
American individualist as he was perceived from the earliest days of
our country: "But the men who appeal most to thinking women are
those with profound and active commitment to causes larger than
themselves" (p. 14). *McCalls's* then documents a growing societal
appreciation of the very qualities that define the befuddled hero:
normality, an ability to laugh at his own absurdity, and a sense of
rightness and duty.

For whatever reason, the befuddled hero has captured our
imaginations and, indeed, the new television season as well. He
appears as Matt Houston (a crime fighter from Texas, of course),
Jake Cutter of "Tales of the Golden Monkey," and Frank Buck of
"Bring 'Em Back Alive" to name the most obvious examples. The
growing popularity of this new hero demonstrates just how
pervasive the cultural shift is, for television is perhaps the most
homogenized and pasteurized of our cultural art forms. Its product is
not innovation, but success. It relies on proven formulas. The
appearance of the befuddled hero on TV, especially in growing
numbers, testifies to the acceptability of the synthesis of the hero
and the clown; as a culture we are ready for the blend.

The befuddled hero, while new on television, draws deeply from
our cultural heritage. His ancestors are impressive, his forerunners
beloved parts of our society. He is a welcome change from the
simplistic stereotypes of the television formula, for he shows more
facets of his personality. He is the more human hero who reflects our
changing cultural outlook.

Journalist As Hero: The Adulation of Walter Cronkite

Robert G. Picard

*I*n bars, offices, stores and homes from New York to California and Minnesota to Texas, groups of people—steelworkers, electronic assemblers, executives, housewives and students— huddled near television sets to witness the historic event. They awaited with anxious anticipation, and when the broadcast began, they quickly "shushed" each other. It was March 6, 1981.

These "Goodbye, Walter" gatherings were held to mark the last time CBS Evening News would open its broadcast with anchorman Walter Cronkite feverishly editing copy until the last seconds before delivering the news. In the background recorded sounds of teletype machines, long-ago retired in favor of quieter and more efficient equipment, clattered while credits rolled and the dean of television news was introduced by an off-camera voice.

Anticipation of Cronkite's last broadcast had been building for months, and newspapers and magazines increased that anticipation by giving him the kind of coverage reserved for the world's greatest public figures.

For nineteen years Cronkite had delivered word of the world's events in his distinctive, soothing, paternal manner, a style that had led one observer to note earlier that "Walter Cronkite reads the news as though it were part of a long narrative with jaunty moments of optimism and despair."[1]

That blend endeared him to audiences, earning him their acclaim as the television newsman they believed the most and as the most trusted man in the United States.[2] It also brought him five Emmys and numerous other awards including the Presidential Medal of Freedom.

196

Cronkite's spring 1981 retirement set off a loud round of adulation in the nation's press, continuing earlier praise he had received and casting him as a saintly and godlike character. The adulation represented the ultimate triumph of celebrity as hero, and in this particular case, journalist as hero.

The rise of the celebrity hero has been well documented by social critics who have noted the passage of hero worship from mythological heroes to saintly heroes, from the common man as hero to the bum as hero, and finally to the celebrity as hero.

Dorothy Norman noted that the actions of mythological heroes exemplified behaviors that were to be the goals for the average man to pursue and that the acts of faith of saintly heroes made them serve as symbolic mediators between heaven and earth, providing enlightened direction for men who had little control over their lives and thus allowing them to make the most of the lives. The age of the common man brought a change in heroes, making inner-directed individuals, who strove for personal achievement, the characters worthy of adulation and emulation.[3]

That stress on personal achievement led to the development of "captains of industry" as heroes after the industrial revolution, Leo Lowenthal has noted, placing a stress on work and other individual success. More recently, that stress has shifted to "captains of consumption," leading the public to consider heroes' tastes, dress and leisure activities, but at the cost of trivializing heroic figures.[4]

Orrin Klapp has also observed the changing face of heroes across time, calling it the "deterioration of the hero." Today, he said, celebrity heroes are gimmick heroes, without "character," who exhibit little innate "goodness."[5] If heroes are the image rather than the individual upon which reverence is bestowed, as Moses Hadas and Morton Smith have maintained,[6] it is not surprising that celebrity heroes occupy an exalted position for a short time, soon displaced by another hero whose image lives up to the shadowy new image of what a hero should be.

Raphael Patai has argued that there has never developed a central, national myth in the United States, consisting of the qualities and characteristics expected of heroic man. As a result, he says, the incomplete national myth has disparate mythical features created by *Augenbliksgotter*, i.e., momentary gods.[7]

If that is the case in the development of celebrity heroes, and there is no evidence to the contrary, perhaps Daniel Boorstin is correct in his observation that celebrities are not true heroes, but pseudo-heroes. The "hero was distinguished by his achievement; the celebrity by his image or trademark. The hero created himself; the celebrity is created by the media. The hero was a big man; the celebrity is a big name."[8]

Given the transitory status of the celebrity hero, it is remarkable, then, that Walter Cronkite was able to attain and maintain such status over so long a period of time. Cronkite started to attain celebrity status when he began to anchor the CBS Evening News in 1962. A year later he made television news history when his show became the first newscast to be lengthened from fifteen to thirty minutes each night.

Without doubt Cronkite's status was created by the media, as Boorstin observed, but achievement and activity as a newsman and careful attention on his part helped nurture and maintain his status. Unlike most celebrity heroes, he was careful not to trivialize his life and when articles on his activities appeared in the popular press, he was careful to ensure that his appearance there reflected the image of a thoughtful, stable and trustworthy personality. We learned he had a heart—through his devotion to his family and his springer spaniel, Buzzy—and of his individuality and need to battle the elements—through his love of the sea and his days on his 42-foot yawl, Wyntje.

But he was not without a sense of humor which led him to make a circumspect celebrity appearance on the TV comedy *Mary Tyler Moore Show*, in which he made a cameo appearance at the WJM-TV newsroom where Mary Richards was employed.

Cronkite's public image as a professional journalist and active, credible and calm purveyor of the world's events contrasted markedly with the image of journalists portrayed in media prior to and during much of his tenure as anchorman. Films, plays and television shows, such as the film *His Girl Friday*, had regularly portrayed journalists as unscrupulous, undisciplined, immoral, heartless and disrespectful individuals. It was not until the last decade of Cronkite's career as anchorman that journalists began to be celebrities who were heralded for their activities, a development brought about, in part, because of the adulation of journalists in such films as *All the President's Men* and television shows such as *Lou Grant*.

Perhaps one of the factors that separated Cronkite from the standard celebrity hero was that he was not a "talking head" personality, devoid of exemplary personal attributes and ideas. He reflected the feelings of the age, engaged in critical discussions of issues, and seemingly took part in the whirlwind of events that shook the world during his term as anchorman. He was portrayed as an active television journalist when he rode a Canberra jet that dive-bombed Viet Cong in the jungle above Danang, Vietnam in 1965. Later he began showing doubts about the conflict that were reflected in a special report about the Tet Offensive in 1968 when he said, "To say that we are mired in stalemate seems the only realistic, yet unsatisfactory conclusion. The only rational way out ... will be to negotiate [and] not as victors."[9]

That broadcast reportedly led Lyndon Johnson to observe, "Well, if I've lost Cronkite, I've lost Middle America."[10]

His excitement about space exploration was well known and he did little to conceal his love for the moon exploration flights. His "Oh, boy," scream of delight as Apollo II lifted off mirrored the emotions of the audience. His affinity and identification with space travel, and his celebrity status, were affirmed by cartoonist Garry Trudeau, who depicted the takeoff of a moon shot being delayed until Cronkite said the word "liftoff."

His celebrity status was later reaffirmed by editorial cartoonist Paul Conrad who placed Cronkite's likeness on a wanted poster, as being hunted by President Nixon for reporting the Watergate break-in and other White House related scandals during the 1972 presidential election.

His coverage of political conventions and apparent enjoyment of the pageantry and intrigue of the gatherings earned him the status of *the* convention reporter and once again reveals his intimate participation in and relationships to the developments he covered. His coverage of the 1968 Democratic convention in Chicago contained outbursts at authorities for the physical attacks upon the press, as well as displeasure at the party for permitting the disturbances—both inside the convention hall and on the streets surrounding it—to continue unabated.

In 1980 his unabashed pursuit of a Reagan-Ford ticket at the Republican convention gained great notice and brought him some disapproving criticism from colleagues who felt he had become too involved in the selection process. The incident did him no apparent public harm, however, and seemed to be perceived more of evidence of his high standing in the country and of his concern about politics rather than undesirable journalistic meddling in public affairs.

But Cronkite was not without critics during his career. He drew a public outcry when he allowed the use of the phrase "god damn" twice in an interview about the problems of housing for blacks in Chicago. He later apologized for allowing the interview containing those words to be broadcast without editing the words out, a self-deprecating act that only helped to reinforce his image as an approachable and responsive journalist.[11]

Cronkite's journalistic career, of course, did not begin with CBS Evening News. He covered the Second World War for United Press, and was one of the handful of correspondents selected to land with the D-Day invasion. After the war he covered Moscow, before leaving UP to join CBS. In 1953 he was made host of the *You Are There* series, in which he conducted fictional interviews with historical figures. He later became host of *The Morning Show*, before moving on to *The Twentieth Century*, where he narrated historical documentary films. Later the show was transformed into *The Twenty-First Century* which concentrated on technological advances and futurism.

Those same concerns have emerged in *Universe*, a show begun before Cronkite's retirement, which once again permits him to utilize his knack for explaining high technology.

This ability—the capacity to explore the complexities of science and technology and convey its meaning and impact in an understandable way to the average man—allowed him to serve as a sympathetic conduit and translator of knowledge between participants in the development of the high technology society and the men and women who would have to learn to cope with the changes it would bring.

He has become synonymous with conflict and disaster because of his ability to calmly react and report events, however disturbing. This ability helped make CBS the major outlet for such news and led *Newsweek* to conclude recently that "America seems conditioned to turn to the CBS eye whenever events are of historic dimension."[12]

Cronkite's coverage of the John Kennedy assassination (in which he was unable to hold back tears, an "unprofessional" act which revealed a caring and concerned man beneath the calm exterior), the Martin Luther King Jr. assassination, Watergate and its aftermath, the hostage situation in Iran (for which he started the counting of the days of captivity) all earned him the respect and admiration of audiences and peers. And even after his retirement from the anchor position, CBS turned to him for help when Anwar el-Sadat was assassinated—sending him to Egypt instead of Dan Rather to cover and explain the occurrence ("to put this thing in perspective," Dan Rather said[13]).

His ability to handle such situations, and the television medium itself, brought Cronkite mythical status, Curt McCray has argued:

> Forms and heroes are inextricably bound together, as any
> reader of the epic knows, and the pleasure of watching a news
> program whose content may be grisly, is the pleasure of seeing a
> hero, our hero, stride through the landscape which is his form.[14]

Anticipation of the departure of Cronkite as such a hero and of the impact of his absence induced the media to explore the situation, to review his career and his personal life, and to interview him about the state of journalism.

Before his departure *Esquire* talked of the "post-Cronkite emptiness" American people were expected to feel "as if a vital part of their life-support nutrient mix were being deprived them."[15]

Cronkite had criticized the growing celebritization of journalists and the trivialization of news some years before his retirement,[16] and he expressed similar misgivings about the furor caused by his departure and its obvious tie to personality newscasters. The future of broadcast journalism worried him because of what he called the increasing role of "pretty people" who enter broadcast news not as journalists but as actors.[17]

In 1974 Cronkite asked that a group which had organized a Walter Cronkite fan club shut down the organization. "I don't think news people ought to have fan clubs," he said later. "It smacks of show business and all the things that are wrong with television news. It's just not right."[18]

Despite his victorious one-man battles against such celebration of journalists, Cronkite lost the war. In an industry where 40 percent of the audience chooses news shows based solely on the anchor person and where ratings translate directly into revenue, Cronkite struggled in vain because network executives viewed newsmen as celebrities—stars to be promoted just like Erik Estrada and Catherine Bach.

Don Hewitt, executive producer of CBS News' "60 Minutes," recently noted that few broadcast journalists are anything but celebrities. "The news divisions of the networks have press departments that put out news releases when reporters change beats," he said. "When you have a press agent, you *are* a personality."[19]

Cronkite's importance as a news celebrity, despite his protestations against such status, has been aptly described by one observer:

> The man *is* television news: Mr. Anchorman, Mr. Space
> Shot, Mr. Convention, and more important—because we're

talking network TV here—Mr.Ratings. For the past thirteen years, season after season, the *CBS Evening News With Walter Cronkite* has won the largest share of the television-news audience. Owned it. America's curious love affair with "Uncle Walter" has driven several generations of NBC and ABC news executives to despair—or into other lines of work.[20]

Cronkite's departure, ironically, mixed personal desires with the problem of the celebration of newsmen. Although his retirement was announced a year in advance, it was moved up to give the anchor position to Dan Rather, who was considering a defection to another network to gain an anchor post. Cronkite graciously agreed to change his plans, step down early, and keep Rather at CBS. "America expects such honorable sacrifices from its folk heroes," one observer noted.[21]

On the night of his final broadcast as anchorman, no one watching network news was denied the opportunity to see Cronkite's final "And that's the way it is ...." Both ABC and NBC news broadcast feeds of his final farewell in their newscasts, preceded by a review of his career. ABC even took out full-page magazine and newspaper ads wishing him well (in hopes his audience would switch channels in his absence).

Cronkite's old friend Johnny Carson didn't let the event go by unheralded. On that evening's edition of *The Tonight Show*, "The Mighty Carson Art Players" presented Carson's comedy version of the journalists's last newscast, in which Cronkite uncharacteristically told off his staff and CBS network executives.

In the weeks following, a wave of articles appeared about his departure. *National Review* called him the "last of the great radio-TV newsmen."[22] *Time* dubbed him "The best-known and most respected broadcast journalist of his era."[23] *Newsweek* was even more eloquent. The seat he occupied, it said, had "acquired the eminence of high government office, the mystique of religious ritual and the corona of TV megastardom."[24] The impossibility of replacing him was regularly asserted.

In the articles published about his departure, scores of phrases and words were used to imbue him with heroic attributes and these descriptions provide clues to the personal factors that made this journalist a hero (Table 1).

A review of these descriptions reveals that they can be synthesized into groups of characteristics, identified by previous studies as exemplary of certain types of heroes (Table II). These provide a much clearer view of what made Walter Cronkite the

Table I
Descriptions of Qualities and Attributes of
Walter Cronkite in Selected Articles

"a national monument"

"has touched all our lives in some way"

"symbol of decency and good character"

"synonomous with news"

"has stature and authority"

"kind open face"

"has self-restraint"

"reputation for neutrality"

"was a pro and his bias was usually muted"

"believes what he is saying himself"

"low-key delivery"

"stature approaching the president's"

"inspired faith"

"easy going amiability"

"holding self-importance at bay"

"old-fashioned newspaper-men"

"conservative broadcast tradition"

"no other star of his magnitude"

"had calm and sensible responses to events"

"genuinely cared about the world he brought us"

"one of the best known men in the nation"

"The fellow next door who'd invite you to his backyard barbecue, and a world statesman at the same time"

"TV's foremost anchor man"

"a national father figure"

"a kind of public institu-tion"

"ubiquitous part of the American scene"

"inspired unquestioning, sober trust"

"matter of fact style"

"a revered and exalted American icon"

"integrity and courage"

"gift for making bad news sound not so bad"

"a center of calm in the whirlwind"

"old-fashioned approach"

"obvious belief in the country and its people"

"benign, avuncular manner"

"steady seriousness that has earned him vast credibility"

"last of the great radio-TV newsmen"

"not just a speaking head but a great reporter"

"best known, most respect-ed broadcast journalist of his era"

"grown from a father figure to a grandfather figure right before our eyes"

"never relinquished his sense of values"

"Mr. Reality: It hasn't happened unless he re-ports it"

"His almost mystical bond of trust with the viewing public"

"a legend"

"stamina"

"integrity"

"credibility"

"sagacity"

"geniality"

"brilliant"

"sentimental"

"eccentric"

"a paragon"

"reassuring"

"professional"

"irreplaceable"

"charismatic"

"a presence"

"avuncularity"

"businesslike"

"believability"

"soothing"

"naturalness"

"solidity"

"suave"

"informed"

"attractive"

"comfortable"

"sense of values"

"benevolent"

"source of reassurance"

"stability"

"awesome stature"

"journalistic pro-fessionalism"

"nearly canonized"

Table II
Condensed Descriptions of Qualities and Attributes
of Walter Cronkite in Selected Articles

Psychologically Comfort ing

"believes what he is saying himself"
"inspired faith"
"had calm and sensible responses to events"
"genuinely cared about the world he brought us."
"a national father figure"
"gift for making bad news sound not so bad"
"a center of calm in the whirlwind"
"obvious belief in the country and its people"
"benign, avuncular manner"
"steady seriousness that has earned him vast credibility"
"grown from a father figure to a grandfather figure right before our eyes"
"never relinquished his sense of values"
"Mr. Reality: It hasn't happened unless he reports it"
"reassuring"
"believability"
"avuncularity"
"soothing"
"comfortable"
"sense of values"
"benevolent"
"source of reassurance"
"His almost mystical bond of trust with the viewing public"

Social Acceptability

"kind open face"
"easy going amiability"
"The fellow next door who'd invite you to his backyard barbeque, and a world statesman at the same time"
"geniality"
"sentimental"
"attractive'"
"suave"

Splendid Performer/Professional

"synonomous with news"
"reputation for neutrality"
"was a pro and his bias was usually muted"
"low key delivery"
"old-fashioned newspaper man"
"conservative broadcast tradition"
"no other star of his magnitude"
"TV's foremost anchor man"
"matter of fact style"
"old-fashioned approach"
"last of the great radio-TV-newsmen"
"not just a speaking head but a great reporter"
"professional"
"businesslike"
"naturalness"
"informed"
"journalistic professionalism"

Qualities to be Emulated

"symbol of decency and good character"
"has self-restraint"
"holding self-importance at bay"
"integrity and courage"
"stamina"
"integrity"
"credibility"
"sagacity"
"stability"

Leadership

"has stature and authority"
"stature approaching the president's"
"one of the best know men in the nation"
"inspired unquestioning, sober the nation"
"inspired unquestioning, sober trust"
"best known, most respected broadcast journalist of his era"
"brilliant"
"irreplaceable"
"charismatic"
"awesome stature"

Myth

"a national monument"
"has touched all our lives in some way "
"a kind of public institution"
"ubiquitous part of the American scene"
"a revered and exalted American icon"
"a legend"
"a paragon"
"a presence"
"nearly canonized"

quintessential journalist as hero.

Of the six categories which emerged in the condensation of the descriptions, four involve personal characteristics and attributes of Cronkite himself: 1) professionalism and performance descriptions, 2) descriptions of attributes and qualities that are psychologically comforting to others, 3) descriptions of qualities and attributes to be emulated, and 4) descriptions of traits which made him socially acceptable. The remaining two classifications of descriptions involve descriptions of leadership qualities and of a mythical nature, characteristics imbued or placed directly upon him rather than inner qualities.

A review of the characteristics leads me to suggest that the mythical and leadership characteristics stem from the other four types of characteristics used to describe him, emerging from and built upon those basic qualities.

The differences between heroes and celebrities—as pointed out by Boorstin—need to be recalled because the descriptions of Walter Cronkite clearly involve both personal achievement and mediated image. While the existence of a public "image" of Cronkite, nurtured by the networks and Cronkite himself, cannot be denied and thus make him a celebrity, he has also achieved a pinnacle of professionalism that allows him to transcend mere celebrity status to enter the hero classification as well. Cronkite's achievement is what Klapp called the splendid performance—mastery of the skills and techniques necessary to make one foremost in one's field of endeavor.

Cronkite also meets the criteria of hero since he typified goals to be approached—seen in his exemplification of personal qualities to be emulated, and in activities that made him a symbolic mediator between heaven and earth—in more current terms, Cronkite's mediation between science, technology and ruling elites and the common man.

Cronkite has been both a "captain of industry" and a "captain of consumption," a la Lowenthal, in that he worked his way up the journalistic ladder, making his own success, and that he became a celebrity figure about which we learned his favorite foods, colors and hobbies.

Sidney Hook has argued that heroes have been created throughout history because of 1) the indispensability of leadership, 2) the creation of myths through cultural institutions, 3) the psychological needs of man, and 4) the need for heroes to save men from crises that arise.[25] Cronkite has filled the requirements of all these criteria. He was partially created by media, provided psychological comfort through his stability and other attributes, helped the public weather and understand crises—although he may not have actually solved them—and, finally, provided leadership strength, although not actually leading the people, by inspiring trust and exhibiting qualities to be emulated.

Those elements help explain how Cronkite became a hero, not merely a celebrity, and how he managed to survive as a revered symbol when other celebrities and journalists rarely gained such status, or faded quickly after doing so.

Throughout his career, Cronkite never forgot his audience or their hopes and fears as he reported and explained the tumultuous and frightening events in the world. He guided Americans through war and peace, bad times and prosperity, and failures and successes with a continuity that reassured them of their ability to survive and conquer obstacles in making better lives for themselves.

When Walter Cronkite delivered his final "And that's the way it is," applause broke out at the gatherings of people across the country, masking the sadness and emptiness of knowing one's hero would no longer be present to safely guide one through the hazardous course of events to come. Their hero was falling and no other stood ready to take his place.

Notes

[1] William Hawes, *The Performer in Mass Media* (New York: Hastings House, 1978), p. 69.

[2] A 1973 Oliver Quale poll put Cronkite at the top of the list of the nation's most trusted public figures, surpassing the nearest competition by 16%. A Doyle, Dane Bernbach survey found him to be the most believable newscaster.

[3] Dorothy Norman, *The Hero: Myth, Image, Symbol* (New York: World, 1969).

[4] Leo Lowenthal, "Biographies in Popular Literature," *Radio Research, 1942-43,* Lazarsfield and Stanton eds. (New York: Duell, Sloan and Pearce, 1944). See also "The Triumph of Mass Idols," in *Literature, Popular Culture and Society* (Englewood Cliffs, N.J.: Prentice-Hall, 1961).

[5] Orrin E. Klapp, *Heroes, Villains and Fools, the Changing American Character* (Englewood Cliffs, N.J.: Prentice-Hall, 1962).

[6] Moses Hadas and Morton Smith, *Heroes and Gods* (New York: Harper & Row, 1972).

[7] Raphael Patai, *Myth and Modern Man* (Englewood Cliffs, N.J.: Prentice-Hall, 1972).

[8] Daniel J. Boorstin, *The Image: A Guide to Pseudo-Events in America* (New York: Atheneum, 1975), p. 61.

[9] Michael C. Emery and Ted S. Smythe, *Readings in Mass Communication*, 3rd ed. Dubuque, Iowa: Brown, 1977), p. 424.

[10] H.F. Waters, "A Man Who Cares," *Newsweek*, March 9, 1981, p. 58.

[11] Peter M. Sandman, David M. Rubin and David B. Sachsman, *Media*, 2nd ed. (Englewood Cliffs, N.J.: Prentice-Hall, 1976), p. 306.

[12] H.F. Waters, Eric Gelamn, George Hackett and Lucy Howard, "TV's War After Cronkite," *Newsweek*, March 9, 1981, p. 56.

[13] Janice Castro and Janice Simpson, "Groping for News from Cairo," *Time*, Oct. 19, 1981, p. 62.

[14]Curk McCray, "Kaptain Kronkite: The Myth of the Eternal Frame," in Horace Newcomb, ed., *Television: The Critical View* (New York: Oxford, 1976), p. 66.

[15]Bob Greene, "Anchors Away," *Esquire*, Dec. 1980, p. 19.

[16]Ron Powers, "The Curator Reacts: Walter Cronkite," *The Newscasters* (New York: St. Martins, 1977).

[17]Interview with Walter Cronkite: "What's Right, Wrong with Television News," *U.S. News and World Report*, March 16, 1981, p. 45.

[18]Timothy White, "Walter, We Hardly Knew You," *Rolling Stone*, Feb. 5, 1981, p. 76.

[19]"Celebrity Journalism:..." *U.S. News and World Report*, Jan. 18, 1982, p. 56.

[20]Edward Tivnan, "The Cronkite Syndrome," *The Dial*, Nov. 1980, p. 44.

[21]Waters, p. 58.

[22]"The Meaning of Cronkite," *National Review*, March 20, 1981, p. 266.

[23]"The New Face of TV News," *Time*, Feb. 25, 1980, p. 64.

[24]Waters, p. 52.

[25]*The Hero in History* (New York: Day, 1943).

Roles, Rituals and Romance: The Appeal of the Soap Opera Heroine

Vicki Abt

*I*ncreased sensitivity to issues relating to women and changing sex role behavior has made the soap opera a legitimate subject of analysis and debate. We are certainly less likely to ignore this most popular of television forms that focuses on, and is watched primarily by, women.[1] (In the recent past "closet" soap opera fans often denied watching the dramas, (*Time*, 1976) suggesting that both men and women still tend to believe that women's traits and interests are generally inferior to those of men and not really worthy of serious study) (Braverman, 1972).

The women's movement may have, inadvertently, forced us to take women's soap opera as seriously as we do male cultural forms (if only to criticize them). In a 1965 attack on soap opera, Betty Friedan argued that the image of women on these shows exemplified the "feminine mystique." Soap opera, she said, feeds on, and reinforces cultural sexism in its portrayal of immature, sick and dependent women (*TV Guide*, 1965). Friedan's views may have been extreme; yet the leaders of the woman's movement generally have dismissed the soaps as presenting a cultural ideal lauding the housewife role and generally stereotyping women's needs and goals.

This preoccupation with women's concerns and the world of primary relationships, on the other hand, has been said to constitute the new feminist perspective. Gordon argues that the soap opera challenges prime time masculine-centered television genres. Rather than aping male sex roles that value bureaucratic, secondary impersonal relations, soap opera is seen as constructing a world that refuses to trivialize traditional feminine interests (Gordon, 1981). It emphasizes intense, emotional, kinship-oriented ties that pervade both public and private world of soap opera characters. Conflict is resolved through informal face to face interactions rather than through any hierarchical bureaucratic structures (these last simply don't exist on soap operas). In effect the split between public and private spheres that characterizes life since the Industrial Revolution dissolves, and family and community are once again merged. (While this may be a large appeal of soap opera, it is by no means certain that this distorted image actually constitutes an ideal of feminism or rather a sexist powerless one of separatism. Power and authority, unhappily, do seem to be attached to the world of capital investments and political decision-making, not to the domestic world.) Nevertheless, the world of soap opera is surely one of small talk, of the forming and breaking and reforming of various intimate relationships within a stable community setting. Analyzing soap opera enables us, at least, to pay attention to this informal world regardless of one's ideological position on its ultimate meaning. Despite Simmel, Goffman and a few others, sociology, in the past, not unlike prime time television, has focused primarily on the male-dominated public and official aspects of social organization. The sociology of women, of the interpersonal, private and informal is rarely examined (Walum, 1977: 95).

In our own content analysis of four soap operas[1] the plots of the soap opera seem to revolve around the informal dynamics and constraints involved in maintaining the individual within a closed society. It has been pointed out that "soap opera is oxymoron, reflecting change and no change simultaneously" (Fine, 1981: 106). Throughout the stories, the characters do not develop as personalities (although they do age). The only thing that develops, vacillates, includes new people and circumstances—is the plot. (This is the essential characteristic of melodrama and, of course, the soap opera genre.)

The soap opera "heroine" in this ahistorical world is primarily preoccupied with maintaining a delicate, if impossible, balance between the society of conformity to traditional norms and the potential disruptive appeal of individual transgression. She may "change" but she doesn't grow. With no memory of past lessons learned, she must, like Sisyphus, constantly repeat her efforts. Yet, unlike another literary lesson, she *can* go home again. Her *unending* involvement with role definitions in terms of the tensions between group demands and individual, rather arbitrary nonpolitical, expressions of personal rebellion (her "consciousness" is *never* finally raised) manages to appeal to many different women in contemporary America.

There is need then for an analysis of how soap operas deal with the contradiction of stability and constant crisis, with these never-ending cycles of tensions and conflicts within a stable, normative system. This is especially pertinent in conjunction with the audience perceptions of four female soap opera characters on the popular day-time serial *All My Children* (ABC).

Roles and Rituals: The Soap Opera Community

Since the soap opera is aimed primarily at women, the women characters are most clearly depicted and more frequently "spotlighted" than the male characters. Men appear as foils, underscoring the concerns and behavior of the heroines. Perhaps the term "heroine" is not appropriate because soap opera resolves conflict by emphasizing society rather than the individual, as Fine says:

> Soap operas present us with a world in which men and women live together in intimacy and harmony. That is not to say that conflict is absent from the soap opera. Jealousy and rage are interpersonal staples; and divorce is frequent. But conflict exists only in terms of individual relationships; the soap opera community, as a whole, remains harmonious. (Fine, 1981: 105)

The very appeal of soap opera lies in its ultimate celebration of the cohesive group over the individual. Again, from Fine's study of soap opera conversations: "The soap opera creates a warm enclosed community, a womb in which the participants receive continual nourishment from each other (p. 106)." Unlike most plays and books written about a particular person or persons, soap opera tells of a miniature society where individuals are indeed replaceable, in this they are more historical than biographical. Life in society goes on even as characters begin and end. If soap opera characters are preoccupied with the relationship of the individual to others it is in Durkheim's sense of collective restraint or collective conscience. Human excesses are controlled through the helpfulness of the cohesive group and constraining daily rituals. Soap operas are *not* anomic. Obviously characters are quite dependent upon one another and these relationships both reinforce women's position within the social structure ("keeping her in her place" rather than allowing her to follow her whims without consequence) and serve as backdrops for the receiving and giving of the cultural script. Characters say things like "I only want to keep you from making a mistake," or "If you want my advice . . .," and then proceed to deliver proscriptive or prescriptive messages about the woman's appropriate courses of action. If the characters are not anomic, it is also true that the soap opera itself may function to provide a feeling of community among its viewers. Audience analyses reveal that some viewers watch soaps because they perceive them as resembling their own lives (Fine, 1981). Women talk of their favorite soap opera character often with the same knowledge as their neighbors and family. *Time* described soap operas as constituting "folk tales that tug at the soul of a nation of strangers for whom television itself is a bond" (*Time*, 1976: 47).

Although studies have shown that the majority of conversations on soap operas revolve around the kinship system, of the extended family, (Fine, 1981; Buerkle-Rothfuss, 1981) it is really primarily the woman's role in the family that is being delineated. It is this aspect of sex roles that appear most antithetical to the woman's movement. However, while the woman is closely watched and involved with her family, clearly being told her duties, they are strangely unbalanced duties. The woman as a family member, a wife and mother, sister and daughter, is depicted, not as woman as homemaker or housewife. Soap opera women rarely if ever concern themselves with cleaning, cooking, mending, washing dishes or any of the other assorted tasks associated with the woman as the wife and mother.[2] In fact she doesn't even babysit her children, rarely is she unavailable for serious adult talk because the baby is crying or needs his diaper changed (baby if upset goes off camera "to bed"). Children don't keep interrupting mother with demands for attention, nor is the mother forced to repeat herself until ready to explode. Even more amazing and delightful to some, baby grows up almost overnight and by himself. He reappears when he is old enough to participate in the adult world. None of this rather lopsided view of the role of wife and mother is accidental. For good or bad, the culture of the soap opera is clearly supporting the expressive, verbal dimensions of women's traditional status (there is very little physical movement on soap opera and much conversation and analysis; this cannot all be explained by low budgets for exterior action shots in that the genre itself needs small spaces and sets for intimacy—Newcomb, 1974). But on the other hand, they are minimizing the more boring drudgery of these roles. Perhaps the enduring nature of sex roles owes something to this rather romanticized view which support their desirability.

Romance: The Tie that Unbinds

If women are not tied to the work involved in the house, what is she like, what concerns her? I have already mentioned the importance of giving and receiving norms in the form of advice, and her role as both socializing agent and conformer to other agents within the family. It is interesting that while most of the conversations deal with family issues only a small portion deals with the husband/wife relationship, the core of the nuclear family (Katzman, 1972: 211; Fine, 1981). It is as if the writers were aware of the unstable nature of this relationship and chose instead to focus on the more enduring forms of kinship. Yet the woman is supposed to be capable of great emotion, passion and love. In fact, romantic love is the only thing the *individual* is allowed to break the norms to protect. One is allowed to "lose control," to trespass against society (i.e., the family) for the sake of intimacy or love only. Seclusion, isolation, or solitude is not permitted. The woman is also supposed to recover from divorce or "a broken heart" by trying her hand at the love game time and time again. Divorces are commonplace but not disillusionment with love and marriage. Love is also the great leveler. There is no age barrier to love. Women of all ages marry, divorce, and remarry, almost always for love. It is true that some "bad" characters marry for social status or personal gain; but such a woman usually leaves the man for a true love or comes to love him in the end.[3]

The soap opera "heroine" is 1) interested in family, 2) interested in finding romantic love which allows her to escape the group for a while, 3) interested in understanding people, in talking through problems, the same problems over and over again which tends to make us believe she is ahistorical, never really learning from her mistakes, but 4) always forgiving and being forgiven. In this she exists in a grey area of mature life, she is never totally evil, but may be reborn through the magic of love or the family. She is forgiven if only she admits her errors or her "humanness." It is comforting to see that society can be so tolerant, or perhaps as Durkheim would suggest, it allows transgressions in order to reaffirm its boundaries.

Soap opera has often been criticized for its noninvolvement in major social or political issues. In this, it maintains its timeless nature, transcending current events. Sometimes social issues are discussed, but *always* within the context of having personally affected a member of the family or close family friends. Soap operas are also comforting in that everyone has a place within the system, strangers coming to the imaginary community are immediately befriended and if not distantly related to someone, then they are "adopted" by a local family. Only individualism and privacy are really taboo; one is supposed to seek community.

A study of the 1970 soap opera plots indicated that sexism, as stereotypic behavior, existed in so far as soap opera women tended to marry older men (rather than the opposite being the rule), most children produced in soap opera marriages were boys, and men initiated discussions with women more often than women would initiate talking with men. In addition, while 60% of the men were engaged in high status occupations such as being doctors, lawyers of businessmen, only 5% of the women were engaged in such professions. While 45% of the married women worked outside the home, 62% of these were engaged in stereotypic low status, supportive occupations such as nursing, clerical jobs and the like (Katzman, 1972: 200-205). While men were talking among themselves, the object of the discussion was most likely to be business, women were rarely depicted as being occupationally ambitious and were quite willing to give their jobs up upon marriage. Time and again women were berated on soap operas for putting their aspirations, such as they were, above the needs of their lovers, husbands or children. When women lawyers and doctors talk on soap operas, it is inevitably about lovers, husbands or children. In these aspects soap operas tend to reinforce traditional sex roles and interests, in line with Friedan's argument.

Soap opera has also been attacked for presenting women in terms of the so-called "double standard." It has been asserted that women are either "good" or "bad" largely depending upon their sexual conduct with men. Moreover, the very casting of women as either "good" or "bad" in itself would constitute a caricaturing process—a process that would deny the variability of women. In addition one such article said the "good" or "bad" women are differentiated in terms of their commitment to or lack of commitment to the housewife role itself: "The worst people of all in the soaps however are the career women, unnatural creatures who actually enjoy some activity other than reproducing the species" (McQuade, 1974: 307). I have not seen either of these characterizations to be the rule. First, I have already mentioned that soap operas rarely depict characters as either always "good" or "bad"; characters change, motivation is shown as a complicated process. All adult women characters are sexually involved with men at some time. In fact much of the "promiscuous" behavior of characters is seen as resulting from a need for love and affiliation. Career women are not considered "unnatural" as long as they remain capable of caring about family ties and commitment to a one-to-one relationship with a man. It is just the stereotype of the cold unloving career woman type that is *not* presented. All women are shown to have similar needs for affiliation, career oriented or not.

Other things should be pointed out that would seem to support Gordon's view of feminism on soap opera and undermine Friedan's view of sexism. For example, women almost equally turn to women for advice as they do to men. The best person to look to for advice is any family member, regardless of sex. A great deal of conversation is not sex-based. Both men and women spend a good deal of time talking about feelings and thoughts. Men are not shown being more physically active than women, nor are they often shown in exclusively male company. At parties men and women intermingle rather than segregating and talking about "men's interests" versus "women's interests." It is as if women have taken on the dominant roles so that men wish to be like them rather than in actual society where the minority group (women) try to take on the dominant group's (men) characteristics and interests. Furthermore, a current survey of soap opera would, I believe, show that more women are engaged in positions of authority even in the public (job) sector. The six years since Katzman's content analysis seems to have made a difference in that aspect of sexism. Sexism as a caste-like system is, clearly, not the totality of soap opera. (Further, neither men nor women, it was mentioned, concern themselves with housework or childcare.)

Viewer's Characterizations of 4 Soap Opera Heroines

As part of a larger study of soap operas, we asked women viewers in the fall of 1979 to respond to questions concerning the characterization of soap opera heroines.[4] Soap opera has been studied from many vantage points, i.e. through an analysis of plot, of character motivation and conversation, physical appearance and behavior. However, the audience's perceptions of and identification with the female characters (heroines) includes their interpretations of all the elements and would seem to have the greatest potential for analyzing, simultaneously, the content and impact of the soap opera message.

McQuade had suggested that heroines are perceived as undimensional beings embodying either totally good or bad characteristics. Moreover, he had suggested that homemakers would be seen as "good" and career women as "bad," unlikeable and not identifiable (1974: 307). From our own viewing we found this difficult to accept, as characters appeared flexible and changing which would seem to mitigate against stereotyping of this sort. The key theme seemed to be "understanding" and "forgiveness" for past mistakes. Although we had data concerning 4 characters on 4 different soap operas (16 characters total), in analyzing the data we soon realised that we would have to limit discussion to characters appearing on a single soap opera. Almost 70% of the total sample watched "All My Children."[5] Over 27% of the "All My Children" viewers said they were regular watchers, 22% said they often but not regularly watched. The 4 female characters who are regulars on the program do not seem very different from those on the other three soap operas included in this survey. Responses to these 4 characters can be seen as indicative of those we would expect for characters on similar soap operas.

Summary and Implications

Soap opera, although one of the most popular types of all television programming, has been attacked by a myriad of political and cultural critics. It is often characterized as having little if any redeeming social value. The prime time caricature "Mary Hartman, Mary Hartman" depicted the soap heroine as obsessed with housecleaning and consumerism. Attacks by critics of the soaps include the argument that these dramas serve to reinforce sexist stereotypes; that they are poor substitutes for declining family and community ties and that they probably serve as kindergarten pap to keep the little woman occupied while the husband concerns himself with the more important tasks of confronting the "real world."

Our own research, does not leave us with this simplistic characterization. If soap operas are viewed as social drama rather than as biographical novels even the repeated crises are not unrealistic. It is true that most of us do not go through divorce after divorce or get indicted for murder but these things do happen regularly within the total community. The major theme of soap opera is communication and community. The plots are excuses for the working out of normative solutions to human relationships. They may be seen as constituting daily socio-dramas. Although the characterizations revolve around the family, the average soap opera character is not obsessed with housework or consumerism. Heroines in novels may "live happily ever after," but soap opera heroines live forever, albeit with many personality and status changes. There is no "happily ever after," but they do survive, they cope and they cope.

The soap opera audience is quite heterogeneous. Many are working women, employed outside the home, many have children, many have rather high family incomes. The audience appears to have firm community and family ties. The majority viewers of soap opera favor the national Equal Rights Amendment. Sexism does exist on soap opera in the form of having characters consumed with the idea of "romantic" love as a single most important fulfilling relationship rather than attempting to depict fulfilling occupational relations. Soap opera is probably less sexist than the movies or even most other prime time television. Women in the soaps keep striving to achieve the American Dream by any means available. The popularity of soap opera may have something to do with the audience being allowed to identify with less than perfect characters; in fact, even "bad" characters are identifiable as human beings.

It has been suggested that the soap opera plot conveys normative scripts which the audience utilizes in their own lives. Our data do not fully support this theory. The issue of audience identification with the characters as role models has not been resolved.

Nevertheless it seems clear that the heroine in soap opera constantly changes and keeps up with the changing mores of American society, though there may be a time lag in this concurrency. As such she is less out of touch and tune with mainstream American life than many critics, for their own reasons, like to stress.

References

Braverman, I.
1972   "Sex Role Stereotypes: A Current Appraisal." *Journal of Social Issues* 28 (2): 59-78.

Buerkel—Rothfuss, N. and S. Mayes
Summer 1981   "Soap Opera Viewing: The Cultivation Effect." *Journal of Communication* 31 (3): 108-115.

Downing, M.
Spring, 1974   "Heroine of the Daytime Serial." *Journal of Communication*
24 (2): 130-137.

Fine, M.
Summer, 1981   "Soap Opera Conversations: The Talk That Binds." *Journal of Communication* 31 (3): 97-107.

Gordon, D.
1981   "The Modern TV Soap Opera: A Feminist Perspective." Paper
presented to the Popular Culture Association annual convention, Cincinnati, Ohio,
1980

Horner, M.
1972   "Toward an Understanding of Achievement-related Conflicts in
Women." *Journal of Social Issues* 28 (2): 157-176.

Kaplan, F.
1975   "Intimacy and Conformity in American Soap Opera." *Journal of
Popular Culture* 9 (3): 622-626.

Katzman, N.
1972   "Television Soap Operas: What's Been Going On Anyway?" *Public
Opinion Quarterly*: 200-212.

Lowry, D.T. et. al.
Summer, 1981   "Sex on the Soap Operas: Patterns of Intimacy." *Journal of
Communication* 31 (3): 90-96.

McQuade, D.
1974   *Popular Writing in America*. New York: Oxford, p. 307.

Newcomb, H.
1974   "Soap Opera: Approaching the Real World." *TV: The Most Popular
Art*. 161-182.

1976   "Sex Roles: Persistence and Change." *Journal of Social Issues* 32 (3).

1976   "Sex and Suffering in the Afternoon." *Time* Vol. 107, p. 47.

March, 1965   "The Soaps Anthing but 99 44/100 Percent Pure," *TV Guide*.

Rose, B.
Autumn, 1979   *"Thickening the Plot." Journal of Communication* 29 (4): 81-
84.

Walum, Laurel
1977   *The Dynamics of Sex and Gender: A Sociological Perspective*.
Chicago: Rand McNally.

Notes

[1] This paper is part of an ongoing study of images of women on televsion. We did a content analysis utilizing several categories concerning relationships among major characters on soap operas as well as a rather lengthy survey of audience perceptions of plot and character of these daytime serials.

[2] The soap opera character is invariably too well turned out, too well dressed (in designer dresses rather than jeans) to be believable doing housework. This makes her fantasy but she is also acting out desired goals ... freedom from certain aspects of the woman's role but not all.

[3] One very popular character named Rachel on "Another World" (NBC) has been married four times and is married to a man old enough to be her father. He is exceedingly wealthy, the wealthiest man in the community, and she was depicted as having shed her bitchy selfish character all for the love of him. Except at this writing she has left her husband, Mac Corey, for a younger lover. The miracle of love is that it can happen again and again.

[5] Over a 2 month period we administered questionaires to a total of 90 women at various locations in the Philadelphia area. Approximately 120 women were approached, some refused to be interviewed, a few stated they never watched soap operas. Ninety respondents indicated they watched soap operas (31% watched at least three times a week). Sixty-five of the 90 respondents watched "All My Children" which is the soap opera used for the present analysis.

Heroes in American Political Film

Harry Keyishian

*E*lectoral politics has always been a popular subject in American films. Movies about electioneering and campaigning contain great spectacles—parades, crowd scenes, mass meetings—which satisfy our yearning for faith and inspiration. They permit us as well to peek in on our "betters," the powerful and the ambitious, and to see that they are no happier or more virtuous than ourselves, thus confirming our skeptical side. And they portray characters under extreme stress, contesting for power and testing their ideals.

For Hollywood the main challenge of political life is the struggle to maintain personal integrity despite the lure of corrupting power, a struggle only the exceptional person can win. The protagonists, even the successful ones, must endure disillusionment, self-doubt and temptation along the way; they must bring to the struggle qualities of character—idealism, determination, honest passion— rather than qualities of mind, for only these will overcome the forces of corruption within and without.

In films of the 1930s the political hero stayed in politics and stayed honest—like Jefferson Smith in Frank Capra's 1939 film *Mr. Smith Goes to Washington.* Post-war films, apparently finding such optimism hard to sustain, took three different paths with political themes. The hero, like Grant Matthews in Capra's *State of the Union* (1948), might keep his integrity by leaving the political arena. Or else, following the pattern of John Ford's *The Last Hurrah* (1958), the films might endorse certain forms of amiable "corruption," accepting them as benign alternatives to inhumane extremes of propriety and self-righteousness. Finally, there is the vision that has come to dominate the political film since Robert Rossen's *All the King's Men* (1949), that of the hero who succumbs to and embraces corruption for the sake of power.

These films have really been about the problem of community in America—the capacity for moral health, its ability to sustain itself and bind its citizens into a functioning social unit. The post-war loss of faith in the individual's ability to reconcile personal honor and political involvement marks a significant shift in our sense of ourselves as a nation.[1]

The core story of these films may best be described as the myth of the redeeming hero.

The community is basically healthy, founded on ideals which are sound and will sustain development. But it is threatened by moral corruption in its leadership, which has lost touch with those life-sustaining ideals. Unless the situation changes, the community will eventually suffer decay and disintegration.

And so, a rescuer comes. Of the community, his primary power to heal comes from his faithful commitment to those original ideals with which the leadership has lost touch. He has, as well, some special additional power, a skill or source of mystical strength which raises him to heroic stature.

But the hero also has a weakness: he is ignorant about the workings of the political structure, in its corrupt form; he does not know how to function in the world of power, where he must work his cure. He needs help from within the system, and he gains it through an ally, a convert to idealism who teaches him strategy and gives him the weapons he needs to pursue his fight.

The hero faces a period of trial; he is tempted to give up the struggle or to join the corruption. But eventually he gathers his resources, regains contact with his mystic source of strength and, with his ally, wins the day. The community is restored to its original health.

Two early examples appear in Norman Taurog's *The Phantom President* (1932) and Harold Lloyd's *Cat's Paw* (1934). In the former, an out-of-work vaudevillian who is the exact double of a stodgy political candidate—both parts played by George M. Cohan—uses show business techniques to pull together and revitalize the nation, winning the love of Claudette Colbert in the process. In *Cat's Paw* a missionary's son who was raised in China and trained by an oriental sage becomes mayor of an American city—put in place by a corrupt machine which wishes to use him for its own ends—and cleans it up by applying his mentor's teachings.

These films were only sketches for the fully developed story of the redeeming political hero in Capra's *Mr. Smith Goes to Washington* (1939), starring James Stewart and Jean Arthur. The corrupt governing unit is the Senate of the United States, where complacency and tolerance of evil flourish and corrupt "deals" are made against the best interests of the people. Senator Paine (Claude Rains) had, years before, gone to Washington full of idealism but after a time had succumbed to expediency and ambition. Now fully under the control of boss Jim Taylor (Edward Arnold) and his gang, Paine is being touted for vice-president by Taylor, who plans to enrich himself through a corrupt land deal.

In comes Jefferson Smith, appointed Senator after the death of Paine's colleague. Thought an ignorant, malleable yes-man, Smith is deemed no threat to the land deal being negotiated. When he finds out about it—somewhat slowly, because of his faith in Senator Paine, who had been his idealistic father's close friend years before—Smith tries to expose the motives behind the project.

Smith wishes to have a boys' camp built at the location where Taylor and Paine plan to build their profitable but unnecesary dam. They frame him with documents that seem to prove that he had a financial interest in the land. Smith fights back through a filibuster, hoping to clear his name. The corrupt machine, which controls the press in his home state, destroys his reputation and crushes his supporters. In the end Senator Paine, in a sudden and somewhat Euripidean reversal, is driven by his conscience to confess his forgeries and to clear Smith's name.

Smith had come to the Senate with a deep knowledge of American history and a faith in American ideals. These are the sources of his strength, renewed on his first arrival in Washington when he visits the monuments. The knowledge he needs about the workings of the Senate comes from Saunders (Jean Arthur), a hard-bitten secretary who had, like Paine, come to Washington with noble ideals but who is now only anxious to use her knowledge of the system. Smith's idealism renews her faith and enlists her in his fight. She gives him the knowledge he needs to conduct his struggle, clear his name and induce Paine's confession.

The film's turning point occurs at the Lincoln Memorial, to which the discouraged Smith has gone before giving up the struggle and leaving for home. Saunders there reminds him of his own statements of belief: "Lost causes are the only ones worth fighting for," and "All the good in the world comes from fools with faith."

These formulas, which had first reawakened in Saunders her lapsed idealism, she uses to rekindle Smith's flagging dedication. After that encounter he returns to the Senate to make his last stand in defense of his cause. The many allusions in the film to Christ—both verbal and visual—reinforce the notion of a redeeming hero come to cleanse the world. In the end, government is healed and society is restored to its health by being reminded of its original ideals.

Hollywood tried this formula once more after the war, in H.C. Porter's *The Farmer's Daughter* (1947), but though the story of a Swedish housemaid's congressional victory over a corrupt machine won Loretta Young an Oscar, it was so sentimentalized as to be fundamentally unserious in its view of politics.

More typical of postwar American attitudes was Capra's *State of the Union* (1948), based on a Pulitzer-Prize-winning Lindsay and Crouse play, in which an honest, plain-spoken industrialist who tries to set the country on a productive path by inducing all factions to transcend their separate interests, finds himself instead succumbing to the methods of his corrupt political managers.

Candidate Grant Matthews, played by Spencer Tracy, begins with a trust in the public which is returned by them. He understands that in order to be happy he needs a cause nobler than merely "beating out the other fellow." In the course of his campaign he is told that ordinary "people" mean nothing and that he must seek the support of influence peddlers, bosses representing divisive special interests. Matthews eventually becomes more than willing to "soft-soap a few idiots" in order to win.

On the other side, Mary—Katherine Hepburn—is contending for him both romantically and spiritually, and a powerful newspaper publisher, Kay Thorndike (Angela Landsbury), sees in Matthews a chance to gain great influence in the nation. Mary reminds Grant of his original ideals, but she is overshadowed by Thorndike's hardline view of the electorate. In the end Mary campaigns for her husband in the hypocritical style he has adopted, but the sight of her compromising herself on his behalf brings him to his senses. Aware that his loss of integrity has cost him the public's affection, he pulls out of politics, vowing to remain an independent voice of reform outside the political system.

Preston Sturges' *The Great McGinty* (1941) had, rather light-heartedly, taken a similar tack in its tale of an opportunistic hobo who became governor of a state through the machinations of a corrupt political machine, but who is crushed when he reforms and tries to run an honest administration.

Franklin Schaffner's 1964 film *The Best Man*, based on Gore Vidal's play, forced its hero, Bill Russell, into the position of deciding whether to blackmail his major opponent, Joe Cantwell, for his homosexual past, even as Cantwell was planning to blackmail him with information about a mental breakdown he had suffered. In the end, Russell (played by Henry Fonda) is disgusted by the corruption he has been forced to practice and endorses a bland nonentity, sacrificing his own chances for the presidency in order to ensure the defeat of the corrupt and unscrupulous Cantwell.

Vincent Canby, in his review of the film, summed up its message: that in politics the best man can't win; if he wins, he's not the best man. But the film offers as an alternative the best *possible* man—Art Hockstader, the former president who is capable of Machiavellian duplicity and manipulation, but who lives according to some simple and humane rules: that there are "no ends, only means"; and that "all that matters is how you feel about people and how you treat them." As a person and friend, Hockstader prefers candidate Russell, but fears he lacks the decisiveness of Cantwell, a Nixon-style, low-hitting political roughneck (played by Cliff Robertson). In the end, Russell's removal from the race defeats Cantwell. In defeat Cantwell sounds a dire warning about politics and community, challenging Russell: "You don't understand me; you don't understand politics; you don't understand this country. The way it is and the way we are. You're a fool." The movie does not reassure us that Cantwell is wrong.

In these films the redeeming hero cannot reconcile political success and personal honor, nor can he cure the ills of the community; his magic power does not suffice.

In the "Eisenhower era" films, the choice faced by the hero is set forth in more casual terms. The test he undergoes is more one of geniality than morality. In John Ford's *The Last Hurrah* (1958) and Otto Preminger's *Advise and Consent* (1962) a moderate amount of corruption is countenanced and even celebrated as necessary spice to the political process.

The community under Mayor Frank Skeffington, played by Spencer Tracy in Ford's version of O'Connor's novel, is as healthy as it ought to be. The ethnic politicians who have wrested power from the representatives of the Puritan past have established a comfortable, unfussy code of live-and-let-live. The Old Guard, non-ethnic protestants, are trying to make a comeback through a young generation of television-oriented political wimps. Skeffington is not saintly, but he does demonstrate human decency and shows an appreciation for ethnic diversity, the rights of the poor and the struggle for dignity. He is defeated at the polls by his callow opponent, but as we witness his last campaign through the eyes of his nephew, Adam, we are invited to mourn the passing of an era of humane values.

Advise and Consent also assumes that the soiled community is the only possible one. The Senate's health depends upon its stability as a unit. It can tolerate a good deal of variation—liberals and conservatives, the charming and the abrasive, the devious and the direct, the homosexual and the heterosexual—as long as each individual holds the good of the unit above personal ambitions and plays according to the rules. "He knows how to be a Senator," it is said of one character, and that fact excuses a multitude of sins; but the one who does not—Van Ackerman, the nasty liberal from Wyoming who ruins the reputation of his political foes to advance his cause—is destroyed by his colleagues for his merciless excesses.

The film's main action concerns the efforts of a dying president to appoint an able liberal as Secretary of State. But Robert Leffingwell, the candidate, had a communist past which he has covered up. Exposed, he must withdraw as a nominee. The Senate forgives him his errors and recognizes his strengths. At the death of the president, the modest, unassuming vice president takes over. He is no hero, but he is honest and tolerant and will not disturb the ecology of the political system, through which chief executives may rise to the stature required of their offices, aided by a Senate which can sanely temper, advise and guide.

These films deny the basic premises of the myth of redeeming hero, that the community needs to be healed, and that the cure can only be worked by someone of exceptional moral rectitude. Extremes of any kind—virtue or vice—are equally suspicious; the community is held together by the ideal of mutual toleration.

In the final version of the myth to be discussed here, the redeemer does face a social order in need of cleansing and fully intends to work a cure. But unlike Jefferson Smith or Grant Matthews the protagonists of these films surrender to corruption.

The idealist who succumbs to the temptations of power and demagoguery appears fully formed in Robert Rossen's *All the King's Men* (1950), based on Robert Penn Warren's novel. Willie Stark (Broderick Crawford, in an academy award winning performance) begins as a naive honest reformer, determined to speak intelligently to the electorate, trusting them to appreciate the logic of his enlightened tax proposals and the morality of his reasoned arguments against corrupt politics.

At first successful, Willie attracts a following after the death of some children in a schoolhouse about whose faulty construction he had warned the voters. His fame catapults him into a campaign for the governorship, but he conducts it badly and loses by a wide margin.

The turning point for Willie comes when he learns that he had been "set up" by political bosses, his campaign having been secretly supported by one establishment candidate to drain off votes from his major rival. In reaction Willie delivers a savage and rousing campaign speech which for the first time puts him in touch with the electorate—with their underlying resentments and their sense of being downtrodden: "Listen to me, you hicks. This is the truth. You're a hick and I'm a hick. I was sent to split the hick vote. But even a dog can stand on its hind legs. . . . Here it is, you hicks. Nail up anyone who stands in your way; if they don't deliver, give me the axe and I'll do it myself."

Willie's "magic" lies not in his ideals but in his anger, his ability to articulate the grievances and class antagonisms of his electorate. Through his identification with the resentments of the common people he gains their passionate support. Though he loses the election, he knows he has gained something: he "learned how to win." His next campaign sweeps him into the governorship and a reign of corruption, opportunism and tyranny.

Instead of curing the community, Willie becomes its worst symptom; instead of reinvigorating Willie with their innate good sense and sound ideals, the deracinated public merely becomes more corrupt. Those who were his mentors are also corrupted: for Willie's sake, Jack digs up information that will destroy his childhood idol Judge Stanton. Anne Stanton does worse; she betrays the Judge, her uncle, after she has replaced Sadie as Willie's mistress. It is Adam Stanton, her brother, who brings Willie's career to a halt by assassinating him on the eve of his greatest victory, when he has overcome an effort to impeach him.

In the end the community is liberated from Willie, but we are given no sense that it is in health again, or ever will be. The willing victims of Willie's egotism, Jack and Anne, turn to each other but it is a pale sense of renewal that we get from their final union. The community is no longer a certain source of moral health and insight; it has merely been saved from one tyrant for a time.

The corrupted political hero later turns up in Michael Ritchie's *The Candidate* (1972) and Alan Alda's *The Seduction of Joe Tynan*

(1979). In both, actors associated in their public lives with liberal causes and proud of their reputations for personal integrity—Robert Redford and Alan Alda—portray figures who succumb to the temptations of power.

Like *State of the Union, The Candidate* gives us a story of an outsider called upon by the political establishment to run for office because he has some special, non-political appeal. This time it is not a wealthy industrialist with a pragmatic turn of mind, but an idealistic young lawyer, Bill McKay, who runs a street-front free legal services office for the poor. Although he generally believes, with his radical followers, that "politics is bullshit," and is reasonably sure that he has no chance to win, he runs for the Senate in order to articulate his ideals.

As the campaign develops, so does his desire to win and so do his chances, though only at the cost of blurring or softening his opinions. As the movie shrewdly shows, the very technology through which the candidate conveys his message modifies both the message and him. Also, as the momentum of the campaign grows, pressure is put on McKay to seek the endorsement of his father, a former governor, and therefore a power in the state, but an opportunist and reactionary, unsympathetic to his son's ideals. The father is induced to endorse his son when he sees his success as a television personality, and a sound political "commodity." ("I think he's going to get his ass kicked," says the leader of a major union; "He's not. He's cute," says the elder McKay, effectively played by Melvyn Douglas.) Finally, McKay gets the ultimate accolade from his father—and confirmation of his loss of integrity—when he is told, with a congratulatory grin, "Son, you're a politician." At the film's end, McKay, who has won the election, turns to his campaign manager and asks, plaintively, "What do we do now?" In the process of winning, he forgot why he was running.

In the case of Alda's hero, the moral issues are far from clear-cut. A U.S. Senator, Joe Tynan considers mounting a campaign against a Supreme Court nominee with a racist past. His Senate colleague, an old friend and mentor (Melvyn Douglas) pleads with him to moderate his opposition, because he wants the nominee to be eliminated as an active force in politics: he fears having to run against him for the Senate. Tynan is put into the position of choosing between principle and friendship; but even that choice is not clear-cut, since the candidate has long since modified his racist opinions, and those opposing him are revealed to have, in their turn, opportunistic motives. Tynan fights against the appointment and wins, gaining for himself a groundswell of support for the presidency, though in the process driving his friend to a mental collapse.

On the domestic front, at the same time, Tynan's political ambitions are tearing his family apart. He keeps from his wife his presidential plans: she wishes to pursue training as a psychotherapist, and a campaign for the presidency would interfere with her progress. At the same time, their troubled and rebellious daughter drifts into alienation as a result of his inattention. Finally, Tynan embarks on a strenuous love affair with a political aide (played by Meryl Streep) who encourages his presidential ambitions.

At the film's conclusion the affair ends, but Tynan's wife, winning her domestic struggle for his affections, begins to understand for herself the lure of power and gets drawn into the orbit of his ambitions. It is as if *State of the Union* ended with Tracy chucking his morality for the sake of success and welcoming Hepburn's help in soft-soaping the gullible public.

In this version of the myth, the ills of the community finally overwhelm the hero: he comes to redeem, but he stays to join the corruption. His magic power, whatever it was, has failed to work its cure. In the spirit of the New Deal and in the face of a darkening international scene, the early political hero found salvation in American ideals, and was enriched by the larger community. Post-war films lost that vision; the most hopeful view they could muster was based not on expectations of curing our political ills but on acceptance of our imperfections in the hope that matters will get no worse.

However their visions have varied, these films have tried to confront problems of community and character in the way Hollywood knows best—in mythic terms. If the easy faith in the redeeming hero of the 1930s was to give way to a more pessimistic view of political life, there was usually an underlying sense that politics mattered, that there was a right way, or at least a liveable way, to conduct political life. Lurking beneath that level of expectation are such absurdist or farcical products as Stanley Kubrick's *Dr. Strangelove* (1963) or *The First Family* (1981) with their visions of imbecile presidents leading imbecile nations.

The core myth of the redeeming hero, however, remains the authentic American vision. If the nation never returns to it with the wholeharted innocence of the 1930s, it will remain the great original pattern from which we will always feel we have fallen.

Note

Films like John Cromwell's *Abe Lincoln in Illinois* (1940), Henry King's *Wilson* (1944) and Vincent Donehue's *Sunrise at Campobello* (1960) are best thought of as pageants. The exception may be John Ford's *Young Mr. Lincoln* (1939).

For discussion of American political films see Dwight Macdonald "Cinematic Politics," *Esqure*, June 1964; a follow-up article in August 1964; and Andrew Sarris, *Politics and Cinema* (New York: Columbia Univ. Press, 1978), pp. 16-18. Robert Sklar's *Movie-Made America: A Cultural History of American Movies*, relates mass culture and movie culture.

Little Miss Poker Face

Nancy B. Bouchier and John E. Findling

O ne does not hear much these days about "Little Miss Poker Face." Her reputation soared in the 1920s; she was almost as great a national treasure as Charles Lindbergh in those days of gin and roses. Yet she retired in the 1930s and lives in virtual obscurity in the 1980s. The wheel turns: it may be that the reputation and stature of Helen Wills will soar as feminism provides a new vision of America's past.

Helen Wills was born in Centreville, California, in October 1905, the daughter of a well-to-do doctor, C.A. Wills. Raised in Berkeley, she was an active child who did not take up tennis until the age of thirteen. On her fourteenth birthday, her father, whom she was now beating regularly at the game, bought her a membership in the prestigious Berkeley Tennis Club, where she began training and playing in junior tournaments under the guidance of Coach William "Pop" Fuller, a retired druggist. Her training regimen was relaxed, based on the attitude that tennis was a game to be played for pleasure alone, and much practice was accomplished through actual game situations and match play rather than serving and volleying drills. Wills preferred to practice against male players, because she strongly believed that women players were inferior to males, a point of view with which other champion female athletes occasionally took issue. At 5'7 ½" in height and weighing about 139 pounds, Wills developed the strength to play a game based on hard serves and powerful ground strokes. She also possessed unusual powers of concentration on the court, where she was so stony-faced that she often disarmed her opponents and earned the nickname, "Little Miss Poker Face."[1]

Wills showed promise from the beginning, won her first junior title at the age of fifteen (just two years after she had taken up the game), and attained national prominence in 1923, when at seventeen, she won her first U.S. women's singles title and the USLTA's number one ranking. By this time, sports writers had begun to tout her as the great American hope to win Wimbledon (no American woman had since 1907) and to dethrone Suzanne Lenglen, the reigning empress of women's tennis. Frequent comparisons were made between the styles of the two, and there was great disappointment when illness forced Lenglen out of Olympic competition in 1924. But Wills' triumph over Emilienne "Didi" Vlasto of France for the Olympic gold medal clearly established her as the pre-eminent challenger to Lenglen.[2] Late in the year, Lenglen stated in an interview, "I must get back into form before spring because I am very anxious to play Miss Wills next summer. If I am to lose my titles, there is no one in the world to whom I would rather pass them on than her."[3]

In 1925, however, Wills passed up the major European tennis tournaments, choosing instead to pursue her art studies at the University of California. There she was a diligent student, studying with the same concentration that would become her hallmark on the tennis court. In an article written years later, she pointed out that she decided to earn a Phi Beta Kappa key in college, studied hard and succeeded, but at the regrettable cost of not really learning anything. She admitted that she was only a "cup hunter in the field of scholarship," unconcerned with human nature, other people, or learning for its own sake. Nonetheless, her talent at sketching tennis players and costumes and painting water colors was well regarded. She gave her first art exhibition in 1929, and art study and patronage came increasingly to dominate her life.[4]

In January, 1926, Wills traveled to France, hoping to continue her art studies and to meet Lenglen in one of the winter tournaments held annually on the French Riviera. The Wills-Lenglen match, held finally on February 15, 1926, became a media event of incredible proportions, due in large measure to the marvelous contrast between the two. Press from all over the world crowded southern France; the Argentines paid the famous author Blasco-Ibanez $15,000 to cover the match, even though he had never seen tennis played before. Lenglen, the champion who had not lost a single match since defaulting to Molla Mallory in the 1921 U.S. Nationals, was high-strung, hot-tempered and imperial in manner, appearing on court with an entourage of retainers trailing behind. Her costume was colorful and sensual (she wore no petticoats underneath her tennis dress), and included an ermine-tripped wrap, and she was known to take sips of cognac between games. Apart from tennis, moreover, Lenglen was famous for her monumental sulks and temper tantrums and was alleged to lead a racy private life. Helen Wills, on the other hand, seemed worlds apart. Her intense concentration and lack of emotion on court were well known by this time, and her white school-girl tennis outfit was a symbol of purity and innocence. Off-court, her behavior was examplary, even under the intense scrutiny of the press, then operating at an all-time high on the curiosity index. But the New York *Times* could report that it was "a source of pride and justification to Americans to read of the manner in which Miss Wills has conducted herself in the face of the most flattering reception that has probably ever been accorded a woman athlete bent on foreign conquest." Throughout the weeks before the match, sports reporters made much of an imaginary feud between the two rivals, discussing the various excuses each had made to avoid meeting the other in earlier tournaments and emphasizing an apparent lack of mutual affection. Still, a New York *Times* editorial concluded that Wills "seems to be behaving the better of the two."[5]

In the match itself, Lenglen won, 6-3, 8-6, but the outcome was almost inconsequential. Wills had won—the match was described as "furious" and Lenglen tired badly toward the end of the second set—and when Lenglen turned professional later in the year, the American was acknowledged to be the best woman amateur player in the world. Since Wills adamantly refused all offers to turn professional (only amateurs play for fun; professionals work), there was never an opportunity for a Wills-Lenglen rematch.[6]

Helen Wills confirmed her position at the top with her first Wimbledon victory in 1927. A *Times* editorial rejoiced not just because she was an American, but also because she had "worked hard and hung on so persistently through former defeats that one feels she has earned her honors." From 1927 to 1933, Wills was the unchallenged champion of woman's amateur tennis. She won Wimbledon and the U.S. Nationals every year she entered, played on several Wightman Cup teams, and never lost a significant match in tournament competition. She married a wealthy young stockbroker named Frederick Moody in 1929 after a storybook romance—Moody supposedly first met Wills at the Lenglen match in 1926 and followed her around the tournament trail whenever he could. But in 1933, she faced a threat to her tennis supremacy posed by Helen Jacobs, another California tennis star who not only grew up on the same street as Wills but also attended the same university, played at the same tennis club and learned from the same coach. Jacobs was, however, the daughter of a butcher rather than a doctor, and was not at all a close friend of Wills and the press made almost as much of this contrast as it had seven years earlier in the Wills-Lenglen rivalry.[7]

The natural drama of the Wills-Jacobs confrontation, which came about in the finals of the 1933 U.S. Nationals was heightened by an unexpected event. Early in the year, Wills had injured her back, either from lifting heavy rocks in her garden, or as Ted Tinling, the tennis fashion designer, revealed in his gossipy memoirs, from "fooling around with Freddie in the surf." Although Wills continued her victory string during the early tournaments in 1933, she played with increasingly severe back pains. In the climactic match with Jacobs, Wills lost the first set, 6-8, won the second, 6-3, and was losing the third, 0-3, when she calmly walked over to the umpire and informed him that she was unable to play any longer, and was retiring from the match. Failing to shake Jacobs' hand at this sudden end to the match, Wills received hisses and catcalls from the crowd; these were followed up in the next several days by unsubtle remarks and insinuations from the press. Her retirement from the match was compared with Lenglen's controversial and unpopular default to Molla Mallory in the 1921 Nationals. But Wills' own account of the incident is straightforward and believable:

> In the third set of my singles match, I felt as if I were going to faint because of the pain in my back and hip and a complete numbness in my right leg. The match was long and by defaulting I did not wish to detract from the excellence of Miss Jacobs' play .... I still feel that I did right in withdrawing because I felt that I was on the verge of a collapse on the court.[8]

The reaction to the default was, as might be expected, sensational though short-lived. Certainly there were those who maintained that Wills' default was warranted, on the grounds that her untimely injury could in no way have been avoided. Others believed that despite her injury, she should have played out the match, fighting, as a true champion would, until the end. In London, front page coverage was given to the incident, and Wills' American critics were characterized as "giving her no more sympathy than a Roman crowd gave a defeated gladiator," leaving the clear impression that the English temperament was more generous than that of the American skeptics.[9]

After the default, Wills returned home to California and entered the hospital for tests and x-rays. Medical diagnosis revealed that her injury was a displaced vertebra. Her father began supervising a rehabilitation program for her, but it was not until 1935, after almost two years of convalescence, that she returned to competitive tennis, winning both the Wimbledon and U.S. Nationals crowns. In the latter tournament, she defeated her arch-rival Helen Jacobs, in the finals. After this victory, Wills was again inactive for two years, devoting her time to her artwork and giving art exhibitions across the United States. In 1938, however, she re-entered tournament tennis and achieved the distinction of being the first and only woman to win eight Wimbledon singles titles. After her final retirement in 1938 Helen Wills spent her time involved in her artistic activities with the same single-minded dedication that had been the hallmark of her tennis at the height of her career. Although she wrote an autobiography, *Fifteen-Thirty*, in 1937, she has written nothing on tennis and given relatively few interviews since then. Today, she lives quietly and reclusively in southern California.[10]

*   *   *

Helen Wills may be considered an authentic American sports heroine. There are several avenues by which she rose to attain that status. First, she was a champion of the 1920s, a period in American history was peculiarly given to hero-worship and to the promotion of organized sports. Second, she was a winner, an unchallenged champion over a remarkable length of time in her sport. Third, she had "style," both on the court and off, a style that was distinctive enough and attractive enough to win her a great number of admirers among the press and thus among the public. Fourth, she was an American champion in an international sport at a time when the American press and public was especially anxious to discover and nurture such a champion. By virtue of her skill with a tennis racket, Helen Wills was unquestionably a great champion, but the times in which she won her championships helped greatly to make her the sports heroine she was.

While heroes have always been a part of the cultural make-up of America, one is struck by the emphasis placed on them in the years immediately following World War I. A documentary film, *Chronicle of America's Jazz Age*, identifies no fewer than 104 personalities in its hour-long coverage of the 1920s; a similar film on the 1930s names only twenty-five or thirty. Most analysts attribute this unusually high level of hero-worship to a combination of factors. Many people were disillusioned with the unsatisfactory results of the war to end all wars and looked for someone in whom to place their shaken faith; others were disturbed by the rapid economic and technological changes of the decade and sought heroes of simple virtues who represented a safer and saner past. Still others were caught up in the very technological revolution their friends and relatives feared and found heroes created for them by the new media of popular culture—film, radio and mass circulation magazines.[11]

Much of the information spread by these new media concerned another new phenomenon of the 1920s: organized sport, now becoming an important cultural factor. Large numbers of sports personalities, mostly from baseball and boxing, joined the pantheon of American heroes. Frederick W. Cozens and Florence S. Stumpf have described this as the result of the emphasis on military athletics during World War I, a greater concern with college sports (particularly football), a general increase in prosperity and leisure time, and an inclination after the war toward the "pursuit of pleasure . . . a reaction to the grimness of the war just ended." Sports journalism began to expand greatly, individual sports writers such as Grantland Rice earned national recognition, and colorful sports personalities received unprecedented media attention as newspapers and magazines pandered to popular taste in order to increase circulation.[12]

Not only were sport personalities prominent for the first time among those whom America admired; women too (at least the right sort of women) were playing an increasingly important role in the public limelight, as they increased their stature and visibility in national life. The 1920s saw more and more women in politics, and the notion of the "working girl" was more respectable than ever. Schoolgirls were permitted to discover something about their individuality and at the same time encouraged to experience "the period of girlhood when romance is associated with heroes of history, with great living personages, and with causes and ideas, rather than with individuals of the opposite sex." Hence, if boys could identify with Babe Ruth or Jack Dempsey, then girls could seek a role model in Gertrude Ederle or Helen Wills. And it seems as though girls did. Writing in *Century* magazine, Ida Clyde Clark, a pioneer woman suffragist, suggested that a woman could be president, but admitted that most young women would vote for Mary Pickford or Helen Wills instead of more realistic candidates such as Alice Roosevelt Longworth or Ruth Hanna McCormick.[13]

Had Dixon Wecter in his book *The Hero in America* turned his attention toward the sports world of the 1920s he would hardly have found a better hero to fit his model than Helen Wills. By any standard of measurement, she was a person who attained great individual achievement. Her eight Wimbledon singles and three doubles titles, seven U.S. National singles and four doubles championships, and four French National crowns, together with scores of lesser tournament championships and gold medals in singles and doubles at the 1924 Olympics, all in the fifteen years between 1923 and 1938 is a record that may never be surpassed. She was, in the most literal sense of the word, a winner. Moreover, in her victories, she usually overwhelmed her opponents. At Wimbledon, for example, she played 56 singles matches over the years, and won 55; she played 117 sets, and won 111, she played 952 games, and won 698. Not only did she win tournaments in abundance, but she also won them in heroic style, a style of play on the court and a lifestyle off the court that was distinctive and attractive enough to the press and public to assure her a place in their hearts for many years.[15]

Wills was the first woman to play a power game of tennis. Her size and strength enabled her to dominate opponents with an intimidating serve and powerful groundstrokes played from the baseline. These attributes compensated for a relative lack of speed on the court by denying most of her opponents the ability to hit controlled spin shots to precise locations, usually far away from the opponent. Wills' game, when it was at its peak, could be awesome. In the 1925 U.S. Nationals, for example, she lost the first set of the finals against the highly regarded British player Kitty McKane and then came back to win the next two sets in a total of just twenty-five minutes.[16]

Even more remarkable was Wills' ability to concentrate. In 1921, Suzanne Lenglen had written a series of articles for the New York *Times*, and in one of her pieces she described the ideal tennis player as one who could, during a match, "shut out all of the world except tennis." While it is not known whether Helen Wills ever read Lenglen's articles, it is clear that she took these precepts to heart. More than any other tennis player of her time, Wills maintained two separate and distinct personalities. Her on-court personality was dominated by imperturbability and intense concentration. An example of this concentration is seen in an account of Wills' unsuccessful first attempt to capture the Wimbledon singles title in 1924 against Kitty McKane:

Wills won the first set and had [to win] four points to lead 5-1

in the second set. This should have given her a certain hold on
the cup but she faltered and the patriotic crowds, not having
seen a British winner since before World War I, cheered Kitty to
a memorable comeback victory. It was symptomatic of Wills'
mental detachment that after the most important match of her
life at that time, she asked the umpire the score!

Wills described her concentration in her own words in a July 1926
interview:

> I never plan ahead of my matches, and never remember
> them afterward. I play all my tennis on the court, and while I am
> playing, I am enjoying the fun of the game, and I am looking no
> further ahead than the next point. I find games exciting whether
> I am winning or losing and no more nerve-wracking at set point
> than at first point.[17]

Her concentration did not allow for facial expression while playing,
the feature of her game which earned her the nickname "Little Miss
Poker Face," which she later came to like. In a recent (and rare)
interview in *World Tennis Magazine*, Wills justified her renowned
impassiveness on the court and said that it was the result of
numerous lectures from her father who had given her strict orders
not to wince or screw up her face for fear that she would develop
unsightly lines. Whether or not this was the case, some interpreted
her cool impassivity to coldness, arrogance, and indifference to the
public. Thus it was headline news when after defeating Helen
Jacobs in the finals of the 1935 U.S. Nationals and succeeding in her
comeback effort following the controversial retirement from her
match with Jacobs two years earlier, she exuberantly threw her
racquet into the air and dashed forward to put her arm around
Jacobs' shoulder. When questioned later about her uncharacteristic
racquet-tossing response to victory, she replied, "Really, did I do
that? Well, it was bad manners. Nobody should throw a racquet."
Some concentration.[18]

Off the court, however, Wills was a different person altogether,
pleasant, articulate and interested in the world around her. She was
an excellent interview subject, who would happily talk about her
tennis game, her opponents' skills or weaknesses, or her abiding
interest in art. At the peak of her career, there was praise everywhere
for the "simple, unostentatious" Miss Wills, who was described in a

New York *Times* Sunday feature article:

> A healthier and more attractive picture of American
> girlhood could not be imagined than Miss Wills made as she
> came out on the turf dressed in her white tennis costume topped
> off by the inevitable visor. Her flawless skin, ruddy and glowing
> with health; the sparkle of her eyes, the springiness of her step,
> and the lightness of her mood all testified to the fact that this 21-
> year old girl, who returned just a year ago from Europe a
> convalescent, was in the perfection of physical condition.[19]

Finally, one aspect of Wills' style which received almost as
much attention as her concentration was her tennis costume.
Throughout her career, she invariably wore the same outfit,
consisting of modest white, pleated skirt falling to just below the
knees, a short-sleeved white "middie" blouse, and a white eyeshade
or visor. In the fashion-conscious 1920s, when there were
predictions that within a decade tennis players would be dressed
like bathing beauties, Wills simply said, "I'll wear the dress I like,",
and ignored the European players, like Lenglen, who were adopting
shorter skirts and sleeveless blouses. "The hard-hitting girls of
today want the sheerest silken garments, dainty and diaphonous,
and they want no more of them than the law demands," noted one
sportswriter in 1928, pointing out that Wills' style was two years
behind the times but suggesting at the same time that her outfit
concealed her hard-driving style, while briefer costumes revealed
every arm and shoulder movement.[20]

There is another way to think of the heroic "style" of Helen
Wills, and that is to use the model devised by various theorists such
as Leo Marx in *The Machine in the Garden*. In America, a heroic
person is one who can successfully mediate the natural state of
tension between power, symbolized by the Machine, and innocence,
symbolized by the Garden. Edison, for example, was a cultural hero
in the early twentieth century because he was perceived as having
achieved a balance between the powers of his inventiveness and the
innocence of his simple origins, lifestyle and value system. In the
same vein, Helen Wills combined tennis and her personality in a
way that made for a successful blending of the Machine and the
Garden.[21]

Wills' fiercely competetive game was nearly mechanical in its
execution, a feature that was constantly fascinating to
sportswriters and intriguing to a public living in a society
undergoing rapid technological change. Her game, built on

powerful strokes and absolute concentration, evoked words and phrases applicable to the machine. Allison Danzig of the New York *Times* was the outstanding tennis writer of the day. Consider the terms he used in an article describing Wills' game: "Hardest hitter...speed and depth .... power ... cold war ... without a trace of emotion ... tremendous power... hammered opponents into submission."

At the same time, articles about Wills off the court emphasized her beauty, style, grace and modest demeanor. Her behavior was impeccable, her outside activities in art were well regulated, and even her illnesses and injuries were of a nature to bring her sympathy. Consider Danzig's choice of words in his description of Wills' appearance: "Fair-skinned ... classic features ... poise ... lovely picture of young womanhood ... stately."[22]

A fourth aspect of Wills' cultural heroism, and one that is particularly pertinent to the 1920s, is the fact that she was an American and represented America explicitly in such matches as the Wightman Cup and the 1924 Olympics, and implicitly in any match she played against a foreign competitor. In the 1920s, the United States pursued a foreign policy that was aggressively nationalistic. Shunning international political organizations like the League of Nations for fear of being forced into undesirable or unwanted entanglements in international political or military adventures, the United States nevertheless promoted her commercial interests around the world, making loans and investments and selling American products abroad at record levels. Connected to this policy was a strong feeling of resentment toward European ex-allies. Many people were annoyed at suggestions that the United States should forgive war debts, at the bickering and turmoil that followed the Armistice and permeated the peace conference, and at the clear indications that the victors were greedy and vengeful. Returning soldiers came back disillusioned about the people and culture of Europe, and especially France, where most had served. Upon their return, these soldiers encountered a brief but sharp postwar economic slump which made jobs hard to find, and a government unsympathetic to their problems. This only served to deepen their disillusionment and anti-foreignism, which did not evaporate when prosperity came to many Americans by the mid-1920s.

At this time tennis was the most international of organized sports. Baseball, football and basketball were totally American, the Olympics were held only every four years, and the only foreign golf tournaments of any concern to Americans were the British Open and the British Amateur. Foreign golfers seldom competed in American tournaments. But in tennis, the premier tournament for all players was Wimbledon, and the U.S. Nationals and the French Open were close behind. Most ranked American players competed in the major European tournaments, and most of the better Europeans made annual trips to the States for competitive play. By the early 1920s, Bill Tilden had secured American dominance in men's tennis, but women's tennis continued to be controlled by Suzanne Lenglen and the other better French and British players. Not since 1907 had an American won the women's singles at Wimbledon, and sportswriters seldom let their readers forget it. So it was a major nationalistic victory for the United States when Wills won the tennis singles gold medal at the 1924 Olympics, but the victory was not quite complete, because of the illness that had forced Lenglen out of Olympic competition.

Hence the Wills-Lenglen match in 1926 became more than just a contest between two excellent tennis players. It was an international grudge match between the United States and France, and Wills and Lenglen were the designated warriors for each rival. Nearly every American newspaper article on the match described it in nationalistic terms, and because Helen Wills was the person she was, the contrasts were invariably flattering to her and subtly critical of Lenglen. The fact that Wills lost the match was almost buried under the news about the social activities peripheral to the match and the personalities involved, and when Wills had an attack of appendicitis and was forced to undergo surgery later that year, it was almost as if she had been a heroic war casualty. By the late 1920s, other Americans, including Helen Jacobs, had come along to insure continued American dominance of international women's tennis, but being the first to prevail on the European circuit after World War I helped Wills to reach the level of cultural heroism that she reached.

By the late 1930s, Wills' star qualities had faded. She began skipping major tournaments as early as 1931, and by the time of her final retirement in 1938 she was nearly thirty-three, a divorcee, and younger, more attractive players had come on the scene, many of whom played a hard-hitting power game modeled after her own. Moreover, the depression-ridden decade of the 1930s provided a much more hostile environment for American cultural heroes than the 1920s had. But for fifteen years, Wills had combined a superior style of tennis with a winning personality to establish herself as an authentic heroine. Had she maintained contact with the sport after 1938 as a teacher or writer, she would certainly be better remembered today. But her total withdrawal from the world of tournament tennis (and largely from the world itself) has meant that there have been no biographies, authorized or unauthorized, save her own, and very few interviews. Without a continual flow of information, we tend to forget even the finest of heroes, and we have largely forgotten Helen Wills.

Notes

[1]Wills, Helen, *Fifteen-Thirty* (New York, 1937), pp. 1-7.

[2]*Fifteen-Thirty*, pp. 48-51. This was of course the last time tournament tennis was played at the Olympic Games. See also the New York *Times*, July 21, 1924.

[3]New York *Times*, Oct. 4, 1924.

[4]Moody, Helen Wills, "Education of a Tennis Player." *Scribner's* 99 (May, 1936) pp. 267-270, (June,1935), pp. 336-37.

[5]New York *Times*, Jan. 25, 28, 31; Feb. 14-18, 1926; *Fifteen-Thirty*, pp. 84-85; Danzig Allison "Tennis," in Danzig, Allison and Peter Brandwein, eds., *Sport's Golden Age* (New York, 1948); Tinling, Ted (with Rod Humphries), *Love and Faults* (New York, 1979), pp. 33-38, 43-49.

[6]New York *Times*, Feb. 17, 1926; July 9, 1927.

[7]New York *Times*,July 4, 1927; Dec. 24, 1929; *Fifteen-Thirty*, pp. 163-168.

[7]Tinling, p, 132; *Fifteen-Thirty*, pp. 260-261 for description of match and withdrawal. See also Minton, Robert, *Forest Hills: An Illustrated History* (Philadelphia, 1975), pp. 133-135.

[9]See for example, *Newsweek* 2 (Sept. 2, 1933), pp. 18-20, and Jacobs, Helen Hull, *Gallery of Champions* (New York, 1949, pp. 30 ff.

[10]*Fifteen-Thirty*, pp. 288-294; Tingay, Lance, *100 Years of Wimbledon* (Enfield, Middlesex, 1977), pp. 68-71.

[11]Adler, Selig, *The Isolationist Impulse* (New York, 1957), pp. 98-100.

[12]Cozens, Frederick W. and Florence S. Stumpf, *Sports in American Life* (Chicago, 1953), pp. 116-119; 132-136.

[13]Cozens and Stumpf, pp. 132-136; Carter, Paul A., *Another Part of the Twenties* (New York, 1977), pp. 114-119; Clark, Ida Clyde, "Women in the White House: Have We a Presidential Possibility?" *Century*, 113 (March, 1927), pp. 590-598.

[14]Wecter, Dixon, *The Hero in America* (New York, 1941), pp. 415-430.

[15]See Tingay, pp. 68-69; and Marshall Fishwick, "The Hero in the Context of Social Change," in Hague, John A. (ed.) *American Character and Culture in a Changing World* (Westport, Ct., 1979), pp. 339-348.

[16]*Fifteen-Thirty*, pp. 62-64.

[17]See also *Fifteen-Thirty*, pp. 161-162.

[18]*Fifteen-Thirty*, pp. 288-294; "Helen Wills Takes a Rare Look Back with World Tennis" *World Tennis* (Feb. 1982), p. 82.

[19]New York *Times*, July 17, 1927.

[20]New York *Times*, July 8, July 20, 1929.

[21]Wachhorst, Wyn, *Thomas Alva Edison, An American Myth* (Cambridge, Ma., 1981), pp. 30-31; Merz, Charles, *The Great American Band Wagon* (New York,1928), pp. 222-228.

[22]Danzig, "Tennis," pp. 225-226. See also the description of Wills' game in the September 1929 *Literary Digest*, quoted in *Fifteen-Thirty*, pp. 153-161.

The Man Who Made
"Casey" Famous

Roberta J. Park

...And now the pitcher holds the ball, and now he lets it go,
And now the air is shattered by the force of Caseys blow...

*T*he game of baseball has fascinated millions of Americans for well over one hundred years. A kind of compelling logic stands out in Allen Guttmann's analysis of "Why Baseball Was Our National Game."[1] Even though many sports enthusiasts (and some sociologists, historians and sports writers) might disagree—holding, as has Glen Waggoner[2], for example, that football has become the pre-eminent spectator sport in America[3]— baseball has a rich tradition which embodies values which many Americans hold in high regard. In 1869, the year of the now famous tour of the Cincinnati Red Stockings, generally acknowledged to be the first all-professional baseball team.[4], *The Nation* declared:

> After sighing for generations that Providence should vouchsafe us a 'truly American' literature and 'truly American' architecture, and 'truly American' schools of painting and music, Providence, it appears, at length answers us (with the usual Providential derision of lofty aspirations) with a truly American game of ball.[5]

We have no way of knowing if the author of this article had the slightest idea of how "American" the notion of the game of baseball would soon become. Whatever the author's motives, the words were somehow startlingly prophetic. In less than a decade The National League of Professional Baseball Clubs would be established and baseball would have evolved to the stage where for many it had become "the national pastime"[6]—an appellation which seems totally appropriate if the context for the term is defined as spectator and participant sport.

Heroes and a few villains, whose exploits and misadventures have often been greatly magnified in the retelling of their deeds, have traditionally been an important part of baseball. In addition to the many flesh and blood figures who have passed through the annals of the game's history, one wholly mythical "hero" ("anti-hero" would be a more descriptive term) became an integral part of baseball lore. The suspense, the drama, even the majesty of the realistic images evoked of "the national pastime" are startingly, but not devastatingly, *shattered* by Casey's swinging third strike. Somehow, we all secretly "know" that in another place, another game, Casey—and Mudville—will win. As Ted Vincent recently noted in *Mudville's Revenge: The Rise and Fall of American Sport*, the Brooklyn Dodgers are fondly remembered for "wait till next year" and Casey is remembered far more for his strikeout than the home run he hits in the poem's sequel.[7]

In his comprehensive *American Baseball: From Gentleman's Sport to the Commissioner System*, David Voigt characterized the 1880s as baseball's "Golden Age."[8] John Betts has noted the rapid rise of baseball in the decades immediately following the Civil War, describing the earnestness with which local teams were formed and their activities followed by devoted fans.[9] Pride in the home club had become important for many towns and cities by the 1880s. Publications like the *Spirit of the Times, New York Clipper, Beadle's Dime Baseball Player* and *Police Gazette* romanticized the game and its players; baseball cards were as popular at the turn of the century as they would again become in the 1940s and 1950s. The depiction of the manliness and prowess of those who played the game quickly became a valued aspect of what Ralph Andreano has called the "Folk Hero Factor" in baseball.[10] In addition to the hero-worship which attached itself to such colorful real-life late 19th century figures as Adrian "Pop" Anson, Mike "King" Kelly and William "Buck" Ewing, the legendary "Casey" of the ballad-poem *Casey At The Bat* captured the imagination of thousands of the nation's baseball fans. To this day Casey's exploits are reflected in baseball lore. (The Stockton, California *Ports* Baseball Club assumed the title "Mudville" Ports in 1982; Vincent's 1981 book is titled *Mudville's Revenge;* and *No Joy in Mudville* is the title of Andreanos 1965 work.) Who was Casey? How did his story originate? How was it initially popularized? Who was the poem's most articulate spokesman? These are the questions with which this paper deals.

The 52-line comic ballad *Casey At The Bat* was the creation of a young Harvard graduate named Ernest Lawrence Thayer. It reflects the joys, hopes, sorrows, defeats and the inescapable drama of competitive sport. Lee Allen, author of *The Hot Stove League*, described Casey as a thoroughly fictitious character who embodies the essence of our national dream,[11] and the poem's most famous interpreter, DeWolfe Hopper, once declared: "There are one or more Caseys in every league, bush or big, and there is no day in the playing season that this same supreme tragedy, as stark as Aristophanes for the moment, does not befall some field."[12] Numerous attempts have been made to assign to Casey the personality of some real-life player, but Thayer insisted throughout his life-time that his Casey was an entirely fictional player.[13]

Ernest L. Thayer had been an outstanding philosophy student at Harvard, where he studied under William James. He was editor of the *Harvard Lampoon*, the author of the annual Hasty Pudding play, and a devoted baseball fan. Thayer's best friend at Harvard is said to have been Samuel E. Winslow, captain of the senior baseball team. In 1886 another of Thayer's friends at Harvard, William Randolph Hearst, who had recently taken over the direction of his father's *San Francisco Examiner*, invited Thayer to write a humor column for the paper's Sunday supplement. Writing under the by-line "Phin" (short for "Phinny," a name by which he had been known at Harvard), Thayer provided a column for the *Examiner* until ill-health forced him to return home to Massachusetts. He continued to send material to the *Examiner* for some time, however, and his final contribution was the now famous *Casey At The Bat* which appeared on Sunday, June 3, 1888.[14] The comic commentary on baseball's hopes and despairs might quickly have been forgotten had it not been for a chance sequence of events.

The man who made Casey famous—and who would claim in 1928 that he had recited the poem to captivated audiences at least "10,000 times"—was William DeWolf Hopper. In an era before radio and television had made it possible to reach enormous listening audiences, Hopper's continuing renditions of Casey were of inestimable value in spreading—if not more properly, creating—Casey's fame. After Hopper's recitations had begun to make Casey famous, newspapers and magazines all over the United States started to reprint the poem.

For some years the poem's authorship remained unclear, and Hopper acknowledged that he had been unaware that it was Thayer until the early 1890s when a Mr. Hammond introduced the two men.[15] Martin Gardner, author of *The Annotated Casey At The Bat,* recorded twenty-seven variations of the original ballad and maintained that many more exist—some of which could not be reproduced in polite literature.[16] (There are many versions which Gardner has not reported, including one humorous parody involving a character which Hopper had played for many years in light opera—"Dead-Eye Dick" of *H.M.S. Pinafore.* This particular version was composed by Edward F. O'Day for a luncheon at San Francisco's Bohemian Club in honor of Hopper, June 4, 1931).[17] Hopper first recreated Casey on Victor records in 1906 (reissued in 1913) and made a new recording in 1926 with *O'Toole's Touchdown* on the reverse side. Casey was the subject of the third of a series of articles which Hopper and Wesley W. Stout contributed to the *Saturday Evening Post.* (These were reprinted in Hopper's 1928 autobiography *Once A Clown Always A Clown*). Casey has also been the subject of at least two stories—a silent film in 1916 starring Hopper and another silent film in 1927 starring Wallace Beery. An opera entitled *The Mighty Casey* had its world premier in Hartford, Connecticut, on May 4, 1953.[18]

William DeWolfe Hopper was born to a prosperous New York family on March 30, 1858. His father had hoped that his son would pursue a career in law, but after passing the Harvard examination, the younger Hopper left college in favor of a career in acting. During the last two decades of the 19th century and first three decades of the 20th century he was considered to be one of the most brilliant figures on the American stage, making his professional debut in 1878 in *Our Boys.* He was a member of the original Weber and Fields Company, played London for eight months in John Philip Sousa's comic opera *El Capitan,* and created dozens of roles during his career. Among his best-known were Gilbert and Sullivan operettas, in which he played such comic figures as "Dead-Eye Dick" (*Pinafore*), "Ko-Ko" (*Mikado*) and the "Lord High Chancellor" (*Iolanthe*). He founded his own company in 1921.[19]

Ever since boyhood, baseball had been one of Hopper's primary interests. In *Comical Confessions of Clever Comedians,* which he helped edit in 1904,he declared: "Of all pastimes ... there is none that appeals to me more than baseball.... When I developed into boyhood, I used to go out in lots and knock out 'fungoes' and window panes."[20] He credited his friend and fellow actor Digby Bell with converting him to organized baseball and the two spent many afternoons at New York's Polo Grounds. When the New York actors and newspapermen played a benefit game at the Polo Grounds in

1889 Hopper played first base for the actors.[21] He regularly listened to baseball on the radio when this new medium made the transmission of games possible.[22] Although a keen fan, Hopper did not advocate exercise for himself. A *Chicago Evening Post* interview in 1932 reported: "Although he eschews exercise, .. Hopper admits having spent most of his time watching the Giants in action."[23] For many years he received a seasonal pass compliments of the National League. (For example, his number in 1923 was 46; in 1932 it was 33).[24] The Testimonial Dinner to Mr. DeWolf Hopper on the Occasion of His 50th Year on the American Stage included among its endorsers such baseball notables as Judge Kenesaw M. Landis, Commissioner, and John J. McGraw, Vice-President and Manager of the New York Baseball Club.[25]

It was probably on August 4, 1888 that Hopper first recited Casey, inserting the poem into the second act of *Prince Methusalem* at Walleck's Theater, 13th and Broadway, New York. During its infancy organized baseball was often in need of financial support. Hopper and Digby Bell had been giving Sunday-night benefits for the New York Giants for two years. They suggested to Colonel John A. McCaull, for whom they were then working—and under whose management Hopper made his metropolitan debut in comic opera— a "baseball night" at which the Chicago White Sox and the New York Giants would be feted. The announcement of this event, Hopper claimed, was seen by Archibald Clavering Gunter, author of over thirty novels, including the then best-selling *Mr. Barnes of New York*, who supposedly told McCaull: "I've got just the thing for your baseball night," providing him with a copy of Casey clipped from the San Francisco paper.[26] Hopper's own description of his initial recitation of Casey is worth repeating verbatim: "On his debut Casey lifted this audience, composed largely of baseball players and fans, out of their seats. When I dropped my voice to B flat, below low C, at 'the multitude was awed', I remember seeing Buck Ewing's (catcher Ewing was a favorite of Hopper) gallant mustacios give a single nervous twitch. And as the house, after a moment's startled silence, grasped the anticlimactic denouement, it shouted with glee."[27]

It is, indeed, the final resolution of the plot which gives to *Casey At The Bat* its particular, and quite probably its lasting, appeal. Everyone who has not previously heard the poem expects the mightly slugger to blast the ball out of the park, and when he strikes out there is a universal gasp of stunned disbelief. In his 1928 autobiography Hopper observed that fans go to parks when the

Yankees are playing not only to see Babe Ruth hit home runs but for the chance that the "King of Swat" might strike out.[28] (Whether today's sports fans would tolerate such ineptness from their heroes is quite another question. But perhaps they would, for many sports sociologists, psychiatrists and historians have suggested that it is the tension between the uncertainty of success and defeat which is one of sport's most captivating elements.)

Hopper seems not to have appreciated immediately the immense potential of Casey, and did not routinely use the poem until the second season of *Wang* (1892-93). He then tried Casey on his audience and again found it to be a huge success. In February 1893 the *New York Dramatic News* featured the young actor on its cover and pointed out the techniques by which Hopper had built, and would continue to build, his stage successes. In addition to his superb talents, the paper declared, it was his ability to "keep in touch with his public," "to learn and cater to popular fancies" and "to keep ahead of the times in the production of novelties."[29] Clearly, in the era of the rise of big-league baseball, Casey did cater to popular interest, and the recitations of this tragi-comic piece during regular productions, as well as during the increasingly popular "Evenings with DeWolf Hopper," proved salubrious for both Casey and Hopper. Here was an ideal means by which the actor could combine his sense of "good theater" with his love of the "national sport."

With the development of radio, Hopper was able to bring Casey to an even larger audience. The *New York American* stated in 1933 that DeWolf Hopper had proven to be an excellent choice for this rapidly developing form of mass communication because, in addition to his "... fine sense of dramatic art, he possesses a superb speaking voice."[30] Will Rogers declared in a 1933 syndicated column: "It was good today to hear our old friend DeWolf Hopper recite his epic *Casey At The Bat* .... The radio pays for itself every Fall during the world series."[31] Hopper, who had begun a new career in radio broadcasting in the early 1930s with the Kansas City symphony orchestra, was well aware of the debt he owed to Casey. In February 1935, only eight months before his death at the age of seventy-eight, he was quoted in the *Chicago Herald and Examiner*: "It was *Casey At The Bat* who first made my voice familiar to radio listeners. I owe a lot to Casey and I love him. He is the best friend I ever had."[32] William DeWolf Hopper, indeed, did owe a lot to Casey, but it seems reasonable to contend that Casey owes a lot to Hopper too.

Notes

[1]Allen Guttmann, *From Ritual to Record: The Nature of Modern Sports* (New York: Columbia Univ. Press, 1978).

[2]Glen Waggoner, "Money Games: The True Story About the Crazy Economics of Professional Sports," *Esquire*, June 1982, pp. 49-60.

[3]Certainly the annual income from professional football considerably exceeds the income from either professional baseball or professional basketball.

[4]Harold Seymour, *Baseball: The Early Years* (New York: Oxford, 1960), pp. 56-57.

[5]"The Philosophy of 'The National Game'," *The Nation*, August 26, 1869, pp. 167-168.

[6]See John A. Lucas and Ronald A. Smith, *Saga of American Sport* (Philadelphia: Lea and Fibeger, 1978), Chapter 11.

[7]Ted Vincent, *Mudville's Revenge: The Rise and Fall of American Sport* (New York: Seaview Books, 1981), p. 5.

[8]David Q. Voigt, *American Baseball: From Gentleman's Sport to the Commissioner System* (Norman: Univ. of Oklahoma Press, 1966), Vol. I, pp. 99-122.

[9]John R. Betts, *America's Sporting Heritage: 1850-1950* (Reading, Mass.: Addison-Wesley, 1974), pp. 92-97; 114-124.

[10]Ralph Andreano, *No Joy in Mudville: The Dilemma of Major League Baseball* (Cambridge, Mass.: Schenkman Publishing Co, 1965).

[11]Lee Allen, *The Hot Stove League* (New York: Barnes, 1955).

[12]DeWolf Hopper and Wesley Winans Stout, *Once a Clown; Always a Clown: Reminiscence of DeWolf Hopper* (Boston: Little, Brown, 1927), p. 93.

[13]Ibid., p. 85; Martin Gardner, *The Annotated Casey At The Bat: A Collection of Ballads About the Mighty Casey* (New York: Clarkson N. Potter, 1967), pp. 3; 175.

[14]*San Francisco Examiner*, June 3, 1888.

[15]Hopper and Stout, p. 85; undated typewritten manuscript entitled "Concentration Difficult" (by DeWolf Hopper. In possession of author).

[16]Gardner also records "O'Toole's Touchdown," a poem constructed with the same meter as "Casey," in which the hero crosses the *wrong* goal line, pp. 167-169.

[17]"Dick Dead-Eye at the Bat" (Typewritten manuscript dated June 4, 1931. In possession of author.)

[18]George Lorimer, Editor of *The Saturday Evening Post*, declared of these articles: "I don't think that I have ever read three more entertaining theatrical articles than those which greeted me upon my return from Europe last week." (Letter from George H. Lorimer to DeWolf Hopper, August 16, 1925. In possession of author.) Gardner, pp. 10-14.

[19]Harry P. Harrison presents "An Evening With DeWolf Hopper." (Souvenir Program.)

[20]DeWolf Hopper and F.P. Pitzer, *Comical Confessions of Clever Comedians* (New York: Street and Smith, 1904).

[21]Hopper and Stout, p. 82.

[22]See, for example, *Chicago Herald and Examiner*, July 23, 1934.

[23]*Chicago Evening Post*, August 23, 1932.

[24]The National League of Professional Baseball Clubs season pass cards inscribed with the name of DeWolf Hopper, 1923, 1929, 1932, 1934. Silver medallion inscribed "New York Giants, Season Pass, 1931." (In possession of author.)

[25]Souvenir program, *Testimonial Dinner to Mr. DeWolf Hopper on the Occasion of His Fiftieth Year on the American Stage*. The Hotel Savoy-Plaza, New York, October 21, 1928. President Coolidge also sent congratulations to Hopper for a half century of "clean and wholesome entertainment." (Letter from U.S. President Calvin Coolidge, October 18, 1928, in possession of author.)

[26]Hopper and Stout, pp. 76-80. Gardner disputes the date given by Hopper.

[27]Ibid., pp. 80-81.   [28]Ibid.

[29]*New York Dramatic News*, Feb. 11, 1893, p. 4.

[30]*New York American*, March 1, 1933. See also *Chicago Tribune*, Sept. 4, 1932.

[31]*Chicago American*, Sept. 29, 1932.

[32]*Chicago Herald and Examiner*, Feb. 10, 1935. DeWolf Hopper, Celebrated American Comedian and the DeWolf Players and Singers,, "An Evening with DeWolf Hopper," Souvenir Program, 1933.

"America's Greatest
Sports Figures"

David L. Porter

mericans have glorified numerous sports heroes. Athletic
figures often have fit the mold of the typical national hero:
self-reliant, industrious, courageous, adventurous,
determined, honest individuals achieving financial success
through dynamic action rather than intellectual prowess. Brilliant
performers, they have risen from modest socio-economic class
backgrounds to secure success. No study of the hero is complete
without them.[1]

The mythical Frank Merriwell, a dauntless character
popularized in the early twentieth century by Gilbert Patten,
typified the athletic hero our culture idolizes. Americans admired
Merriwell for basing sports achievements on hard work,
intelligence, courage, boldness, perseverance, diligence and high
moral principles. Merriwell's dramatic exploits on the diamond,
gridiron and track at a preparatory school and Yale University
thrilled readers. Overcoming countless obstacles, Merriwell
managed to hit game-winning home runs, dive for winning
touchdowns and edge opponents in track events.[2]

Who have been America's greatest real-life heroes? As a sport
historian I became curious about who have made the most
signficant contributions. A survey of sport historians seemed to be
the best way to find out. I polled 40 leading sport historians, asking
each to select our ten greatest sports figures. Thirty-one (78%)
responded, most belonging to the North American Society for Sport
History.[3]

Participants were not asked to rank their choices in numerical order. Two criteria were suggested: 1) the accomplishments of the sports figure and 2) his or her long-range impact on American sports. After tabulating the votes, I determined the order of the ten greatest sports figures in the eyes of these voters (table):

Table
Numerical Tallies and Rank

Rank	Sports Figure	Tallies
1	Babe Ruth	29
2	Babe Didriksen Zaharias	22
3	Jackie Robinson	18
4	Billie Jean Moffitt King	17
5	Muhammad Ali (Cassius Clay)	14
6	Jim Thorpe	13
7 (tie)	Walter Camp	12
7 (tie)	Joe Louis	12
9 (tie)	Red Grange	11
9 (tie)	Jesse Owens	11
11	James Naismith	9
12 (tie)	Avery Brundage	8
12 (tie)	Ty Cobb	8
12 (tie)	George Halas	8
15	Albert Spalding	7
16 (tie)	Branch Rickey	6
16 (tie)	Amos Alonzo Stagg	6

Fifty-eight other sports figures received votes.

1. *Babe Ruth (1895-1948)*: An outstanding pitcher for the Boston Red Sox (1914-1919) and slugging outfielder for the New York Yankees (1920-1934), Ruth was considered America's leading sports figure. Named by over 90% of the respondents, Ruth dominated professional baseball. He pitched brilliantly for the Red Sox, winning 93 of 137 decisions. The best left-handed pitcher in the American League, he helped his club capture three pennants and World Series and hurled around 30 consecutive shutout innings in post-season competition. In 1920 Ruth was sold to the New York Yankees. Nicknamed "The Bambino" and "The Sultan of Swat" he quickly established several home run marks and changed baseball from a scientific, strategy-oriented game to a power sport. Ruth in 1923 was selected the American League's Most Valuable Player and

in 1927 set the home run record for a 154 game season with 60. He developed the Yankees into baseball's greatest dynasty, helping them win seven pennants and four World Series. Besides compiling a career .342 batting average and .690 slugging percentage, Ruth hit 714 career home runs, knocked in 2,217 runs, and walked over 2,000 times. He made baseball the nation's most popular sport, rescuing it from a severely tarnished image following the Chicago Black Sox scandal. The best paid professional baseball player of his era, Ruth earned $80,000—a higher salary than President Herbert Hoover. Despite being undisciplined, he became the greatest folk hero of that generation and was adored by children. Ruth devoted much time to charity and established the Babe Ruth Foundation for underprivileged children. One of the first members of the National Baseball Hall of Fame, he was named by professional baseball in 1969 as its greatest player.[4]

2. *Babe Didrikson Zaharias (1914-1956)*: A superb all-round sport performer from 1932 to the mid-1950s, she remains America's greatest female athlete. Excelling in an era before many women competed in sports, she was named the Associated Press female athlete of the first half-century. The slim, muscular, long-legged Didrikson led the Dallas Golden Cyclone Basketball Club to a National Amateur Athletic Union championship and was selected an All-American in 1930. At the 1932 AAU women's national track and field championships, she won five events and smashed three world records. At the 1932 Olympic games, Didrikson captured gold medals and set world marks in the 80 meter hurdles and the javelin. She also established a world standard in the high jump, but was disqualified. Subsequently she earned $50,000 to $100,000 annually from advertisements, exhibitions and barnstorming tours with basketball and baseball teams. Zaharias later became the nation's premier amateur female golfer, winning 22 tournaments from 1944 to 1947. After turning professional in 1947, she captured 34 more tournaments, helped form the Ladies Professional Golf Association, and won three U.S. Open titles. Six times Zaharias was named by the Associated Press as the female athlete of the year. Despite battling cancer, she won the U.S. Open and the All-American Open in 1954. The following year Zaharias published an autobiography, *This Life I've Led*. Through her brilliant athletic record, she helped win recognition for women in sports.[5]

Jackie Robinson (1919-1972): Robinson played a pivotal role in desegregating professional sports as a premier infielder for the Brooklyn Dodgers (1947-1956). A determined, outspoken, fiery competitor, he starred in four sports for the University of California at Los Angeles and as shortstop for the Kansas City Monarchs of the Negro National League. In August, 1945 Dodger president Branch Rickey signed 26-year-old Robinson because of his outstanding athletic ability and character, making the latter the first twentieth century black participant in organized baseball. Robinson in 1946 starred for the Montreal Royals farm team, leading the International League in batting and stolen bases. The next season he joined the Dodgers as regular second baseman, winning *The Sporting News* Rookie of the Year honors. A clutch hitter, sure-footed infielder, and explosive base runner, Robinson braved the taunts of teammates, opposition players, executives and spectators to become one of the best and most exciting National League players. In 1949 he led the National League in batting and was selected Most Valuable Player. During an abbreviated major league career, Robinson compiled a .311 batting average and twice led the National League in stolen bases. The six-time All-Star helped the Dodgers win six pennants and one World Series title. Through Robinson's pioneering accomplishments, blacks gained acceptance into professional team sports. Robinson was the first black player elected to the National Baseball Hall of Fame and was selected by *Sport* as the premier athletic figure of the 1946-1971 era.[6]

Billie Jean Moffitt King (1943-   ): The youngest member of the distinguished group, she was a dominant female tennis player of the late 1960s and early 1970s and provided skillful leadership for and improved the quality of women's athletics. An articulate, flamboyant, dynamic competitor, she won the Wimbledon Doubles title at age 17 and subsequently captured more major tennis championships than any woman to her time. King not only won four U.S. Singles and six Wimbledon Singles titles, but numerous other individual and doubles championships. During the late 1960s, she helped form the Women's Tennis Association. King also secured improved monetary prizes for female athletes and achieved equity in prize money with male professionals at the Wimbledon and U.S. Open Tournaments. In 1971 she became the first lady to earn over $100,000 in annual prize money, thus enabling her to establish a women's sports magazine. King the next year organized a ladies' tour, the biggest financial bonanza in female athletic history. She in September, 1973 defeated Bobby Riggs in straight sets before a prime time television audience at the Houston Astrodome. Although Riggs had passed his prime, the match showed that women could achieve high level competitive performance with men in sports. She twice was chosen female athlete of the year and, as a spirited feminist, encouraged other women to pursue professional sports.[7]

5. *Muhammad Ali (1942-   )*: Born Cassius Marcellus Clay, Jr., he attracted world renown in the 1960s and 1970s as a flamboyant heavyweight champion, Black Muslim and war critic. A scientific fighter, Clay triumphed in 100 of 108 amateur bouts and in 1960 won the Olympic gold medal in the light-heavyweight division. He attracted national publicity by winning 19 consecutive professional fights, writing verse and recording an album. In February 1964, Clay upset Sonny Liston to capture the heavyweight title, converted to Black Muslim beliefs, and changed his name to Muhammad Ali. In March 1965, Ali retained his crown by knocking out Liston in one minute in the shortest bout in championship history. The next two years he successfully defended his title eight more times. During the Vietnam War, Ali refused military induction because of his religious beliefs and was sentenced to a five-year prison term. The World Boxing Association stripped Ali of his crown, although the U.S. Supreme Court eventually overturned his conviction. Ali in March 1971 lost a classic 15 round unanimous decision to heavyweight Joe Frazier before a huge audience over closed-circuit and satellite-transmitted television. In October 1974, he became the second heavyweight to regain the title by knocking out unbeaten George Foreman. Ali successfully defended his crown ten times before Leon Spinks in February, 1978 upset him. Later that year, he defeated Spinks to regain the title for an unprecedented third time. Ali, the "most talked about, written about, argued about, photographed athlete in history," lost only five of 61 bouts and grossed over $45 million. *The Ring* ranked him as the ninth greatest heavyweight, while the Associated Press selected him best Athlete of the 1970s.[8]

6. *Jim Thorpe (1888-1953)*: Thorpe, an undisciplined Sac and Fox Indian from Oklahoma, starred in football and track and remains the nation's greatest all-around athlete. A 6 foot, one inch 190 pounder, he consistently won a half dozen track events per meet, led the baseball team in hitting, and dominated several other sports at Carlisle Indian School in Pennsylvania. Under renowned coach Pop Warner, Thorpe excelled in football as a runner, passer, blocker, tackler and kicker. He helped Carlisle defeat formidable eastern

teams, meriting his selection twice as a halfback on Walter Camp's All-American squads. In 1912 Thorpe led the nation with 25 touchdowns and 198 points and was chosen Player of the Year by the Helms Athletic Foundation. At the 1912 Olympic Games at Stockholm, Sweden, he won gold medals in the decathalon and pentathalon. No other Olympian has accomplished that remarkable feat. Since these events required speed, strength, skill, stamina and all-around physical prowess, King Gustav V of Sweden proclaimed Thorpe the world's greatest athlete. The Olympic Committee stripped Thorpe of his medals and world records because he had played semi-professional baseball for $15 a week in the summer of 1909 in North Carolina. Subsequently he played professional baseball for New York, Cincinnati and Boston of the National League and professional football for the Canton Bulldogs. The popular, high-salaried Thorpe served as first president of the American Professional Football Association. Thorpe, who was selected by the Associated Press in 1950 as the greatest athlete of the half-century, belongs to the Professional Football Hall of Fame.[9]

7. *(tie) Walter Camp (1859-1925):* Camp played the most instrumental role in the early development of intercollegiate football. A 6 foot 200-pound halfback, he played for Yale University from 1876 to 1881. Twice captain of the squad, Camp exhibited exceptional speed, extraordinary strength and superb kicking skills. The author of three football books, he coached at Yale and Stanford University and had several undefeated teams. Amos Alonzo Stagg and other premier coaches played under Camp's tutelage. From 1876 to 1925 Camp attended nearly all football conventions and rules committee meetings. An innovator, he proposed reducing the number of players from 15 to 11, arranged the scrimmage line with seven linemen, established the quarterback position and introduced signal calling. Besides developing the scoring system, Camp encouraged strategy, physical conditioning, sportsmanship and eliminating dangerous formations. Football injuries increased alarmingly, prompting Camp in 1906 to form the American Intercollegiate Rules Committee. This committee reformed the sport by limiting massed interference, legalizing the forward pass, establishing neutral zones and requiring that teams move the ball ten yards in four downs to retain possession. From 1889 to 1924 he selected All-American squads recognizing the premier football players at each position.[10]

8. *(tie) Joe Louis (1914-1981):* Louis, a boxer named "The Brown

Bomber" became one of the nation's most popular black athletes. As an amateur, he won the Golden Gloves and National AAU light heavyweight titles. After turning professional in 1934, he defeated former heavyweight champions Primo Carnera, Max Baer and Jack Sharkey. In June 1936, German Max Schmeling upset Louis in 12 rounds to inflict the latter's first professional loss. Louis knocked out James Braddock in the eighth round in June, 1937 to win the heavyweight title, making him the second black and youngest fighter to hold the championship. The following year he demolished Schmeling in one round at Yankee Stadium before 70,000 spectators and a vast radio audience. The Nazis had utilized the fight for political propaganda purposes, as Hitler preached Aryan supremacy. Louis defended his title 25 times, knocking out 21 challengers. He held the championship 12 years, longer than any other heavyweight, and grossed an estimated $4.2 million. During World War II, Louis fought exhibitions for the military troops and donated his earnings to the armed forces. After retiring undefeated in 1949, Louis made unsuccessful comeback attempts against Ezzard Charles and Rocky Marciano. In 71 professional bouts, he lost only three times and was knocked out only once. *The Ring* selected Louis, a member of the Boxing Hall of Fame, as the nation's greatest heavyweight titleholder. Unlike controversial black heavyweight champion Jack Johnson, Louis followed a strict behavioral code, gave blacks someone to emulate and was well accepted by the dominant white society.[11]

9. (tie) Red Grange (1903-   ): Nicknamed "The Galloping Ghost" for his remarkable speed and agility, he popularized intercollegiate and professional football. Grange played halfback from 1923 to 1925 at the University of Illinois, where he scored 31 career touchdowns, ran over 3,600 yards and was three-time All-American. In October 1924 he helped Illinois upset the University of Michigan, winners of 20 consecutive games. Before 67,000 spectators, Grange gained 363 yards and scored three touchdowns against the formidable University of Pennsylvania. Grange, who drew record crowds, became the "most famous, most talked-about, most photographed, and most picturesque player that the game has ever produced." After the 1925 season, Grange signed a $30,000 contract with the Chicago Bears of the fledgling National Football League. Grange popularized and stabilized professional football, smashing attendance marks on a barnstorming tour. Although never achieving his college statistics, Grange remained an explosive runner and developed into a fine defensive back. During the 1930s, he helped the Bears win three division titles and one league championship. Besides having a lucrative professional football salary, Grange earned considerable income from movies, vaudeville, commercial endorsements, an insurance agency and television commentating. The game's first broken field runner, he was selected to the National Professional Football Hall of Fame.[12]

9. *(tie) Jesse Owens (1913-1980)*: Owens, who excelled in track and field, was a popular black athlete. At Fairview Junior High School and East Technical High School in Cleveland, he displayed exceptional speed in the 100 yard dash. In 1933 Owens won three track titles in the National Interscholastic Championships in Chicago. After enrolling at Ohio State University, he in May, 1935 made the greatest individual track and field performance in the nation's history. At the Big Ten Championships, Owens decisively shattered world records within about 45 minutes in the broad jump (26 feet, 8 1/4 inches), 200 yard dash (20.3 seconds), and 220 yard low hurdles (22.6 seconds), and tied the world standard in the 100 yard dash (9.4 seconds). No runner had set more than one world track record in a single day. At the 1936 Olympic games in Berlin, Germany, the Nazis ridiculed the black members of the American team. Despite this propaganda, Owens dominated the individual competition by winning four gold medals. He tied the Olympic record in the 100 meter dash, set an Olympic mark in the broad jump, and established world standards in the 200 meter dash and the 400 meter relay run. Owens impressed whites and blacks alike with his humble, dignified manner and encouraged other blacks to participate in track. An articulate speaker, he made good will tours for the U.S. State Department, established the junior sized Olympic games, and started a sports clinic for boys in Illinois. His records remained intact until the 1960s, although he ran on clay or cinder tracks, did not have starting blocks, and did not have rubberized runways in the broad jump.[13]

These ten sports figures met the criteria for greatness. As athletic performers, they made exceptional accomplishments and achievements. Zaharias and Thorpe starred in several sports, while others excelled in at least one major sport. Collectively they compiled many outstanding, enduring statistical records and made an enormous long range impact on the development of American sports. Ruth and Camp profoundly changed their sport's strategy or rules; Ruth, King, Ali, Louis and Grange popularized particular sports; Zaharias and King expedited the development of women's athletics; Ali, Louis and Owens became embroiled in major political controversies and, along with Robinson, encouraged blacks to enter sports; Zaharias, Ali, Thorpe and Owens starred in the Olympic games; and Robinson, King, Ali and Camp exhibited bold, dynamic leadership.

These sports figures fit the mold of the typical national hero. From humble socio-economic class backgrounds, they demonstrated self-reliance, determination, courage, adventure and honesty. These heroes thrilled spectators with incredible athletic performances and usually were well paid for their efforts.

Other sports figures fared quite well in the survey (table). James Naismith (basketball), Avery Brundage (Olympics), Ty Cobb (baseball), and George Halas (football) nearly made the list of ten greatest. Finishing further down the list were Albert Spalding (baseball, sporting goods), Branch Rickey (baseball), Amos Alonzo Stagg (football, basketball), Bobby Jones (golf), Tex Rickard (boxing promotions), Knute Rockne (football), Jack Johnson (boxing), Vince Lombardi (football), Arnold Palmer (golf), John L. Sullivan (boxing), Bill Tilden (tennis), Jack Dempsey (boxing), and Bill Russell (basketball).

These poll rankings will provoke controversy and debate. Some will argue that certain sports figures in the table should be included among the ten greatest. Sports notables, including Hank Aaron, Walter Johnson, Willie Mays and Cy Young (baseball); Jimmy Brown and Bear Bryant (football); Wilt Chamberlain and Kareem Abdul Jabbar (basketball); Jack Nicklaus (golf) and Mark Spitz (swimming) strikingly are absent from the list. A poll taken in a future generation might produce dramatically different results. Only time will tell.

Notes

[1]Marshall Fishwick, *American Heroes Myth and Reality* (Washington: Public Affairs Press, 1954), p. 157; John A. Lucas and Ronald A. Smith, *Saga of American Sport* (Philadelphia: Lea and Febiger, 1978), pp. 294-295.

[2]Stewart H. Holbrook, "Frank Merriwell at Yale Again—And Again and Again," *American Heritage,* XII (June, 1961), 24-28, 78-81; John R. Betts, *America's Sporting Heritage* (Reading, Mass.: Addison-Wesley, 1974), p. 237.

[3]I am deeply indebted to the 31 sport historians who participated in the survey. For an overview of American sport history, see Lucas and Smith, *Saga of American Sport*; Betts, *America's Sporting Heritage*; Wells Twombly, *200 Years of Sports in America: A Pageant of a Nation at Play,* (New York: McGraw-Hill, 1976); Foster Rhea Dulles, *A History of Recreation: America Learns to Play* 2nd ed. (New York: Appleton-Century-Crofts, 1965); and Earle Zeigler, *A*

History of Physical Education and Sport in the United States and Canada (Champaign, Ill.: Stipes Publishing Co., 1975).

[1]Robert Creamer, *Babe: The Legend Comes to Life* (New York: Simon & Schuster, 1974); Marshall Smelser, *The Life that Ruth Built: A Biography* (New York: Quadrangle Books, 1975); Robert Smith, *Babe Ruth's America* (New York: Crowell, 1974); Kal Wagenheim, *Babe Ruth: His Life and Legend* (New York: Praeger, 1974); Kenneth Sobol, *Babe Ruth and the American Dream* (New York: Ballantine, 1974); Babe Ruth as told to Bob Considine, *The Babe Ruth Story* (New York: Dutton, 1948). For shorter sketches, see David Q. Voigt, "George Herman (Babe) Ruth," in John A. Garraty and Edward T. James, eds., *Dictionary of American Biography*, Supp. Four, 1946-1950 (New York: Scribner's, 1974), pp. 709-712; "Babe Ruth," *Current Biography*, V (August, 1944), 571-575; *New York Times*, August 17, 1948; Jack Sher, "The Babe Ruth You Never Knew," in Ernest V. Heyn, ed., *Twelve Sport Immortals* (New York: Bartholomew House, 1949), pp. 280-304; Roger Kahn, "The Real Babe Ruth," *Esquire*, 50 (August, 1959); Paul Gallico, *Farewell to Sport* (New York: Knopf, 1938); Lawrence S. Ritter and Donald Honig, *The 100 Greatest Baseball Players of All Time* (New York: Crown, 1981); Robert Smith, *Baseball's Hall of Fame* (New York: Bantam, 1973). For background on baseball in Ruth's era, see Frederick G. Lieb, *The Boston Red Sox* (New York: Putnam's, 1947); Frank Graham, *The New York Yankees: An Informal History* (New York: Putnam's, 1943); Harold Seymour, *Baseball: The Golden Age* (New York: Oxford, 1971); David Q. Voigt, *Baseball: From the Commissioners to Continental Expansion* (Norman: Univ. of Oklahoma Press, 1970); Lawrence S. Ritter and Donald Honig, *The Image of Their Greatness: An Illustrated History of Baseball from 1900 to the Present* (New York: Crown, 1979); Richard C. Crepeau, *Baseball: America's Diamond Mind, 1919-1941* (Gainesville: Univ. Presses of Florida, 1980); Glenn Dickey, *The History of American League Baseball* (New York: Stein and Day, 1980).

[5]Babe Didrikson Zaharias, *This Life I've Led* (New York: Barnes, 1955); Ralph Adams Brown, "Mildred ('Babe') Didrikson Zaharias," in John A. Garraty, ed., *Dictionary of American Biography*, Supp. Six, 1956-1960 (New York: Scribner's, 1980), pp. 722-723; "Babe Didrikson Zaharias," *Current Biography*, VIII (April, 1947), 701-723; *New York Times*, Sept. 18, 1956; Betty Hicks, "Babe Didrikson Zaharias," *women Sports*, II (Nov., 1975); Paul Gallico, *The Golden People* (Garden City: Doubleday, 1965); Paul Gallico, "Farewell to the Babe," *Reader's Digest*, 70 (Jan., 1957), 21-23; Grantland Rice, *The Tumult and the Shouting: My Life in Sport* (New York: Barnes, 1954). For background on Olympics, see John A. Lucas, *The Modern Olympic Games* (New York: Barnes, 1980); John Kieran and Arthur Daley, *The Story of the Olympic Games: 776 B.C. to 1976* (Philadelphia: Lippincott, 1977); John Durant, *Highlights of the Olympics*, 5th ed. (New York: Hastings House, 1977); Lord Kilanin and John Rodda, eds., *The Olympic Games: 80 Years of People, Events and Records* (New York: Macmillan, 1976). For background on golf, see Henry Cotton, *A History of Golf Illustrated* (Philadelphia: Lippincott, 1975); Herbert W. Wind, *The Story of American Golf*, 3rd ed. (New York: Knopf, 1975); Will Grimsley, *Golf: Its History, People and Events* (Englewood Cliffs, N.J.: Prentice-Hall, 1966).

[6]Jackie Robinson, *I Never Had It Made* (New York: Putnam, 1972); Jackie Robinson, *Baseball Has Done It* (Philadelphia: Lippincott, 1964); Carl T. Rowan with Jackie Robinson, *Wait Till Next Year: The Story of Jackie Robinson* (New York: Random House, 1960); Milton J. Shapiro, *Jackie Robinson of the Brooklyn Dodgers* (New York: Julian Messner, 1966); Arthur Mann, *The Jackie Robinson Story* (New York: Grosset and Dunlap, 1956); Roger Kahn, *The Boys of Summer* (New York: Harper & Row, 1971); Robert W. Peterson, *Only the Ball was White* (Englewood Cliffs, N.J.: Prentice-Hall, 1970). For shorter sketches see "Jack Roosevelt Robinson," *Current Biography*, VIII (Feb., 1947), 544-547; *New York Times*, Oct. 25, 1972; Lucas and Smith, *Saga of American Sport*, pp. 386-390; Ritter and Honig, *100 Greatest*; Smith, *Baseball's Hall*; "Jack Roosevelt Robinson," in Charles Van Doren, ed., *Webster's American Biographies* (Springfield, Mass.: Merriam, 1979), pp. 881-882. For background on baseball in Robinson era, see A.S. "Doc" Young, *Negro Firsts in Sports* (Chicago: Johnson Publishing Co., 1963); Donald Honig, *Brooklyn Dodgers* (New York: St. Martin's, 1981); Tommy Holmes, *Baseball Dodgers* (New York: Macmillan, 1975); Lee Allen, *The National League Story* (New York: Hill and Wang, 1961); Ritter and Honig, *Image of Their Greatness.*

[7]Billie Jean King and Kim Chapin, *Billie Jean* (New York: Harper & Row, 1974); "Billie Jean (Moffitt) King," *Current Biography*, XXVIII (Dec., 1967), pp. 225-227; Grace Lichtenstein, *A Long Way, Baby: The Inside Story of the Women in Pro Tennis* (New York: Morrow, 1974); Trent Frayne, *Famous Women Tennis Players* (New York: Dodd, Mead, 1979). For background on tennis see Angela Lumpkin, *Women's Tennis: Historical Documentary* (Troy, N.Y.: Whitston, 1981); Herbert W. Wind, *Game, Set & Match: Great Moments in Tennis* (New York: Dutton, 1979);

Lance Tingay, *Tennis: A Pictorial History* (New York: Hastings House, 1977); Richard Shickel, *The World of Tennis* (New York: Random House, 1975); Will Grimsley, *Tennis: Its History, People and Events* (Englewood Cliffs, N.J.: Prentice-Hall, 1971).

⁸Muhammad Ali and Richard Durham, *The Greatest: My Own Story* (New York: Random House, 1975); Robert Lipsyte, *Free to Be Muhammad Ali* (New York: Harper & Row, 1978); Budd Schulberg, *Loser and Still Champion: Muhammad Ali* (New York: Doubleday, 1972); Don Atyeo and Dennis Felix, *The Holy Warrior: Muhammad Ali* (New York: Simon & Schuster, 1975); "Through the Years with Ali," *Sports Illustrated*, XLV (Dec. 20-27, 1976, 104-120; "Muhammad Ali," *Current Biography*, XXXIX (Nov., 1978), 8-12. For background on boxing, see Nat Fleischer and Sam Andre, *A Pictorial History of Boxing*, rev. ed. (Secaucus, N.J.: Citadel Press, 1975); John Durant, *The Heavyweight Champions*, 6th ed. (New York: Hastings House, 1976); John Grombach, *Saga of the Fist* (New York: Barnes, 1977); John McCallum, *The World Heavyweight Boxing Championship: A History* (Radnor, Pa.: Chilton, 1974.

⁹Robert W. Wheeler, *Jim Thorpe: World's Greatest Athlete* (Norman: Univ. of Oklahoma Press, 1975); Gene Schoor, *Jim Thorpe Story: America's Greatest Athlete* (New York: Julian Messner, 1951); Allison Danzig, *Oh, How They Played the Game: The Early Days of Football and the Heroes Who Made it Great* (New York: Macmillan, 1971); Frank Scully and Norman L. Sper, "Jim Thorpe: The Greatest Athlete Alive," *American Mercury*, 57 (August, 1943), 210-215; Al Stump, "Jim Thorpe: Greatest of Them All," in Ernest V. Heyn, ed., *Twelve More Sport Immortals* (New York: Bartholomew House, 1951), 281-303; Arthur Daley, *Pro Football's Hall of Fame* (New York: Quadrangle Books, 1963). For shorter sketches, see Ralph Adams Brown, "James Francis Thorpe," in John A. Garraty, ed., *Dictionary of American Biography*, Supp. Five, 1951-1955 (New York: Scribner's, 1977); *New York Times*, March 29, 1953. For background on college football, see Allison Danzig, *History of American Football: Its Great Teams, Coaches and Players* (Englewood Cliffs, N.J.: Prentice-Hall, 1956); Alexander Weyand, *The Saga of American Football* (New York: Macmillan, 1955); Ivan D. Kaye, *Good Clean Violence: A History of College Football* (Philadelphia: Lippincott, 1973); John Durant and Les Etter, *Highlights of College Football* (New York: Hastings House, 1970); Robert Leckie, *The Story of Football* (New York: Random House, 1965). For background on professional football, see Robert Smith, *Pro Football: The History of The Game and the Great Players* (Garden City: Doubleday, 1963); George Sullivan, *Pro Football's All-Time Greats: The Immortals in Pro Football's Hall of Fame* (New York: Putnam, 1968).

¹⁰Harford Powel, Jr., *Walter Camp: The Father of American Football* (Boston, 1926); Walter Chauncey Camp, *American Football* (New York: Harper's, 1894); *New York Times*, March 15, 1925; Parke H. Davis, *Football: The American Intercollegiate Game* (New York: Scribner's, 1911); N.G.O. "Walter Chauncey Camp," in Allen Johnson, ed., *Dictionary of American Biography*, Vol. III (New York: Scribner's, 1929), pp. 444-445; Danzig, *Oh, How They Played;* Guy Lewis, "The American Intercollegiate Football Spectacle, 1869-1917," (Ph.D. dissertation, Univ. of Maryland, 1964). For background on college football, see Danzig, *History;* Weyand, *Saga;* Kaye, *Good Clean Violence;* Durant and Etter, *Highlights;* Leckie, *Story.*

¹¹Anthony O. Edmonds, *Joe Louis* (Grand Rapids, Mich.: William B. Eerdmans, 1973); Anthony O. Edmonds, "The Second Louis-Schmeling Fight: Sport, Symbol and Culture," *Journal of Popular Culture*, VII (Summer 1973), 42-50; *New York Times*, April 13, 1981; Bill Libby, *Joe Louis: The Brown Bomber* (New York: Lothrop, Lee and Shepard, 1978); Joe Louis, *Joe Louis: Biography of a Champion* (New York: Harcourt Brace Jovanovich, 1978); Jack Sher, "The Saga of Joe Louis," in Heyn, ed., *Twelve Sport Immortals*, pp. 260-279. For background on boxing, see Fleischer and Andre, *Pictorial History;* Durant, *Heavyweight Champions;* Grombach, *Saga of Fist;* McCallum, *World Heavyweight.*

¹²Harold Red Grange, *Zuppke of Illinois* (Chicago: Glaser, 1937); Harold Edward Grange, *The Red Grange Story* (New York: Putnam's, 1953); Danzig, *Oh, How They Played;* Ed Fitzgerald, "Red Grange—The Galloping Ghost," in Heyn, ed., *Twelve More*, pp. 79-105; Mervin D. Hymen and Gordon S. White, Jr., *Big Ten Football: Its Life, Times, Great Coaches, Players and Games* (New York: Macmillan, 1977); "Football History as Made by the Illinois Iceman," *Literary Digest*, LXXXVII (Dec. 26, 1925), 29-34; Myron Cope, *The Game That Was: An Illustrated Account of the Tumultuous Early Days of Pro Football*, Rev. Ed. (New York: Crowell, 1974); Daley, *Pro Football's.* For shorter sketches, see "Harold Edward Grange," in Van Doren, ed., *Webster's American*, p. 421; Sullivan, *Pro Football's All-Time.* For background on college football, see Danzig, *History;* Weyand, *Saga;* Kaye, *Good Clean Violence;* Durant and Etter, *Highlights;* Leckie, *Story.* For background on professional football, see Smith, *Pro Football;* Roberts, *Story.*

¹³Jesse Owens with Paul Neimark, *Jesse: The Man Who Outran Hitler* (Plainfield, N.J.: Logos International, 1978); Richard D. Mandell, *The Nazi Olympics* (New York: Macmillan,

1971); Young, *Negro Firsts*; "The Black Olympian," *Black Sports*, II (May-June, 1972), 58-62; Lawrence N. Snyder, "My Boy Jesse," *Saturday Evening Post*, 209 (Nov. 7, 1936), 14-15. For shorter sketches, see "Jesse Owens," *Current Biography*, XVII (Nov. 1956), 475-477; *New York Times*, April 1, 1980; Stephen E. Ambrose, "Jesse Owens Breaks 4 Track Records," *American History Illustrated*, I (June 1966), 51-52. For background on Olympics, see Richard Espy, *The Politics of the Olympic Games* (Berkeley: Univ. of California Press, 1979); Lucas, *Modern Olympic*; Kieran and Daley, *Story of Olympic;* Durant, *Highlights*; Kilanin and Rodda, eds., *Olympic Games*.

The Astro-Political Hero

David S. Bertolotti

Heroes used to look to heaven; now they use space as a
stage. They are becoming astro-political.

Perhaps a paraphrase of biblical admonition best explains
how professionals in a technologically complex world
become cultural heroes: "Many are considered but few are
chosen." This was especially so in the early days of the Mercury
program selections. But who are the chosen and how are they
converted into the super-heroes? According to Willy Ley's *Rockets,
Missiles, and Men in Space* one needs to meet specific physical and
professional requirements. An astronaut candidate had to be
between twenty-eight and forty years old—twenty-eight because an
amount of accumulated knowledge was essential, under forty for no
apparent reason. Five feet-eleven inches was the maximum height
requirement and "excellent" physical condition—a rather arbitrary
measure—was deemed essential.[1]

Experience with machinery was also required, as was
experience in "extricating himself from difficult situations." In
December of 1958, then-President Eisenhower had concluded that
military pilots provided an acceptable pool from which a choice
would be made; therefore, the foundation was laid for a heroic
military elite, members of which had personal totals of 1500 hours
flying time, had graduated from test pilot school and were qualified
jet pilots. Such requirements naturally reduced the number of
potential candidates; however, in addition to creating a heroic elite,
the sociologically identifiable process of astropolitics was
beginning to develop and take shape. A further limitation resulted
from the fact that a Bachelor's degree or the equivalent, plus an I.Q.

of 125 or better was essential.[2]

The selection process was engaged: 508 screened service records resulted in 110 who met the stated requirements (58 Air Force, 47 Navy and five Marines). There were no Army candidates because none considered were graduates of test pilot school. Through a process of testing and examination, the number was reduced from sixty-nine to thirty-six to eighteen, and finally to the chosen seven, although the original plan was to have one-third of eighteen, or six, Mercury astronauts.[3]

Of course, as soon as the selections were made public, the press reported. *Life* carried features on those chosen for the first Mercury missions: "All are brave and patriotic, and all are supremely willing to make the trip."[4] John Glenn was described as being "kind to strangers, jovial with friends and tender with his family," in addition to being "moral and strongly religious" and "a determined realist."[5] He was shown in an accompanying photo "Helping his daughter Lyn shape hamburgers ... for the outdoor grill in the family's backyard."[6] Gus Grissom was portrayed as a "quiet little fellow who scoffs at the chance of being a hero" and readers were informed that his "silence is not the result of the politeness he learned as a Boy Scout back home in Mitchell, Indiana." Alan Shepard indicated, with some impatience: "We were asked to volunteer, not become heroes."[8] However, the time had come for astro-heroes, with no option, for heroes were to be created for the astropolitical machine; and, importantly, the machine guaranteed that the heroes would not be female, black, civilian or any combination thereof.

Ebony editorialized that the plight of women and blacks was once again the result of the myth of white male superiority "which has made the 'inferior race' and the 'weaker sex' miss the space ship."[9] Black comedian Nipsy Russell was shown holding up the *Life* issue which featured the Mercury seven and commented in his nightclub act: "Not a Mau Mau in the bunch. They're fixing to go off and leave us again."[10] The absence of women in the space program was in effect dictated by the Eisenhower decision to include only military test pilots. The *Science News Letter*, speaking of the astronauts only with male pronouns, contained the statement that "to defend themselves, the astronauts must maintain an intellectual rather than [an] emotional attitude toward what was going on around them."[11] NASA officials were more direct with their criticism of women in space. In one instance, on June 17, 1962, some announced that they believed space was "for men only." One official, who refused to be identified, said, "the talk of a proposed American space woman makes me sick to my stomach."[12] Using bureaucratic jargon, another stated: "We have no openings for female astronauts."[13]

NASA informed members of the House Science and Aeronautics subcommittee that "women astronauts would be a waste of space [pun?], a luxury the United States space effort cannot afford"[14] Not stopping there, the astropolitical machine also reinforced itself with its own humor, as well as its self-serving logic. Witness the following from one subcommittee session:

> If we find any women that demonstrate they have better qualifications for going into a program than we have ... we would welcome them with open arms, so to speak.[15]

The astronauts who said the above, when informed that a group of women had passed both the physical and the psychological examinations in Albuquerque, New Mexico, at the Lovelace Foundation, said "people don't qualify automatically by passing a test. My mother could pass the physical exam at Lovelace."[16]

Ebony, well-acquainted with techniques similar to those used by the astropoliticians, claimed the committee "even brought up the oldie about the cost of adding 'separate facilities'."[17] Readers were told that:

> Women use less oxygen, need less food, have a higher radiation tolerance. They also have greater endurance. Hence, space ladies, not withstanding the added cost of powder rooms, would be of far greater value to the satellite program than men.[18]

But how could non-members of the astropolitic machine compete with the media image of one astronaut portrayed as a "model of the old West hero who rode through his native Colorado, or at least through the pages of Owen Wister and Zane Grey."[19] Or another described "as American as apple pie, brought up in a place no more exotic than New Concord, Ohio; and who was self-reliant, modest and courageous."[20] Perhaps an editorial in the New York *Times* best crystallizes the general attitude of the press toward the astropolitical hero:

> This is the kind of talk you might hear from the guy next door, that is about what most of these astronauts turned out to be ... a remarkable number of them in the old athletic, moral,

Church-going mold—not self-righteous priggish characters but
not wild sophisticates either.[21]

In part the astronauts did not "turn out to be" as the editorial
suggests for the inscription was implicitly written into the selection
process as determined in 1958. In effect, the hero of the Space Age
simply filled an already prefabricated mold. Many questions
consequently arose, questions for which there are few
comprehensive answers. For instance, did the press advance a
heroic myth? Indeed, was the press duped by NASA publicity? Or,
worse yet, did the press actively engage in deliberate space
propaganda? Perhaps the following gives some indication of how
the press, like other elements of the astropolitic machine, worked.
Perhaps the press simply fulfilled a normal function, as did
government:

> What philosophy, theology, and art have been in the past—
> the major contexts of human creativity—technology is today.
> Each age produces its own type of hero: soldier, diplomat,
> theologian, statesman or businessman. Today who would deny
> that the technology occupies a hero's niche? Nobel Laureates,
> National Academy members, scientist-administrators, all
> possess a prestige that makes front page news and carries them
> past the highest councils of government and society.[22]

Assuming this to be somewhat accurate, the astronaut was a
logical candidate for technological hero; and, the astropolitical
system assured such results. Walter Cunningham, former
astronaut, in *The All American Boys*, which is an insider's look at
the space program, emphasizes the role of astropolitics in the early
years of the space program.

> In the beginning, though, it had to be a clean and simple
> world. There were seven, "we seven," all-for-one-and-one-for-all.
> They paraded together, went to the White House together, and
> lunched with the Shah of Iran together. They were a package.[23]

Of course, some myths had to be perpetuated: those of physical
fitness, intelligence, discipline and many others designed to create
the super-hero. Cunningham in part challenges the media with
what he terms "a few obvious commandments . . . a buyers guide to
how astropolitics was played." Four of these commandments—
there are ten in all—are directly related to the selection process:

If you were one of the boys you didn't necessarily have to be terribly competent.

Physical fitness, other than injuries or death, had no bearing on your status, opportunities, or accomplishments.

First impressions, even those formed before you joined the program, could affect your career almost forever.

Scientist-astronauts stayed at the bottom of the pecking order.[24]

In summary, Thomas Carlyle, who in the nineteenth century could in no manner predict the nature of the astropolitical hero, did, in effect, adequately condense the general condition of hero selection: "The Hero can be a Poet, Prophet, King, Priest or what you will according to the kind of world he finds himself born into."[25]

In retrospect, the view from the 1980s toward those early days of the space program provide some curious perspectives, especially relative to John Glenn, the popular hero who may become President of the United States. Indeed, the times may be ripe for "a heroic president," which, although not identical to "a hero for president" still is appropriate since not many people have proven themselves heroic before the fact. In other words, Glenn already is a national hero with a historic and a documentable personality. Where else can a nation find a real, non-Hollywood hero? And, importantly, one who is also respected internationally. Where else can a nation find a hero of science and technology so appropriate for a nation of increasing science and technology? In effect, a heroic personage is available as the nation is indeed searching for a president of heroic potential. Glenn has the political aspirations, the required ambition which has marked his life, and the present opportunity.

In a real sense, the depth of Glenn's heroic achievement can be measured by the following. Glenn has served in the United States Senate longer than he was an astronaut. Yet few Senators would be considered heroic enough to be president, if heroic at all. It is Glenn's adventure as astro-heroic which may win him the presidency, not his tenure as Senator from Ohio. The media during the early space program is in part responsible for this, so are the history books, as are the John Glenn Junior High Schools; and another factor of significant proportions need be considered.

Past U.S. Presidents have not been especially heroic. Perhaps Washington, Lincoln, Teddy Roosevelt, Franklin D. Roosevelt and Eisenhower qualify. Some would argue for Truman. But in general those with charisma, of whatever duration, were not very heroic. PT-

109 was not D-Day, the Great Society lacked the heroic adventure of San Juan Hill, and telephone calls to winning football coaches cannot compete with the New Deal.

It somehow seems logical and appropriate that John Glenn Astro-hero become John Glenn President of the United States, not so much because of the historical or technological significance of his space adventure but because of the romantic and idealized perceptions of that accomplishment. In the final analysis, how often does a generation have the opportunity to vote for its own hero, myth and all?

Notes

[1]Ley, Willy, *Rockets, Missiles, and Men in Space* (New York: Viking), p. 374.
[2]Ibid.   [3]Ibid.
[4]"The Chosen Three for the First Space Ride," *Life*, 3 March 1961, 50: 24-31.
[5]Ibid.   [6]Ibid.   [7]Ibid., p. 29.   [8]Ibid., p. 30.
[9]"In the Same Boat," *Ebony* Oct. 1962, 17: 72-73.
[10]Loc. Cit.
[11]"Oneness with the Universe," *Science News Letter*, 13 May 1961 79: 293.
[12]New York *Times*, June 17, 1962, Sec. A, p. 16.
[13]"Ladies in Space," *Saturday Evening Post* 25 August 1962, 235: 86.
[14]"Space Women Expensive," *Science News Letter*, 4 August 1962, 82: 70.
[15]"Astronettes," *Newsweek*, 30 July 1962, 60: 17-18.
[16]"Space Women Expensive," et al.
[17]"In the Same Boat," et al.
[18]Loc cit.
[19]"Playing it Cool: The Astronaut and His Wife," *Newsweek* 4 June 1962, 59: 22.
[20]"John Glenn: One Machine That Worked Without a Flaw," *Newsweek*, 5 May 1962, 59: 19-24.
[21]Reston, James, "Halfway to Heaven in Living Color," New York *Times*, 21 February 1962, p. 44.
[22]Douglas Jack D. *The Technological Threat* (Englewood Cliffs, N.J.: Prentice-Hall, 1971), p. 40. Chapter "The Import of Technological Decision Making," by Robert Nisbet.
[23]Cunningham, Walter, *The All-American Boys* (New York: Macmillan, 1977), p. 83.
[24]Ibid., p. 98.
[25]Carlyle, Thomas, *Heroes and Hero-Worship.*

Archetypal Alloy:
Reagan's Rhetorical Image

Sarah Russell Hankins

We are threatened by a new and a peculiarly American menace,... the menace of unreality.... We risk being the first people in history to have been able to make their illusions so vivid, so persuasive, so 'realistic' that they can live in them. We are the most illusioned people on earth.[1]

*I*n the October, 1979 issue of *The Reader's Digest,* a eulogy appeared entitled "Unforgettable John Wayne." The author was a friend of Wayne and a celebrity in his own right. He spoke of their companionship, the values they held in common, his wife's admiration for the man. In a most skillful whitewash of the McCarthy era, he cited the time when they nearly singlehandedly stopped "the determined bid by a band of Communists to take control of the film industry,"[2] and their humanity toward and forgiveness of those who admitted they were wrong. The personalities and goals of the two men seem to meld into a single heroic spirit. The writer stated that Wayne "gave the whole world the image of what an American should be,"[3] and supported his friend's assertion that "one day those doctrinaire liberals will wake up to find the pendulum has swung the other way."[4]

Thirteen months later the author of this article was elected President of the United States.

In 1980 the American people elected Ronald Reagan, a seventy-year-old actor, to the highest position in the land, a man who "bears the fingerprints of a lifetime of selling an image, a rehearsed product."[5] In casting Reagan in the role of president, a drama has unfolded in which a mortal can play the part of the hero while retaining his limited human capacities. It is an ironic heroism in which all parties involved know the story, enter the fiction, and draw strength from its portrayal—the pageant of the rugged individualist enacted on the American political stage.[6]

Attraction to Reagan can be traced by exploring the rhetoric of the archetypal hero as portrayed in the media for thirty years and the stylistic changes which that hero has adopted to reflect the political climate and the president. Within this analogic analysis, two points become clear. First, archetypal, heroic characteristics (or the lack thereof) have traditionally been assigned to a president after his election to office. Mythic characterizations of Reagan, however, were created before Reagan's election, and the drama has been reinforced so intently that one critic remarked, "As his first year in office draws to a close, Ronald Reagan's Presidency resembles one of those flamboyant Hollywood movies in which he once starred."[7] Second, this exploration of American media mythology, political celebrities, and exigencies since the era of the classic Western reveals a social structure clinging to the fictional notion of an all-powerful heroic figure. This portrayal persists despite the realization of America's increasing vulnerabilities and the conflict of ideologies between the autonomous hero and democratic equality. The presidential choice in 1980 was an attempt to align the human with the illusion of the heroic, a person who could act the part of the leading man and who has cultivated a persona that is quintessentially American—the classic hero of the Old West.

I

The Hero

Every human time has had its Super Dudes. They attest to the peculiar intelligence and aspirations of a culture. They are communal dream work.[8]

Let's return to the heyday of Western genre in America.[9] *The Gunfighter* appeared in 1950, *High Noon* in 1952, *Shane* in 1953. In 1958 fifty-four feature-length Westerns were made and in 1959, eight of the top ten television shows were Westerns. This was the age of the classic Western hero, the embodiment of the rugged individualist. In the 1960s, however, the hero of the Western changed. Increasingly the outlaw was portrayed in the hero role, as in *Butch Cassidy and the Sundance Kid* and *Left-Handed Gun*. In another aberration of the classic Western, small armies of men were pitted against each other as in *The Wild Bunch*. The archetypal hero of the West was riding into the sunset. Even John Wayne turned from his Western role in 1969 to make *True Grit*, where his character took on unherolike characteristics.

In the late 60s a new popular hero appeared, the cult figure Jesus, who took the nation by storm through the early 70s, inspiring lapel buttons, wristwatch faces and bumper stickers urging, "Honk If You Love Jesus!"[10] With the advent of the rock opera *Jesus Christ Superstar* in 1971 the Jesus Movement was in full swing. By 1973, however, press reports started dwindling, and by 1976, the Jesus of the streets had been reinstitutionalized.

As the Jesus Movement was moving indoors, Superheroes were gaining popularity. Marvel and DC Comics found they were appealing on an adult level to the same kids they had entertained thirty years before.[11] *The Six Million Dollar Man, The Bionic Woman, The Incredible Hulk* and *Wonder Woman* appeared on TV. The most popular Superhero is Superman, originally born in 1933, revived during the 1950s and presently reaching new zeniths of popularity with two feature-length movies, dolls, lunchboxes, T-shirts, posters, capes and telephone booth cookie jars.

The Heroic Archetype

It is monumentally difficult to separate the hero from his story. After all, that is how he makes his mark on society. Cawelti sees myth as an archetypal pattern.[12] Campbell calls the hero's story a "monomyth" and follows his journey through separation or departure, trials and victories of initiation, and a return and reintegration with society.[13] Frye describes the myth's central form as a dialectic between good and evil, formalizing it as "the perilous journey and the preliminary minor adventures, the crucial struggle, usually some kind of battle in which either the hero or his foe, or both, must die; and the exultation of the hero."[14] The paradigmatic structure of the classic hero's story is comforting in its redundancy, satisfying our need for a "sense of tradition, the norms of associative living, moral principles, the valid rules of proper deportment."[15]

As the hero's narrative unfolds, however, five generic qualities of the hero emerge. These qualities are found in virtually every archetypal hero and distinguish him from the mortals he must save.

First, the hero comes from outside the society in which he operates. The Western hero is described as a "transcendent figure."[16] Superman is labelled "not from earth."[17] Jesus and Superman, compared in a religious article, are referred to as coming "from the heavens."[18] Origins such as those witnessed in the Bible or in the womb-like structure that propels the baby Superman to earth in *Superman I* may not be as important as rebirth, however, when superpowers are gained or regained. The Lone Ranger's mystic relationship to Tonto (a popular culture Good Samaritan), Jesus' baptism by John the Baptist, and Superman's trek to regain his hero status from Mother in *Superman II* all attest to an outside source validating a rebirth into herohood. Every week over the credits on *The Six Million Dollar Man* re-runs, the audience is reminded of Steve Austin's technological baptism which gave him his extraordinary powers.

Second, the hero always has an ascetic quality, an austerity that seems related somehow to his virtue. Campbell describes this denial as "self-achieved submission.'[19] Warshow states that the hero's "loneliness is organic, not imposed on him by his situation but belonging to him intimately and testifying to his completeness."[20] The hero has no regard for material belongings or for money; we never see Clark Kent's apartment in the Superman films. Jesus and the Western hero are just assumed to have a bed for the night. They each have only one change of clothes (though Superman needs two). Gurko describes the hero's attitude toward life as one of "sublime indifference."[21]

A third characteristic is the hero's aversion to women.[22] Mary Magdelene laments, "I don't know how to love him," in *Jesus Christ Superstar*. The Western hero rides off leaving the girl behind, and poor Superman gives up his powers to the temptations of the flesh, only to be beaten up at a truck stop five minutes later in the movie *Superman II*. Clearly the classic hero was not meant to fool around.

Fourth, the hero exhibits compassion for the society of which he is not really a part. In *Superman II* the villains from Krypton recognize this as a weakness in the hero. "Why, he actually likes those creatures," marvels General Zod. "Probably like pets," Ursa replies incredulously. Jesus heals the sick and the lame, reveres the little children, rescues the woman at the well; Shane fights to save the town which has rejected him; the Lone Ranger flits in and out long enough to vanquish the bad guys while remaining aloof to society in general, always moving on its periphery.

Fifth, the hero is always in the business of conquering evil.[23] Eco contends that each hero "is gifted with such powers that he could actually take over the government, defeat the army or alter the equilibrium of planetary politics. On the other hand, it is clear that each of these characters is profoundly kind, moral, faithful to human and natural laws, and therefore it is right (and it is nice) that he uses his powers only to the end of good."[24]

These five archetypal characteristics are intrinsic to the Western hero, Jesus and Superhero. Although their narratives differ to form a reciprocal bond with the era in which they gain popularity, the hero's mythic journey also remains basically unaltered, and has invited several analysts to directly compare variations of the archetypal hero's story. For example, Homans wonders whether revivalist religion produced the Western.[25] Shane is described as "the new Christ, the frontier Christ, coming down from a Western Olympus to help the cause of the farmers against the ranchers.[26] Brown acknowledges a similarity between the Superman and Jesus stories.[27] Joseph Campbell successfully weaves the story of Jesus into a worldwide structure of mythic heroes in *The Hero With a Thousand Faces*.

Mythic Heroes and Presidents

> Within each [horizontal] period the structure of the myth corresponds to the conceptual needs of social and self understanding required by the dominant social institutions of that period; the historical changes in the structure of myth correspond to the changes in the structure of those dominant institutions.[28]

In *Six Guns and Society*, Will Wright analyzes the changes in the structure of the Western in terms of evolving economic, familial and educational systems within society. In the ebb and flow of institutional actions, he finds a corresponding structure in social mythology. The same analogic correspondence can be found in the reciprocal interaction between the media hero of an era and the Man-Who-Would-Be-National-Hero, the president. This interaction reveals itself both through the direct symbolization of President-equals-Hero or President-doesn't-equal—Hero, and indirectly through societal adoption of media heroes who either reflect or are the antithesis of the presidential image.

In 1953 Dwight Eisenhower became the first Republican president in twenty years. In 1945, he had led the Allied Armies to victory in World War II and became president of Columbia University in 1948, NATO Commander in 1950. He was a proven leader, a patriarchal figure. His landslide victories in 1952 and 1956 established his credibility as the American people's overwhelming choice. Although history has labelled him a do-nothing president, at the time he was seen as successful. He promised to end the Korean conflict, and did so shortly after inauguration. His early years in office were a time of relative tranquility for an America which had too long been fighting. When Ike was caricatured, it was often as a statesman above reproach.[29] Shoemaker portrayed him in startling realism as the Captain of the Ship.[30]

Not incidentally, the popular Western hero of the day mirrored the presidential qualities. It was an era when personal sacrifice to a cause was applauded, and a mortal could still rise to greatness, even hero status, through determination and hard work. Although society was portrayed as weak, strong stewardship was at hand to lead the flock. In Lenihan's words, "Traditional American ideals and the system of government worked out by the nation's enlightened forefathers were adequate to meet present-day challenges, if only Americans would recall and live up to the national heritage."[31]

Toward the end of Ike's second term, America was restless. Racial conflict was causing riots and taking lives. Although we launched a space satellite in 1958, we were in second place to the Russians. The McCarthy witch hunts had undermined America's sense of fair play. By the end of Eisenhower's second term, the image of the guy-in-the-white-hat was dusty and we needed a new vision.

It appeared for a time that Kennedy could step into the hero role. He was young and idealistic. In his inaugural address he captured the imagination of a changing social structure, proclaiming that "a new generation of Americans" had taken leadership of the country, and that we would "pay any price, bear any burden, meet any hardship, support any friend, oppose any foe to assure the survival and the success of liberty."[32] In the era of the New Frontier, political cartoons captured him directly as the romantic Western hero or the frontier hero in the Davy Crockett tradition.[33] Kennedy established the Peace Corps, man flew in space, the Freedom March inspired new unity in minority groups eager for equality.

By 1963, however, some of the shine had worn off the Kennedy star. The Cuban Missile Crisis nearly flung us into war with the Russians, the Berlin Wall produced a cold war cynicism, rumblings were heard in South Vietnam. Disillusionment also followed in the political cartooning of 1963, where Kennedy was portrayed as the Western hero shot up with arrows, and a covered wagon he was driving labelled "New Frontier" was shown losing a wheel.[34] Clifford Baldowski pictured a boy scout Kennedy carrying a little old lady across the street; she is hitting him with her umbrella and screaming, "I don't wanta cross the street, dammit!"[35]

On November 22, 1963, John F. Kennedy was assassinated. With him died the New Frontier, and soon the classic hero of the Western frontier died, too, replaced by the outlaw as anti-hero in movies such as *Hud* and *Hombre*. Cunning, savagery and revenge marked the Westerns of the 1960s with Clint Eastwood rising to stardom in *A Fistful of Dollars, The Good, The Bad and The Ugly* and *Hang 'Em High*. The lone gunman hero was replaced with armies of men, frontier S.W.A.T. teams as it were, portrayed in such films as *The Professionals* and *The Wild Bunch*.

This change in Western genre was a reflection of the social upheaval in progress in America.[36] In 1965, troops were sent to Vietnam, polarizing the American population. Racial rioting reached into the North and the West, as the sociopolitical climate of America underwent change. Johnson was caught in this cultural maelstrom and never could shake his image of the conniving, crass buffoon. Although political cartoons portrayed him in Western garb, he was the big-talking Texan, not the romantic hero. He seldom made it to a horse, but was seen riding a bull or a jackass.[37] In 1968, Martin Luther King and Bobby Kennedy were assassinated, the Vietnam War was raging, civil strife was rampant, and Johnson declined to run for a second term as president, saying there was such "division in the American House" that he was withdrawing in the name of national unity.[38] It was at this moment in history when a new popular hero emerged who was the antithesis of the presidential image, the cult figure Jesus.

Although evangelism had been steadily gaining converts since the Billy Graham televised crusades were started in the late-50s, suddenly in 1968 and 1969, articles in the popular press concerning a kind of "storefront Christianity" escalated sharply. Followers were called "Jesus Freaks," a name they wore proudly until *Look* coined the phrase "Jesus Moment" to describe the phenomenon.[39] Early articles cited social unrest as the breeding ground for the evangelical movement.[40] David Gordon saw the movement as allowing the participants a reconciliation between childhood codes of morality and youth-oriented styles of living.[41] Hundreds of people were baptized at a time in the Pacific Ocean; thousands attended rallies in Madison Square Garden.

Rev. David Wilkerson, a New York urban minister, explained that "the kids are discovering that they have to find something bigger than themselves and bigger than the world that they can believe in and follow."[42] America's archetypal hero had adopted a touch of the divine. More important, in an age when bloodshed and war were unpopular, America chose a pacifist hero to follow. Although the basic hero's pilgrimage story was the same, Jesus always took the peacemaking route, even when it meant his death, because he knew there would be ultimate redemption and eternal life. Young people, drawn between personal morality and patriotism, ostracized or banished from their native land, sought visionary hopes of that same future redemption and adopted a conciliatory romantic hero as the symbol of the era.

Several religious analysts forecast that the biggest danger for the Jesus Movement was "the eternal temptation to turn spontaneity into drill."[43] By 1973, cultism was being exposed. Of thirteen articles on religion and evangelism that appeared in the popular press in that year, five concerned deprogramming.[44] In 1975 and 1976 the death knell was sounded when "Whatever Happened to..." articles appeared in national magazines.[45] Jesus had seen America through the political corruption of the Nixon administration, a messy war and a bitter aftermath for returning veterans and their friends who "didn't go." The pacifist hero Jesus was replaced with what people perceived to be his counterpart in real life—the "nice guy" image of Gerald Ford.

However, without the divine clout in the archetypal hero image of Jesus, "nice guys" in public office are usually characterized as ineffectual and bumbling. Many angry Americans had expected the swift justice of an avenging Yahweh toward a villainous Richard Nixon. Instead Ford proved too Christlike when he pardoned Nixon's offenses. After only two years, Ford was replaced in 1976. Carter came from outside the Washington establishment, was unknown to the society he was to serve, and seemed to have the answers. However, Carter also proved too nice in the office. His Human Rights Credo was laughed at in the global community. He was ineffective during the hostage crisis, botched the rescue mission in Iran and appeared impotent in dealing with the Ayatollah.

Meanwhile on the media scene, Americans were getting mad as

hell, and were not going to take it anymore. Superheroes emerged, ready to match right with might. The Superhero was no bully, but you could push him only so far before he took physical action. America was getting shoved around and needed a return to the no-nonsense, don't-cross-that-line nation of the past. A particularly poignant political cartoon shows a forlorn Carter standing in a Superman suit that is several sizes too big for him.[46] Once more, the reactionary media hero was the antithesis of the presidential image.

Significantly the Superhero adaptation of the popular hero role combines the physical action of the Western hero of the 1950s with the divine powers of the Jesus figure of the late 60s. In our global embarrassment and seeming cowardice, America envisioned a mythic hero who could protect us from all dangers and recreate national pride. The stage was set for the entrance of Reagan, who in 1976 was defeated in the presidential primary because he was perceived "as someone who 'shoots from the hip,' a man of action," and four years later was elected for that same reason.[47]

A landslide victory ushered in the Reagan era in much the same spirit that Ike entered office nearly thirty years before. During the campaign voters experienced an eerie *deja vu* as the Reagan political themes echoed the rhetoric of the 1950s—returning America to her rightful glory, reestablishing traditional values, stressing an omnipotent rightness of cause rather than an impotent niceness of intentions. David Henry points out that these themes have formed Reagan's "Speech" since his days with *G.E. Theater* in the late 50s.[48] Fisher feels that Reagan expounds the rhetoric of "romantic democracy" and argues that we may have a potential romantic hero in the White House.[49]

Reagan's image seems the political embodiment of the mythic Westerner. Fisher cites his origins, his love for Western clothing and horseback riding, his film and television roles, his rugged appearance and his personal virtues of honesty, sincerity, innocence, optimism and certainty as contributing to an image of "Town Marshal."[50] *Maclean's*, Canada's popular magazine, has used references in its titles to the Western hero concept in virtually every article about Reagan, even though the contents of the stories have nothing to do with Reagan's Western style.[51] Political cartoonists overwhelmingly favor a Western hero caricature for Reagan.[52] The assassination attempt did much to fortify the Reagan legend. Walking into the hospital with a bullet in his chest, Reagan seemed the real-life counterpart of his Western film image.

In truth, only six of the fifty-three movies which Reagan made were Westerns. America's lasting perception of him as the Westerner came from his short two-year stint as host on *Death Valley Days* from 1964 to 1966. Reagan's Western persona appears much of the time to be more hype than reality. Ritter claims that Reagan became governor of California in 1966 because of his outstanding public relations efforts.[53] Certainly his eulogy to John Wayne one month before his announcement as candidate for the presidency is an example of brilliant PR work which enhanced his Western hero image. A biting analysis of the Reagan style is offered by Allan Fotheringham: "Most politicians spend their lives learning to be actors. Here is an actor learning to be a politician. The arts merge. Subterfuge and guile fold and meld, fuzz into one. There is no DMZ. Mushification reigns."[54]

Boorstin distinguishes between a hero, who is famous because he is great, and a celebrity, who seems great because he is famous.[55] Are we bumping into a potential romantic hero, as Fisher would claim, or "The Cardboard Messiah: Starring Ronald Reagan as the Giant Replica of a Statesman"?[56]

Myth and Reagan

Each sociopolitical era must have a human representation as the embodiment of cultural values. Although these heroic images are archetypally the same, their style is determined by social and political events of the moment and those events which immediately preceded the emergence of the hero persona. When this embodiment of social values loses rhetorical significance for an age, a stylistically different variation of the archetype emerges to become the cultural talisman for the new era.[57] Thus in the 1950s and early 60s, the time of Eisenhower and Kennedy, the president was mirrored in the media is hero of the day. In the late 60s and early 70s, a hawkish Johnson and a corrupt Nixon were countered with the pacifistic, pure image of Jesus. This hero, in turn, ushered in the presidencies of Ford and Carter. In the late 70s the backlash against the "nice guy" image in the White House was the Superhero, an avenging yet compassionate god.

The Superhero as national savior presents a study in paradox. The might and right hero as Carlyle saw him is the antithesis of democratic stewardship, in which all the people have a voice in the government. It smacks of dictatorship or monarchy. "American democracy," argues Boorstin, "is embarrassed in the charismatic presence."[58] At the same time, as Eco states, "in an industrial society ... where man becomes a number in the realm of the organization which has usurped his decision-making role, .. the positive hero must embody to an unthinkable degree the power demands that the citizen nurtures but can not satisfy."[59]

Enter the Superhero, bigger than life, more powerful than a locomotive, able to leap tall buildings at a single bound. His is a beguiling, utterly fictional presence, for although Americans are aware of our vulnerability in a nuclear world, we would not ever want real persons with superpowers among us, even if they were on our side. They could too soon rule us, as the bad guys from Krypton (the Shadow of Superman) pointed out in *Superman II.*

The illusion of Superman shows as well disillusionment in the notion of mortals as heroes that was entertained with the Western hero. We have not returned to the Western genre as our means of escape. The only true Western movie of late, *The Lone Ranger*, would reveal in close analysis that with his never-ending supply of silver bullets, a Pegasus-like steed, and an immaculate masked presence, the Lone Ranger is more Superhero than Wild West figure.

Instead, to reflect a nostalgic though uncertain belief in the value system of the Old West, we have adopted the aura of *Urban Cowboy*, a sterile, uptown Western culture where the bucking bulls run on electricity. In this costume party setting, the boots are made of iguana skin, cowboys smoke Marlboros and smell of "Chaps" cologne rather than the corral, and our jeans have some Frenchman's name across the rear end. If Ronald Reagan fits into this milieu, then he is playing our game, the game of cultural make-believe.

We do not expect Reagan to be the Western hero; we are content to have him play the part. We do not want to return to the 1950s; we just need the comforting rhetoric of that era. In 1982, to extend McLuhan's thought, the medium of Ronald Reagan is his message. Yet it is not the verified message of an Eisenhower, the visionary message of a Kennedy, or the sincere if inept message of a Ford or Carter. It is a xeroxed message, a copy of the original, once removed from reality.

The election of Reagan was a grand experiment. Could a leading man carry off a magnificent improvisation in life? Could he make us believe, if only for a time, that this was the America of the past? Could he make us believe hard enough to regain some of those old values?

If Reagan succeeds in this portrayal of statesman and hero, it will be superb acting. "No man can be a hero to his valet," Carlyle wrote. The American public is the valet to the president via the news media, which report sneezes, curses, stumbles and gastrointestinal upsets with relish. The modern president must play the part to make us believe the role. If Reagan can do this, he will be a hard act to follow. If he does not succeed in his portrayal, it may well mark the end of the celebrity president. The homely, Lincolnesque figure might seem a relief to an over-indulged, media literate public.

In a recent poll, 49% of the people rated Reagan's performance in office as excellent or good, while 46% felt his performance thus far was only fair or poor. The same poll showed 46% of those polled saying that cuts in his social programs had gone too far.[60] This would indicate that the scale is balanced almost evenly between those who view Reagan's policies with nostalgic relief and those who have benefitted by the social revolutions of the 1960s and 70s and have no intention of turning back the clock. It would seem that much of Reagan's future success will depend on whether he can make the past a move forward.[61]

Meanwhile, to paraphrase Wister in *The Virginian*, this time will never come again. But for the moment, we ride in our historic yesterday.

Notes

Reprinted with permission from *Central States Speech Journal*, 33 (Spring 1983). Copyright 1983, Central States Speech Association.

[1]Daniel J. Boorstin, *The Image* (New York: Atheneum, 1962), p. 240.
[2]Ronald Reagan, "Unforgettable John Wayne," *The Reader's Digest*, Oct. 1979, p. 117.
[3]Ibid., p. 116.   [4]Ibid., p. 118.
[5]Allan Fotheringham, "A Lifetime of Rehearsals from Stagecoach to Stage," *Maclean's*, July 28, 1980, p. 56.
[6]For an insightful examination of the presidency as "real-fiction," see Walter R. Fisher, "Rhetorical Fiction and the Presidency," *Quarterly Journal of Speech*, 66 (April 1980), 119-126.
[7]Loye Miller, Jr., "Reagan Year Marked by Success, But Path Strewn with Obstacles," *The Denver Post*, Dec. 27, 1981, p. 8A.
[8]Keith D. Mano, "Super Freaks," *National Review*, May 13, 1977, p. 566.
[9]The genre of the Western is traced in greater detail in Thomas H. Pauly, "What's Happened to the Western Movie?" *Western Humanities Review* 28 (Summer 1974), 260-269. See also John Cawelti, *The Six-Gun Mystique* (Bowling Green, Ohio: Popular Press, 1971), and Will Wright, *Six Guns and Society* (Berkeley: Univ. of California Press, 1975).
[10]Edward E. Plowman, "Whatever Happened to the Jesus Movement?" *Christianity Today*, Oct. 24, 1975, p. 46.
[11]See especially "Heroes of Our Times," *Maclean's*, May 15, 1978, pp. 30-44, and Ivor Davis, "Marketing the Man of Steel," *Maclean's* Dec. 11, 1978, pp. 46-50.
[12]Cawelti, p. 27.
[13]Joseph Campbell, *The Hero With a Thousand Faces* (Princeton Univ. Press, 1968), pp. 49-243.
[14]Northrup Frye, *Anatomy of Criticism* (Princeton Univ. Press, 1957), p. 187.

[15]Umberto Eco, "The Myth of Superman," *The Role of the Reader* (Bloomington, IN: Indiana Univ. Press, 1979), p. 121.

[16]Peter Homans, "Puritanism Revisited: An Analysis of the Contemporary Screen-Image Western," *Studies in Public Communication*, No. 3 (Chicago: Dept. of Sociology, Univ. of Chicago, Summer, 1961), rpt. *Focus on the Western*, ed. Jack Nachbar (Englewood Cliffs, N.J.: Prentice-Hall, 1974), p. 84.

[17]Eco, p. 107.

[18]O.J. Brown, "Superman on the Screen: Counterfeit Myth?" *Christianity Today*, April 20, 1979, p. 26. For accounts of extraordinary birth and childhood in hero figures, see Campbell, pp. 297-311.

[19]Campbell, p. 16. Homans also treats this subject, p. 91.

[20]Robert Warshow, *The Immediate Experience* (Garden City, N.Y.: Doubleday, 1962), p. 137.

[21]Leo Gurko, *Heroes, Highbrows and the Popular Mind* (New York: Bobbs-Merrill, 1953), p. 175.

[22]See Cawelti, pp. 49, 61-62; Homans, pp. 85, 90; Campbell, pp. 65, 120-126. To replace women, Leslie Fiedler describes the hero's relationship with other men of lesser stature as "the pure marriage of males—sexless and holy, a kind of counter-matrimony," in *Love and Death in the American Novel* (1960; rpt. New York: Stein and Day, 1966), p. 211.

[23]See Pauly, pp. 265-266; Eco, p. 108; Homans, p. 91.

[24]Eco, p. 122.   [25]Homans, p. 91.

[26]Michael Marsden, "Savior in the Saddle: The Sagebrush Testament," *Focus on the Western*, p. 97. Other allusions to Christ in this article include the Starrett's names, Joe and Marion, and Shane being wounded in the left side.

[27]Brown, pp. 26-27.   [28]Wright, p. 14.

[29]See especially Edison B. Allen, *Of Time and Chase* (New Orleans: Habersham Corporation, 1969), pp. 89, 91.

[30]Vaughn Shoemaker, *Shoemaker* (Chicago: Chicago Tribune-New York Times News Syndicate, 1966), n.p.

[31]John H. Lenihan, *Showdown* (Urbana, Il: Univ. of Illinois Press, 1980),p. 116. Lenihan sees mass media as precursive rather than reflective of historical eras, and *Showdown* presents a thorough analysis of Western genre and an intriguing synthesis with societal happenings not seen in other books on the subject.

[32]John F. Kennedy, Inaugural Address, Jan. 20, 1961.

[33]See especially Clifford Baldowski's cartoons in *The Atlanta Constitution*, Jack Howells Ficklen's in the *Dallas Morning News* and Frank Miller's in *The Des Moines Register*, during 1961 and 1962.

[34]Lou Grant, *Oakland Tribune* and Daniel E. Holland, *Chicago Tribune* in *Today's Cartoon*, ed. John Chase (New Orleans: The Hauser Press, 1962), n.p.

[35]Clifford Baldowski, *The Atlanta Constitution*, 1963.

[36]See Wright, p. 154-163, and Lenihan, pp. 148-176. Also see John Cawelti, "Reflections on the New Western Films," *Focus on the Western*, pp. 113-117.

[37]See Jim Berry, *Berry's World* (New York: Four Winds Press, 1967), pp. 14, 78, 103, and Joseph E. Parrish, *Chicago Tribune*, 1961, in *Today's Cartoon*, n.p.

[38]Lyndon Johnson, nationally televised speech, March 31, 1968.

[39]Brian Vachon, "The Jesus Movement is Upon Us," *Look*, Feb. 9, 1971, pp. 15-21.

[40]See especially L. Ford, "Evangelism in a Day of Revolution," *Christianity Today*, Oct. 24, 1969, pp. 6-12.

[41]David Gordon, "The Jesus People: An Identity Synthesis," *Urban Life and Culture*, 3 (July 1974), 159-178.

[42]"New Life for Old Time Religion," *U.S. News and World Report*, Oct. 19, 1970, p. 87.

[43]"Street Christians," *Time* August 3, 1970, p. 32.

[44]See especially "Defreaking Jesus Freaks: Activities of Ted Patrick," *Newsweek*, March 12, 1973, p. 44; "Deprogramming Jesus Freaks and Others," *Christian Century*, May 2, 1973, pp. 510-511; "Kidnapping for Christ: Deprogramming Members of the Jesus Movement, *Time*, March 12, 1973, pp. 83-84; "Kidnapping the Converts," *America*, May 19, 1973, p. 456; "Devil vs. Mr. Patrick: Can Your Parents Have You Brainwashed?" *Senior Scholastic,* Jan. 10, 1974, pp. 14-17.

[45]See "Whatever Happened to Young 'Jesus People'?—Coming of Age," *U.S. News and World Report*, March 29, 1976, p. 49. Also see Plowman, pp. 46-48.

[46]Bert Whitman, *Phoenix Gazette* in *Best Editorial Cartoons of the Year*, ed. Charles Brooks (Gretna, La: Pelican Publishing Co., 1981), p. 46. Also see Pat Oliphant, *The Jelly Bean Society*

(Kansas City: Andrews and McMeel, 1981), p. 11.

[47]Walter Fisher, "Romantic Democracy, Ronald Reagan and Presidential Heroes," *Western Journal of Speech Communication,* 46 (Summer, 1982), p. 301. For further discussion of the hero as a man of action see Dixon Wecter, *The Hero in America: A Chronicle of Hero-Worship* (1941; rpt. New York: Scribner's, 1972), pp. 486-487.

[48]David Henry, "Once More, With Feeling: Reagan and 'The Speech' In 1980," paper presented at the Western Speech Communication Association Convention, San Jose, Ca., 1981, p. 1. Also see Kurt Ritter, "Ronald Reagan and 'The Speech': The Rhetoric of Public Relations Politics," *Western Speech* 32 (Winter, 1968), pp. 50-58.

[49]Fisher, "Romantic Democracy," p. 302.

[50]Ibid.

[51]For example, see "Tall in the Saddle Again," *Maclean's,* April 14, 1980, pp. 40-41; "No Gunfight on the Rio Grande," *Maclean's,* Jan. 19, 1981, pp. 30-31; "America's High Noon Mentality," *Maclean's* April 13, 1981, pp. 23-27.

[52]*Best Editorial Cartoons of the Year,* p. 14, 15, 20, and the cover. See also Oliphant, *Jelly Bean* p. 48, 101, 139.

[53]Ritter, pp. 50-51.

[54]Fotheringham, p. 56.

[55]Boorstin, p. 48.

[56]Pat Oliphant, *Oliphant: An Informal Gathering* (New York: Simon & Schuster, 1978), p. 88.

[57]See treatment of this change in the style of the archetypal hero in Janice Hocker Rushing and Thomas S. Frentz, "The Rhetoric of 'Rocky': A Social Value Model of Criticism," *Western Journal of Speech Communication,* 41 (Spring 1978), 63-72; and Frentz and Rushing, "The Rhetoric of 'Rocky': Part Two," *Western Journal of Speech Communication,* 42 (Fall 1978), 231-240.

[58]Boorstin, p. 50.

[59]Eco, p. 107.

[60]"Poll Discounts Influence of Reagan in Jersey Vote," *New York Times,* Oct. 7, 1981, p. B7. Another poll in December confirmed these findings. See "Poll Shows Women Lead Shift Toward Democratic Party," *The Denver Post,* Dec.27, 1981, p. 12A.

[61]Fisher also agrees with this assessment. See "Romantic Democracy," p. 310.

Marilyn Monroe: Cult Heroine

Lesley Dick

Marilyn Monroe (1926-1962) starred in only eleven movies during the fifties' placid decade. Yet, in her personal behavior and movies, she created a heroine and cult figure which has grown since her death. She created an image of the child-woman, sexy but innocent, experienced yet vulnerable, which both she and the onlooker could mold into any fantasy or reality which fitted the occasion. She could fulfill one man's dreams without demanding anything in return. The facts of her life, her image, photographs, films and other paraphernalia, and her early and mysterious death, all played a part in transforming her into the role of a present day hero-cult figure. However, it was her media exploited rise from rags to riches and untimely death which evoked the enormous sympathy for her and the interest in her life which exists today and is still growing.

Monroe's recognized illegitimate birth of a woman who lived in an asylum most of her life created a tragic beginning, a quality which automatically endeared her to the American public who love the under-dog, the poor and deprived of the world. Monroe, realizing this aspect of American society, exploited this proclivity. On screen she was the picture of success, although off-screen she presented a different image. She constantly proclaimed with total frankness her illegitimacy, the poverty of her childhood, the insanity in her family and her ignorance which she was always clearly striving to overcome.

This *complete* figure was sympathetic in its child-likeness. She was never fully rounded, always a foil to men. As such she became the picture of Everywoman as sex object, the complete body and spirit. She sophisticated the act of the unknowledgeable portrayal of sex. As Alexander Walker in in *The Celluloid Sacrifice* points out:

> No sooner did the 'woman' bring out the wolf in a man than the 'child' side of her turned him into a big hearted guard dog.

Thus she democratized sex and leveled the sexual aggressiveness in men.

This then was the image Monroe had created by the time of her death. By dying on Sunday, August 5, 1962 in clouded circumstances, possibly of an overdose of barbituates, she in effect threw herself into the mysterious realm of mythology. As with John F. Kennedy and his premature death, Monroe's early death seemed a senseless loss of great promise to America. Her death epitomized the stress of American life to all people and perhaps suggested that her suicide threatened the security of all.

The hero-cult that grew up after her death was and is an expression of that fear, and of America's love of the youth that died too early. All forms of worship of Monroe deal with the two personalities that she embodied. Her openness about her real early life reinforced her success story. The public listened with enormous interest to her constant revelations about the deprivations of her youth; such is the cradle in which heroes are born and nurtured. Monroe, realizing this hunger on the part of her public, over-dramatized her life, and stressed the strangle-hold it had held on her. At the time of her death, the New York *Times* expressed America's attitude toward the frustrated and bent life:

> The sad and ironic realization is that Miss Monroe aspired to creativity.... But the effort to overcome the many obstacles ... was apparently too great for her. Therein lies her tragedy and Hollywood's.

This attitude epitomizes the fascination with Monroe and with ourselves that has continued since her death in both books and dramatizations. Over twenty books have been published. All spend much time developing her passage from orphan to factory girl to superstar. One of the best, Fred L. Guiles' *Norma Jean* (1969), plays on the two sides of the person:

> Norma Jean Baker was the frightened insomniac whose

> barbiturates had finally worked. And Marilyn Monroe was the
> ghost goddess who rose from the little girl's ashes.

In other words, the vulnerability of the split personality which never could meld into a secure one frightened while fascinating the public.

Norman Mailer's tribute, *Marilyn* (1973) continued to build up the momentum. He used photographs from an exhibition by Larry Schiller, a Los Angeles journalist and photographer, a collection of 185 photographs of her by about fifteen top photographers entitled *Marilyn Monroe: The Legend and the Truth*. Opening in 1973 at the David Stuart Galleries in Los Angeles, it toured thirty cities in the United States. Blow-ups of the photographs sold for $250 to the thousands of the faithful who viewed the exhibit. The photographs romanticized the tribute of Monroe as the ultimate sex object and the ultimate victim. Mailer's book, using these photographs, emphasized the theme: "Everyman's love affair with America," and expressed the country's reaction to her death when he stated, "What a jolt to the dream life of the nation that the angel died of an overdose." This book was published in over 12 countries, including France and Japan. It was both huge—31 lbs. 6 oz. and 9'x11" and expensive at $19.95. But it has continued to be a bestseller; its latest printing in hardcover was in 1981, and since then it has come out in paperback with an additional chapter.

One does not question the status of a hero with impunity, as Norman Mailer discovered in his second book on Monroe, *Of Women and Their Elegance* (1980). In this second photographic essay, he adopted the persona of Monroe and described her experiencing every type of sexual activity from the ordinary to the fantastic. Critics thought this throwing of mud at the goddess was disgusting.

This deification of Monroe was continued in twenty-four plays, twenty-seven films and various documentaries that have been produced since her death using her character. The main theme running through all is that of a poor orphan child who through her own abilities rose to fame and fortune and was destroyed by her inability to cope with her life—it smacked too much of everybody in America. Where this theme differs there has been a public outcry. Arthur Miller's *After the Fall* (1964) bases the character Maggie on the author's ex-wife. Miller appears to be attempting to exorcize his wife's ghost. Monroe is characterized as a schizophrenic surviving on drugs alone and blackmailing the main character—whose likeness to Miller is unmistakeable—by threats of suicide. The play was received badly by press and public alike. The public could cope with her drug abuse and bad behavior as an indication of her inability to cope and her weak hold on life, but not when represented in this way.

Expressions of the hero-cult have not been limited to books, plays, movies and documentaries. The songs from her movies have been released to a receptive audience. These have been augmented by other statements by poets and songwriters. Norman Rosten, a close friend, wrote a poem; Edwin Morgan, a stranger, did also. Songs have followed suit, Elton John's "Candle in the Wind," sung by himself, continues to reflect the sympathetic theme:

> It seems to me you lived your life
> Like a candle in the wind
> Never knowing who to cling to
> When the rain set in.

Other artists have paid their tribute in various forms. In 1968, six years after her death, the Sydney Janis Gallery exhibited a "Homage to Marilyn" consisting of fifty-two works by thirty-six artists. Billboard artists such as James Rosenquist used her as an icon; his *Marilyn Monroe* reflects the public life she led and the constant mention of her in the press. Andy Warhol did a series of paintings depicting her in which he was examining the contemporary American folk hero. Sculptor George Segal's *Film Poster* consists of a plaster figure of a man with a briefcase under his arm nonchalantly studying a poster of Marilyn Monroe wearing an outfit from the movie *Some Like It Hot* (1956). Both the loneliness and mystery of the man and Marilyn Monroe in a poster version are suggested, and it is Marilyn as victim that is emphasized. Claes Oldenburg sculpted *Giant Lipstick* (ceiling sculpture for Monroe) in 1967 and *String Wardrobe—Long Dress, Short Dress and Bathing Suit for Marilyn Monroe*. The slick style of the first turns it into a tool suitable for a technicolor goddess. The second work is made up entirely of string and wire. Its looseness and disconnection from reality suggest both eroticism and object or victim rather than reality.

The magnitude of the hero-cult figure has continued to grow through the sale throughout the world of all kinds of pictorial works. Although the posters and postcards of Monroe is aligned with the movie paraphernalia trade which in the seventies and early eighties reached national and international importance—transactions at auctions—this does not in itself explain the thousands of postcards, posters and photographs on sale today depicting her. In any shop selling these kinds of things today, the two movie stars who will be included will be Humphrey Bogart and Marilyn Monroe; she is starred on literally hundreds. Part of this intensity can be explained by the fact that because of their pictorial quality they are timeless and people today appreciate her beauty as much as her contemporaries did. However, it is yet another expression of the hero-cult that has grown up around her—cult figures need tangible figures constantly before the public.

To the younger generation today there might be something of a mystery about the heroic status of Monroe. Yet, although they have not seen her films and are not fully aware of her biography, they are conscious of her stardom and of the mystery of her "suicide." She can be grouped with the other figures in the pantheon of youth today, Elvis Presley, Jim Morrison, James Dean and Sid Vicious, and generate a sympathetic appeal. Presenting the embodiment of a beautiful woman with the ultimate in sexuality, she strengthens her claim to immortality by fleshing out the American dream and the weakness of its value to some people.

The American Dream flourishes well in mystery. Sometimes mystery defies reality. There is still some question of whether Monroe committed suicide or was murdered because of her involvement with the Kennedys. Facts have been discovered about her bad behavior and destructive drug abuse. There was at the time and still is a bitter taste in her public's mouth about her desire to become a "serious" actress.

But such insinuations merely cast the right kind of light on the figure of the hero in the temple, where the vigil is still kept. She still remains the quintessential picture of the child-adult, innocent-wanton, private-public possession who articulates America and Americans.

There is one interesting development in January 1983 which might threaten Monroe's future as hero. As goddess of democracy she is being picked up by at least one element of the elite, and is being made the subject of *haute couture,* with gowns designed for the beautiful people and sold in some thirty exclusive shops designed to be spread throughout the United States.

The elite always steal from the demos. But the people do not give up their own without a fight. Monroe is the hero of the people. Perhaps the elite can trail along, or even crowd in front of the people but they can never take Monroe from the masses.

Leaders of the American West: Who Are Their Heroes?

John J. Gardiner & Kathryn E. Jones

All history resolves itself very easily into the biography of a few stout and earnest persons.

Ralph Waldo Emerson

Steadily the frontier of settlement advanced and carried with it individualism, democracy, and nationalism.

Frederick Jackson Turner

Our democratic problem is statable in ultrasimple terms: Who are the kind of men from whom our majorities shall take their cue?

William James

During the early summer months of 1982, in anticipation of the second annual Southwest Cultural Heritage Festival, the authors decided to conduct a national study of American heroes. It had been contended widely in the literature that the absence of heroes was a mark of our age.[1] The absence of heroes, the authors speculated, might have indicated more about the kind of people that we as Americans had become than about the absence of great men and women in our midst. Was it possible that we were no longer able or fit to recognize the heroes among us? Had the American definition of heroism itself changed during the past one or two decades? A national study of American heroes might also allow for another test of Frederick Jackson Turner's thesis that the American frontier promoted individualism, democracy, and "the freedom of an individual to arise under conditions of social mobility."

If a new definition of the American hero was emerging, how might its parameters be best determined? The authors decided, as part of the study, to send a survey instrument consisting of five open-ended questions to approximately three hundred national political and educational leaders. The questions would encourage these leaders to identify their heroes, as well as the common characteristics shared by the people they admired. Thus, national leaders might assist in the process of constructing a more contemporary American definition of heroism. Following are the five questions asked of the national leaders:

1) Please list the names of three people whom you regard as your heroes.
2) What characteristics, if any, do you see these people as sharing?
3) If you have children, please list the names of three people whom you believe your children regard as heroes. If you do not have children, please list the names of three people whom you believe young people today regard as heroes.
4) What characteristics, if any, do you see your children's (our youth's) heroes as sharing?
5) It is commonly believed that today's young people have fewer heroes than their parents did. Do you agree or disagree? Why or why not?

The authors hoped that, as a result of an analysis of these responses, the outline of a contemporary definition of American heroism might emerge.

The sample for the study consisted of one hundred and fifty political leaders (50 State Governors and 100 United States Senators) and one hundred and forty educational leaders (50 State Chancellors of Higher Education, 50 presidents of leading American universities, and 40 educational leaders identified in a national survey conducted by *Change Magazine*). For purpose of analysis, the country was divided into two parts. Using the Mississippi River as boundary line, and excluding border states, the following nineteen states were considered Western for the purposes of this study: Alaska, Arizona, California, Colorado, Hawaii, Idaho, Kansas, Montana, Nebraska, Nevada, New Mexico, North Dakota, Oklahoma, Oregon, South Dakota, Texas, Utah, Washington and Wyoming. The other states were considered Eastern for purpose of analysis. It was hoped that a review of the data might lead to an identification of the heroes of current leaders of the American West, as well as an opportunity to contrast these heroes, and their definitions of American heroism, with those of the leaders of the American East.

Ralph Waldo Emerson in his essay on heroism noted that "self-trust is the essence of heroism . . . the characteristic of heroism is its persistency." Emerson's emphasis on persistence and self-reliance exemplified early American definitions of heroism. Once he or she had chosen a part in the human drama, the individual who would be heroic did not weakly try to reconcile him- or herself with the world at large. The early American hero could not, therefore, be considered an ordinary person in the sense that he or she had, in the words of Emerson, "done something strange and extravagant and broken the monotony of the decorous age." Thomas Carlyle, a contemporary of Emerson's, wrote in his classic work, *On Heroes, Hero-Worship and the Heroic in History,* that "the greatest of faults (on the part of the potential heroes) is to be conscious of none." Carlyle's emphasis on humility added another dimension to this nineteenth century definition of heroism. All greatness had to be unconscious or it was considered less than heroic. Sidney Hook, in his 1943 study on *The Hero in History: A Study in Limitation and Possibility*, emphasized another perspective of the earlier definition of American heroism. Hook noted that "the hero in history is the individual to whom we can justifiably attribute preponderant influence in determining an issue or event whose consequences would have been profoundly different if he had not acted as he did." Heroes made their marks during times of crisis. Lest we fear, Emerson reminded us, that "whoso is heroic will always find crises to try his edge." In describing the potential hero in a democracy, Hook noted that "his will to action is stronger; his knowledge of what must be done to realize what he sees is surer. For these reasons, he finds himself, more likely than not, in a minority." The classic definition of the democratic hero then appears to be a solitary, action-oriented person, loyal to the democratic ideal, persistent and self-reliant, with the good fortune to confront sufficient crises to challenge his or her courage and perseverance.

The *Unabridged Webster's Third New International Dictionary* defined hero as "a man of courage and nobility, famed for his miltary achievements; a man admired for his achievements and noble qualities and considered a model or ideal." *The American Heritage Dictionary of the English Language* defined hero as "any man noted for feats of courage and nobility of purpose; especially, one who has risked or sacrificed his life." A secondary definition offered by the *American Heritage Dictionary* viewed the hero as "a person prominent in some event, field, period, or cause by reason of his special achievements or contributions." Modern definitions of hero reduce the stature of the individual fulfilling that role from historical proportions. From demigod, the hero is transformed into "much, if not more, a product of the public mood as the creator of that mood." This emphasis of Arthur Levine, in his 1980 work on *When Dreams and Heroes Died: A Portrait of Today's College Student*, minimized the role of the man on horseback in human history. Less self-reliant, more manipulative of the public mood, the modern American hero is viewed as a flawed character. It would appear that the modern age denies the desirability or need of great people. The modern hero becomes difficult to idealize; he or she becomes, at best, someone we might admire. Our modern lack of faith makes it difficult for us to elevate mere human beings to the level of heroes. A cynical view of traditionally accepted great men and women has cut us off from our heroic past. Levine noted this basic trend in his review of Gallup's surveys which stated that "confidence in the leaders of the major social institutions, including medicine, higher education, organized religion, the U.S. Supreme Court, major companies, the executive branch of government, the press, Congress, organized labor, and advertising agencies declined from an average of 45% in 1966 to an average of 21% in 1979." American confidence in political, social and economic institutions and in their leaders had declined to an all-time low. Were our heroes, if they existed at all, failing us? Or, were our current perceptions clouding from us the heroes in our midst? John W. Gardner noted that "the ideas for which this nation stands will not survive if the highest goal free men can set themselves is an amiable mediocrity ... the plain fact is that never in our history have we stood in such desperate need of men and women of intelligence, imagination and courage."

In an analysis of the questionnaires returned by American educational and poltical leaders, distinct Western and Eastern definitions of the American hero emerged. The Western definition emphasized commitment, integrity, compassion and courage. The Eastern definition focused on intellectual capacity, leadership ability, compassion and integrity. Though there are similarities in the two orientations described by today's educational and political leaders, differences stand out. This is particularly apparent in the selections of Abraham Lincoln and Harry Truman as the dominant heroes of the Western block; and Thomas Jefferson and Franklin D.

Roosevelt as the leading heroes of the Eastern block. The Eastern emphasis on intellectual, well-born leadership countered the Western emphasis on courageous, self-made men. Frederick Jackson Turner's thesis that "frontier individualism has from the beginning promoted democracy" was reinforced by survey returns. Forty-two percent of the Western Governors responded to the survey, while only 10% of the Eastern Governors did; twenty-four percent of the national educational and political leadership of the West responded to the survey, while only 8% of the leadership group from the East completed the questionnaire. Interestingly, the most common reason given for non-participation was that of standard policy "not to complete questionnaries of any kind." This pattern of nonresponsiveness of leaders was particularly notable in the United States Senate. If the responsiveness of leaders is a characteristic of democratic society, then Levine's statistics regarding declining public confidence in American institutions and their leaders becomes more understandable. Furthermore, it is interesting to consider the large difference between the response rates for the Eastern and Western portions of our country. Frontier individualism, as once contended by Turner, may still be promoting American democracy in the Western states in at least the sense of greater responsiveness on the part of Western public officials.

Turner's thesis that "the advance of the frontier decreased our dependence on England" was also supported by survey returns. Eastern political and educational leaders tended to identify such English leaders as Edmund Burke and Winston Churchill. Eastern United States Senator William S. Cohen of Maine identified William Shakespeare, Oliver Wendell Holmes, Jr., and Julius Erving, offering as the rationale for his selection that "each has set the highest standard possible in their respective fields."

A typical Western political response was that of Governor Edherschler of Wyoming who selected Harry Truman, Abraham Lincoln and Theodore Roosevelt on a rationale of honesty, initiative, daring and humility; or Governor J.S. Hammond of the State of Alaska who selected Meriwether Lewis and William Clark as on a rationale of dedication, resourcefulness and great courage. U.S. Senator Barry Goldwater of Arizona typified the individualism of the West in his selection of the three people he regarded as heroes, Jim Doolittle, John Wayne and General Sandy Patch, on the singular rationale of honesty. Rhodes scholar U.S. Senator David L. Boren of Oklahoma, was the single Western exception in his selection of Englishman Winston Churchill as one of three people he most regarded as heroes.

Among educational leaders, Chancellor Barbara Uehling of the University of Missouri identified Eleanor Roosevelt, Madame Curie and Alice Rivlin on a rationale of determination, intellectual capacity and courage. Also representing the Eastern portion of the United States, Father Theodore M. Hesburgh, President of the University of Notre Dame, selected Pope John XXIII, Mother Teresa of Calcutta and Winston Churchill on a rationale of leadership, dedication to others and vision. Association Presidents Dale Parnell and Allan Ostar presented contrasting views of heroism as perceived by two Eastern educational leaders. Dale Parnell, President of the Association of Community and Junior Colleges, identified Jesus Christ, Harry Truman and Mother Teresa on the rationale that these individuals were positive, compassionate and possessed personal integrity. Allan W. Ostar, President of the American Association of State Colleges and Universities, selected Thomas Jefferson, Herman B. Wells and Anwar Sadat on the basis of these individuals' extraordinary courage to translate ideals into practical results to mankind. "In short," Ostar noted, "they all made a difference."

Harvard University's Professor of Sociology David Riesman presented a particularly insightful analysis of heroism in his selection and defense of Anton Chekhov, George Washington and George Kennan. His emphasis on the quality of risk-taking evident in the lives of these heroes was shared by several Western educational and political leaders who identified Meriwether Lewis and William Clark, the courageous team of Northwest explorers.

Herman B. Wells, former President of Indiana University, was the major educational leader to be selected as hero by participants in the national survey. A dedicated president, Wells was elevated to his position of leadership from service as the young dean of Indiana University's School of Business in 1938. He introduced a revolutionary age in university management at his institution which converted it from a respectable provincial college into one of broad international influence. In Volume III of Indiana University's historical study entitled *Years of Fulfillment*, Wells was described as a man who "personally blended the native sense of everyday practicality with a dreamer's vision." As president, he laid no claims to broad or intensive scholarship, but rather he supported a campuswide appreciation for the superior human and intellectual qualities of his faculty, thus promoting excellence throughout Indiana University. Interestingly, Wells was selected as hero by educational leaders of both the East and the West. Typical of the rationale for his selection was that offered by Edward Moulton, Chancellor of the Ohio Board of Regents. Wells, according to his assessment, possessed integrity, talent and a compassion for people.

Mother Teresa of Calcutta was the major female hero identified by national educational and political leaders. Her compassion for people and commitment to excellence were cited by several surveyed participants. Governor Bruce King of New Mexico typified survey participants who selected their mothers and/or fathers as personal heroes. The Governor of New Mexico identified his parents' heroic characteristics as ones of great leadership coupled with a concern for all living things.

The dominant western models of Abraham Lincoln and Harry Truman, along with the primary Eastern paradigms of Thomas Jefferson and Franklin Roosevelt, require further attention. The Chancellor Emeritus of a major northeastern university, who preferred not to be identified by name, offered as his rationale for the selection of Jefferson and Roosevelt their great concern for the preservation of democracy, their unwaivering determination in the face of national and personal crises, their ability to persuade, and their strong senses of compassion. Chancellor Chalmers Gail Norris of the State of Washington defended his selection of Lincoln and Truman on the basis of character, wit and common touch. Both Lincoln and Truman represented self-made leaders nurtured on American frontier individualism. The selection of these two American presidents by the educational and political leaders of the West confirmed Frederick Jackson Turner's thesis that Western democracy "tended to the production of a society of which the most distinctive fact was the freedom of the individual to rise under conditions of social mobility." The heroes of the West were, and are, common folk. Common, that is, in their origins among America's solid, rural, Protestant stock. Lincoln was born in a small log cabin; Truman's folks could not afford to send him to college. Yet both men rose to the highest elective office of their land, and both are recognized today as good and faithful servants of their people. In his classic work on *The Hero in America*, Dixon Wecter described the development of America's earliest heroes. Regarding Lincoln, Wecter noted that "from a soil of poverty on the prairies of Indiana and Illinois sprang his fierce ambition, his lack of conventional dignity, his sympathy for the common man, his humility which blended with a sturdy and serene self-confidence." Rising from the hardship of the American frontier, Lincoln and Truman remain folk heroes to the educational and political leaders of the American West.

Thomas Jefferson and Franklin Roosevelt, the heroes selected by America's most responsive educational and political leaders of the East, represent an alternative model of the American hero. American aristocrats by birth, both men took up the cause of America's common people. Their appeals were more reflective and more intellectual. Yet, they shared a deep compassion that crossed class lines.

All four leaders were self-respecting, honorable people with confidence in their leadership ability. All brought America through significant national and international crises. All represented viable forms of the American hero. From the identification of the two regional models of American heroism, however, it would appear that "the American frontier, simply by being there, forged a different kind of person out of foreigners and Americans who faced it," a possibility alluded to by Ray B. Browne in a recent essay on regional cultures.

The heroes of the children of American educational and political leaders presented another interesting facet of the evolving definition of American heroism. The only name selected with any consistency by children among American leaders was that of President John F. Kennedy. His name led the list in all categories of region and occupation. Great diversity characterized the selection of other heroes identified by American youth. Professor Lewis B. Mayhew of Stanford University identified John Kennedy, Jane Fonda and Ansel Adams as heroes of his children. These heroes were all seen as pragmatic men and women who stressed consistent principles. Selection of Roger Staubach by U.S. Senator Don Nickles of Oklahoma, as the only major hero of his children, is typical of the sample's broad professional diversity; as was Allan W. Ostar's identification of Captain Kirk of Star Trek, Hawkeye of $M*A*S*H$ and the Beatles as the heroes of his children. These latter heroes were assessed to be wise, compassionate, idealistic and entertaining. Did the people selected as heroes of the children of America's leaders represent an emerging trend in the evolving definition of the American hero? Had mass media transformed the hero in the minds of American youth from an idealized model to a flawed celebrity? Had mass media, which "emphasized everyone's warts," in the words of Allan W. Ostar, reduced the American hero to smaller stature? Had a "greater concern with their own personal welfare," as observed by John D. Millett, President Emeritus of

Miami University and Chancellor Emeritus of the Ohio Board of
Regents, redirected the focus of American young people regarding
heroism? Was democratic leadership more difficult today as a result
of a narrowing perspective of heroism on the part of American
youth, as noted by Howard R. Bowen, Professor of Economics and
Education at Claremont Graduate School? Was the reason for fewer
heroes on the part of young people in America today simply a result
of a fact that there were "too few around today," as stated by Father
Theodore M. Hesburgh, President of the University of Notre Dame.

Possibly the answer, in the tradition of academe, was
somewhere in-between. K. Patricia Cross, Professor of Education at
Harvard University, pointed out that "if their heroes are rock stars
and football players, as we are sometimes led to believe, we (the
parent generation) may be unable to accept them as heroes." Young
people today might not have fewer heroes, but rather fewer people
that would be categorized as heroes by America's adult population.
Youth's perceptions of heroes may appear to adults to be more
transient and more narrowly focused. Had greater affluence led to a
lesser need to identify with fantasies on the part of the young as
suggested by Chancellor Uehling of the University of Missouri?
Have the television and movie heroes of mass media replaced the
real-live heroes of the past? Has an emphasis on self-reliance
associated with an earlier definition of the American hero faded in
the minds of American youth? Governor Lee Shermond Dreyfus of
Wisconsin emphasized the point that "teams now do almost
everything—no 'Lone Eagle' can fly to the moon." Has mass
communications created an overload of public figure images and
resulted in the advancement of those who lack heroic quality, as
suggested by Lawrence K. Pettit, former Commissioner of Higher
Education for the State of Montana and current Associate
Commissioner of Higher Education for the State of Texas? U.S.
Senator David L. Boren of Oklahoma, offered some useful advice.
"We have done too much de-mythologizing in our time. We need
heroes, symbols, and traditions. They hold our society together."
The sense of belonging—of history—of a tie to the past—is not as
strong today as it once was. Consequently, "many of today's youth
honor heroes in the sports and entertainment worlds," as noted by
Arvo Van Alstyne, Commissioner of the Utah System of Higher
Education. William S. Thorpe, Executive Director of Nebraska's
Higher Education System, suggested that the heroes of American
youth are more pragmatic and less romantic.

Mass media focus on the faults of people, thus resulting in less hero-worship on the part of Americans today. How much independence of judgment can we expect from American youth who daily confront society's pressures of materialism, techology and mass media? The observations of Governor John Spellman of Washington regarding the heroes of his own children may provide a valuable insight regarding the heroes of the young. "Every generation," Spellman noted, "has its heroes. It's just that the older generation always thinks that the kids' popular heroes are weird, kooky or far-out." Interestingly, Governor Spellman identified the heroes of his own children as Robert Kennedy and Henry Kissinger. He saw his children's heroes as sharing the characteristics of candor, competence and inspirational leadership. Wherever America's future takes us, whatever specific definitions of American heroism evolve, the future of our nation remains hopeful. In the words of Dixon Wecter, "The people's choice of heroes for America has been prevailingly sound; our major favorites are those that any nation might be proud of. They go far toward vindicating the whole democratic theory of careers open to talents." America's great heroes of "Jefferson and Lincoln remain giants, symbols so durable that they could be broken only by an America which deliberately renounced its great past, its independence, and its democratic faith." On the basis of this study of American heroism, the authors conclude that this repudiation is not likely to come to pass.

Note

[1] For a comprehensive, philosophical treatment of the absence of heroes as a mark of our age, see Thomas Carlyle, *On Heroes, Hero-Worship and The Heroic in History* (London: Oxford University Press, 1946). For two insightful, modern treatments of the theme, see Arthur Levine, *When Dreams and Heroes Died: A Portrait of Today's College Student* (San Francisco: Jossey-Bass Publishers, 1980) and Henry Fairlie, "Too Rich for Heroes," *Harper's* 257, 1942 (November 1978), 33-43, 97-98.

Here's a Real Hero

Art Buchwald

*T*here are two kinds of people who don't pay any income taxes in America; the very poor and the very rich. One tends to look down on the poor when they don't pay taxes, because they're a burden on society, but show me a rich man who doesn't pay any money to the Government and I'll show you a real American hero.

My role model is Harvey Ripplemyer, a millionaire many times over, who has hardly paid a cent in income taxes to the Federal Government for 10 years.

"How do you do it?" I asked Harvey the other day.

"I don't do it myself," he answered modestly. "I pay people to do it for me. I believe it's an American right, I might add duty, to take advantage of every loophole our tax laws offer.

"I'm sure every taxpayer feels the same way. But not many of us can achieve the ultimate of not paying any taxes as all. What is your secret?"

"You need money not to pay money to the IRS. The more money you have, the less you have to give them. What you have to do is find paper tax losses to offset your real income. Then you prove that you've actually lost money in the fiscal year and therefore you owe the Government a pittance."

"OK, but how do you find a way to do that?"

"You hire the best tax lawyers that money can buy. They usually happen to be former IRS attorneys who know all the loopholes. They're experts on what will fly and what won't."

"What happens when the IRS closes a tax loophole for somebody like you."

"Then my tax lawyers find another loophole. Fortunately our tax laws are such that when the IRS thinks it has you trapped, you can always crawl through a hole it left open. It's really a poker game, but you have a big pot going in to play. What you need are large carryover losses, huge interest deductions, big depreciation write-offs, and solid tax shelters. Now, the average person doesn't have the stakes to acquire all these things, so he has to pay his taxes."

"What about your attorneys' fees? They must be very high."

"Not really. They're tax deductible"

"Does anyone have any guilt if he can beat the tax system? Go through your newspapers and magazines—half the ads are from people who claim they can help you beat the IRS. The best-seller lists always have a new book on ways you can keep your tax money. The only people who feel guilty in this country are those who have to pay their full share."

"It's lucky we can have them or there wouldn't be any money in the Treasury."

"Now I don't want you to get the idea that just because I pay hardly any taxes that I'm not a good American. I serve on the Committee for a Strong National Defense, I'm against large government deficits, and I don't believe in social programs that are bleeding this country to death."

"I never questioned your patriotism"

"Do you know why this is the greatest country on earth?"

"I think I do, but I'd like to hear it from you."

"Because if a man can beat the tax system he can keep everything he has. And it's possible to do it here without violating the law. You don't have to be born rich to avoid paying taxes. This country allows you to become rich and not give any of it away. That's why I love America."

"And that's why everyone loves you, Harvey. You're an inspiration to every taxpayer in America who aspires to be in your position right now."

"Anyone can do it," Harvey said. "With a little luck, a lot of money, and a good tax lawyer who really knows what he's doing and has your interests at heart."

Did Anyone Ever See Washington Nude?

Marshall W. Fishwick

Washington, the Father of our Country, *nude?* "It is inconceivable!" Nathaniel Hawthorne answered categorically. "He had no nakedness, but was born with clothes on, and his hair powdered, and made a stately bow on his first appearance in the world."

"The first word of infancy should be Mother," Horatio Weld wrote, "the second Father, and the third Washington." How could one describe or picture George Washington? "A human angel," humorist Ward wrote, "in a three-kornered hat and knee britches."

Over the years George Washington has been turned from a man into a monument—a man in the white marble toga. To contemporary poet Robert Lowell he seems as distant and aloof as his monument. These lines from Lowell's "The March" commemorate the October 23, 1967, sortie by peace demonstrators on Washington:

> Under the too white marmoreal Lincoln Memorial
> the too tall marmoreal Washington obelisk,
> gazing into the too long reflecting pool,
> the reddish trees, the withering autumn sky,
> the remorseless, amplified harangues for peace....

Why dismiss the George Washington in whom there burned a mad hell, which, on the few occasions when it was freed, seared the souls of those who stood in its path? There was hotter blood in his veins than the DAR dreamed of. Small vignettes indicate how human the man they never called George really was.

The young teen-ager, hickory-tough and backwoods-minded, was forced to copy off *Rules of Civility and Decent Behavior* from an English adaptation of a French guide—the kind of assignment that sent a latter-day kindred spirit, Huck Finn, onto a raft and down the river. But George gritted his teeth and copied:

> Put not another bit into your Mouth til the former be Swallowed.
> Cleanse not your teeth with the Table Cloth, Napkin, Fork or Knife.
> Kill no Vermin as Fleas, lice ticks & in the Sight of others.

What interested him deeply as he grew into manhood was not pithy thoughts, but pretty girls. We know some of their names: Betsie Fountleroy, Frances Alexander, Lucy Grymes, Mary Cary, Mary Philipse. When he showed interest in Sally Cary her father thundered, "Remember! You are accustomed to your coach and six!" She chose wealthy coach-conscious George Fairfax. Could Sally have been scared off by young Washington's poetry, of which this is a painful sample:

> Xerxes wasn't free from Cupid's Dart
> And all the greatest heroes felt the smart.

Or was she, like Lucinda Lee, more afraid of his actions than his words? One day Lucinda was walking in the garden with her sisters, Nancy and Molly. "We were cutting thistles to try our sweethearts," she wrote in her *Journal*, "when Mr. Washington caught us, and you can't conceive how he plagued us—chased us all over the garden and was quite impertinent." On another occasion: "While we were eating the apple pye in bed, God bless you! Making a great noise, in came Mr. Washington, dressed in Hannah's short gown and petticoat, and seazed me and kissed me twenty times, in spite of all the resistance I could make; and then Cousin Molly." What sort of marble is this?

Now that few can or want to be squires, it is easy to dismiss the copybook world of George Washington. But we do so at the peril of not understanding how our country came into being and what it stood for. Simply to learn a few eighteenth-century phrases, "Give me liberty or give me death....life, liberty, and the pursuit of happiness .... a government of laws, not men," will not suffice in the revolutionary electronic twentieth-century world. When we look back we should see not only abstract phrases, but real men, real events. Lifestyles are not the products of airy nothings and high rhetoric. They are made out of mud, blood and sweat.

So look again at the General Washington who wanted "news on the spur, for I am all impatience," and who found New Englanders "an exceedingly dirty and nasty people." Hearing that a sword had been broken over the head of a deserting officer, Washington deemed it "a mild punishment"; Bismark was not the first leader to think blood and iron were the only national foundations.

Recall what the painter Gilbert Stuart saw when he studied the weathered face of Washington: "All his features were strong, indicative of the most ungovernable basic passions, and had he been born in the forest he would have been the fiercest man among the savage tribes."

This is the Washington who suffered and squirmed under the symbolic trappings as first President of the Republic. Look at him at an afternoon reception, wearing his black-velvet suit with silver knee and shoe buckles, yellow gloves, a glittering sword in a scabbard of polished white leather. An old Revolutionary soldier approaches in buckskin. He has walked from Kentucky to Philadelphia for the meeting. Both the President and his lady recognize him from the window and hurry to the door to greet him cordially.

"I never was better treated," the veteran reported. "I hadn't believed a word against him. I found out that he was still Old Hoss."

Old Hoss had become "our demigod" by 1800. That same year a Pennsylvania German farmer wrote *Washington Ankunft in Elisium*, in which the General strolled around heaven chatting with Columbus. How could artists, cartoonists, sculptors hope to portray such a figure?

Yet portray him they did, even when he still wore the red uniform of a British officer. Charles Willson Peale did the first major portrait about which there is no question of authenticity in 1772. Washington the colonial militiaman now hangs in Washington & Lee University. The two prints of Washington issued in London in 1775 made their way throughout Europe, once the American Revolution broke out. In 1778, Voltaire ordered a Washington medal struck in Paris, but the head was fictitious. John Trumbull, a young painter-patriot, served as an aide to General Washington, and did an engraving in 1781 and numerous subsequent portraits. The best-known portraits, however, were done by Gilbert Stuart, who did not have his first sitting from Washington until 1795. The portrait known as "Lansdowne," done for the Marquis of Landsdowne, portrays Washington standing by a table; the "Athenaeum" is of the head alone. Stuart made so many copies of it that he came to refer to it as "my hundred dollar bill." We have Rembrandt Peale's word that in it the features were inaccurately drawn, and the character "heavily exaggerated." But this is the face that we remember—as the pictures which follow illustrate.

They are only a handful from the hundreds of portraits, busts, cartoons and covers that have been forthcoming. As the country changes, so does its historic and symbolic Father. Historians need to consider images as well as words when they are interpreting our heritage. On many different levels, and in many media, Washington *is* the hero in transition; and so is every other hero. See for yourself.

That famous face, fixed forever in the American imagination, appeared everywhere in the young Republic. He was first in everything—and still is. With the classical goddess and laurel teeth, this anonymous folk painting shows its American origin. Old Glory flies proudly over the whole scene.

What did Washington *really* look like? Most authorities believe that Charles Willson Peale and Gilbert Stuart give the best clues. Washington was 47, at the height of his power, when Peale painted the oval portrait (left). Stuart did a famous series in Washington's last years. By then, Washington had no teeth, and the "letterbox mouth" was a Stuart trademark (right).

Was Washington a Greek god, or the noblest Roman of them all (complete with toga) in the giant statue by Horatio Greenough (1852-52)? So gigantic was the neo-classical statute that it crashed through the floor of the Capitol, and for many years was stored away. But now it greets myriads of visitors in the foyer of the new Museum of American History on Washington's mall.

During the Civil Rights movement, Black leaders saw Washington as the epitome of the Establishment, and the white elitism that had kept them in bondage for so long. In this 1970 work, James Gadsen has a white ominous Washington (still shaped in the Stuart profile) looming over black Americans of humble origin.

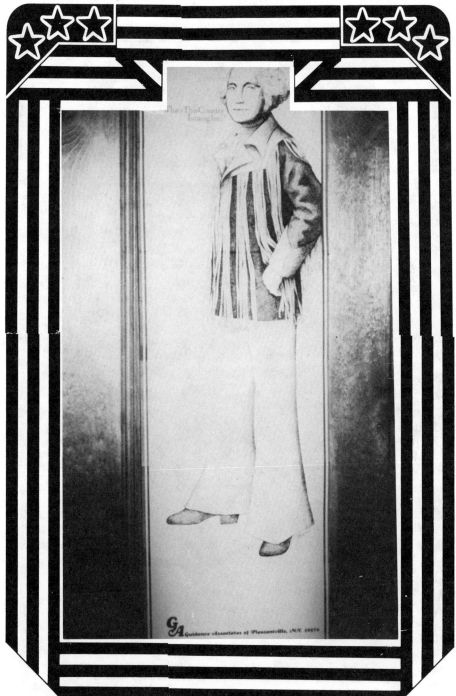

Heroic images may be used to show dislike as well as approval. In the 1960s Washington was shown as disapproving of the counter-culture and its life-style. Here we see the Father of Our Country dressed in leather thong jacket, bell bottoms, and platforms. He stares out and asks: "What's This Country Coming To?"

Washington's face underwent considerable changes before making the front cover of
Mad Magazine during the Bicentennial Year, 1976. Washington has been crossed
with J. Alfred Neumann and recovered his teeth—though a key one is missing. There
is also a short letter for Gilbert Stuart:

"Dear Mr. Stuart: I really do not believe this to be a good likeness of me. It would
best remain unfinished.

George Washington."

By 1978, America was being "kicked around" both at home and abroad. When *Time* struck the "To The Rescue!" theme, it pictured George Washington, paladin of old-time virtues, the advocate of strength at home, no entangling alliances abroad. Even with one black eye, he managed an assuring smile.

Lincoln in the Bosom
of Familiarity

Ray B. Browne

Humor is not kind to heroes; few can survive it. It washes over the hero the truth of ridicule and laughter. As Napoleon said that no man is a hero to his valet, he might have said that few people are heroes to the humorist. Humor casts a strong light in which shadows obscure few warts, and the warts of the hero are the points of entry for the scalpel of truth which exposes the complete individual. When a person is able to withstand this revelation favorable or unfavorable (or favorable *and* unfavorable) he has achieved a stature that nobody else can achieve.

Lincoln was such a person. Nobody in American history has been the subject of so much humor, and has undergone so many changes in that humor. He was a diamond with so many facets that he reflected every kind of humor invented by fertile imaginations. He was a rich subject for humor and caricature. Ugly, tall, ungainly, uneducated (though wiser than his contemporaries), diffident, shy, unassuming and apparently indifferent to his critics, he allowed his warts to be all too evident. No aspect of Lincoln's character escaped the humorist. He was godlike and satanic; he was a heartless monster and a saint; he loved his enemies and forgave his attackers; he was a loving parent who sent America's sons off to war. Perhaps the greatest asset the humorists had was Lincoln's love of humor. The editor of *Wit and Humor* said: "Nothing that can be written about Lincoln can show his character in such a true light as the yarns and stories he was so fond of telling, and at which he would laugh as heartily as anyone." The editor of *Wit and Humor of Abraham Lincoln* insisted that Lincoln's stories always had "a moral, which every good story should have." The President's anecdotes, this editor added, contain "lessons that could be taught so well in no other way. Every one of them is a sermon. Lincoln, like the man of Galilee, spoke to the people in parables." And the people answered, if not in parables and symbols, at least partially in kind. To a certain number of them, at least, although apparently not the serious, important people in government, it was understandable that he had to maintain his sense of humor during the heart-breaking days of the Civil War or he could not have stood the strain.

Heroes are ordinarily olympian--distant, cold, unapproachable and, at times, indifferent, although people make every effort to humanize them. When heroes are hugged to the bosom of familiarity they reach an even higher and deeper level of heroism than the conventional olympians. The hero treated with love, respect, familiarity—though sometimes bloodied in the fray—reaches a stature of importance no other can achieve. Lincoln is our best example.

The stories about Lincoln are legion; the collections of them are numerous. The collections of caricatures of Lincoln are plentiful. Lincolniana has long been a growth industry; and it seems that it will never slack off. Of all our presidents, and citizens, Lincoln is the one nearest and dearest to us. He is a part of the very fabric of the nation and of every individual, even though sometimes only in wish-projection. Washington may have been first in war, first in peace and first in the hearts of his countrymen. But Lincoln's stature overshadows Washington's. At his death it was remarked prophetically, "Now he belongs to the ages"—and it might have been added, "to the world." No American has ever belonged so much to the world as Lincoln does.

In the few sketches that follow—which span his whole career— we easily see the many aspects of Lincoln that funsters— professionals and amateurs, lovers and haters—found amusing and which provided them with material for their laughter.

Too Deep

During the Black Hawk War, when the valiant Illinoisians were in hasty retreat from what they thought certain scalping, and the roads exclusively bad, in fact, unfathomable mud.—In this predicament, the corps in which Uncle Abe was, became somewhat scattered, when the officer commanding, called out to the men to form *two* deep. "Blast me!" shouted Abe from a slough, in which he was nearly buried, "I am too deep already; I am up to the neck." (*Lincolniana*)

The Running Sickness

In the Black Hawk war, Uncle Abe belonged to a militia company in the service. On a scout, the company encountered the Indians, and in a brisk skirmish drove them some miles, when, night coming on, our forces encamped. Great was the consternation on discovering that Lincoln was missing. His absence, or rather his stories, from the bivouac was a misfortune. Suddenly, however, he came into camp. "Maj-Abe, is that you? Thought you were killed. Where've you been?" were the startling speculations. 'Yes," said Uncle Abe, "this is me—ain't killed either." "But where have you been all this time?" "Oh, just over there." "But what were you over there for? Didn't run away, did you?" "No," he said deliberately, "I don't think I run away; but, after all, I reckon if anybody had seen me going, and had been told I was going for a doctor he would have thought somebody was almighty sick." (*Lincolniana*)

The Questions of Legs

Whenever the people of Lincoln's neighborhood engaged in dispute; whenever a bet was to be decided; when they differed on points of religion or politics; when they wanted to get out of trouble, or desired advice regarding anything on the earth, below it, above it, or under the sea, they went to "Abe."

Two fellows, after a hot dispute lasting some hours, over the problem as to how long a man's legs should be in proportion to the size of his body, stamped into Lincoln's office one day and put the question to him.

Lincoln listened gravely to the arguments advanced by both contestants, spent some time in "reflecting" upon the matter, and then, turning around in his chair and facing the disputants, delivered his opinion with all the gravity of a judge sentencing a fellow-being to death.

"This question has been a source of controversy," he said, slowly and deliberately, "for untold ages, and it is about time it should be definitely decided. It has led to bloodshed in the past, and there is no reason to suppose it will not lead to the same in the future.

"After much thought and anxiety, it is my opinion, all side issues being swept aside, that a man's lower limbs, in order to preserve the harmony of proportions, should be at least long enough to reach from his body to the ground." (*Wit and Humor*)

Uncle Abe Swapped as a Baby

Abe when asked whether he could account for his excessive homeliness said, "When I was two months old I was the handsomest child in Kentuck, but my nurse swapped me off for another boy just to please a friend who was going down the river whose child was rather plain looking." (*Lincolniana*)

Uncle Abe's Nose

Uncle Abe being asked once why he walked so crookedly, said, "Oh my nose, you see, is crooked, and I have to follow it!"

The Ugliest Man

Mr. Lincoln enjoyed a joke at his own expense. Said he: "In the days when I used to be in the circuit, I was accosted in the cars by a stranger, who said, 'Excuse me, sir, but I have an article in my possession which belongs to you.' 'How is that?' I asked, considerably astonished.

"The stranger took a jackknife from his pocket. 'This knife,' said he, 'was placed in my hands some years ago, with the injunction that I was to keep it until I had found a man uglier than myself. I have carried it from that time to this. Allow me to say, sir, that I think you are fairly entitled to the property'." (*Lincolniana*)

Old Abe, My Jolly Jo
Air—"John Anderson, My Jo John"

Old Abraham, my jolly Abe,
　When we were first acquaint,
I thought you were an honest man,
　But nothing of a saint;
But since you wore the Spanish cloak,
　You love the negro so,
And hate the white man, so you do,
　My jolly Abe, my Jo.

Old Abraham, my jolly Abe,
    What do you really mean?
Your negro proclamation is
    A wild fanatic's dream.
The war you did begin, old Abe,
    And that you surely know;
You should have made a compromise,
    My jolly Abe, my Jo.

Old Abraham, my jolly Abe,
    Your negro plan has failed,
Ere this you know that cruel war
    And taxes you've entailed.
In this unhappy land, old Abe,
    Is weeping, wail, and woe,
That you can't cure, nor we endure,
    My jolly Abe, my Jo.

Old Abraham, my jolly Abe,
    The blindest man can see
The Union you will not restore
    Till every negro's free,
And equal with the best of men,
    In arm and arm they go
To vote as you wish them to,
    My jolly Abe, my Jo.

(Copperhead Minstrel)

The Despot's Song
By "Ole Secesh"

With a beard that was filthy and red,
    His mouth with tobacco bespread,
Abe Lincoln sat in the gay White House,
A-wishing that he was dead,—
    Swear! swear! swear!
Till his tongue was blistered o'er;
Then in a voice not very strong,
He slowly whined the Despot's song:—
    Lie! Lie! Lie!
I've lied like the very deuce!
    Lie! Lie! Lie!

THE PRESIDENT LISTENED PATIENTLY.

Too many Brigadiers.

"GIVE MY COMPLIMENTS TO BIDDY, JOHN, AND TELL HER I'LL THINK SERIOUSLY OF WOMEN-SUFFRAGE."

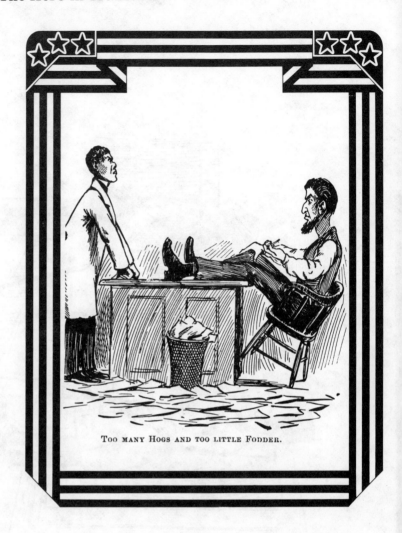

Too many Hogs and too little Fodder.

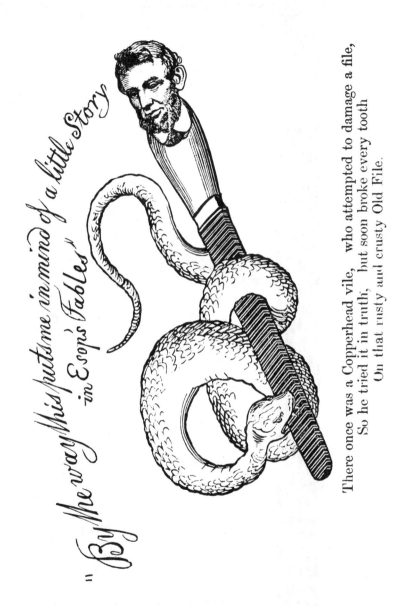

"By the way this puts me in mind of a little story" in Æsop's Fables"

There once was a Copperhead vile,   who attempted to damage a file,
So he tried it in truth;   but soon broke every tooth
On that rusty and crusty Old File.

ABRAHAM

AFRICANUS I.

His Secret Life,

AS REVEALED UNDER THE

MESMERIC INFLUENCE.

Mysteries of the White House.

J. F. FEEKS, PUBLISHER
No. 26 ANN STREET, N. Y.

As long as lies were of use;
But now that lies no longer pay,
   I know not where to turn;
For when I the truth would say,
   My tongue with lies will burn!

   Drink! drink! drink!
Till my head feels very queer!
   Drink! drink! drink!
Till I get rid of all fear!
Brandy, and whiskey, and gin,
   Sherry, and champagne, and pop,
I tipple, I guzzle, I suck 'em all in,
   Till down dead-drunk I drop.

   Think! think! think!
Till my head is very sore!
   Think! think! think!
Till I couldn't think any more!
And it's oh! to be splitting of rails,
   Back in my Illinois hut:
For now that everything fails,
   I would of my office be "shut!"
   Jeff! Jeff! Jeff!
To you as a suppliant I kneel!
   Jeff! Jeff! Jeff!
If you could *my* horrors feel,
You'd submit at discretion,
   And kindly give in
To all my oppression,
   My weakness and sin!

          (*Rebel Rhymes and Rhapsodies*)

ABRAHAM AFRICANUS I

(*Of all the extended attacks on Lincoln, probably the cleverest and most interesting is this one which changes the President into King. Published anonymously in 1861 by J.F.Feeks, who specialized in violent anti-Administration diatribes, it exploited outstanding or prominent characteristics of the President and his adminstration. Typically, Lincoln is pictured, like Faust before him, as having trafficked with Satan. Naturally such a low and unprincipled character as Lincoln would try to outsmart the arch Demon. The fact that he did not succeed undoubtedly represents a profound hope on the part of the author and his fellows. As was usual in this kind of attack, the names of Lincoln and his Cabinet were only thinly disguised.*

Only a portion—the introductory verse and the first few lines of the succeeding prose—is reprinted here.)

CHAPTER I
THE GREAT MAN'S FRIEND

One stormy night in chill November,
As cold a night as folks remember,
'Twas ten o'clock and every street
Was cold and damp with rain and sleet.
Old chimneys rocked and tiles were cast
At mercy of the fitful blast;
And houses shook and shutters slammed,
And stray curs yelpt and hackmen damned;
And tavern signs were heard to creak
As if their very hearts would break,
And leafless trees swayed to and fro
As if they'd nothing else to do.
Still grew the darkness, deep, profound,
O'er root and dome and all around,
And froze the rain, and moaned the blast
Like gibbering spirits as it passed.
Each straggler hugged his friendly cloak,
As home his lonely way he took,
While all the smiles which blessed his home
Seem'd brighter 'mid the deep'ning gloom;
And oft he started as he passed,
At shadows which the street lamp cast;—
The sleeping watchman snug and tight
Forgot to hail the passing night;
And wind and rain and driving sleet
Soon held possession of the street.

Within his arm-chair, snug and warm,
Bram, dozing sat, nor heard the storm,
Of, if he heard, he thought, no doubt,
How very cold it must be, out.
The warm full bed and cozy curtain
Made pleasant rest and slumber certain;
And the warm arm chair, as you'll suppose,
Seemed almost courting him to doze.
Within the broad hearth where he gazed,

A gladsome fire creaked and blazed,
And rose and fell with cheering sound,
Dispensing light and heat around.
The clothes he wore and all his pride
Were both together laid aside,
And in his night gown, at his ease,
He felt his comfort much increase;
Small care had he for rain or snows;
His Excellency viewed his toes,
And took his punch, as grateful heat
Came running through his lanky feet.
Bram warmed his toes and sipped his liquor,
Until his thoughts and tongue grew thicker;
Nor could he think, small brains he boasted,
Whether his feet were warmed or roasted.
Thus in his mind confusion grew
Until he neither thought nor knew;
Yet, tho' he slept, his master mind,
(These common folks are always blind)
Beheld what passed. "What's that I see?
The very andiron bows to me!"
And so it was; the andiron grew
Beneath his Excellency's view,
And as it grew he could but note
Its brass arms stuck beneath its coat;
He wondered if 'twould next have wings,
For rum and dreams can do strange things.
"Great God!" quoth Bram, "what do I see?
The very andiron bows to me!"

"Yes, Bram," quoth it, "I bow; you'll find
A fellow feeling makes us kind.
I am the Devil, and I feel
Of all the rogues who wrong, who steal,
Who murder, intrigue, violate,
I love the rogue who rules a State,
Because, when he does wrong or says it,
A thousand knaves and fools must praise it,
And all the efforts preachers make
Will not avail, *'tis bound to take*;
I love you Bram, your high position
Gives hope to knaves of mean condition,
When gazing on your strange success,
They think their own fate can't be less.
Make 't easy men should find a flaw
In codes of morals and of law;
And on their wits in firm reliance,
Set all of virtue at defiance;
They think that he who like yourself,

The Hero in Transition

Concentres all and all in self,
Will find that fate and luck conspire,
Both, that the knave may rise the higher,
Both, that a strange success in life,
May be of knave, fool, fortune, rife;
That Justice, being blind, must lag;
That Luck's by far the fastest nag,
And on her back in hope they'll vault,
To carry Fortune by assault.
This serves my ends. It proves when past,
Knave, fool, and fortune, all won't last,
And while it hides the sure defeat,
Mine is the profit and the cheat;
I've ruled the world and still must rule
As long as there's a knave or fool."

"Stop, stop," cried guilty Bram, "suppose
Instead of jingling verse we chat in prose.

"Agreed," said Satan, "though it's my conviction
You'll find the prose as difficult to face as fiction."

"Well, the fact is," said Abraham, handing old Nick a chair and pushing the decanter towards him, "it comes more natural. I can defend myself a good deal easier; your word to the contrary notwithstanding. This reminds me of a western story."

"Ah," said Satan, pouring himself out a pretty stiff horn and gazing at the fire through its amber transparency with the air of a connoisseur, "a joke?"

"Yes, what I should call a d--n good joke, for it served my purpose elegantly."

"Don't swear it"; interrupted Nick, "forget your old habits for once, and behave yourself while in the presence of a gentleman *as a* gentleman" ....

(All these examples are from Ray B. Browne, ed., *Lincoln-Lore: Lincoln in the Contemporary Popular Mind* [Bowling Green, OH: Bowling Green University Popular Press, 1974]).

Contributors

Marshall W. Fishwick is in the Communications Department at Virginia Tech, Blacksburg, Virginia.

Roger R. Rollin is in the English Department at Clemson University, Clemson, South Carolina.

Bruce A. Beatie is on the faculty of the Department of Modern Languages, Cleveland State University, Cleveland, Ohio.

Robert Inchausti is a Visiting Lecturer of English at the University of California, Davis, California.

Linda B. Martin is a professional writer and photographer, living at 14 Buckingham Place, Great Neck, NY 11021. Besides contributing to many newspapers and magazines, Mrs. Martin is co-author of the book, *Nassau County, Long Island in Early Photographs* (Dover, 1981).

David Manning White is retired living in Richmond Virginia.

Ray B. Browne is Chair of the Popular Culture Department at Bowling Green State University, Bowling Green, Ohio.

Richard Shereikis is professor in the Literature Program, Sangamon State University, Springfield, Illinois.

Gary L. Harmon is in the English Department at the University of North Florida, Jacksonville, Florida.

Peter Rickman is in the Philosophy Department at the City University, Northampton Square, London

Gary Hoppenstand is a Ph.D. candidate in American Culture at Bowling Green State University.

Hanna B. Lewis teaches in the Division of English, Foreign Languages and Journalism at Sam Houston State University, Huntsville, Texas.

William Nelson specializes in Contemporary Fiction

Rita C. Hubbard chairs the Arts & Communications Department at Christopher Newport College, Newport News, Virginia.

Hal Blythe and Charlie Sweet teach in the English Department at Eastern Kentucky University, Richmond, Kentucky.

Elizabeth S. Bell teaches English, at the University of South Carolina at Aiken.

Robert G. Picard is in the School of Journalism at the University of Missouri at Columbia.

Vicki Abt teaches Sociology at Penn State University, Ogontz Campus.

Harry Keyishian is in the English Department at Fairleigh Dickinson University, Madison, New Jersey.

Nancy B. Bouchier is at the University of Western Ontario and *John E. Findling* is Professor of History at Indiana University Southeast, New Albany.

Roberta J. Park teaches at the University of California, Berkeley.

David L. Porter is in the History Department at William Penn College, Oskaloosa, Iowa.

David S. Bertolotti is in the Humanities Department at GMI, Flint, Michigan.

Sarah Russell Hankins is on the faculty of the Communications Department at the University of Colorado, Boulder.

Lesley Dick is a Ph.D. candidate in American Culture at Bowling Green State University.

John J. Gardiner is an associate professor and director of graduate studies for the Department of Educational Administration and Higher Education, Oklahoma State University, Stillwater and *Kathryn E. Jones* is a doctoral candidate in the department and serves as an assistant to the Dean of the College of Education, Oklahoma State University.